# discover
# NEW
# ZEALAND

**CHARLES RAWLINGS-WAY**
**BRETT ATKINSON, SARAH BENNETT,**
**PETER DRAGICEVICH, SCOTT KENNEDY**

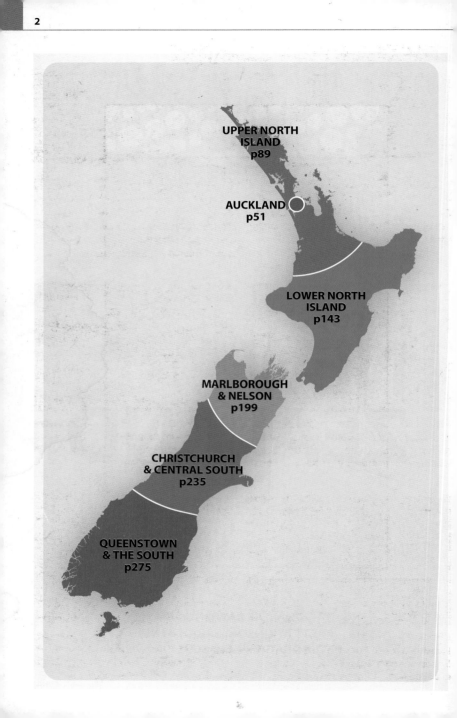

UPPER NORTH
ISLAND
p89

AUCKLAND
p51

LOWER NORTH
ISLAND
p143

MARLBOROUGH
& NELSON
p199

CHRISTCHURCH
& CENTRAL SOUTH
p235

QUEENSTOWN
& THE SOUTH
p275

# DISCOVER NEW ZEALAND

**Auckland (p51)** New Zealand's big smoke is a real soap-opera hero: hip, gritty and really good-lookin'.

**Upper North Island (p89)** Rotorua's geysers and Maori culture, Waitomo's caves and Napier's art deco...here is a mixed-bag of Kiwi surprises.

**Lower North Island (p143)** Cafes, bars, restaurants...Wellington rocks! Further afield lie photogenic mountains, and the sunshine and wine of the East Coast.

**Marlborough & Nelson (p199)** The sunny side of the south offers wine, whale-watching and the fabulous Abel Tasman National Park.

**Christchurch & Central South (p235)** Head from civilised Christchurch, the South Island's biggest city, to the ice-clad heights of Aoraki/Mt Cook.

**Queenstown & the South (p275)** Peaks, glaciers, fiords and sounds are ground zero for adrenaline junkies (bungy jumping, skiing, white-water rafting...).

# ⬊ CONTENTS

UPPER NORTH
ISLAND
p89

AUCKLAND
p51

LOWER NORTH
ISLAND
p143

MARLBOROUGH
& NELSON
p199

CHRISTCHURCH
& CENTRAL SOUTH
p235

QUEENSTOWN
& THE SOUTH
p275

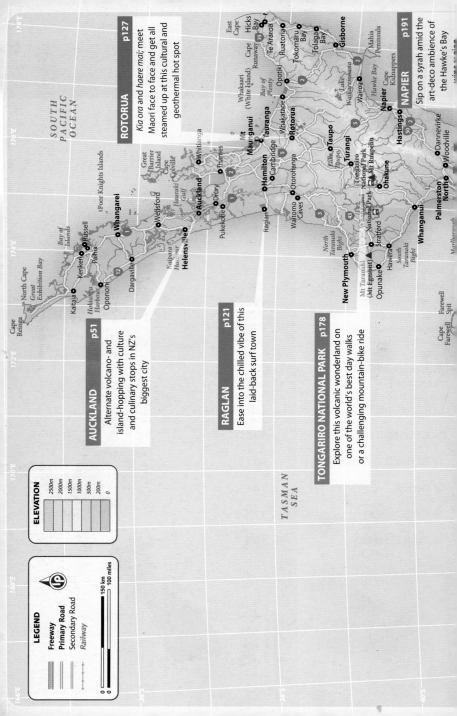

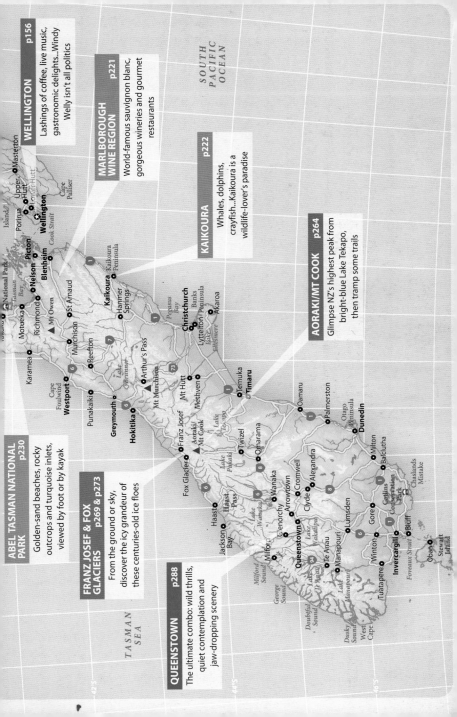

### WELLINGTON p156

Lashings of coffee, live music, gastronomic delights...Windy Welly isn't all politics

### MARLBOROUGH WINE REGION p221

World-famous sauvignon blanc, gorgeous wineries and gourmet restaurants

### KAIKOURA p222

Whales, dolphins, crayfish...Kaikoura is a wildlife-lover's paradise

### AORAKI/MT COOK p264

Glimpse NZ's highest peak from bright-blue Lake Tekapo, then tramp some trails

### ABEL TASMAN NATIONAL PARK p230

Golden-sand beaches, rocky outcrops and turquoise inlets, viewed by foot or by kayak

### FRANZ JOSEF & FOX GLACIERS p269 & p273

From the ground or sky, discover the icy grandeur of these centuries-old ice floes

### QUEENSTOWN p288

The ultimate combo: wild thrills, quiet contemplation and jaw-dropping scenery

SOUTH PACIFIC OCEAN

TASMAN SEA

# ↘ THIS IS NEW ZEALAND

**You probably already know how ludicrously photogenic New Zealand is. You may also know that adventure sports rule here (bungy jumping, skiing, skydiving, white-water rafting etc).**

**Then there's NZ's antinuclear stance, its rich Maori culture, its passion for rugby, its abundant sheep, its sauvignon blanc…**

But there's one aspect of Aotearoa that you probably haven't counted on – the extent to which the average Kiwi will genuinely want you to have a really, really good time. Perhaps it's just insecurity, but whatever the motivation, it's in the interactions with everyday, eager-to-please Kiwis that lasting memories are made. As a Maori proverb suggests: *He aha te mea nui o te ao? He tangata! He tangata!* (What is the most important thing in the world? It is people! It is people!).

Politically and economically, recent years have seen a lot of changes down here. In 2008, just as the US was trading in George Bush for Barack Obama, Helen Clark's centre-left Labour government was ousted after nine years in power, and John Key's centre-right Nationals took the stage. Then the global economy went belly-up. Will affable, laid-back Key be able to pull NZ out of the gloom?

But enough politics – most Kiwis are more interested in the rugby. In 2011 NZ will host the Rugby World Cup. New Zealand's All Blacks are the most successful rugby team in history (with a 74% winning record) but they've only snagged the Cup once. After yet another dazzling failure in France in 2007, the pressure is on the All Blacks to redeem themselves on home soil. Whether you're visiting before, during or after the event, expect to hear a *lot* about it.

'It's in the interactions with everyday, eager-to-please Kiwis that lasting memories are made'

Whatever the economic or rugby prognosis, you can be guaranteed of a warm welcome in NZ. Kiwis love sharing their gorgeous country with visitors, and in turn seeing it anew through foreign eyes. You're in for a treat.

↘ NEW ZEALAND'S TOP
25 EXPERIENCES

**1**

## ↘ EXTREME QUEENSTOWN

On the South Island, Queenstown (p288) has a reputation for extreme sports, unjustly taking precedence over the city's beauty. The extreme sports are fun, though: jumping from 134m above a river is one of the more ridiculous ways our species has invented to entertain ourselves.

Daniel Corbett, Lonely Planet staff

## ↘ TE PAPA

Dominating the Wellington waterfront, **Te Papa** (p157) is New Zealand's national museum. It's an inspiring, interactive repository of historical and cultural artefacts…and best of all, it's free! Expect plenty of Maori heritage and a slew of innovative displays celebrating all things Kiwi.

Charles Rawlings-Way, Lonely Planet author

## ↘ MARLBOROUGH WINE REGION

It's hard to avoid Marlborough sauvignon blanc in the world's liquor stores these days – it's crisp, zesty and drinkable. Whether by minibus, bicycle or on the back seat of someone's car, touring the cellar doors of the **Marlborough Wine region** (p221) is a decadent delight.

Charles Rawlings-Way, Lonely Planet author

1 EMILY RIDDELL; 2 COURTESY OF TE PAPA; 3 MTMEDIA

1 Bungy jumping, Queenstown; 2 Our Space map, Te Papa, Wellington; 3 Vineyard, Marlborough region

## ➘ RUGBY

**Rugby** (p11) is New Zealand's national game and governing preoccupation. If your timing's good you might catch the revered national team, the All Blacks, in action. If not, yell along with the locals in a small-town pub as the big men collide on the screen.

Charles Rawlings-Way, Lonely Planet author

**4**

**5**

## ➘ KAYAKING ABEL TASMAN

Kayaking in **Abel Tasman National Park** (p233) is a must. We only had one day, but it was plenty of time to paddle the aqua-coloured waters up the coast from Kaiteriteri to spectacular caves, secluded beaches and curious seals. If the wind is on your side, you may even be able to sail back!

Phillipa Ellis, Lonely Planet staff

## ⬊ MAORI ROTORUA

Most people visit **Rotorua** (p127) to see the town's iconic geothermal geysers, but Rotorua is also a hot spot for Maori culture. Join in a *haka*, chow down at a traditional *hangi*, or check out an authentic cultural performance with song, dance, legends, arts and crafts.

Charles Rawlings-Way, Lonely Planet author

6

4 HOLGER LEUE; 5 MICHAEL GEBICKI; 6 RICHARD I'ANSON

4 Junior rugby players, Canterbury; 5 Sea kayaking, Abel Tasman National Park; 6 Maori carving, Rotorua

# ↘ WELLINGTON

**Wellington** (p156) is beautiful, with a striking waterfront surrounded by bush-clad hills. It's easy to get around, and there are plenty of great cafes and restaurants. Wellingtonians are friendly and ready to help visitors experience the city.

Tana Umaga, former All Blacks captain (NZ's men's rugby team)

7

8

## WHALE-WATCHING IN KAIKOURA

Off the coast of Kaikoura (p222), drifting among gently rolling waves, we pulled up some distance from a giant sperm whale. The nose of the whale came up and then it dived, ever so slowly and gracefully. The last sight was its tail, which flipped out of the water then gently submerged. It was mesmerising.

Lucy Monie, Lonely Planet staff

## DOUBTFUL SOUND

9

Our yacht motors between the steep, wooded sides of Doubtful Sound (p317). Seals dive in the surf, and we canoe to see orchids and plants growing among the trees and cracks of the rocks. Spray washes our faces. Dolphins race with us, waterfalls cascade over cliffs, penguins swim by and birds sing.

Nigel Sentence, traveller, UK

7 DAVID WALL; 8 DAVID WALL; 9 MICAH WRIGHT

7 City centre and harbour, Wellington; 8 Sperm whale, Kaikoura; 9 Doubtful Sound, Fiordland

## ⬎ URBAN AUCKLAND

**10**

Whether it's a cool organic cafe, slick fine dining or an indulgent shopping fix that you're after, the urban utopia of Ponsonby is within a stone's throw of central Auckland (p60): perfect for a business breakfast or fuelling-up before a day of island-hopping.

Chris Zeiher, Lonely Planet staff

## ⬎ WAITOMO CAVES

**11**

The best way to experience the Waitomo Caves (p124) is by blackwater rafting. It's really hands-on, requiring some agility and the guts to jump backwards down small waterfalls. Finish off the trip quietly drifting through the caves in your tube, looking at the glowworms with your headlamp turned off.

Dr Farah Rangikoepa Palmer, former Black Ferns captain (NZ's women's rugby team)

## ⌐ SAILING THE BAY OF ISLANDS

12

Learning to sail in the **Bay of Islands** (p102) is definitely one of the highlights of New Zealand. Anchoring at night in a deserted bay for a bit of skinny-dipping, sea-chilled-beer drinking and snapper fishing was blissful; and sailing while surrounded by dolphins is something I will never forget.

Ian Drew, traveller, UK

## ⌐ RAGLAN SURF SAFARI

13

Laid-back, hippified and surprisingly multicultural, little **Raglan** (p121) is the mythical surf village you always knew was out there but could never find (until now…). A few kilometres south of town are some of the best point breaks on the planet.

Charles Rawlings-Way, Lonely Planet author

10 COURTESY OF TOURISM AUCKLAND; 11 DAVID WALL; 12 MANFRED GOTTSCHALK; 13 PAUL KENNEDY

10 Dining out, Auckland; 11 Abseiling into the Waitomo Caves; 12 Sail boats, Bay of Islands; 13 Surfer, Raglan

**14**

## ↘ NAPIER'S ART-DECO ARCHITECTURE

The art-deco wonderland of Napier (p148) feels like a cross between a film set and a 1930s time capsule. Deco buildings abound, including a sculpted live-music shell and even an art-deco backpackers. The wine and welcome are bang up-to-date, even if the charming architecture is firmly rooted in the past.

Tom Hall, Lonely Planet staff

# ↘ WAIHEKE ISLAND

A 50-minute ferry ride from central Auckland transports you to culinary heaven on **Waiheke Island** (p54). It's easy to watch a day disappear at one of the wineries, savouring the incredible views of Oneroa Bay and the Hauraki Gulf while sipping the local pinot gris and nibbling from an organic tasting plate.

Chris Zeiher, Lonely Planet staff

15

14 JOHN HAY; 15 PAUL KENNEDY

14 Art-deco hotel, Napier; 15 Palm Beach (p85), Waiheke Island

## ↘ HIKING FRANZ JOSEF GLACIER

Walking between crevices of different shades of blue ice, listening to the various noises the ice makes, before climbing up to the surface of **Franz Josef Glacier** (p269) into bright sunshine to see the rainforest and the sea – a truly magnificent experience.

Bethan Drummond, traveller, UK

16

17

## ⬎ DOWNTOWN CHRISTCHURCH

The centre of Christchurch (p246) may be Cathedral Sq, but the best part of the inner city is a short stroll down Worcester St. I like to explore the Arts Centre and Botanic Gardens, check out the striking Christchurch Art Gallery, then head back for a locally brewed beer at the Dux de Lux.

Chris Girdler, Lonely Planet staff

## ⬎ AKAROA

18

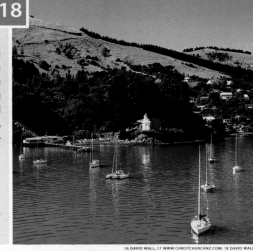

On our last two days in New Zealand we headed down to Akaroa (p258). Eating fish and chips at dusk on the pier, hiking through grazing land and turning in for the night at a local farmhouse was a perfect, peaceful ending to a whirlwind three-week trip.

Rana Freedman, Lonely Planet staff

16 DAVID WALL; 17 WWW.CHRISTCHURCHNZ.COM; 18 DAVID WALL

16 Blue ice, Franz Josef Glacier; 17 Christchurch Art Gallery (p251), Christchurch; 18 Akaroa Harbour, Canterbury

## ↘ DUNEDIN'S MUSIC SCENE

For any half-keen fan of live, independent music, the eclectic live-music venues of **Dunedin** (p308) are a mandatory part of a NZ itinerary. Follow the thrum of guitars to old-school bars where rock gods reign, or head to hidden, backstreet clubs and relax with seriously laid-back dub and reggae sounds.

Errol Hunt, Lonely Planet staff

19

20

## ↘ AORAKI/MT COOK

At a cloud-piercing 3754m, **Aoraki/Mt Cook** (p264) is New Zealand's crowning peak. Take a walk around the rumbling glaciers and moody lakes dappling its flanks, carve up the snow on a ski trip, or get closer to the summit on an eye-popping scenic flight.

Charles Rawlings-Way, Lonely Planet author

19 IAN JORGENSEN; 20 JOHN ELK III

19 Dunedin band Die! Die! Die!; 20 Aoraki/Mt Cook

21

## ↘ MT TARANAKI

Mt Taranaki (p185) is beautiful on a clear day – an almost perfect cone on the skyline. We drove up through native bush to the visitors centre. From there you can see Taranaki farmland stretching out towards the rugged coast, and there was enough snow for a snow fight before a hot chocolate in the cafe.

Suzannah Shwer, Lonely Planet staff

## ↘ HOT WATER BEACH

22

Get yourself into hot water on the Coromandel Peninsula at legendary Hot Water Beach (p116). Warm geothermal springs bubble up through the sand: with some creative digging, you can kick back in your custom-made spa pool and watch the surf lap along the beach.

Charles Rawlings-Way, Lonely Planet author

## OTAGO PENINSULA WILDLIFE

23

On a day trip from Dunedin, tour around the bends, bays and beaches of the Otago Peninsula (p310). Along the way are opportunities to see penguins, sea lions and seals. Taiaroa Head, at the peninsula's eastern tip, has the world's only mainland colony of royal albatrosses.

Charles Rawlings-Way, Lonely Planet author

24

## TRANZALPINE RAIL JOURNEY

The TranzAlpine (p271) is one of the world's great train rides. The train rolls across the Canterbury Plains before climbing to Arthur's Pass: I had to be dragged off the viewing carriage before we entered a huge tunnel on the descent to Greymouth. Don't start your West Coast adventure any other way.

Tom Hall, Lonely Planet staff

21 DAVID WALL; 22 NOBLEIMAGES/ALAMY; 23 DAVID WALL; 24 TOURISM NEW ZEALAND

21 Mt Taranaki; 22 Hot Water Beach, Coromandel Peninsula; 23 Yellow-eyed penguins (p311), Otago Peninsula; 24 TranzAlpine train

# ↘ TONGARIRO ALPINE CROSSING

Beat the summer crowds on a winter traverse of **Tongariro Alpine Crossing** (p180) in Tongariro National Park. An excellent tramp leads from Mangatepopo Hut to Oturere Hut via the Emerald Lakes. Turn right at the lakes and spend the night at Oturere among lava flows. Retrace your steps the next day.

Steve Waters, Lonely Planet staff

**25**

25 JOHN ELK III

25 Emerald Lakes, Tongariro National Park

# NEW ZEALAND'S TOP ITINERARIES

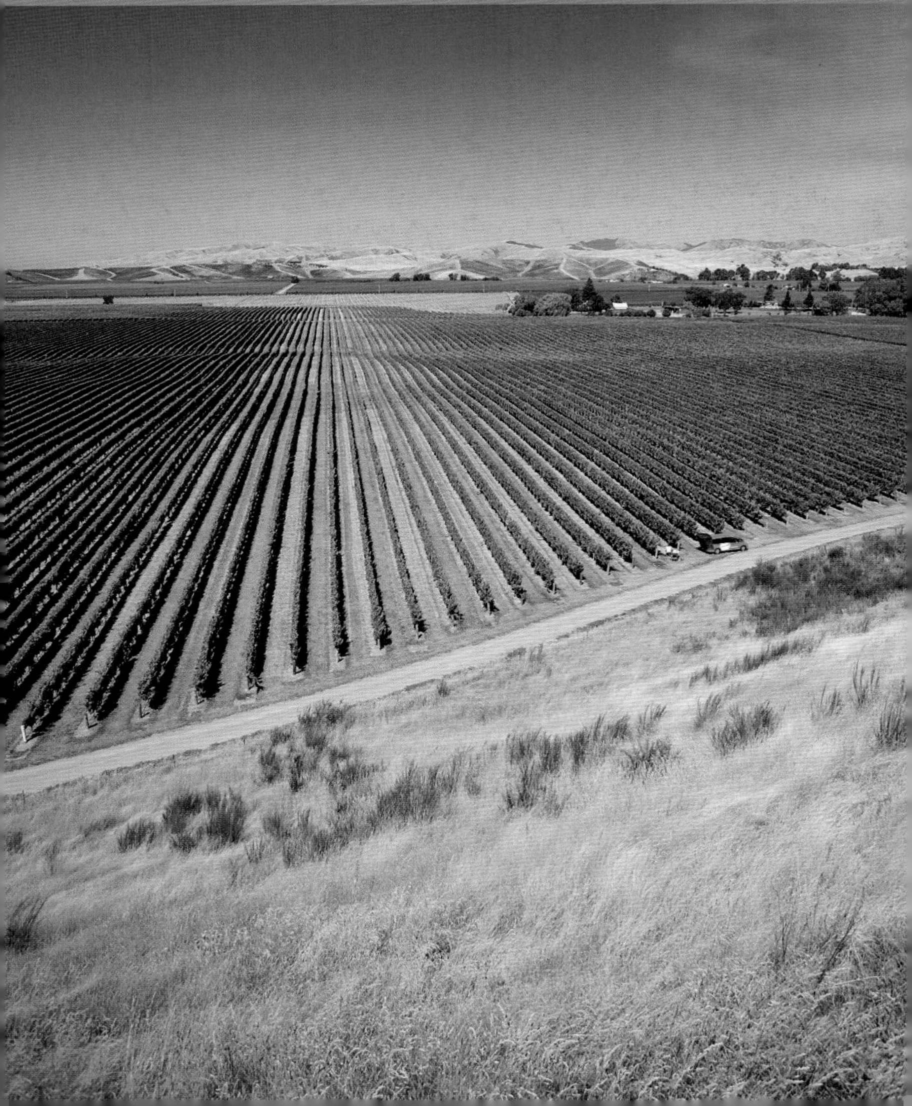

# WINTER WANDERER

## FIVE DAYS QUEENSTOWN TO CHRISTCHURCH

**Yes, we know a whole bunch of you are here for one thing only: snow! Hit Queenstown on the South Island for perfect powder, and great bars and restaurants. Further north, Kaikoura's winter days are crisp, the whales are wallowing and you'll get the place all to yourself.**

### ❶ QUEENSTOWN

Take a direct flight to Queenstown (p288) and get ready for some seriously snowy fun, with access to world-class skiing, cool bars and restaurants, and a kickin' nocturnal scene. If you're here in late June or early July, the Queenstown Winter Festival (p48) goes berserk, with live music, comedy, parades and lots of family fun. When you've had your fill of snowy slopes, the extreme activities (p289) on offer in Queenstown will keep the winter chills at bay: try kayaking, paragliding, jetboating, white-water rafting, skydiving or mountain biking.

### ❷ CORONET PEAK & THE REMARKABLES

These two ski fields are the epicentre of the Queenstown ski scene. Coronet Peak (p327) is the region's oldest ski field, with a multimillion dollar snow-making system, treeless slopes, consistent gradient and excellent skiing for all levels (great for snowboarders too). The visually remarkable Remarkables (p327) are more family-friendly – look for the sweeping run called 'Homeward Bound'.

### ❸ WANAKA

As an alternative to Queenstown, head to Wanaka (p299). It's like Queenstown's little brother – all the benefits without the hype. Ski

Fox Glacier (p273), Westland Tai Poutini National Park

MICHAEL GEBICKI

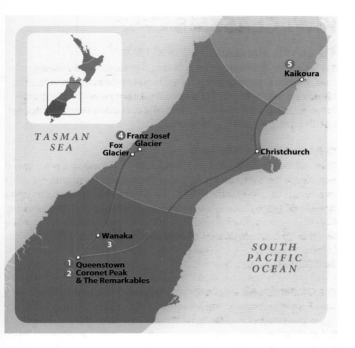

fields near here include **Treble Cone** (p327), with steep intermediate and advanced slopes, plus snowboarding half-pipes and a terrain park; **Cardrona** (p327), with high-capacity chairlifts, beginners' tows and extreme snowboarding terrain; **Snow Farm New Zealand** (p327), the country's only commercial Nordic (cross-country) ski area; and **Snow Park** (p327), the only dedicated freestyle ski and board area in New Zealand, with pipes, terrain parks, boxes and rails.

## ❹ FRANZ JOSEF GLACIER & FOX GLACIER

If you want something different, take a drive to Westland Tai Poutini National Park on the West Coast to check out **Franz Josef Glacier** (p269) and **Fox Glacier** (p273).

## ❺ KAIKOURA

From Queenstown, fly north to **Christchurch** (p246) – keep a look out the aeroplane window for **Aoraki/Mt Cook** (p264). From Christchurch, drive a few hours north to **Kaikoura** (p222), a photogenic town on the South Island's northwest coast. In winter (especially), migrating humpback and sperm whales come close to the shore – check them out up close on a whale-watching tour while the summer crowds are a million miles (or at least a few months) away.

# KIWI CLASSICS

## 10 DAYS AUCKLAND TO AUCKLAND

Classy cities, geothermal eruptions, fantastic wine, Maori culture, glaciers, extreme activities, isolated beaches and forests. These are just a few of NZ's favourite things, and what you'll want to see if you're a first-time, short-trip visitor. It's the best of the country, north and south.

### ❶ AUCKLAND & AROUND

The City of Sails, **Auckland** (p51) is a South Pacific melting pot – spend a few days here shopping, eating, drinking and savouring NZ at its most cosmopolitan and worldly. Truck north to the winterless **Bay of Islands** (p102) for a dose of aquatic adventure – sailing, surfing, kayaking and scuba-diving – or scoot over southeast to explore the forests and beaches of the **Coromandel Peninsula** (p110).

### ❷ ROTORUA

Further south is **Rotorua** (p127), where you can giggle at volcanic mud bubbles, gasp as geothermal geysers blast boiling water into the sky and get a nose full of egg-gas. Rotorua is also a great place to experience Maori culture via a *haka* (war dance), *hangi* (feast) or legend-loaded cultural performance.

### ❸ WELLINGTON

Down in **Wellington** (p156), the coffee's hot, the beer's cold and wind from the politicians generates its own low-pressure system. Clinging

Viaduct Harbour precinct (p68), Auckland

COURTESY OF TOURISM AUCKLAND

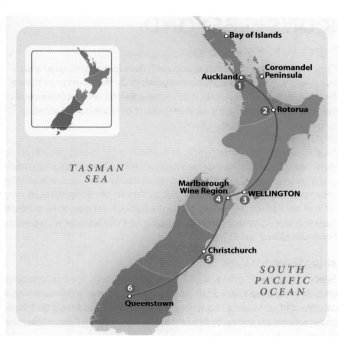

to the hillsides like a mini–San Francisco, NZ's capital city is the place for serious arts, live music and hip street culture.

## ❹ MARLBOROUGH WINE REGION
Swan over to the South Island for a few days (even the ferry trip is scenic) and experience the best the south has to offer. Start with a tour through the Marlborough Wine Region (p221) – the sauvignon blanc they produce in this cool microclimate is world class.

## ❺ CHRISTCHURCH
Further south is classy Christchurch (p246), the South Island's biggest city, from where you can meander southwest.

## ❻ QUEENSTOWN
Bungy-obsessed party town Queenstown (p288) is a must-visit for adrenaline junkies. From here you can hop on a flight directly back to Auckland.

# ICONS & BEYOND

## TWO WEEKS AUCKLAND TO CHRISTCHURCH

Check some big-ticket attractions off your list on this trip, with kayaking, caving and tramping breaking up the road trip. Take a little time on this well-travelled route – switch into holiday mode, embrace nature and savour the flavours of dual-island travel.

### ❶ AUCKLAND

Cruise the hip, inner-city streets of Auckland (p51) and get a feel for Maori culture at the Auckland Museum (p63). Take your pick of the many lunch spots along K Rd. Dinner at Ponsonby (p76) will attune your tastebuds to NZ's brand of 'Pacific fusion' cooking. After dinner hit the bars around Viaduct Harbour (p78). Next day, take a break from the streets with a ferry ride out to the beaches and wineries on Waiheke Island (p83).

### ❷ WAITOMO CAVES

A few hours south of Auckland, beyond Hamilton, are the amazing Waitomo Caves (p123) – an underground labyrinth of glowworm-filled caverns. Put on a wetsuit and headlamp and dive in for some blackwater rafting, abseiling, or floating along on an inner-tube in the inky blackness. There are a couple of good eateries to refuel at afterwards.

### ❸ TAUPO & TONGARIRO NATIONAL PARK

From Waitomo, hook southeast to idyllic Taupo (p170) and try skydiving (you know you want to), or go tramping around the triple-peaked, volcanic wilderness of Tongariro National Park (p178).

DAVID WALL

Auckland city (p51) viewed across Waitemata Harbour

## ❹ MT TARANAKI

If time is on your side and the sun is shining, take SH43 west to New Plymouth and catch an eyeful of photogenic Mt Taranaki (p185) – if there's a better-looking mountain on the planet, we want to know about it.

## ❺ WELLINGTON

Watch the nocturnal freak show pass by in late-night, caffeinated Wellington (p156), then chug across Cook Strait to the South Island.

## ❻ MARLBOROUGH SOUNDS

Track west from Picton and disappear into the abstract waterways and woodlands of the Marlborough Sounds (p217) for a day, or continue on to the golden-sand bays of Abel Tasman National Park (p230).

## ❼ WEST COAST

Heading west, track down the rain-swept, lonesome West Coast (p266; this ain't Kansas no more Dorothy...) and check out its iconic glaciers (p269 and p273). There are dozens of hikes to tackle around the icy valleys, or take a helicopter ride up onto the glaciers them-

DAVID WALL

Mitre Peak, Milford Sound (p318)

selves: a sure-fire way to develop feelings of insignificance. En route, stop at **Greymouth** (p268) to taste the West Coast's own Monteith's beer. Drive up over Haast Pass to adrenaline-addicted **Queenstown** (p288) for a night or two of partying Kiwi-style.

## ❽ MILFORD SOUND
Mix and match highways to Te Anau for the beguiling side-road to **Milford Sound** (p318) – you might want to do a bit of kayaking here, or take a boat trip around the craggy inlets and mirror-topped waterways. This is NZ at its most pure, pristine and perfect.

## ❾ AORAKI/MT COOK
Weave your way onto the SH8 for an up-close look at sky-scraping **Aoraki/Mt Cook** (p264), NZ's highest peak (3754m). You can do some hikes here (long or short) or take an aerial sightseeing flight to really get to know the mountain. Brooding, changeable and cloud-shrouded – it's a mysterious and evocative place.

## ❿ CHRISTCHURCH & AROUND
Veer back east to cathedral-centred **Christchurch** (p246), where you can whittle away a day or two shopping and gallery-hopping. The comprehensive **Canterbury Museum** (p251) and up-to-the-minute **Christchurch Art Gallery** (p251) are must-sees. Take an afternoon to explore the quirky harbour town of **Lyttelton** (p257) or the amazing **Banks Peninsula** (p258) south of the city, with its French-influenced town of Akaroa.

# PLANNING YOUR TRIP

# NEW ZEALAND'S BEST

## EXTREME ACTIVITIES

- **Bungy jumping** (p289) Hurl your-self off a perfectly good bridge/canyon/highwire in Queenstown.
- **Skydiving** (p171) Head to Taupo, the skydiving capital of the world.
- **Skiing** (p327) Hit the perfect pow-der on South Island slopes.
- **Rafting, abseiling & rock climb-ing** (p123) Visit Waitomo Caves for black-water rafting, abseiling and rock climbing.
- **Mountain biking** (p130) For 100km of NZ's best mountain-bike tracks, get to the Redwoods – Whakarewarewa Forest.

## MAORI EXPERIENCES

- **Whakarewarewa Thermal Village** (p129) Weaving, carving and cul-tural performances in Rotorua.
- **One Tree Hill (Maungakiekie)** (p64) This volcanic cone is an important historical site.
- **Waipoua Kauri Forest** (p109) Maori-run tours among spiritually significant kauri trees.
- **Te Papa** (p146) Maori *marae* (meet-ing house), galleries and guided tours at NZ's national museum.
- **Parihaka** (p46) & **Matariki** (p48) Culturally significant Maori festivals in January and June.

## TRAMPS

- **Abel Tasman Coast Track** (p230) Walk through Abel Tasman National Park. Three to five days, 51km.
- **Tongariro Alpine Crossing** (p180) Tramp Tongariro National Park and see volcanic vents, alpine vegeta-tion and lush forest. One day, 18km.

LEFT: GERARD WALKER; RIGHT: TOURISM BAY OF PLENTY

Left: Bungy jumping (p289), Kawarau Bridge, Queenstown; Right: Rafting on the Wairoa River (p130), Bay of Plenty

- **Milford Track** (p318) Rainforest and towering mountains at Milford Sound. Five days, 54km.
- **Queen Charlotte Track** (p218) Hike through the scenic Marlborough Sounds. Three to five days, 71km.
- **Lake Waikaremoana Track** (p191) Circuit the lake and scale spectacular Panekiri Bluff. Four days, 46km.

## MUSEUMS

- **Te Papa** (p146) Interactive Kiwi culture, history and performance, plus Maori artefacts and a *marae*.
- **Canterbury Museum** (p251) Brilliant collation of Kiwi artefacts, both Maori and Pakeha.
- **Auckland Museum** (p63) This shiny Greek temple is a great introduction to Maori culture.
- **Otago Museum** (p304) Otago culture and landscapes: dinosaurs, geology, wildlife and Maori heritage.
- **Waikato Museum** (p118) Science, art, Maori treasures, Hamilton history and a Waikato River exhibition.

## FOOD & DRINK

- **NZ lamb** Chops on the barbecue or a roast in the oven.
- **Kiwifruit** Roadside farm stalls sell bags-full for next to nothing.
- **Seafood** Kaikoura crayfish, Bluff oysters, mussels, whitebait or fish and chips by the beach.
- **Maori hangi** A Maori essential: pork, chicken and vegetables cooked in an underground fire-pit.

- **Beer & wine** Zingy sauvignon blanc and microbrewed stouts, ales and pilseners.

## GEOTHERMAL HOT SPRINGS

- **Hot Water Beach** (p116) Dig your own spa pool in the Coromandel sand.
- **Polynesian Spa** (p130) Rotorua's long-running bathhouse has lake-edge hot pools.
- **Hanmer Springs** (p261) Let it all hang out at this sub-alpine hotspot.
- **Huka Falls Walkway hot springs** (p171) Free-and-easy swimming at Taupo's thermal swimming hole.
- **Tokaanu Thermal Pools** (p176) Low-key hot springs and a mud-pool boardwalk.

## CITY LIFE

- **Live music in Dunedin** (p308) Reggae, garage, dub, hip-hop… Dunedin rocks.
- **Wellington's caffeine scene** (p163) Wide-awake Wellington cranks out serious coffee.
- **Shop in Auckland** (p80) Buy up big brands, rummage for retro or browse the bookshelves.
- **Party in Queenstown** (p297) Cuddle-up with après-ski drinkers.
- **Cultured Christchurch** (p246) Refined, liveable, easy going: 'Chch' is cultured and civilised.

# THINGS YOU NEED TO KNOW

## AT A GLANCE

- **ATMs** In large cities and most towns.
- **Credit cards** Visa and MasterCard are widely accepted; American Express less so.
- **Currency** New Zealand dollar.
- **Electricity** Three pin, 230V AC, 50Hz.
- **Tipping** Not expected, but tip 5-10% for good restaurant service.
- **Visas** Required for some but not all countries (p371).

## ACCOMMODATION

- **B&Bs** (p358) Bed down in a locally-run cabin/house/mansion, with breakfast included (DB&B means dinner is also included).
- **Camping & holiday parks** (p358) NZ is brilliant for campers: pitch your tent in spectacular isolation or park your campervan at a functional holiday park.
- **Farmstays** (p359) Help out on a Kiwi farm and chow-down at the family dinner table.
- **Hostels** (p359) Spartan and decent or beery and oversexed – Kiwi backpacker hostels cover all the bases.
- **Hotels** (p359) From cheap pub rooms with shared bathrooms to ritzy five-star hotel chains.
- **Motels** (p359) Cookie-cutter sameness but reliable standards of comfort and cleanliness in reasonably central locations.

## ADVANCE PLANNING

- **Three months before** Look into visa requirements (p371) and shop around for the best deal on flights.
- **One month before** Book accommodation and regional flights, trains, ferries etc.
- **One week before** Book a bungy jump/surf lesson/caving tour/ Maori cultural experience.
- **Day before** Reserve a table at a top Auckland/Wellington restaurant and make sure you've packed your hiking boots.

## COSTS

- **Up to $100 per day** Camp or stay in hostels, cook your own meals, repress the urge to drink beer, tackle attractions independently and travel on a bus pass.
- **$100–200 per day** Do some sightseeing, eat out once or twice a day, stay in midrange motels or B&Bs, and have the odd glass of wine.
- **Over $200 per day** Hire a car, see the sights, eat when and where you want, and stay in decent digs.

## EMERGENCY NUMBERS

- **Ambulance, fire & police** (☎ 111)

## ⤷ GETTING AROUND

- **Bus** (p375) Accessible and well-organised links between towns and cities for mid-distance trips.
- **Drive** (p379) Car hire is available from major cities and many airports – really the best way to see the country.
- **Ferry** (p375) Daily ferries cross Cook Strait between the North and South Island.
- **Fly** (p374) Save yourself some time by flying between major city hubs with domestic carriers.
- **Train** (p381) A scenic option across the Southern Alps and between some major cities.
- **Walk** Long and short, easy and challenging tracks thread through magnificent scenery around NZ.

## ⤷ TRAVEL SEASONS

- **Summer** December to February is when Kiwis come out to play: sunshine = crowds.
- **Autumn** From March to May the crowds thin and the water is still warm(ish).
- **Winter** The beach is empty but the mountains are full: ski season runs from June to August (and beyond).
- **Spring** NZ gears up for summer from September to November: it's still chilly, but the sun is starting to shine.

PLANNING YOUR TRIP

THINGS YOU NEED TO KNOW

TOURISM BAY OF PLENTY

Camping riverside, Bay of Plenty (p126)

## ⬐ WHAT TO BRING

- **Driver's licence** (p378) The best way to see NZ is under your own steam.
- **Insect repellent** Bites from Kiwi sandflies just keep on giving.
- **Power-plug adaptor** To keep your gadgets charged.
- **Travel insurance** (p366) Make sure you're covered for 'high-risk' activities (skiing, surfing, helicopter rides etc).
- **Visa** (p371) Confirm the latest visa situation.

## ⬐ WHEN TO GO

- **Beat the crowds** September to November and March to May are shoulder seasons.
- **Hit the beaches** Sunny days from December to February.
- **Hit the ski slopes** Winter wipe-outs from June to August.
- **Festival frenzy** December to March is prime time for food and wine festivals, concerts and sporting events.
- **School holidays** Run from mid-December to late January, mid- to late April, early to mid-July, and mid-September to early October – avoid if possible!

LEFT: TOURISM BAY OF PLENTY; RIGHT: TOURISM BAY OF PLENTY

**Left:** Mt Maunganui (p141); **Right:** Maori performer

# → GET INSPIRED

## ↘ MUSIC

- **Don't Dream it's Over** (Crowded House, 1986) Neil Finn tries to catch a deluge in a paper cup – timeless melancholia.
- **Six Months in a Leaky Boat** (Split Enz, 1982) The Enz at their quirky, catchy and oddly nationalist best.
- **Slice of Heaven** (David Dobbyn with Herbs, 1986) South Pacific smash-hit from veteran Dave.
- **Not Many** (Scribe, 2003) Hot Kiwi hip-hop: 'How many dudes you know flow like this?'
- **Home Again** (Shihad, 1997) Riff-driven power from NZ's guitar-rock kings.

## ↘ FILMS

- **Once Were Warriors** (1994, director Lee Tamahori) Brutal, tragic, gritty: Jake 'the Muss' Heke in urban Auckland.
- **The Piano** (1993, director Jane Campion) Betrayal and passion on an 1850s NZ frontier: a mute woman, her daughter and her piano.
- **The Lord of the Rings trilogy** (2001–03, director Peter Jackson) Hundreds of hobbits: *The Fellowship of the Ring*, *The Two Towers* and the best picture–winning *The Return of the King*.
- **Whale Rider** (2002, director Niki Caro) Maori on the North Island's East Coast are torn between tradition and today's world.
- **Sione's Wedding** (2006, director Chris Graham) Samoan marital mayhem in the Auckland suburbs.

## ↘ BOOKS

- **The Bone People** (Keri Hulme, 1984) Maori legends, isolation and violence: Hulme's Booker Prize–winning novel explores traumatic family interactions.
- **Mister Pip** (Lloyd Jones, 2007) Reflections of Dickens' *Great Expectations* in an isolated Bougainville community. Booker Prize–shortlisted.
- **The Carpathians** (Janet Frame, 1989) A New Yorker in rural NZ; disturbing interplay between reality and imagination.
- **Bulibasha: King of the Gypsies** (Witi Ihimaera, 1994) On the North Island's East Coast, two Maori leaders are in conflict to become king.
- **The 10pm Question** (Kate De Goldi, 2009) Twelve-year-old Frankie has many questions; Sydney has some difficult answers.

## ↘ WEBSITES

- **100% Pure New Zealand** (www .newzealand.com) NZ's official tourism site; comprehensive visitor info.
- **Department of Conservation** (www.doc.govt.nz) Parks, recreation and conservation info.
- **DineOut** (www.dineout.co.nz) Restaurant reviews across NZ.
- **Living Landscapes** (www.living landscapes.co.nz) Maori tourism operator listings.
- **Muzic.net** (www.muzic.net.nz) Gigs, reviews, band bios and charts.

# CALENDAR

## ↘ JANUARY

### BIG DAY OUT
Hurl yourself into the international music moshpit at this rock extravaganza held in Auckland every summer. Big names such as Muse, Dizzee Rascal, the Red Hot Chilli Peppers and Metallica crank out the tunes; see www.bigdayout.com.

### WORLD BUSKERS FESTIVAL
National and international buskers, including jugglers, musos, sword swallowers and unicycle riders, hit Christchurch's city streets for 10 days in late January. Be prepared for audience participation and don't forget to drop a few coins in the hat; see www.worldbuskersfestival.com.

### PARIHAKA
This culturally and historically significant music and arts festival happens at Parihaka, a small Maori settlement east off Taranaki's Hwy 45. The town was the centre of peaceful resistance to European land confiscations after the violence of the Taranaki Land Wars; see www.parihaka.com.

### HARVEST HAWKE'S BAY
The fab Harvest Hawke's Bay festival is an indulgent wine and food celebration, focussing on the wineries around Napier and Hastings. But it's not just chardonnay and syrah: local produce, personalities and musicians abound. See www.harvesthawkes bay.co.nz.

## ↘ FEBRUARY

### TE MATATINI NATIONAL KAPA HAKA FESTIVAL
This Maori *haka* competition is held in February in odd-numbered years. There's much gesticulation, thigh-slapping, eye-bulging and tongue extension. Venues vary: in 2011 it will be held at Gisborne on the North island's east coast. See www.tematatini.org.nz for more info.

### MARLBOROUGH WINE FESTIVAL
Marlborough sauvignon blanc is a world-wide wine hit, and this festival is a great excuse to drink some. It features wine from over 50 Marlborough wineries, fine food and entertainment: over-indulgence aplenty. See www.wine-marlborough-festival.co.nz.

### NEW ZEALAND INTERNATIONAL SEVENS
The world's top seven-a-side rugby teams crack heads in Wellington. The regular rugby season happens in winter, so this is a great chance to experience NZ's national game if you're here in the sunny season; see www.nzisevens.co.nz.

### NEW ZEALAND INTERNATIONAL ARTS FESTIVAL
This month-long biennial occupies Wellington's hearts and minds in February/March each even-numbered year. Expect dozens of theatre, dance, music and visual arts performances and exhibitions, with dozens of in-

ternational acts; see www.nzfestival
.nzpost.co.nz.

## FRINGE NZ
Three weeks of way-out-there experimental visual arts, music, dance and theatre in Wellington: everything that's too weird, challenging or non-profitable to make it into the more formal New Zealand International Arts Festival; www.fringe.org.nz.

## ⬋ MARCH

### WOMAD
Following on from its sister event in South Australia, WOMAD (World of Music Arts & Dance) features local and international arts performances at the Bowl of Brooklands in New Plymouth. Bring the kids! Everything from Mongolian nose flautists to Peter Gabriel; see www.womad.co.nz.

### PASIFIKA FESTIVAL
In early to mid-March, Western Springs Park in Auckland hosts the excellent Polynesian Pasifika Festival. Thousands descend to load up on island food, hang out in the sun and catch cultural performances. See www.aucklandcity.govt.nz/whatson/events/pasifika.

## ⬋ APRIL–MAY

### NATIONAL JAZZ FESTIVAL
Bee-bop za-bah-dee-dah: every Easter in Tauranga (the biggest town in the

Food and wine festival (p46), Hawke's Bay

Bay of Plenty), the longest-running jazz fest in the southern hemisphere gets fingers a-snappin'; see www.jazz.org.nz.

### NEW ZEALAND INTERNATIONAL COMEDY FESTIVAL
This three-week comedy festival happens in April and May, in venues across Auckland, Wellington and various regional centres. Plenty of touring giggle-vendors and local laugh-mongers. BYO beret; see www.comedyfestival.co.nz for more info.

# CALENDAR

| JAN | FEB | MAR | APR |

## JUNE–JULY

### MATARIKI

Maori New Year is celebrated on the first new moon in June, with remembrance, education and ceremonial tree plantings. Events are held mainly around Auckland and Northland; see www.taitokerau.co.nz/matariki.htm.

### QUEENSTOWN WINTER FESTIVAL

Up to 60,000 people wax their snowboards and head for the mountains in this 10-day winter fiesta in Queenstown. There are fireworks, jazz, comedy, live music and lots for the kids to do. See www.winterfestival.co.nz.

### NEW ZEALAND INTERNATIONAL FILM FESTIVALS

After separate film festivals in Wellington, Auckland, Dunedin and Christchurch, a selection of hit flicks hits the road for screenings in regional towns from July to November. Get ready for a lot of hours sitting still in the dark; see www.enzedff.co.nz.

## SEPTEMBER–OCTOBER

### WORLD OF WEARABLEART AWARD SHOW

Bizarre in the best possible way, the WOW show started off in Nelson in 1987 but now fills a two-week slot in Wellington every September. Amazing garments by the wardrobe-full (made from wine bladders, car parts, cardboard, venetian blinds) make front-page news across the nation. See www.worldofwearableart.com.

Pasifika Festival (p47)

PAUL KENNEDY

| MAY | JUN | JUL | AUG | SEP | OCT | NOV | DEC |

Toast Martinborough food and wine festival (p49)

### SEAFEST
On the first Saturday in October, Kaikoura's popular annual fish fiesta features seafood and wine, live bands, family entertainment and a big Friday night bash to kick things off. Book tickets and beds well in advance to avoid missing out; see www.seafest.co.nz for more information.

## NOVEMBER

### TOAST MARTINBOROUGH
Wine-swilling Wellingtonians cross the Rimutaka Ranges into the Wairarapa Region for Toast Martinborough – a *looong* day of pinot noir-soaked indulgence and sophisticated good times. See www.toastmartinborough.co.nz.

## DECEMBER

### RHYTHM & VINES
See out the old year in Gisborne (then be the first to see the new year's dawn) at Rhythm & Vines. Wine, music and song (all the good things), with top DJs, hip-hop acts, bands and singer-songwriters; see www.rhythmandvines.co.nz.

AUCKLAND

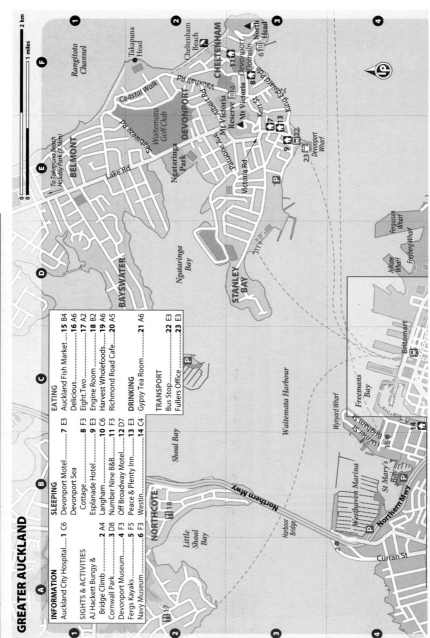

# GREATER AUCKLAND

**INFORMATION**
Auckland City Hospital......1 C6

**SIGHTS & ACTIVITIES**
AJ Hackett Bungy &
  Bridge Climb..............2 A4
Cornwall Park..................3 D8
Devonport Museum..........4 F3
Fergs Kayaks...................5 F5
Navy Museum.................6 F3

**SLEEPING**
Devonport Motel..............7 E3
Devonport Sea
  Cottage......................8 F3
Esplanade Hotel..............9 E3
Langham........................10 C6
Number Nine B&B...........11 F3
Off Broadway Motel.........12 D7
Peace & Plenty Inn..........13 E3
Westin............................14 C4

**EATING**
Auckland Fish Market......15 B4
Delicious.........................16 A6
Eight.Two........................17 A2
Engine Room...................18 B2
Harvest Wholefoods........19 A6
Richmond Road Cafe.......20 A5

**DRINKING**
Gypsy Tea Room..............21 A6

**TRANSPORT**
Bus Stop.........................22 E3
Fullers Office...................23 E3

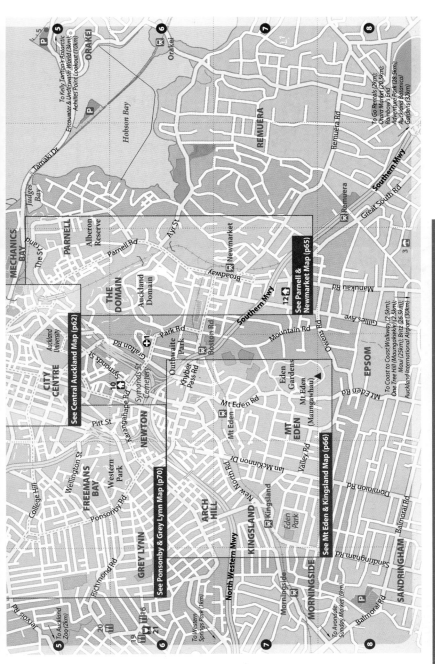

AUCKLAND

AUCKLAND

# HIGHLIGHTS

**1** ## WAIHEKE ISLAND

### BY STEVE & NIGEL ROBINSON, ANANDA TOURS

We often have visitors telling us Waiheke was the highlight of their trip to New Zealand. The island's very easy to get to. You can arrive from Sydney or Los Angeles at breakfast time, and be on Waiheke for lunch at an excellent vineyard restaurant with spectacular views.

HIGHLIGHTS

## ↘ STEVE & NIGEL ROBINSON'S DON'T MISS LIST

### ❶ THE ARTS SCENE

There are lots of artists on Waiheke, and the *Arts Trail* brochure highlights the island's galleries. The **Waiheke Art Gallery** (p85) in Oneroa showcases local artists, and the superb **Connell's Bay Sculpture Park** (p85) features a two-hour walk through installations on a former sheep farm.

### ❷ WINE

Waiheke wine is all about quality over quantity. Wines from **Goldwater Estate**, **Te Motu** and **Stonyridge** (all p85) are included in the book *1001 Wines You Must Taste Before You Die*. Waiheke's also an island of boutique businesses – on wine tours (86) visitors share the passion directly with the winemakers

Clockwise from top: Oneroa Beach; Palm Beach; A Waiheke vineyard

### ❸ BEACHES

On beaches such as **Onetangi**, **Oneroa**, and **Palm Beach** (see p85), we think it's crowded if there are more than 20 people. Visitors arrive and say, 'Where is everybody?' Even in the height of summer, it's easy to find quiet stretches of beach.

### ❹ STONY BATTER HISTORIC RESERVE

This amazing landscape is strewn with huge boulders thrown up by volcanic eruptions 20 million years ago. It's also a historic reserve: the **Stony Batter Fort** (p85) was built in WWII to defend against a naval invasion that never happened. There's more than a kilometre of tunnels 25 feet (7.6m) underground to be explored.

### ❺ WALKING THE COAST

Because the island is so hilly, around every corner there's a new view – usually with sea in it. The local council has put lots of resources into bush and coastal walkways, and there's public access to most parts of the coast. Other activities include horse riding and sea kayaking. See p85 for more info.

### ↘ THINGS YOU NEED TO KNOW

**Quirkiest shopping** Ostend market (Ostend Hall; ⊗8am-1pm Sat) **Bookings essential** Lunch on summer weekends at vineyard restaurants such as Mudbrick, Te Whau or Cable Bay **Best advice** The sign welcoming visitors off the car ferry: 'Slow down. You're here.' **For more on Waiheke Island, see p84**

# HIGHLIGHTS

## ⬐ AUCKLAND MUSEUM

If you have the slightest interest in Maori and Pacific Islander culture, your first stop should be the Auckland Museum (p62). The Maori galleries are loaded with artefacts from around the country, and there are cultural performances daily – see why NZ's All Blacks rugby team uses the *haka* to put the fear of God into their opposition. There's plenty of natural history, war history and kids stuff, too.

## ⬐ RESTAURANTS, CAFES & BARS

Dress up for the classy restaurants and bars around Viaduct Harbour (p68), browse the eateries along Ponsonby Rd (p76), or order some fast sushi downtown. Breakfast and coffee are big business in Auckland – the cafes are kickin' around Parnell & Newmarket (p76). Later on, you'll find plenty of places to wet your whistle: Vulcan Lane, Ponsonby Rd and K Rd are drinking (p78) hot spots.

**4**

## ↘ VOLCANOES

Feel the heat! There's a huge reservoir of molten magma 100km below the streets of Auckland, and there are 50 volcanic peaks (p61) around the city. But don't sweat – there hasn't been an eruption here for 600 years, and most of the cones are dormant. Take a hike up Mt Eden (Maungawhau; p64) or One Tree Hill (Maungakiekie; p64) and see what you can see.

**5**

## ↘ AUCKLAND ART GALLERY

The Auckland Art Gallery (p65) provides a hushed, cultured escape from the streets. The Main Gallery and the New Gallery (predictably) focus on the old and the new respectively: look for European masters and early colonial works in the former, and contemporary Kiwi creations and temporary exhibitions in the latter.

**6**

## ↘ PASIFIKA

Almost 180,000 Pacific Islanders (PI) live in Auckland, making it the world's principal Polynesian city. Samoans are the largest group, followed by Cook Islanders, Tongans, Niueans, Fijians, Tokelauans and Tuvaluans. You'll find PI motifs everywhere in art, architecture, fashion, homewares and music. The Pasifika Festival (p47) celebrates all things south seas.

2 ANDERS BLOMQVIST; 3 DAVID WALL; 4 RICHARD CUMMINS; 5 RICHARD CUMMINS; 6 PAUL KENNEDY

2 Maori meeting house, Auckland Museum (p62); 3 Viaduct Harbour (p68); 4 One Tree Hill (Maungakiekie; p64);
5 Auckland Art Gallery (p65); 6 Celebrations at the Pasifika Festival (p47)

AUCKLAND

BEST...

# BEST...

## ↘ POINTS OF VIEW

- **Mt Eden** (Maungawhau; p64) Killer views from Auckland's highest volcanic cone.
- **Sky Tower** (p65) The southern hemisphere's tallest structure.
- **One Tree Hill** (Maungakiekie; p64) Historic volcanic cone with a 360 degree outlook.
- **On the water** (p69) Cruise onto the harbour and see Auckland from the water.

## ↘ FRESH-AIR FACTORIES

- **The Domain** (p62) Eighty downtown hectares of recreational greenery.
- **Eden Gardens** (p65) Burgeoning blooms on Mt Eden.
- **Albert Park** (p67) Formal Victorian-era garden full of canoodling students.
- **Tamaki Drive** (p67) Tree-lined runway for joggers and the generically good looking.

## ↘ EAT STREETS & DRINKING DENS

- **Ponsonby Rd, Ponsonby** (p76) Busiest restaurant-cafe-bar strip (www.ponsonbyroad.co.nz).
- **Karangahape Rd (K Rd), Newton** (p75) Edgy strip of affordable restaurants and bars.
- **Princes Wharf & Viaduct Harbour, Central Auckland** (p68) Upmarket waterfront eating and drinking.
- **New North Rd, Kingsland** (p76) Emerging eat street with great Thai and French cuisine.

## ↘ FESTIVALS

- **Devonport Food & Wine Festival** (www.devonportwinefestival.co.nz; mid-Feb) Sassy two-day sip-fest.
- **Auckland Festival** (www.aucklandfestival.co.nz; Mar) Auckland's biggest arts party; on odd-numbered years.
- **New Zealand Boat Show** (www.boatshow.co.nz; mid-May) Hoist your spinnaker.

PAUL KENNEDY

**Wintergarden, the Domain** (p63)

# THINGS YOU NEED TO KNOW

## ⬂ VITAL STATISTICS

- **Population** 1.2 million
- **Telephone code** ☎ 09
- **Best time to visit** December to February (summer)

## ⬂ NEIGHBOURHOODS IN A NUTSHELL

- **Central Auckland** Commercial high-rise hub: waterfront eating and drinking, Queen St shopping and K Rd nightlife.
- **Ponsonby & Grey Lynn** Alternative foodie haunts and bars.
- **Parnell & Newmarket** Old-money 'hoods; pricey restaurants and boutiques.
- **Mt Eden & Kingsland** Emerging foodie enclaves south of the centre.
- **Devonport & North Shore** Village vibes and beaches across the harbour.

## ⬂ ADVANCE PLANNING

- **One month before** Book your bed in the city (p72) and transport, accommodation and activities on the Hauraki Gulf Islands (p83).
- **Two weeks before** Book tickets (p79) for concerts and the rugby.
- **One week before** Book a harbour cruise (p69) and a table at a top restaurant (p75).

## ⬂ RESOURCES

- **Auckland i-SITE** (www.aucklandnz .com) Downtown tourist info.
- **Auckland NZ** (www.aucklandnz.com) Official tourist site.
- **DOC Information Centre** (www.doc. govt.nz) National Parks info.
- **MAXX Regional Transport** (www .maxx.co.nz) Public transport details.

## ⬂ EMERGENCY NUMBERS

- **Ambulance, fire service & police** ( ☎ 111)
- **Auckland Central Police Station** (Map p62; ☎ 09-302 6400; cnr Vincent & Cook Sts)

## ⬂ GETTING AROUND

- **Airbus Express** (p82) to/from the airport.
- **Bus** (p82) all around the city.
- **Ferry** (p82) to the islands and North Shore.
- **Hirea car** (p81) when you want to leave town.
- **Train** (p83) to the southwestern suburbs.
- **Walk** around Central Auckland and the waterfront.

AUCKLAND

# DISCOVER AUCKLAND

Paris may be the city of love, but Auckland is the city of many lovers, according to its Maori name, Tamaki Makaurau.

It's hard to imagine a more geographically blessed city. Its two magnificent harbours frame a narrow isthmus punctuated by volcanic cones and surrounded by fertile farmland. From any of its numerous vantage points you'll be astounded at how close the Tasman Sea and Pacific Ocean come to kissing and forming a new island.

As a result, water's never far away – whether it's the ruggedly beautiful west-coast surf beaches or the glistening Hauraki Gulf with its myriad islands. The 135,000 pleasure crafts filling Auckland's marinas have lent the city its most durable nickname: the 'City of Sails'.

Yet the rest of the country loves to hate it, tut-tutting about its traffic snarls and the supposed self-obsession of the quarter of the country's population that call it home. With its many riches, Auckland can justifiably respond to its detractors, 'Don't hate me because I'm beautiful.'.

DISCOVER AUCKLAND

## AUCKLAND IN...

### Two Days

Book ahead for tomorrow night's dinner. Breakfast in Ponsonby (p76) and take the Link Bus to Auckland Museum (p62) for the Maori gallery and culture show. Wander through the Domain (p62) towards K Rd, where you can grab lunch. End with a relaxing drink or meal at Princes Wharf.

On day two, grab breakfast in the city before catching the 9.15am ferry to Rangitoto (p84). This will give you time to explore the volcanic island before it starts to bake. Catch the 12.45pm ferry to Devonport (p68) for lunch. Stay on the North Shore for a memorable dinner at the Engine Room (p77) or Eight. Two (p77).

### Four Days

On the third day, head west. Grab breakfast in Titirangi (p87) before exploring the Waitakere Ranges Regional Park (p88), Karekare (p88) and Piha (p88). Freshen up for a night of eating and drinking your way around Kingsland (p76 & p79).

On day four, breakfast in Mt Eden (p76) and then climb Maungawhau (p64). Catch the train back to Britomart for the 11am ferry to Waiheke Island (p84). Don't miss the last ferry back.

## ORIENTATION

The Auckland isthmus runs roughly west–east, with Waitemata Harbour lying to the north (feeding into the Hauraki Gulf) and Manukau Harbour to the south (feeding into the Tasman Sea). The Harbour Bridge links the city to the North Shore, with the CBD to its east.

## INFORMATION

There are plenty of moneychangers, banks and ATMs, especially on Queen St.

**Auckland City Hospital** (Map p52; ☎ 09-379 0000; Park Rd, Grafton; ☉ 24hr) The city's main hospital; has an accident and emergency (A&E) section.

**Auckland i-SITE** (Map p62; ☎ 09-363 7182; www.aucklandnz.com; Sky Tower Atrium, cnr Victoria & Federal Sts; ☉ 8am-8pm) Tourist info.

**Auckland Metro Doctors & Travelcare** (Map p62; ☎ 09-373 4621; 17 Emily Place, Auckland Central; ☉ 9am-5.30pm Mon-Fri, 10am-2pm Sat) Specialises in health care and vaccinations for travellers.

**DOC information centre** (Map p62; ☎ 09-379 6476; www.doc.govt.nz; 137 Quay St; ☉ 9am-5pm Mon-Fri, 10am-3pm Sat)

**New Zealand i-SITE** (Map p62; ☎ 09-307 0612; 137 Quay St; ☉ 9am-5.30pm May-Oct, 8am-7pm Nov-Apr)

**Wellesley St Post Office** (Map p62; 24 Wellesley St) The place to pick up poste restante mail (ID is required).

## SIGHTS

### AUCKLAND VOLCANIC FIELD

Some cities think they're tough by living in the shadow of a volcano. Auckland's

CLOCKWISE FROM TOP LEFT: RICHARD CUMMINS; RICHARD CUMMINS; MARTIN ROBINSON; PAUL KENNEDY

Clockwise from top left: Princes Wharf; Maori carving, Auckland Museum (p62); Ferry to Devonport (p68); Mt Eden (Maungawhau; p64)

AUCKLAND

ORIENTATION

AUCKLAND

SIGHTS

built on 50 of them and, no, they're all extinct. The last one to erupt was Rangitoto (p84) about 600 years ago and no one can predict when the next eruption will occur. Auckland's quite literally a hot spot – with a reservoir of magma 100km below waiting to bubble to the surface. But relax: this has only happened 19 times in the last 20,000 years.

Some of Auckland's volcanoes are cones, some are filled with water and some have been completely quarried away. Moves are afoot to register the

field as a World Heritage Site and protect what remains. Most of the surviving cones show evidence of terracing from when they formed a formidable series of Maori *pa*.

The most easily accessible and well known of Auckland's volcanic cones are One Tree Hill (Maungakiekie; p64) and Mt Eden (Maungawhau; p64).

## AUCKLAND MUSEUM & DOMAIN
Covering about 80 hectares, the green swath of the **Auckland Domain** (Map

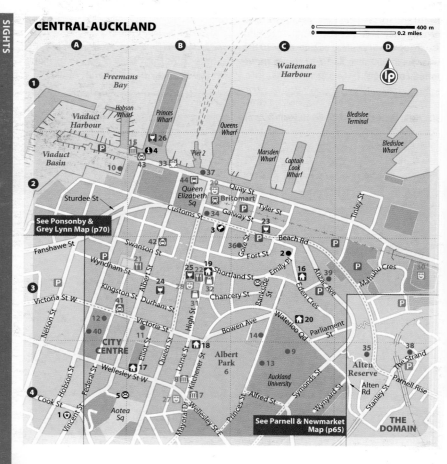

CENTRAL AUCKLAND

AUCKLAND

p65) contains sports fields, interesting sculptures, formal gardens, wild corners and the **Wintergarden** (Map p65; admission free; ⊗ 9am-5.30pm Mon-Sat, 9am-7.30pm Sun Nov-Mar, 9am-4.30pm Apr-Oct), with its fernery, tropical house, cool house, cute cat statue and neighbouring cafe.

Dominating it all is the magnificent **Auckland Museum** (Map p65; ☎ 09-309 0443; www.aucklandmuseum.com; adult/child $5/free; ⊗ 10am-5pm), an imposing Greek temple with an impressive modern dome. Its comprehensive display of Pacific Island and Maori artefacts on the ground floor deserves to be on your 'must see' list. Highlights include a 25m war canoe and an extant carved meeting house from the Thames area that you can enter (remove your shoes first).

Bookings are required for the **museum highlights guided tour** (☎ 09-306 7048; adult/child $10/5; ⊗ 10.30am & 2pm). **Maori gallery tours** (same prices) take place at 11.30am and 2pm. Daily **Maori cultural performances** (adult/child $25/13; ⊗ 11am, noon & 1.30pm) provide a decent (and good-humoured) introduction to things Maori.

WIBOWO RUSLI

SIGHTS

**Wintergarden, the Domain**

AUCKLAND

SIGHTS

**One Tree Hill (Maungakiekie)**

RICHARD CUMMINS

## ↘ ONE TREE HILL (MAUNGAKIEKIE)

This volcanic cone (off Map p52) was the isthmus' key *pa* and the greatest fortress in the country. It's easy to see why: a drive or walk to the top (182m) offers amazing 360-degree views. At the summit is the grave of John Logan Campbell, who gifted the land to the city in 1901, requesting that a memorial (the imposing obelisk and statue above the grave) be built to the Maori people.

Looking at One Tree Hill, your first thought will probably be 'Where's the bloody tree?' Good question. Up until 2000 a Monterey pine stood at the top of the hill. This was a replacement for a sacred totara that was chopped down by British settlers in 1852. Maori activists first attacked the foreign usurper in 1994, finishing the job in 2000. It's unlikely that another tree will be planted until local land claims have moved closer to resolution, but you can bet your boots that this time around it'll be a native.

Auckland's most beloved landmark achieved international recognition in 1987 when U2 released the song 'One Tree Hill' on their acclaimed *The Joshua Tree* album. It was only released as a single in NZ, where it went to number one.

To get here from the city, take bus 328 from Customs St to Manukau Rd (adult/child $4.30/2.40, 21 minutes).

Walking here from the city will take about 30 minutes, or you can catch the Link Bus (p83) to the neighbouring hospital.

## MT EDEN (MAUNGAWHAU)

The view from Mt Eden (Map p66), Auckland's highest cone (196m), is su-perb. The symmetrical crater (50m deep) is known as Te Ipu Kai a Mataaho (the Food Bowl of Mataaho, the god of things hidden in the ground) and is highly *tapu* (sacred); don't enter it, but feel free to explore the remainder of the mountain. The remains of *pa* terraces and storage pits are clearly visible.

On its eastern slopes, **Eden Gardens** (Map p66; ☎ 09-638 8395; 24 Omana Ave, Epsom; adult/child $6/free; ⏰ 9am-4pm) is a horticultural showpiece noted for camellias, rhododendrons and azaleas.

## AUCKLAND ZOO

**Auckland Zoo** (off Map p52; ☎ 09-360 3800; www.aucklandzoo.co.nz; Motions Rd; adult/child $19/9; ⏰ 9.30am-5.30pm) is an excellent modern zoo with spacious, natural compounds. The infrared lighting of the nocturnal house offers a rare chance to see kiwi fossicking about. The big foreigners tend to steal the attention from the timid natives, but if you can wrestle the kids away from the tigers and elephants you'll find tuataras and a large selection of native birds.

From the city, catch any bus (adult/child $3.20/1.80, 16 minutes) heading west via Great North Rd.

## AUCKLAND ART GALLERY

The **Auckland Art Gallery** ( ☎ 09-379 1349; www.aucklandartgallery.com; admission free; ⏰ 10am-5pm) spreads over two neighbouring buildings. The **Main Gallery** (Map p62; cnr Wellesley & Kitchener Sts), built in French chateau style, isn't terribly big, but it houses important works by Pieter Bruegel the Younger and Guido Reni in the European collection, and an extensive collection of NZ art. It's worth calling in for the intimate 19th-century portraits of tattooed Maori subjects by Charles Goldie and Gottfried Lindauer alone. The **New Gallery** (Map p62; cnr Wellesley & Lorne Sts) concentrates on contemporary art and temporary exhibitions (with varying admission charges). Ten commercial galleries can be found in the immediate vicinity.

## SKY TOWER

The impossible-to-miss **Sky Tower** (Map p62; ☎ 09-363 6000; www.skycityauckland.co.nz; cnr Federal & Victoria Sts; adult/child $25/8; ⏰ 8.30am-10.30pm Sun-Thu, 8.30am-11.30pm Fri & Sat) looks like a giant hypodermic giving

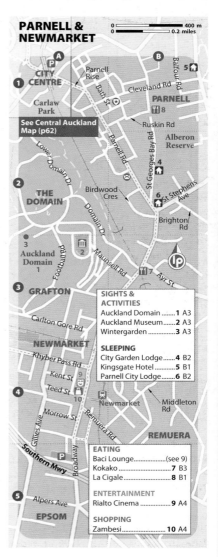

**PARNELL & NEWMARKET**

| SIGHTS & ACTIVITIES | | |
| --- | --- | --- |
| Auckland Domain | 1 | A3 |
| Auckland Museum | 2 | A3 |
| Wintergarden | 3 | A3 |

| SLEEPING | | |
| --- | --- | --- |
| City Garden Lodge | 4 | B2 |
| Kingsgate Hotel | 5 | B1 |
| Parnell City Lodge | 6 | B2 |

| EATING | | |
| --- | --- | --- |
| Baci Lounge | (see 9) | |
| Kokako | 7 | B3 |
| La Cigale | 8 | B1 |

| ENTERTAINMENT | | |
| --- | --- | --- |
| Rialto Cinema | 9 | A4 |

| SHOPPING | | |
| --- | --- | --- |
| Zambesi | 10 | A4 |

AUCKLAND

SIGHTS

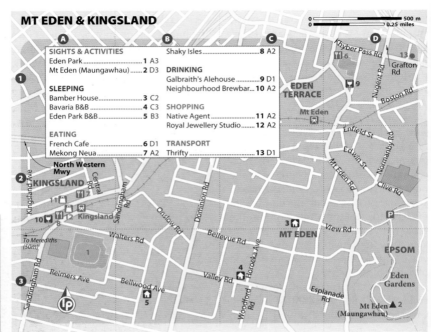

## MT EDEN & KINGSLAND

| SIGHTS & ACTIVITIES | | Shaky Isles ........................ **8** A2 |
| --- | --- | --- |
| Eden Park ........................ **1** A3 | | |
| Mt Eden (Maungawhau) ...... **2** D3 | | **DRINKING** |
| | | Galbraith's Alehouse ........ **9** D1 |
| **SLEEPING** | | Neighbourhood Brewbar .. **10** A2 |
| Bamber House .................. **3** C2 | | |
| Bavaria B&B .................... **4** C3 | | **SHOPPING** |
| Eden Park B&B ................ **5** B3 | | Native Agent ................ **11** A2 |
| | | Royal Jewellery Studio ...... **12** A2 |
| **EATING** | | |
| French Cafe .................... **6** D1 | | **TRANSPORT** |
| Mekong Neua .................. **7** A2 | | Thrifty .......................... **13** D1 |

a fix to the heavens. Spectacular lighting renders it even more space-age at night. The colours change for special events and shooting fireworks make it even more phallic on New Year's Eve.

At 328m it is the tallest structure in the southern hemisphere. A lift takes you up to the observation decks in 40 stomach-lurching seconds; look down through the glass floor panels if you're after an extra kick. See p68 for crazy stuff you can do while you're up here.

## KELLY TARLTON'S ANTARCTIC ENCOUNTER & UNDERWATER WORLD

This unique **aquarium** (off Map p52; ☎ 09-531 5065; www.kellytarltons.co.nz; 23 Tamaki Dr, Orakei; adult/child $32/16; ⏰ 9.30am-5.30pm) is housed in old stormwater and sewage holding tanks. A transparent tunnel runs

along the centre of the tank, through which you travel on a conveyor belt, with the fish, including sharks and stingrays, swimming around you.

The big attraction, however, is the permanent winter wonderland known as Antarctic Encounter. It includes a walk through a replica of Scott's 1911 Antarctic hut, and a ride aboard a heated Snow Cat through a frozen environment where a colony of king and gentoo penguins lives at sub-zero temperatures.

Buses numbered 745 to 769 head here from Britomart (Map p62). There's also a free shark-shaped shuttle bus that departs 172 Quay St (opposite the ferry terminal) on the hour between 9am and 4pm (except 2pm) and SkyCity's atrium 10 minutes later (departing Kelly Tarlton's 40 minutes later).

## TAMAKI DRIVE

This scenic, pohutukawa-lined road heads east from the city, hugging the waterfront. In summer it's a jogging/cycling/rollerblading blur offering plenty of eye candy.

Below the headland is **Mission Bay**, a popular beach with an iconic fountain, historic mission house, restaurants and bars. Safe swimming beaches **Kohimarama** and **St Heliers** follow. Further east along Cliff Rd, the **Achilles Point lookout** (off Map p52) offers panoramic views.

Buses 745 to 769 from Britomart follow this route.

## ALBERT PARK & AUCKLAND UNIVERSITY

Hugging the hill on the city's eastern flank, **Albert Park** (Map p62) is a charming Victorian formal garden overrun by students during term time, some of whom periodically deface the statues of Governor Grey and Queen Victoria. Auckland University campus stretches over several streets and incorporates a row of stately **Victorian merchant houses** (Map p62; Princes St) and **Old Government House** (Map p62; Waterloo Quadrant).

The **University Clock Tower** (Map p62; 22 Princes St) is Auckland's architectural triumph.

**AUCKLAND**

**SIGHTS**

Auckland in bloom

WIBOWO RUSLI

## ↘ IF YOU LIKE...

If you like **Eden Gardens** (p65) we think you'll like these other Auckland green zones.

- **Auckland Botanical Gardens** (off Map p52; ☎ 09-267 1457; Hill Rd, Manurewa; admission free; ⊗ 8am-6pm) These 64-hectare gardens have themed areas, threatened plants, and a hell of a lot of brides and grooms.
- **Cornwall Park** (Map p52; admission free; ⊗ 24hr) On the side of One Tree Hill, Cornwall Park has impressive mature trees.
- **Western Springs Park** (off Map p52; Great North Rd, Grey Lynn; admission free; ⊗ 24hr) Formed by a confluence of lava flows, the lake here was once Auckland's water supply. It's a great spot for a picnic.

PAUL KENNEDY

**View over Devonport**

## DEVONPORT

Located at the bottom of the North Shore, Devonport makes a pleasant day trip by ferry from the city. Quaint without being twee, it retains a village atmosphere, with many well-preserved Victorian and Edwardian buildings and loads of cafes.

The navy is based here, its history on display at the **Navy Museum** (Map p52; ☎ 09-445 5186; www.navymuseum.mil.nz; King Edward Pde; admission by donation; ⏰ 10am-4.30pm). Its civilian neighbours have theirs preserved in the **Devonport Museum** (Map p52; ☎ 09-445 2661; www.devonport museum.org.nz; 33a Vauxhall Rd; admission free; ⏰ 2-4pm Sat & Sun).

Ferries to Devonport (adult/child $10/5 return, 12 minutes) depart from the Auckland Ferry Building every 30 minutes (hourly after 7pm) from 6.15am to 11pm (until 1am Friday and Saturday), and from 7.15am to 10pm on Sundays and public holidays. Some Waiheke Island and Rangitoto ferries also stop here.

### VIADUCT HARBOUR

Once a busy commercial port, the Viaduct Harbour was given a major makeover leading up to the 1999/2000 and 2003 America's Cup tournaments. It's now a fancy dining and boozing precinct for the boat-shoes brigade, and guaranteed to have at least a slight buzz any night of the week.

The well-presented **Voyager – New Zealand Maritime Museum** (Map p62; ☎ 09-373 0800; www.nzmaritime.org; cnr Quay & Hobson Sts; adult/child $16/8; ⏰ 9am-5pm) traces NZ's seafaring history, from Maori voyaging canoes to the America's Cup.

## ACTIVITIES
### SPIDERMAN ACTIVITIES

The wise men of bungy, **AJ Hackett Bungy & Bridge Climb** (Map p52; ☎ 09-361 2000; www.ajhackett.com/nz; Westhaven Reserve, Curran St) offers the chance to climb up or jump off the Auckland Harbour Bridge. Both the 40m bungy leap and the 1½-hour guided tour along the arch (with a harness attached to a static line) cost $120.

Not to be outdone, the Sky Tower offers an ever-expanding selection of pants-wetting activities. If you thought the observation deck was for pussies, **Sky Walk** (Map p62; ☎ 0800 759 925; www.skywalk.co.nz; adult/child $135/100; ⏰ 10am-5.30pm) involves circling the 192m-high, 1.2m-wide outside halo of the tower without rails or a balcony – but with a safety harness (they're not completely crazy). **Sky Jump** (Map p62; ☎ 0800 759

586; www.skyjump.co.nz; adult/child $195/145; 🕙 10am-5.30pm) is an 11-second, 85km/h base wire jump from the observation deck. It's more like a parachute jump than a bungy, and it's a rush and a half. You can combine both in the Look 'n' Leap package ($260).

## CRUISES

**Fullers** (Map p52; ☎ 09-367 9111; www.fullers. co.nz; Ferry Bldg, 99 Quay St) operates ferry services (Birkenhead, Northcote Point, Devonport, Rangitoto, Waiheke Island, Great Barrier Island) and daily harbour cruises (adult/child $35/18, 1½ hours,

10.30am and 1.30pm), which include a stop on Rangitoto, a complimentary cuppa and a free return ticket to Devonport.

**360 Discovery** (Map p62; ☎ 09-307 8005; www.360discovery.co.nz; Pier 4 kiosk, Quay St) also runs ferries (Gulf Harbour, Motuihe, Tiritiri Matangi, Coromandel Town) along with the Harbour Discovery cruise (adult/child $29/15, 1½ hours), departing at 10am, noon and 2.30pm, which stops at Devonport, Rangitoto, Motuihe and Orakei Wharf (for Kelly Tarlton's Antarctic Encounter).

AUCKLAND

ACTIVITIES

HOLGER LEUE

Reverse bungy, Auckland city

## ↘ IF YOU LIKE...

If you like the **AJ Hackett Bungy & Bridge Climb** (p68), we think you'll like these other Auckland adrenaline rushes:

- **Active Sky Hang Gliding** ( ☎ 021 170 3646; www.activeskyhanggliding.co.nz; tandem flight $175) Fly like a kahu (native hawk – NZ doesn't have eagles) in a tandem flight.
- **NZ Skydive** ( ☎ 09-373 5778; www.nzskydive.co.nz; tandem skydive $299) Tandem skydives from 12,000ft (including a 7000ft free fall).
- **Sky Screamer** (Map p62; ☎ 09-377 1328; www.reversebungy.com; cnr Albert St & Victoria Sts; ride $40; 🕙 10.30am-10pm Sun-Thu, 10am-2am Fri & Sat) Get strapped into a seat and reverse-bungied 60m up in the air. Should you hurl, rest assured – you can get a video of it.

**Sail NZ** (Map p62; ☎ 0800 397 567; www.sail newzealand.co.nz; Viaduct Harbour) heads out on genuine America's Cup yachts (adult/child $150/110, two hours). This experienced and highly regarded outfit also offers daily Whale & Dolphin Safaris (adult/child $150/100); dolphins are spotted 90% of the time and whales 75%. Their Pride of Auckland fleet of glamorous large yachts offers tours ranging from the 90-minute Coffee Cruise (adult/child $70/37) to the full-day Sailing Adventure (adult/child $135/110).

### HIKING

The city council's *Auckland City's Walkways* pamphlet has a good selection of urban walks, including the **Coast to Coast Walkway** (off Map p52; 16km, four hours). Heading clear across the country, from Waitemata Harbour to Manukau Harbour, the walk encompasses Albert Park, the University, the Domain, Mt Eden (Maungawhau) and One Tree Hill (Maungakiekie), keeping as much as possible to reserves rather than city streets. Starting from the Viaduct Basin and heading south, it's marked by yellow markers and milestones; heading north from Onehunga there are blue markers. To get back to the city, take bus 328, 334, 348 or 354 from Onehunga Mall ($5.40, 50 minutes).

### OTHER ACTIVITIES

**Fergs Kayaks** (Map p52; ☎ 09-529 2230; www.fergskayaks.co.nz; 12 Tamaki Dr, Okahu Bay; ⏰ 9am-6pm Mon-Fri, 8am-6pm Sat & Sun) hires out kayaks ($15 to $40 per hour or $50 to $120 per day), bikes (per hour/day $20/120) and inline skates (per hour/day $15/30). Day and night guided kayak trips

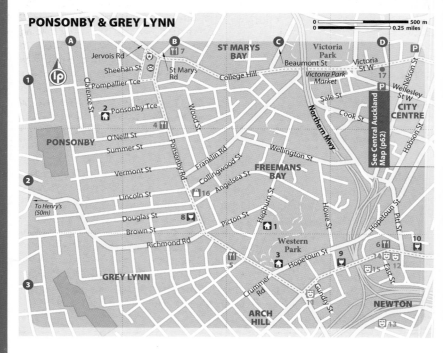

are available to Devonport (8km, three hours, $95) or Rangitoto Island (13km, six hours, $120).

**Rainbow's End Adventure Park** (off Map p52; ☎ 09-262 2030; www.rainbowsend.co.nz; 2 Clist Cres, Manukau; superpass adult/child $45/35; ☺ 10am-5pm) has enough rides (including a corkscrew roller coaster and the 'Power Surge'), shows and interactive entertainment to keep the kids happy all day, plus plenty of sugary snacks to fuel it all. Superpasses allow unlimited rides.

## AUCKLAND FOR CHILDREN

Auckland has plenty to keep kids entertained, whatever the weather. All of the east coast beaches (St Heliers, Kohimarama, Mission Bay, Okahu Bay, Cheltenham, Narrow Neck, Takapuna, Milford, Long Bay) are safe for supervised kids, while Rainbow's End Adventure Park (above), Kelly Tarlton's Antarctic Encounter & Underwater World (p66) and Auckland Zoo (p65) are other favourites.

| SLEEPING | | |
|---|---|---|
| 23 Hepburn | **1** | C2 |
| Great Ponsonby Arthotel | **2** | A1 |
| Verandahs | **3** | C3 |
| | | |
| EATING | | |
| Dizengoff | **4** | B1 |
| Ponsonby Village Food Court | **5** | C3 |
| Satya | **6** | D3 |
| Soto | **7** | B1 |
| | | |
| DRINKING | | |
| Ponsonby Social Club | **8** | B2 |
| Thirsty Dog | **9** | D3 |
| Wine Cellar | **10** | D3 |
| | | |
| ENTERTAINMENT | | |
| Dogs Bollix | **11** | C3 |
| Ink & Coherent | **12** | D3 |
| Kings Arms Tavern | **13** | D3 |
| NZ Film Archives | **14** | D3 |
| Rising Sun & 4:20 | **15** | D3 |
| | | |
| SHOPPING | | |
| Zambezi | **16** | B2 |
| | | |
| TRANSPORT | | |
| Hertz | **17** | D1 |

## TOURS

Three-hour bus tours will typically take you around the city centre, over the Harbour Bridge and out along Tamaki Dr, including stops at Mt Eden, the Auckland Museum and Parnell, for about $67. **Gray Line** ( ☎ 09-307 7880; www.graylinetours.co.nz) and **Great Sights** ( ☎ 09-583 5790; www.greatsights.co.nz) both offer this service.

**Potiki Tours** ( ☎ 09-845 5932; www.potikitours.com) run an excellent Urban Maori day tour (adult/child $195/100) for small groups. It leaves Mt Eden to the buses and heads to One Tree Hill (Maungakiekie) instead, pointing out features of the mountain *pa* site. After a quick lunch it's off to the west-coast beaches, where bush and beach walks are peppered with Maori creation stories, *karakia* (incantations) and explanations of the traditional uses of plants.

The hop-on, hop-off **Explorer Bus** ( ☎ 0800 439 756; www.explorerbus.co.nz; adult/child $35/15) departs from the Ferry Building (Map p62) every hour from 10am to 3pm (more frequently in summer), heading to 14 tourist sites around the central city.

Other options include **Auckland Adventures** ( ☎ 09-379 4545; www.aucklandadventures.co.nz; afternoon/day tours $85/120). This outfit runs an afternoon tour (12.45pm to 5pm) that includes Muriwai gannet colony, an orchard, wineries and Mt Eden; day tours (9am to 5pm) can include a hike or mountain-biking experience.

**Fine Wine Tours** ( ☎ 09-529 5227; www.insidertouring.co.nz) Runs tours of the West Auckland wineries, including lunch: four-hour tour ($149), with cheese ($169); six-hour tour including Muriwai Beach and a microbrewery ($269); food and wine tour with stops at city providores ($199).

# SLEEPING
## BUDGET
### CENTRAL AUCKLAND

**Frienz.com** (Map p62; ☎ 09-307 6437; www.frienz.com; 27-31 Victoria St; dm $23-28, d $72; 🖳 🛜 ) Raising the bar for this part of town, Frienz has actually put an effort into its decor (crazy wallpaper and bright colours) and into organising regular social events (free BBQ nights, poker tournaments etc). Add to that free internet access, fridges in the private rooms and a terrific rooftop terrace and you get one of the inner city's best hostels.

**Aspen House** (Map p62; ☎ 09-379 6633; www.aspenhouse.co.nz; 62 Emily Pl; s $69, d $89-129, tr $99-149, q $219; 🅿 🖳 🛜 ) Located on a sweet, steep street a stone's throw from one of Auckland's most intriguing little parks, the Aspen is split into a renovated wing (high ceilings, en suites) and an older wing (lumpy beds, two toilets between 12 rooms). It's worth paying more for the former. The excellent communal spaces, friendly staff and tucked-away location make this a top inner city hostel.

### PARNELL

**City Garden Lodge** (Map p65; ☎ 09-302 0880; www.citygardenlodge.co.nz; 25 St Georges Bay Rd; dm $28-30, s/d $52/68, tw $58-68; 🅿 🖳 🛜 ) Housed within a character-filled, two-storey house built for Tongan royalty, this friendly and well-run backpackers has a lovely garden and high-ceilinged rooms with solid period features. If you need privacy, a cute double room will do the trick, and if you need to unwind, indulge in some yoga on the front lawn.

### MT EDEN

**Bamber House** (Map p66; ☎ 09-623 4267; www.hostelbackpacker.com; 22 View Rd; dm $25-28, d $66-86; 🖳 🛜 ) The original house here is a mansion of sorts, with some nicely maintained period trimmings. The new pre-fab cabins have less character but come with en suites. There's plenty of space for Bamber's 60-odd guests to stretch out on the lawns and there's a playground for the kids. All in all, an excellent choice.

### PONSONBY

**Verandahs** (Map p70; ☎ 09-360 4180; www.verandahs.co.nz; 6 Hopetoun St; dm $26-28, s $53, d $70-88, tr $90; 🖳 🛜 ) Ponsonby Rd, K Rd and the city are an easy walk from this grand hostel, housed in two neighbouring villas overlooking the mature trees of Western Park. The bunkless dorms sleep a maximum of five people.

### NORTH SHORE

**Takapuna Beach Holiday Park** (off Map p52; ☎ 09-489 7909; www.takapunabeachholidaypark.co.nz; 22 The Promenade, Takapuna; campsites $32, cabins $65, caravans $65-80, units $115; 🖳 🛜 ) Superbly positioned looking onto one of Auckland's most popular beaches, this little park is a smart proposition. The clean, new cabins have decks.

## MIDRANGE
### CENTRAL AUCKLAND & NEWTON

**Quadrant** (Map p62; ☎ 09-984 6000; www.thequadrant.com; 10 Waterloo Quadrant; apt $123-400; 🅿 🖳 🛜 ) Slick, central and full of all the whiz-bang gadgets, this apartment-style complex in the nicest part of the city is an excellent option. The only catch is that the apartments are tiny and the bathrooms beyond small.

**Elliott Hotel** (Map p62; ☎ 09-308 9334; www.theelliotthotel.com; cnr Elliott & Wellesley Sts; apt $139-209; 🖳 🛜 ) Housed in one of the city's grandest historic buildings (1880s), this apartment-style hotel is much plusher than the price implies. Rooms may not be huge but the high ceilings will let your spirits rise.

AUCKLAND

Takapuna Beach

PAUL KENNEDY

SLEEPING

**Langham** (Map p52; ☎ 09-379 5132; www.auckland.langhamhotels.co.nz; 83 Symonds St; r $190-370, ste $470-2420; P ☐ ☎ ☎ ) The Langham may be five-star, but the glamour of the giant chandelier in the reception dissipates somewhat once you reach the low-ceilinged guest floors. Perhaps that's why you can often nab a special and take advantage of the faultless service and heavenly beds at a midrange price.

### PARNELL & NEWMARKET

**Parnell City Lodge** (Map p65; ☎ 09-377 1463; www.parnellcitylodge.co.nz; 2 St Stephens Ave; apt $105-170; P ) Old and newer sections are available in this motel, where every unit is different, some have a bit of character and all have a kitchenette. It's on a busy intersection though, so traffic noise might be a nuisance if you're a light sleeper.

**Off Broadway Motel** (Map p52; ☎ 09-529 3550; www.offbroadway.co.nz; 11 Alpers Ave; units $139-255; ☎ ) The Off Broadway is a dandy little performer in Auckland's accommodation scene and deserves a few

stage-door Johnnies singing its praises. The three small studios are a little dark but the larger studios are a great deal as they have a balcony and bathtub. Executive suites have separate bedrooms and represent very good value.

**Kingsgate Hotel** (Map p65; ☎ 0800 782 548, 09-377 3619; www.millenniumhotels.co.nz; 92 Gladstone Rd; r $140-199, tr $155-229; ☐ ☎ ☎ ) Opposite the Parnell Rose Gardens, this large hotel has generic rooms clustered in landscaped 'Tudor' or 'Colonial' blocks (although they look the same to us), together with a restaurant, pool, spa and plenty of parking. It's popular with tour groups.

### MT EDEN

**Bavaria B&B** (Map p66; ☎ 09-638 9641; www.bavariabandbhotel.co.nz; 83 Valley Rd; s $105-115, d $149-165; ☐ ☎ ) This clean, long-running B&B in a spacious villa has been freshened up with new carpets and a coat of paint. The rooms are big and airy, and there's a decent TV lounge, dining room and deck where guests can mix and mingle.

**Eden Park B&B** (Map p66; ☎ 09-630 5721; www.bedandbreakfastnz.com; 22 Bellwood Ave; s $135-155, d $200-225; 🖳 🛜) If you know any rugby fans who require chandeliers in their bathrooms, send them here. The hallowed turf of Auckland's legendary rugby ground is only a block away and while the rooms aren't overly large for the prices, they mirror the Edwardian elegance of this fine wooden villa.

### PONSONBY & GREY LYNN

**23 Hepburn** (Map p70; ☎ 09-376 0622; www.23hepburn.co.nz; 23 Hepburn St; r $185-205; 🅿 🛜) The three boutique rooms are a symphony in muted whites and creams, inducing the pleasant sensation of waking up inside an extremely chic pavlova. You can sleep in for as long as you like as the continental breakfasts are self-service, left in your in-room fridge the previous evening.

**Henry's** (off Map p70; ☎ 09-360 2700; www.henrysonpeel.co.nz; 33 Peel St; r/apt $200/240; 🛜 🖳) These beautiful wooden villas are what Auckland's inner suburbs are all about. Henry's has been stylishly renovated, adding en suites to the downstairs rooms and a self-contained harbour-view apartment above.

### DEVONPORT & NORTH SHORE

**Devonport Sea Cottage** (Map p52; ☎ 09-445 7117; www.homestaysnz.co.nz/listings/46; 3a Cambridge Tce, Devonport; r $130) Head up the path to your own self-contained cottage, which holds everything you'll need for a relaxing stay near the sea (including a set of French doors opening onto a garden). Excellent weekly rates are on offer in winter.

**Devonport Motel** (Map p52; ☎ 09-445 1010; www.devonportmotel.co.nz; 11 Buchanan St, Devonport; r $130) This minimotel has just two simple, self-contained units in the back garden, but they're modern, clean and in a nice quiet location that's still close to Devonport's action (such as it may be).

**Number Nine B&B** (Map p52; ☎ 09-445 3059; tainui@xtra.co.nz; 9 Tainui Rd, Devonport; r $170) You'll get a warm welcome from

Esplanade Hotel

JOHN ELK III

Christine and Pari at this cosy home that has two attractive rooms for guests, one with a claw-foot tub. If you fancy a game of golf at the nearby club, you can borrow clubs here and have a round organised.

**Esplanade Hotel** (Map p52; ☎ 09-445 1291; www.esplanadehotel.co.nz; 1 Victoria Rd, Devonport; r $200-375, ste $350-750) This beautiful boutique hotel takes pride of place on the corner in a 1903 heritage building. It features lovingly tended period details such as supremely high ceilings, and has much more style than many of the luxury hotels in the city centre. It's perfectly located and achingly romantic, with sumptuous rooms that steadfastly refuse to fall into cookie-cutter territory when it comes to decor.

## TOP END
### CENTRAL AUCKLAND
**Hotel de Brett** (Map p62; ☎ 09-925 9000; www.hoteldebrett.com; 2 High St; r $290-590 incl breakfast; 🖥 🛜 ) Supremely hip, this lavishly refurbished historic hotel has been zooshed up with supercool stripey carpets and clever designer touches in every nook of the extremely comfortable rooms. Prices include breakfast, free broadband and a predinner drink.

**Westin** (Map p52; ☎ 09-909 9000; www.westin.com/auckland; 21 Viaduct Harbour Ave; r $435-710; 🅿 🖥 🐾 ) Auckland's Westin has outdone itself with simple, exquisite design, Maori art and sumptuous furnishings (we love the high-thread-count sheets and goose-down pillows). There's water everywhere you look – in the form of the harbour or tinkling water features – which is very restful, as long as it doesn't induce a constant need to pee.

### PONSONBY
**Great Ponsonby Arthotel** (Map p70; ☎ 09-376 5989; www.greatpons.co.nz; 30 Ponsonby Tce;

r $235-400; 🅿 🖥 ) It's not as slick as the others in this bracket but this deceptively spacious Victorian villa has gregarious hosts, impressive sustainability practices, great breakfasts and it's located a stone's throw from cool Ponsonby Rd in a quiet cul-de-sac. Studio apartments open onto an attractive rear courtyard.

### DEVONPORT
**Peace & Plenty Inn** (Map p52; ☎ 09-445 2925; www.peaceandplenty.co.nz; 6 Flagstaff Tce, Devonport; s $195-265, d $265-350; 🅿 🖥 ) This perfectly located, wonderful five-star period house is stocked with antique furnishings and a thousand conversation pieces – the charming Judith can tell you the provenance of each and every one of them. The romantic, luxurious rooms have en suite, TV, flowers, free sherry/port and local chocolates. A delight, and truly exceptional.

# EATING
Because of its size and ethnic diversity, Auckland tops the country when it comes to dining options. Aucklanders love a good coffee, so you never have to walk too far to find a decent cafe.

## CENTRAL AUCKLAND & NEWTON
**Raw Power** (Map p62; ☎ 09-303 3724; Level 1, 10 Vulcan Lane; mains $7-17; 🕑 7am-4pm Mon-Fri, 11am-4pm Sat; Ⓥ ) Vegetable-shaped salt-and-pepper shakers, superbright walls and the freshest ingredients entice punters to this upstairs eatery, popular with visiting vegetarian/vegan rock royalty. Grab a window seat if you can.

**Satya** (Map p70; ☎ 09-377 0007; 271 K Rd; mains $11-26; 🕑 lunch Mon-Sat, dinner daily; Ⓥ ) Hugely popular, this humble-looking and humbly priced eatery has the best *dahi puri* (an entrée of chickpea, potato and yoghurt on a pappadam cracker) and *masala dosa* (a crepe filled with potato-and-onion curry) in town.

**Grove** (Map p62; ☎ 09-368 4129; St Patrick's Sq, Wyndham St; mains $32-48; ☽ lunch Mon-Fri, dinner Mon-Sat) Romantic fine dining at its best: the room is cosy and moodily lit, the menu encourages sensory experimentation and the service is effortless. If you can't find anything to break the ice from the extensive wine list, give it up mate – it's never going to happen.

**French Cafe** (Map p66; ☎ 09-377 1911; 210 Symonds St; mains $40; ☽ lunch Fri, dinner Tue-Sat) The legendary French Cafe has been rated as one of Auckland's top restaurants for around 20 years now and it still continues to excel. The cuisine is (unsurprisingly) French, but chef Simon Wright manages to sneak in some Pacific Rim touches. Book well ahead if you want to snag a table.

## PARNELL & NEWMARKET

**Kokako** (Map p65; ☎ 09-366 4464; 492 Parnell Rd; mains $8-17; ☽ breakfast & lunch; Ⓥ ) Kokako offers vegetarian, fair trade and organic delights in a smart cafe atmosphere that won't unduly strain the bank balance – a feat nearly as rare as the native bird it's named after. There's a good selection of counter food as well as delicious cooked breakfasts.

**Baci Lounge** (Map p65; ☎ 09-529 4360; Level 1, Rialto Centre, Broadway; mains $9; ☽ 9.30am-10.30pm) Round, padded booths are nestled among the shelves at this very appealing bookshop-cafe. Devour delicious counter food (salads, paninis, fancy pies, gluten-free slices) and literary greats all at the same time.

## MT EDEN & KINGSLAND

**Shaky Isles** (Map p66; ☎ 09-815 3591; 492 New North Rd; mains $8-19; ☽ breakfast & lunch; 🛜 )

Kingsland's coolest cafe has cute cartoons on the wall and free wi-fi. It does excellent breakfasts and salads but it's hard to go past 'good stuff in a bun', the good stuff being mushrooms, avocado, feta, pesto and mayonnaise.

**Mekong Neua** (Map p66; ☎ 09-846 0323; 483 New North Rd; mains $17-24; ☽ dinner; Ⓥ ) Plundering the cuisine of Northeast Thailand and Laos, this welcoming restaurant will fill your head with delicious fragrances and dreams of rice paddies.

**Merediths** (off Map p66; ☎ 09-623 3140; 385 Dominion Rd; mains $38, degustation $100; ☽ lunch Thu & Fri, dinner Tue-Sat) Dining at Merediths is the culinary equivalent of black-water rafting – you're surprised at every turn, you never know what's coming next and you're left with a sense of breathless exhilaration. You'll need to book well in advance to secure a table for the weekend degustation-only sittings; this is one of NZ's best restaurants.

## PONSONBY & GREY LYNN

**Dizengoff** (Map p70; ☎ 09-360 0108; 256 Ponsonby Rd; mains $5-18; ☽ 7am-5pm) This superstylish shoebox crams in a mixed crowd of corporate and fashion types, straights and gays, Jewish families, Ponsonby denizens and visitors. Mouthwatering scrambled eggs, tempting counter food, heart-starting coffee, plus a great stack of reading material if you tire of eavesdropping and people-watching.

**Ponsonby Village Food Court** (Map p70; 106 Ponsonby Rd; mains $8-18; ☽ 10am-10pm; Ⓥ ) The city's best food hall. Choose between Italian, Japanese, Malaysian, Chinese, Turkish, Thai, Lao, Indian, Mexican and the best Vietnamese in the central city.

**Richmond Road Cafe** (Map p52; ☎ 09-360 5559; 318 Richmond Rd; mains $13-29; ☽ 7am-4pm) Auckland's current 'it' cafe, and with good reason. The service is impeccable and the menu is full of well-priced and interesting cafe fare. If it doesn't have a cardamom-cream or lavender-syrup twist it's too boring for this place. Try the spiced banana and rum porridge with fresh coconut.

**Delicious** (Map p52; ☎ 09-360 7590; 472 Richmond Rd; mains $26-29; ☷ lunch Wed-Fri, dinner Tue-Sat) The name doesn't lie. Foodies flock to this neighbourhood eatery for simple but first-rate pasta at reasonable prices. Delicious doesn't take bookings so expect to wait – it's always busy.

**Soto** (Map p70; ☎ 09-360 0021; 13 St Marys Rd; mains $29-31; ☷ lunch Tue-Fri, dinner Tue-Sat) Auckland has a surfeit of excellent Japanese restaurants, but this is the best. The staff glide by in kimonos, leaving a trail of exquisitely presented dishes in their wake – including sushi, sashimi and *zensai* (Japanese tapas).

## NORTH SHORE

**Engine Room** (Map p52; ☎ 09-480 9502; 115 Queen St, Northcote; meals $31-34; ☷ dinner Tue-Sat) A strong contender for Auckland's best restaurant, this informal eatery serves up lighter-than-air goat's cheese soufflés, inventive whiteboard mains and oh-my-god chocolate truffles. It's worth booking ahead and catching the ferry.

**Eight.Two** (Map p52; ☎ 09-419 9082; 82 Hinemoa St, Birkenhead; mains $35-37; ☷ dinner Tue-Sat) Hollowed out of an old villa, this dazzlingly white dining room offers a modern menu and a great wine list. Catch the Birkenhead ferry from the city for a memorable night out.

## SELF-CATERING

**Auckland Fish Market** (Map p52; ☎ 09-379 1490; www.aucklandfishmarket.co.nz; cnr Jellicoe & Daldy Sts; ☷ 7am-6.30pm) No self-respecting city with a position like this should be without a fish market. This market not only has a boisterous early-morning auction, but also a, eateries and a seafood-cooking school

**La Cigale** (Map p65; ☎ 09-366 9361; 69 St Georges Bay Rd; ☷ market 8am-1pm Sat, 9am-2pm Sun) caters to Francophiles and homesick

Dining alfresco

JOHN ELK III

Occidental Belgian Beer Cafe

PETER BENNETTS

Gauls, stocking all manner of French produce (wine, cheese, tinned snails etc), and the in-house cafe (mains $7.50 to $17.50) serves delicious delicatessen platters ($18) throughout the week. Yet it's during the weekend farmers markets that this *cigale* (cicada) really chirps. Lose yourself among stalls laden with produce, home baking, homemade jam, honey and all manner of tasty snacks.

Auckland's legendary organics store **Harvest Wholefoods** (Map p52; ☎ 09-376 3107; 405 Richmond Rd; ⏰ 9am-7pm Mon-Fri, 9am-5pm Sat, 10am-5pm Sun; **V** ), stocks planet-friendly fresh produce, grocery items and cosmetics. It's a meatfree zone, but there's an organic butchery across the road.

# DRINKING

Auckland's nightlife tends to be quiet during the week and positively funereal on Sunday, but wakes up late on Friday and Saturday, when most pubs and bars are open until 1am or later. If in doubt head to Ponsonby, K Rd or the bottom end of the city.

## CENTRAL AUCKLAND & NEWTON

**Agents & Merchants/Racket** (Map p62; ☎ 09-309 5852; 46-50 Customs St) Tucked into their own covered laneway with an outdoor fireplace and sofas, this duo conjures an old-world yet thoroughly modern atmosphere. A&M serves excellent tapas and wine while Racket kicks off a little later with DJs on duty.

**Bluestone Room** (Map p62; ☎ 09-302 0930; 9 Durham Lane; ⏰ 11am-late Mon-Fri, 4pm-late Sat) There's no shortage of character in this 1861 stone building, secreted down a dingy alley in the old part of town (a glassed-over well in the floor dates to 1841). The Rolling Stones played here in the '60s and live blues and rock are still a feature on the weekends.

**Occidental Belgian Beer Cafe** (Map p62; ☎ 09-300 6226; 6 Vulcan Lane; ⏰ 7am-late Mon-Fri, 9am-late Sat & Sun) Belgian beer, Belgian food (plenty of *moules* and *frites* – mussels and chips) and live music are on offer at this historic (1870) pub.

**Pasha** (Map p62; ☎ 09-355 0077; Princes Wharf; ☻ 4pm-late) Awesome cocktails and Moorish exoticism combine in this impressive Viaduct bar.

**Galbraith's Alehouse** (Map p66; ☎ 09-379 3557; 2 Mt Eden Rd; ☻ noon-11pm Mon-Sat, noon-10pm Sun) Brewing up real ales and lagers on-site, this English-style pub offers bliss on tap. The backdoor beer garden trumps the brightly lit bar.

**Wine Cellar** (Map p70; ☎ 09-337 8293; St Kevin's Arcade, K Rd; ☻ 5pm-midnight Mon-Thu, 5pm-2am Fri & Sat) Secreted down some stairs in an arcade, this is the kind of bar that Buffy the Vampire Slayer would have hung out in on Auckland-based assignments. It's dark, grungy and very cool, with regular live music in the neighbouring Whammy Bar.

## KINGSLAND

**Neighbourhood Brewbar** (Map p66; ☎ 09-529 9178; 498 New North Rd; ☻ 11am-late Mon-Fri, noon-late Sat & Sun) With picture windows overlooking Eden Park and a front terrace that's pick-up central after dark, this upmarket pub is guaranteed to be the place-to-be during the Rugby World Cup.

## PONSONBY & GREY LYNN

**Gypsy Tea Room** (Map p52; ☎ 09-361 6970; 455 Richmond Rd; ☻ 4-11.30pm Sun-Thu, 3pm-2am Fri & Sat) No one comes here for tea. This cute wine/cocktail bar has dishevelled charm in bucketloads.

**Ponsonby Social Club** (Map p70; ☎ 09-361 2320; 152 Ponsonby Rd; ☻ 5pm-late) Half-and-half alleyway and bar, the back end of this long, narrow space heaves on the weekends when the DJs crank out classic funk and hip-hop.

# ENTERTAINMENT

The *NZ Herald* has an in-depth rundown of the coming week's happenings in its *Time Out* magazine on Thursday and again in its Saturday edition. If you're planning a big night along K Rd, then visit www. kroad.co.nz for a detailed list of bars and clubs.

Tickets for most major events can be bought from the following:

**Ticketek** (☎ 09-307 5000; www.ticketek. co.nz) Outlets include Aotea Centre and SkyCity Atrium.

**Ticketmaster** (☎ 09-970 9700; www.ticket master.co.nz) Outlets at Vector Arena (Map p62) and Britomart Station (Map p62).

## LIVE MUSIC

**Dogs Bollix** (Map p70; ☎ 09-376 4600; www. dogsbollix.co.nz; cnr K & Newton Rds) This Irish pub is a live-music venue from Tuesday to Sunday but doesn't only play Irish music. Spot local musos here when they're off-duty.

**Thirsty Dog** (Map p70; ☎ 09-377 9190; www.thirstydog.co.nz; 469 K Rd; ☻ 11am-late) This Dog's both thirsty and noisy, with a decent sound system and a regular roster of local bands.

**Kings Arms Tavern** (Map p70; ☎ 09-373 3240; www.kingsarms.co.nz; 59 France St; ☻ 11am-late) One of Auckland's leading small venues for live (and local) rock bands, which play most nights. A rite of passage if you want to get into the local scene.

## NIGHTCLUBS

**Cassette Number Nine** (Map p62; ☎ 09-366 0196; www.cassettenine.com; 9 Vulcan Lane; entry Fri & Sat $10; ☻ 5pm-late) Auckland's most out-there hipsters gravitate to this eccentric bar/club where swishy nouvelle New Romantic guys rub shoulders with girls in short dresses and the music ranges from live indie to international DJ sets.

**Ink & Coherent** (Map p70; ☎ 09-358 5103; www.inkcoherent.co.nz; 268 & 262 K Rd; entry free-$45) These are neighbouring clubs

**AUCKLAND**

for serious dance aficionados, sometimes hosting big-name DJs.

**Rising Sun & 4:20** (Map p70; ☎ 09-358 5643; www.420.co.nz; 373 K Rd) Downstairs is a straight-out nightclub hosting different nights (particularly hip-hop, but also electro, crunk, reggaetron etc), while upstairs there's a large room with a view and another small dance floor.

### CINEMAS
**Academy Cinemas** (Map p62; ☎ 09-373 2761; www.academycinemas.co.nz; 44 Lorne St; adult/concession $15/11) In the basement of the Central City Library, the Academy shows independent foreign and art-house films.

**Rialto Cinema** (Map p65; ☎ 09-529 2218; www.rialto.co.nz; 167 Broadway, Newmarket; adult $10-16, child $8-10) Screens art-house and international films, plus some mainstream fare.

**NZ Film Archives** (Map p70; ☎ 09-379 0688; www.filmarchive.org.nz; 300 K Rd; ⏰ 11am-5pm Mon-Fri, 11am-4pm Sat) A wonderful resource of more than 1000 Kiwi feature films and documentaries dating from 1905, which you can watch for free on a TV screen. See p45 for some recommended Kiwi feature films.

## SHOPPING
Followers of fashion should head to High St, Chancery Lane, Newmarket, Ponsonby Rd and K Rd. The central city area (especially Queen St) has lots of stores selling outdoor clothes and equipment.

### CLOTHING & ACCESSORIES
**Royal Jewellery Studio** (Map p66; ☎ 09-846 0200; 486 New North Rd) Displaying interesting work by local artisans, including some beautiful Maori designs, this is a great place to pick up authentic *pounamu* (greenstone) jewellery.

**Zambesi** (City; Map p62; ☎ 09-303 1701; cnr Vulcan Lane & O'Connell St); (Newmarket: Map p65; ☎ 09-523 1000; 38 Osborne St); (Ponsonby; Map p70; ☎ 09-360 7391; 169 Ponsonby Rd) Handsdown, the most interesting and influential fashion label to come out of the country,

Queens Arcade, Queen St

DAVID WALL

and much sought-after by local and international celebs.

## GIFTS & SOUVENIRS

**Pauanesia** (Map p62; ☎ 09-366 7782; 35 High St) A colourful treasure-trove of Polynesian craft and gifts.

**Native Agent** (Map p66; ☎ 09-845 3289; 507b New North Rd) There's a strong Maori bent to the jewellery, clothing and knick-knacks on offer here, and it's all NZ-made.

## MARKETS

**Otara Market** (off Map p52; ☎ 09-274 0830; Newbury St; ☾ 6am-noon Sat) Held in the car park between the Manukau Polytech and the Otara town centre, this market has a real Polynesian atmosphere, and you can buy South Pacific food, music and fashions. Take bus 497 from Britomart ($5.40, 50 minutes).

**Avondale Sunday Market** (off Map p52; ☎ 09-818 4931; Avondale Racecourse, Ash St; ☾ 6am-noon Sun) A similar vibe to the Otara Market; take the train to Avondale station.

# GETTING THERE & AWAY

## AIR

**Auckland International Airport** (off Map p52; ☎ 09-275 0789; www.auckland-airport.co.nz) is 21km south of the city centre. It has an international terminal and a domestic terminal, each with a tourist information centre. A free shuttle service operates every 20 minutes (6am to 10.30pm) between the terminals and there's also a signposted footpath (about a 1km walk).

Auckland is the major gateway to NZ, and a hub for domestic flights. See p373 for information on international flights.

Domestic airlines operating to and from Auckland and the destinations they serve:

**Air New Zealand** (Map p62; ☎ 09-336 2400; www.airnewzealand.co.nz; cnr Customs & Queen Sts) Kaitaia, Kerikeri, Whangarei, Hamilton, Tauranga, Whakatane, Gisborne, Rotorua, Taupo, New Plymouth, Napier, Whanganui, Palmerston North, Masterton, Wellington, Nelson, Blenheim, Christchurch, Queenstown and Dunedin.

**Jetstar** (☎ 0800 800 995; www.jetstar.com) Wellington, Christchurch and Queenstown.

**Pacific Blue** (☎ 0800 670 000; www.paificblue.co.nz) Wellington, Christchurch, Queenstown & Dunedin.

## BUS

The main long-distance bus company in Auckland, as for the rest of NZ, is **InterCity** (☎ 09-583 5780; www.intercity.co.nz) and its travel and sightseeing arm **Newmans Coach Lines** (www.newmanscoach.co.nz). Services leave from the **SkyCity Coach Terminal** (Map p62; ☎ 09-913 6220; 102 Hobson St).

**Naked Bus** (www.nakedbus.com) buses travel along SH1 as far as Paihia (four hours) and Wellington (12 hours), as well as heading to Waitomo Caves (3¾ hours), Whitianga (3¾ hours), Tauranga (3½ hours), Gisborne (nine hours) and Napier (12 hours).

## CAR

The major companies (Avis, Budget, Hertz and Thrifty) are reliable, offer full insurance and have offices at the airport and all over the country. They are more expensive, but rates are often negotiable for longer hires or off-season.

Some of the more reputable car-hire companies (which may also hire out sleeper vans and campervans):

**Britz** (off Map p52; ☎ 0800 831 900, 09-275 9090; www.britz.co.nz; 36 Richard Pearse Dr, Mangere)

**Budget** (Map p62; ☎ 0800 283 438, 09-529 7788; www.budget.co.nz; 163 Beach Rd)

**Escape** (Map p62; ☎ 0800 216 171, 021 288 8372; www.escaperentals.co.nz; 7 Gore St) Eccentrically painted campervans.

**Go Rentals** (off Map p52; ☎ 0508 246 684, 09-525 7321; www.gorentals.co.nz; 688 Great South Rd, Penrose)

**Hertz** (Map p70; ☎ 0800 654 321, 09-367 6350; www.hertz.co.nz; 154 Victoria St)

**Jucy** (Map p62; ☎ 0800 399 736, 09-374 4360; www.jucy.co.nz; 2-16 The Strand)

**Maui** (off Map p52; ☎ 0800 651 080, 09-255 3910; www.maui.co.nz; 36 Richard Pearse Dr, Mangere)

**Omega** (Map p62; ☎ 0800 525 210, 09-377 5573; www.omegarentals.com; 75 Beach Rd)

**Thrifty** (Map p66; ☎ 0800 737 070, 09-309 0111; www.thrifty.co.nz; 150 Khyber Pass Rd)

## TRAIN

**Overlander** ( ☎ 0800 872 467; www.tranz scenic.co.nz) trains arrive at and depart from **Britomart station** (Map p62; Queen St), the largest underground diesel train station in the world. They depart from Auckland at 7.25am (daily from late September to April, Friday to Sunday May to October) and arrive in Wellington at 7.25pm (the return train from Wellington departs and arrives at the same time). A standard fare to Wellington is $118, but a limited number of *Go Anywhere* discounted seats are available for each journey at $49, $69 and $89 (first-in, first-served).

# GETTING AROUND
## TO/FROM THE AIRPORT

The **Airbus Express** ( ☎ 09-366 6400; www. airbus.co.nz; adult one way/return $16/23, back-packer $14/21, child $6/12) runs every 15 minutes from 7am to 7.30pm and every 30 minutes from 7.30pm to 7am, between the terminals and the city. Reservations are not required and you buy a ticket from the driver. The trip takes less than an hour each way (longer during peak hour).

The convenient door-to-door **Super Shuttle** ( ☎ 0800 748 885; www.supershuttle. co.nz) will charge about $25 for one person heading between the airport and a city hotel. The price increases if you want to go to an outlying suburb.

A taxi between the airport and the city costs around $70.

## BOAT

Fullers and 360 Discovery both run ferries from Quay St in the city. See p69 for destinations.

## PUBLIC TRANSPORT

Due to rampant privatisation during the 1980s, Auckland's public transport system is run by a hotchpotch of different operators, none of which seem to cooperate. As a result there are few integrated public transport passes. The Auckland Regional Council is trying to sort out the mess and runs the excellent **Maxx** ( ☎ 09-366 6400; www.maxx.co.nz) information service, which covers buses, trains and ferries.

### BUS

Bus routes spread their tentacles throughout the city. Many services terminate around Britomart station (Map p62). Bus stops often have electronic displays, giving an estimate of waiting times. Be warned: they're inaccurate.

Single-ride fares in the inner city are 50c for an adult and 30c for a child (you pay the driver when you board), but if you're travelling further afield there are fare stages from $1.60/1 (adult/child) to $9.70/5.80. A one-day pass (which includes the North Shore ferries) costs $11, while a weekly pass costs $45 ($40 from an agent) – there's no reduction for children.

The environmentally friendly **Link Bus** ($1.60, every 10 to 15 minutes, 6am to 11.30pm) is a very handy service that travels clockwise and anticlockwise around a loop that includes Queen St, SkyCity, Victoria Park Market, Ponsonby Rd, K Rd, Newmarket, Parnell and Britomart station.

The red City Circuit bus (every 10 minutes, 8am to 6pm) provides free transport around the inner city from Britomart station, up Queen St, past Albert Park to Auckland University, across to the Sky Tower and back to Britomart.

### TRAIN

Auckland's train service is excellent but limited. Impressive Britomart station (Map p62) has food retailers, foreign-exchange facilities and a ticket office.

There are just three train routes: one runs west to Waitakere, while two run south to Pukekohe. Services are at least hourly and run from around 6am to 8pm (later on the weekends). A $13 Discovery Pass allows a day's travel on most bus, train and North Shore ferry services. Otherwise, pay the conductor on the train (one stage $1.40); they'll come to you.

### TAXI

**Auckland Co-op Taxis** ( ☎ 09-300 3000) is one of the biggest companies. Flagfall is $3, then it's $2.40 to $2.60 per kilometre. There's a surcharge for transport to and from the airport and cruise ships.

# HAURAKI GULF ISLANDS

The Hauraki Gulf, stretching between Auckland and the Coromandel Peninsula, is dotted with *motu* (islands) and gives the Bay of Islands stiff competition in the beauty stakes. Some are only minutes from the city and make excellent day trips: wine-soaked Waiheke and volcanic Rangitoto really shouldn't be missed.

DAVID WALL

Hauraki Gulf Islands

DAVID WALL

Rangitoto Island

If you miss the last ferry, **Auckland Water Taxis** ( ☎ 0800 890 007; www.watertaxis. co.nz) operates a 24-hour water-taxi service (Auckland to Waiheke has a minimum charge of $210; to Rangitoto, $100). See also p69 for cruises and sailing trips.

# RANGITOTO

Sloping elegantly from the waters of the gulf, **Rangitoto** (260m; www.rangi toto.org), the largest and youngest of Auckland's volcanic cones, provides a picturesque backdrop to all of the city's activities.

The island makes for a great day trip. Although it looks steep, up close it's more like an egg sizzling in a pan. The walk to the summit only takes an hour and is rewarded with sublime views. There's an information board with walk maps at the wharf.

**Fullers** ( ☎ 09-367 9111; www.fullers.co.nz; adult/child return $25/13) has 20-minute ferry services to Rangitoto from Auckland's Ferry Building (Map p62; three daily on weekdays, four on weekends) and Devonport (two daily). Fullers also offers the **Volcanic Explorer** (adult/child $55/28), a guided tour around the island in a canopied 'road train', to a 900m boardwalk leading to the summit. Prices include the ferry.

**Reubens** ( ☎ 0800 111 616; www.reubens. co.nz; return $64) operates a shuttle service to Islington Bay on Wednesdays, Fridays, Saturdays and Sundays (also Mondays from November to March).

# WAIHEKE ISLAND

Waiheke is 93 sq km of island bliss only a 35-minute ferry ride from the CBD. Once they could hardly give land away here; nowadays multimillionaires rub shoulders with the old-time hippies and bohemian artists who gave the island its green repute.

On Waiheke's city side, emerald waters lap at rocky bays, while its ocean flank has some of the region's best sandy beaches. While beaches are the big drawcard, wine is a close second. There are 17 boutique wineries to visit, many with swanky restaurants and breathtaking city views. Pick up the *Waiheke Island of Wine* map for a complete list.

The **Waiheke Island i-SITE** ( ☎ 09-372 1234; 2 Korora Rd; www.waihekenz.com; 9am-5pm) and library (with free internet access) are in the Artworks complex (see below). They also have a (usually unstaffed) counter in the ferry terminal at Matiatia Wharf.

## SIGHTS

The **Artworks complex** ( ☎ 09-379 2020; 2 Kororoa Rd) houses a **community theatre** ( ☎ 09-372 2941; www.artworkstheatre.org.nz), an **art-house cinema** ( ☎ 09-372 4240; www.wicc.co.nz) and an attention-grabbing **art gallery** ( ☎ 09-372 9907; www.waihekeartgallery.org.nz; admission free; 10am-4pm).

**Connells Bay** ( ☎ 09-372 8957; www.connellsbay.co.nz; Cowes Bay Rd; adult/child $30/15; by appointment, late Oct to late Apr) is a pricey but excellent private sculpture park featuring a stellar roster of NZ artists. Admission is by way of guided tour.

Waiheke's two best beaches are **Onetangi**, a long stretch of white sand at the centre of the island, and **Palm Beach**, a pretty little horseshoe bay between Oneroa and Onetangi. Both have nudist sections; head west just past some rocks in both cases. **Oneroa** and neighbouring **Little Oneroa** are also excellent.

## WINERIES

Waiheke's hot, dry microclimate has proved excellent for bordeaux reds, syrah and some superb rosés. Because of an emphasis on quality rather than quantity, the premium wine produced here is relatively expensive. It's also NZ's only wine region where all the wineries charge for tastings (from $3 to $10; sometimes free if you make a purchase). Some are spectacularly located and worth a visit for that reason alone. Over summer many extend their

hours, some even sprouting temporary restaurants.

**Goldwater Estate** ( ☎ 09-372 7493; www.goldwaterwine.com; 18 Causeway Rd; noon-4pm Wed-Sun Mar-Nov, daily Dec-Feb) Waiheke's wine pioneers, Goldwater has been producing wine from these 21 acres for more than 30 years.

**Stonyridge** ( ☎ 09-372 8822; www.stonyridge.co.nz; 80 Onetangi Rd; 11.30am-5pm) Famous organic reds, an atmospheric cafe, tours ($10, 35 minutes, 11.30am Saturday and Sunday) and the occasional dance party.

**Te Motu** ( ☎ 09-372 6884; www.temotu.co.nz; 76 Onetangi Rd; 11am-4pm Wed-Sun) Shares the same driveway as Stonyridge and also has a restaurant.

## ACTIVITIES

The *Explore Waiheke Island's Walkways* pamphlet has detailed maps and descriptions of eight excellent coastal hikes that take from one to three hours. Some head to the Royal Forest & Bird Protection Society's three reserves: **Onetangi** (Waiheke Rd), **Te Haahi-Goodwin** (Orapiu Rd) and **Atawhai Whenua** (Ocean View Rd). Other tracks traverse the **Whakanewha Regional Park**, a haven for rare coastal birds.

At the bottom end of the island, the **Stony Batter Historic Reserve** (www.fortstonybatter.org.nz; Stony Batter Rd; admission/tour $8/15; 10am-3.30pm) has WWII tunnels and gun emplacements that were built in 1941 to defend Auckland's harbour. The walk leads through private farmland, and derives its name from the boulder-strewn fields. Bring a torch.

It's the fervently held opinion of Ross of **Ross Adventures** ( ☎ 09-372 5550; www.kayakwaiheke.co.nz; Matiatia beach; 2hr/4hr/day trips $55/85/145, hire from per hour $25) that Waiheke offers kayaking that's every bit as good as the legendary Abel Tasman National Park. He should know – Ross has been offering guided kayak trips for more than 20 years. Experienced sea kayakers can comfortably circumnavigate the island in four days, exploring hidden coves and sand spits inaccessible by land.

## TOURS

**Ananda Tours** ( ☎ 09-372 7530; www.ananda.co.nz) Offers a food and wine tour ($95) and a Wine Connoisseur's Tour ($190). Small-group, informal tours can be customised, including visits to artists' studios.

**Fullers** ( ☎ 09-367 9111; www.fullers.co.nz; Matiatia Wharf) Runs a Wine On Waiheke Tour (adult $115, 4¾ hours, departs Auckland 1pm) that visits three of the island's top wineries and includes a platter of nibbles. Taste Of Waiheke (adult $112, 5½ hours, departs Auckland 11am) includes three wineries plus a visit to an olive grove and a light lunch. There's also a 1½-hour Explorer Tour of the island (adult/child $48/24, departs Auckland 10am, 11am and noon). All prices include the ferry and an all day bus pass.

## EATING

**Te Whau** ( ☎ 09-372 7191; 218 Te Whau Dr; mains $33-40; ☺ lunch Wed-Mon, dinner Sat) Perched on the end of Te Whau peninsula, this winery restaurant has exceptional views, food and service, and one of the finest wine lists you'll see in the country (1982 Chateau Mouton Rothschild, $3000). Try their own impressive Bordeaux blends, merlot and rosé for $3 per taste (11am to 5pm).

**Cable Bay Vineyards** ( ☎ 09-372 5889; www.cablebayvineyards.co.nz; 12 Nick Johnstone Dr; mains $36-49 ☺ lunch & dinner) Impressive ubermodern architecture, sculptures and beautiful views set the scene for this acclaimed restaurant. The food is sublime but the service isn't always so. If the budget won't stretch to a meal, stop in for a wine tasting ($5) or a drink on the terrace.

**Mudbrick** ( ☎ 09-372 9050; 126 Church Bay Rd; mains $38-42; ☺ lunch & dinner) Auckland and the gulf are at their glistening best when viewed from Mudbrick's picturesque veranda. The adventurous menu is crammed with quality ingredients, which are well put together. Mudbrick also offers tours and wine tastings ($5 to $10, from 11am until 5pm).

## GETTING THERE & AWAY

**Fullers** ( ☎ 09-367 9111; www.fullers.co.nz; Matiatia Wharf; adult/child return $32/16; ☺ 5.20am-11.45pm Mon-Fri, 6.25am-11.45pm Sat, 7am-9.30pm Sun) has frequent ferries from Auckland to Matiatia Wharf (on the hour from 9am to 5pm), some via Devonport.

You can pick up the **360 Discovery** ( ☎ 0800 888 006; www.360discovery.co.nz) tourist ferry at Orapiu on its journey between Auckland and Coromandel Town (see p114).

## GETTING AROUND

The island has regular bus services, starting from Matiatia Wharf and heading through Oneroa (adult/child $1.40/80c, three minutes) on their way to all the main settlements, as far west as Onetangi (adult/child $4/2.20, 30 minutes). Enquire through **MAXX** ( ☎ 09-366 6400; www.maxx.co.nz). A day pass (adult/child $8/5) is available from the Fullers counter at Matiatia Wharf.

Mountain bikes (half-/full day $20/30) can be hired at **Waiheke Bike Hire** ( ☎ 09-372 7937; Matiatia Wharf; ☺ 9am-5pm), or you can cheat on the inclines with electric bikes. The i-SITE also rents mountain bikes

HOLGER LEUE

Tide pools at Bethell's Beach, Waitakere Ranges

(half-day/full day $20/30) and scooters (day/overnight $50/60).

**Waiheke Auto Rentals** ( ☎ 09-372 8998; www.waihekerentals.co.nz; Matiatia Wharf; car/scooter/motorbike/4WD from $50/55/75/80) and **Waiheke Rental Cars** ( ☎ 09-372 8635; www.waihekerentalcars.co.nz; Matiatia Wharf; car/4WD from $50/80) offer rentals, but you must be over 21 and pay 65c a kilometre for cars or 4WDs. The insurance excess (deposit) is $1000.

# WEST OF AUCKLAND

West Auckland epitomises rugged: wild black-sand beaches, bush-shrouded ranges, and mullet-haired and black-T-shirt-wearing 'Westies'. The latter is just one of several stereotypes of the area's denizens. Others include the back-to-nature hippie, the eccentric bohemian artist and the dope-smoking surfer dude, all attracted to a simple life at the edge of the bush.

## TITIRANGI

This little village marks the end of Auckland's suburban sprawl and is a good place to spot all of the stereotypes mentioned above over a caffe latte, fine wine or cold beer. Once home to NZ's greatest modern painter, Colin McCahon, there remains an artsy feel to the place.

It is a mark of the esteem in which Colin McCahon is held that the house he lived and painted in during the 1950s has been opened as a mini-museum, **McCahon House** (www.mccahonhouse.org.nz; 67 Otitori Bay Rd, French Bay; admission $5; ☺ 10am-2pm Wed, Sat & Sun), to the public. Look for the signposts pointing down Park Rd, just before you reach Titirangi Village.

## WAITAKERE RANGES

This 16,000-hectare wilderness was covered in kauri until the mid-19th century, when logging claimed most of the giant trees. A few stands of ancient kauri and other mature natives survive amid the dense bush of the regenerating rainforest, which is now protected inside the **Waitakere Ranges Regional Park**.

**Scenic Drive** winds its way 28km from Titirangi to Swanson, passing numerous waterfalls and lookouts. The **Arataki visitors centre** ( ☎ 09-817 0077; www.arc.govt.nz; Scenic Dr; ⌚ 9am-5pm daily Sep-Apr, 10am-4pm Mon-Fri, 9am-5pm Sat & Sun May-Aug) is 6km west of Titirangi and is a brilliant starting point for exploring the ranges.

## KAREKARE

Wild and gorgeously undeveloped, this famous beach has been the setting for onscreen moments both high- and low-brow, from Oscar-winner *The Piano* to *Xena, Warrior Princess*.

Karekare rates as one of the most dangerous beaches in the country, with strong surf and ever-present rips, so don't even think about swimming unless the beach is being patrolled by lifeguards (usually only in summer).

To get here take Scenic Dr and Piha Rd until you reach the well-signposted turn-off to Karekare Rd.

## PIHA

If you notice an Auckland surfer dude with a faraway look, chances are they're day-dreaming about Piha…or just stoned. This beautifully rugged, iron-sand beach has long been a favourite for refugees from the city's stresses – whether for day trips, weekend teenage parties or holidays.

There's no public transport, but **NZ Surf'n'Snow Tours** ( ☎ 09-828 0426; www.newzealandsurftours.com) provides shuttles when the surf's up ($25 one way).

# UPPER NORTH ISLAND

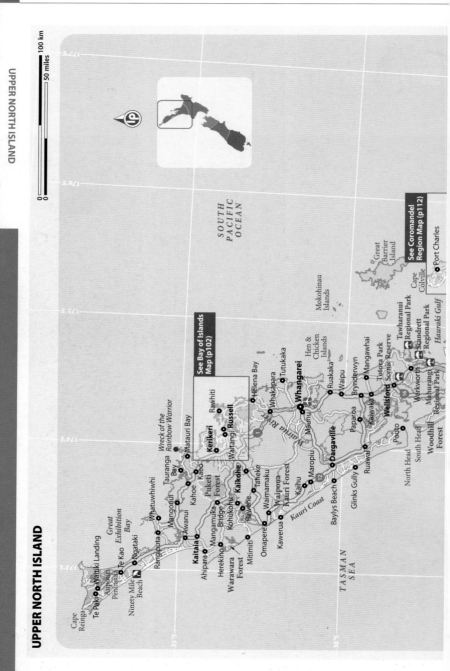

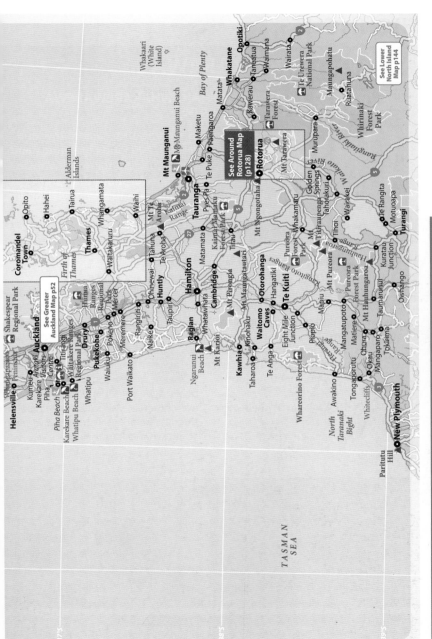

# HIGHLIGHTS

## 1   WHAKAREWAREWA

### BY RENEE NATHAN, WHAKAREWAREWA THERMAL VILLAGE

This 'living village' is significant to Maori: the land is unique, with more than 500 kinds of springs and geyser systems, and the Tuhourangi Ngati Wahiao tribe have been living here for more than 300 years, utilising the natural resources and welcoming visitors since tourism started in Rotorua.

## ⤵ RENEE NATHAN'S DON'T MISS LIST

### ❶ TAKE A GUIDED TOUR

Our tours get a lot of good feedback – they're often the highlight of a visit to the village. Because the guides are from the village, they give their own personal story about how they, or their parents or grandparents, grew up here. The *marae* (meeting house) is usually part of a tour. People can also explore the village at their own leisure.

### ❷ SEE HOW LOCALS LIVE

Whakarewarewa is a living village: there are 25 families here, so about 60 people in all...kids and old people, little babies. One hot pool, Parekohuru, is basically the heartbeat of the village. Visitors see locals cooking their food in steam boxes and the geothermal pools. If we've got any celebrations or even funerals, visitors who are here on the day are able to observe and learn about what is happening.

Clockwise from left: Corn cooking in a hot spring; Maori cultural group performance; Maori man; Pohutu geyser

CLOCKWISE FROM LEFT: DAVID WALL; PAUL KENNEDY; HOLGER LEUE; HOLGER LEUE

## ❸ SEE A CULTURAL PERFORMANCE

The concept of *manaakitanga* has always been upheld here: it means treating visitors not as visitors, but as friends. People say that the village performers don't look bored, they look like they're enjoying themselves during the *haka*, the songs and the *poi* dance. We involve children because that's our way of ensuring the next generation learn the songs. A lot of traditions – such as dancing – are so strong here in Rotorua.

## ❹ TRY OUR FOOD

The pool where our hot corn is cooked has been recognised by geothermal experts as the largest natural cooking pool in the southern hemisphere. We also do *hangi* pies: the ingredients are all cooked inside the steam boxes and hot bowls.

## ❺ WATCH GEYSERS ERUPT

Pohutu (the largest geyser in NZ) and the Prince of Wales' Feathers erupt on average once or twice every hour, but they are natural. You can get a great view from the village.

## ❧ THINGS YOU NEED TO KNOW

**Best time to visit** There are two 30-minute cultural shows daily, at 11.15am and 2pm. Tours take one hour, leaving on the hour. **Best photo op** It's beautiful when it's raining – the atmosphere changes because of the geothermal steam **See our author's review, p129**

# HIGHLIGHTS

**2**

## ↘ BAY OF ISLANDS

When the sun is shining it's easy to forget that the much-touted **Bay of Islands** (p102) isn't just about sailing, swimming, suntans…The area also holds huge historic significance for Maori and Pakeha, both of whom settled here when they first arrived in Aotearoa. You're here today, not yesterday, but at least try and imagine the conflict and resolution of the past as you trim the mainsail.

**3**

## ↘ WAITOMO CAVES

Even if you're not a troll or a spelunker, this incredible network of limestone **caves** (p123) is an absolute must. If you're feeling gung-ho, try 'black-water' rafting (like white-water rafting, only in the dark) or underground abseiling. Not a thrill seeker? Take a slow meander through a glowworm cave and admire the local luminaries. Above ground in Waitomo township, there are some hip places to eat and stay.

### ⤵ WAIPOUA KAURI FOREST

Feel insignificant (and very young) in the presence of some mighty big trees: managed by the local Te Roroa tribe, **Waipoua Kauri Forest** (p109), on Northland's west coast, is all that remains of a once vast swath of huge kauri trees. The big daddy of them all is **Tane Mahuta** – its massive trunk is hard to photograph, let alone circumnavigate.

### ⤵ HOT WATER BEACH

Warm mineral-spring waters bubble up through several beaches around NZ, but **Hot Water Beach** (p109) on the Coromandel Peninsula is the best known and most accessible. Join the other enthusiastic excavators and create your own hot tub in the sand. Stay out of the waves here – there are dangerous rips and undertows.

### ⤵ GO GEOTHERMAL!

It seems wherever you go in this region there's a bubbling pool of mud, a steaming hot spring, an erupting geyser or a plume of sulphurous gas egging its way into your nostrils. Much of it is stand-and-watch-type stuff (too hot to handle!), but don't miss the chance to immerse yourself in some hot springs: try Rotorua's **Polynesian Spa** (p130) for starters.

2 DAVID WALL; 3 OLIVER STREWE; 4 ANDERS BLOMQVIST; 5 HOLGER LEUE; 6 DESTINATION ROTORUA TOURISM MARKETING

2 Bay of Islands (p102); 3 Waitomo Caves (p123); 4 Four Sisters kauri trees (p110), Waipoua Kauri Forest; 5 Hot Water Beach (p116); 6 Polynesian Spa (p130), Rotorua

# BEST...

## ⬎ SWIM SPOTS

- **Bay Of Islands** (p102) Sail to your own island beach or swim with dolphins.
- **Buffalo Beach** (p114) Safe swimming on the Coromandel Peninsula.
- **Ngarunui Beach** (p122) Lifesaver-patrolled kid-sized surf south of Raglan.
- **Tauranga** (p138) Jump in the ocean and splash around with dolphins.

## ⬎ EXTREME ACTION

- **Black-water rafting** (p123) Fast, wet, dark, claustrophobic and subterranean: bring it on!
- **Zorbing** (p138) Roll downhill inside a plastic bubble.
- **Sand tobogganing** (p109) Cape Reinga's massive dunes await.
- **Skydiving** Cross it off your 'Must Do' list in Tauranga (p139).

## ⬎ SURF BREAKS

- **Manu Bay** (p122) Legendary left-hand point break (the world's longest?) near Raglan.
- **Whale Bay** (p122) Like Manu, but harder to get to.
- **Mount Beach** (p141) Awesome artificial surf reef off Mt Mauganui.
- **Hot Water Beach** (p116) Not just hot springs – there are waves here, too!

## ⬎ SMALL TOWNS

- **Raglan** (p121) Multicultural surfie nirvana on the Waikato coast.
- **Mt Maunganui** (p141) Cafe-strewn main street in the shadow of Mauao.
- **Coromandel Town** (p113) Historic hub with quality eats and sleeps.
- **Hahei** (p116) Summery Smallville near Cathedral Cove.

LEFT: DESTINATION ROTORUA TOURISM MARKETING; RIGHT: DESTINATION ROTORUA TOURISM MARKETING

Left: Skydiving (p139), Bay of Plenty; Right: zorbing (p138)

# THINGS YOU NEED TO KNOW

## ⬂ VITAL STATISTICS

- **Population** Rotorua 70,400; Raglan 2700; Russell 820
- **Telephone code** ☎ 09 Northland; ☎ 07 Coromandel, Waikato & Rotorua
- **Best time to visit** December to February (summer)

## ⬂ LOCALITIES IN A NUTSHELL

- **Northland & the Bay of Islands** (p100) History-rich towns, remote coastlines and the famed Bay of Islands archipelago.
- **Coromandel Region** (p110) Peninsular playground with beaches, forests and historic villages.
- **Waikato & the King Country** (p117) Agricultural towns above ground; amazing caves below.
- **Rotorua & the Bay of Plenty** (p126) Volcanic hubbub, Maori culture and laid-back beachiness.

## ⬂ ADVANCE PLANNING

- **One month before** Organise any internal flights and car hire.
- **Two weeks before** Book a Bay of Islands sailing trip (p103) and accommodation across the region.
- **One week before** Book a Maori cultural performance in Rotorua (p131) and a Waitomo Caves adventure (p123).

## ⬂ RESOURCES

For bookings and information on regional accommodation, transport and activities, plus DOC info and contacts:

- **Bay of Islands i-SITE** (www.north landnz.com)
- **Coromandel Town i-SITE** (www. thecoromandel.com)
- **Hamilton i-SITE** (www.waikatonz.co.nz)
- **Rotorua i-SITE** (www.rotoruanz.com)

## ⬂ EMERGENCY NUMBERS

- **Ambulance, fire service & police** (☎ 111)

## ⬂ GETTING AROUND

- **Bus** between the larger towns.
- **Hire a car** for the freedom to explore.
- **Sail** (p103) around the scenic Bay of Islands.
- **Walk** around the Mauao Base Track (p141).

UPPER NORTH ISLAND

THINGS YOU NEED TO KNOW

# UPPER NORTH ISLAND ITINERARIES

## AUCKLAND TO NORTHLAND Three Days

Some say (1) Auckland (p51) is just Sydney for beginners. We think not! Check out the Maori gallery at the Auckland Museum (p62), then cross the Domain to K Rd for lunch. Afterwards, stop by the Auckland Art Gallery (p65) and the impossible-to-miss Sky Tower (p65). Ponsonby (p76) awaits for dinner and drinks.

On day two, set your compass north: explore the iconic (2) Bay of Islands (p100) on board a yacht or cruise boat, and check out the isolated splendour of (3) Ninety Mile Beach (p108). On the tip of the rugged Aupouri Peninsula is (4) Cape Reinga (p108), shrouded in solitude and Maori lore.

On the way back down south on day three, ogle the giant trees at (5) Waipoua Kauri Forest (p109) before you wheel back into the City of Sails.

## HIT THE BEACH Five Days

With a bit more time in (1) Auckland (p51), ferry out to one of the (2) Hauraki Gulf Islands (p83) for some beach- and wine-flavoured R&R. Chug back over to the North Shore and chill out on Cheltenham Beach, then hit Devonport (p68) for dinner.

After breakfast in Mt Eden (p76), meander across to the Coromandel Peninsula and take your pick from surf beaches, safe-swimming bays and geothermal sands. At (3) Hot Water Beach (p116) hot springs seep up through the beach. For safe swimming, try (4) Buffalo Beach (p114) near Whitianga.

The next day, truck further east to the Bay of Plenty, which has, not surprisingly, bays aplenty: head for (5) Mount Beach (p141) in Mt Maunganui, with its gnarly artificial surf reef, good swimming and restaurant-lined main drag.

To complete your beachy break, trundle over the hills to (6) Raglan (p121), which has two legendary surf breaks: Manu Bay (as seen in *Endless Summer*) and Whale Bay.

## HISTORY & CULTURE One Week

Of course, Aotearoa isn't just about sunshine and surf. The Upper North Island in particular holds great historic and cultural significance for both Maori and Pakeha.

In (1) Auckland (p51), hike up One Tree Hill (Maungakiekie), a volcanic cone that was once the site of the greatest *pa* (fortified Maori village) in the country. Mt Eden (Maungawhau), another of Auckland's volcanic cones, is capped by a sacred crater called Te Ipu Kai a Mataaho (the Food Bowl of Mataaho, the god of things hidden in the ground).

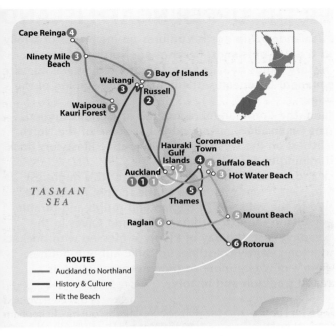

Further north, in the Bay of Islands, **(2) Russell** (p104) was the site of the first European settlement in NZ, and had a fearsome reputation for debauchery. Not far away is **(3) Waitangi** (p105), where Maori chiefs and the British signed the controversial Treaty of Waitangi in 1840, granting the British sovereignty.

The Coromandel Peninsula has a chequered history of Maori settlement and gold rushes. **(4) Coromandel Town** (p113) and **(5) Thames** (p127) are dotted with historic buildings from the gold-rush era.

A real stronghold of Maori culture today is **(6) Rotorua** (p127), where you can take in a Maori cultural performance and experience a *hangi* (feast).

# DISCOVER THE UPPER NORTH ISLAND

For many New Zealanders, 'up north' conjures up memories of family holidays around the Bay of Islands. Beaches are Northland's main drawcard, but history hangs heavily here, too: the region was the site of NZ's first permanent European settlement and the signing of the Treaty of Waitangi.

East of Auckland, the Coromandel region has an aura of rugged individualism. The peninsula's eastern edge has some of the North Island's best beaches; on the western side alternative lifestylers flock to historic gold-mining towns.

South of Auckland, verdant fields fold down into NZ's mightiest river, the Waikato, which lends its name to the region. Adrenaline junkies are drawn to the wild surf of Raglan and rough-and-tumble underground pursuits in the extraordinary Waitomo Caves in the King Country. Heading east, the Bay of Plenty is blessed with buckets of sunshine and a long, sandy coastline. Volcanic hubbub defines the landscape here – nowhere more so than Rotorua, which is a stronghold of Maori tradition and history.

# NORTHLAND & THE BAY OF ISLANDS

## GETTING THERE & AROUND

Whangarei, Kerikeri and Kaitaia have domestic airports, connecting via Auckland to international flights. Northland has no passenger train service, but **InterCity** ( ☎ 09-583 5780; www.intercity.co.nz) and associated buses ply SH1 from Auckland to Kaitaia. **Naked Bus** ( ☎ 0900 62533; per min $1.80; www.nakedbus.com; advance fares from $1) covers the same route as far as Paihia.

## WHANGAREI

pop 45,800

On the pretty-to-ugly continuum, Whangarei sits somewhere in the middle. But beauty is never far away and there are plenty of attractive natural and artistic things to keep you distracted in Northland's gateway.

## INFORMATION

**Whangarei i-SITE** ( ☎ 09-438 1079; www. whangareinz.com; 92 Otaika Rd/SH1; ☼ 8.30am-5pm Mon-Fri, 9am-4.30pm Sat & Sun) Information, cafe, toilets and internet access ($6 per hour).

## SIGHTS & ACTIVITIES

The budget traveller's answer to Waitomo, **Abbey Caves** (Abbey Caves Rd; admission free) is an undeveloped network of three caverns full of glowworms and limestone formations, 4km east of town. Grab a torch, strong shoes and a mate (you don't want to be stuck down here alone if things go pear-shaped) and prepare to get wet.

The **Whangarei Art Museum** ( ☎ 09-430 4240; www.whangareiartmuseum.co.nz; admission by donation; ☼ 10am-4pm Tue-Fri, noon-4pm Sat & Sun) is an interesting little gallery with changing displays in cute **Cafler Park**, which spans Waiarohia Stream.

West of Whangarei, 5km down the road to Dargaville at Maunu, is the **Museum &**

**Kiwi House** ( ☎ 09-438 9630; www.whangarei museum.co.nz; SH14; adult/child $10/5; ☻ 10am-4pm). The complex includes a veritable village of 19th-century buildings and an impressive collection of Maori artefacts. It also offers a rare chance to see a North Island brown kiwi, although he's a bit shy and doesn't always feel the need to face his adoring public.

## SLEEPING

**our pick** **Little Earth Lodge** ( ☎ 09-430 6562; ·www.littleearthlodge.co.nz; 85 Abbey Caves Rd; sites per person/dm/s/d/tr $15/28/54/64/84; ▯ ☜ ) One of the very best hostels, Little Earth might spoil you for all the rest. Set on a farm 4km from town and right next to Abbey Caves (left), the place is brimming with art and Balinese furnishings. Forget dorm rooms crammed with nasty spongy bunks: settle down in a proper cosy bed with nice linen and a maximum of two roommates. Resident critters include miniature horses Tom and Jerry, and the lovable pooch Muttley.

**Whangarei Views B&B** ( ☎ 09-437 6238; www.whangareiviews.co.nz; 5 Kensington Heights Rise; s/d/tr/q $99/160/200/240; ☜ ) The name clearly articulates its prime proposition: views over the city and then some. Modern and peaceful, it has a self-contained two-bedroom flat downstairs and a B&B room in the main part of the house.

**Pilgrim Planet** ( ☎ 09-459 1099; www.pil grimplanet.co.nz; 63 Hatea Dr; r $110-130; ▯ ☜ ) Upmarket rooms open onto a shared kitchen and lounge, giving this smart place the sociability of a hostel but without the German teenagers living off rice and canned corn (not that there's anything wrong with that!).

## EATING & DRINKING

**Bob** ( ☎ 09-438 0881; 29 Bank St; breakfast $6-16, lunch $15-17; ☻ breakfast & lunch) Hey Bob, nice coffee. How would you describe yourself? Deli? Cafe? All that fancy produce spices up the standards – like the kransky sausages in the big breakfast. Nice one, Bob.

ANDERS BLOMQVIST

**Bay of Islands**

`our pick` **à Deco** ( ☎ 09-459 4957; 70 Kamo Rd, Kensington; mains $34-36; ◷ lunch Wed-Fri, dinner Tue-Sat) Northland's best restaurant, with an inventive menu that prominently features local produce: Northland scallops, Tutukaka tuna, Waimate mushrooms, Kaipara flounder, Dargaville kumara (sweet potato) and the native flavours of horopito and manuka. Art-deco fans will adore the setting – a wonderfully curvaceous marine-style villa with original fixtures.

`our pick` **Butter Factory & Butterbank** ( ☎ 09-430 0044; 8 Butter Factory Lane & 84 Bank St; ◷ 4pm-late Wed-Sat) Tucked away in a back lane, Butter Factory is an atmospheric wine bar with stone walls, exposed beams and so-cool-it-hurts staff. As the hours dissolve, DJs kick in and the crowd spills outside. It's proved so popular that the Butter Factory taken over the old bank upstairs and converted it into a nearly as cool tapas and cocktail bar.

# BAY OF ISLANDS

Undeniably pretty, the Bay of Islands ranks as one of NZ's top tourist drawcards. The footage that made you want to come to NZ in the first place no doubt featured lingering shots of lazy, sun-filled days on a yacht floating atop these turquoise waters punctuated by around 150 undeveloped islands.

The Bay of Islands is a place of enormous historical significance. Maori knew it as Pewhairangi and settled here early in their migrations. As the site of NZ's first permanent English settlement (at Russell), it is the birthplace of European colonisation. It was here that the Treaty of Waitangi was drawn up and first signed in 1840; the treaty remains the

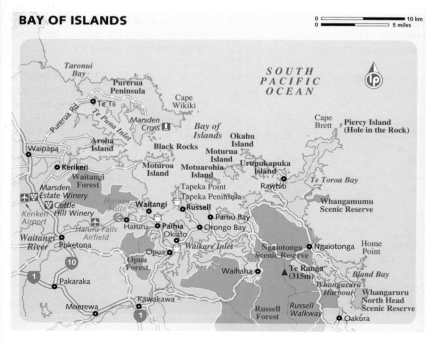

**BAY OF ISLANDS**

linchpin of race relations in NZ today (see p344).

## ACTIVITIES & TOURS

### SEA KAYAKING

**Coastal Kayakers** (☎ 09-402 8105; www. coastalkayakers.co.nz; Te Karuwha Pde, Paihia) Runs guided tours (half-/full-/two-day tours $60/80/130) for a minimum of two people. Kayaks can also be rented (half/full day $30/40).

**Island Kayaks** (☎ 09-402 6078; www.bay beachhire.co.nz; Marsden Rd, Paihia; half-/full-day tour $55/90) Operates from Bay Beach Hire.

### BOAT TRIPS

You can't leave the Bay of Islands without taking some sort of cruise and there are plenty of vessels keen to get you on board, including sailing boats, jetboats and large launches. Boats leave from either Paihia or Russell, calling into the other town as their first stop.

**Fullers** (☎ 0800 653 339; www.dolphincruises. co.nz) runs full-day (adult/child $99/50) and half-day ($89/45) tours, taking in the Hole in the Rock off Cape Brett (passing through it if conditions are right) and stopping on an island. The full day Cream Trip follows the old supply and mail route around the islands and includes dolphin swimming and boom netting (where you can get close to the critters while being dragged through the water in a net).

### OVERNIGHT CRUISES

You just need to roll up to the **Rock** (☎ 0800 762 527; www.rocktheboat.co.nz; 22hr cruise $178), a former vehicle ferry that's now a floating hostel, with four-bed dorms, twin and double rooms, and (of course) a bar. The cruise departs at 5pm and includes a barbecue and seafood dinner with live music, then a full day spent island-hopping, fishing, kayaking, snorkelling and swimming.

**Ecocruz** (☎ 0800 432 627; www.ecocruz. co.nz; cruises dm/d $595/1350) is a highly recommended three-day/two-night sailing cruise aboard the 72ft ocean-going yacht *Manawanui*, which has an emphasis on the marine environment. Prices include accommodation, food, fishing, kayaking and snorkelling.

### SAILING

Recommended boats offering day trips:

**Carino** (☎ 09-402 8040; www.sailingdolphins. co.nz; adult/child $99/60) A 50ft catamaran offering swimming with dolphins and a barbecue lunch ($6 extra).

**Gunghall** (☎ 0800 478 900; www.bayofislands sailing.co.nz; trips $85) A beautiful 65ft ocean yacht with a friendly crew offering freshly made sandwiches.

**On the Edge** (☎ 09-402 8234; www. explorenz.co.nz; adult/child $120/79) NZ's fastest commercial catamaran, capable of speeds of more than 30 knots. It also has a licensed bar.

**Phantom** (☎ 0800 224 421; www.yacht phantom.com; adult/child $99/50) A 50ft racing sloop, known for its wonderful food (10 people maximum; BYO allowed).

**R Tucker Thompson** (☎ 09-402 8430; www. tucker.co.nz; adult/child $120/60) A majestic tall ship with daily tours that include a barbecue lunch. Run by a charitable trust with an education focus, it partners with the Historic Places Trust and DOC for special sailings.

### DOLPHIN SWIMMING

**Dolphin Discoveries** (☎ 09-402 8234; www. explorenz.co.nz; adult/child $89/45) was the first to offer dolphin-swimming trips in the bay. The price includes a four-hour trip, with an additional $30 payable if you choose to swim.

As well as the Cream Trip, Fullers offers a three-hour dolphin-swimming cruise (adult/child $89/45, $30 extra for the swim). The only yacht to be licensed for dolphin swims is *Carino*.

## CAPE REINGA TOURS

It's cheaper and quicker to do trips to Cape Reinga from Ahipara, Kaitaia or Doubtless Bay (see p108). But if you're short on time, there are several long day trips (10 to 12 hours) that leave from the Bay of Islands.

**Fullers** ( ☎ 0800 653 339; www.dolphin cruises.co.nz) runs regular bus tours and backpacker-oriented versions, both stopping at Puketi Forest. Their standard, child-friendly version (adult/child $115/58) includes an optional barbecue lunch at Houhora ($23). Otherwise there's **Awesome NZ** ( ☎ 0800 653 339; www.awesomenz.com; tour $99), which has louder music, more time sandboarding and includes stops to chuck a frisbee around at Taputaputa Beach and devour fish and chips at Mangonui.

## HOKIANGA & WAIPOUA FOREST TOURS

**Crossings Hokianga** ( ☎ 0800 653 339; www. dolphincruises.co.nz; adult/child $93/47) leaves Paihia at 8.30am and heads to the forest for a one-hour tour with a Footprints Waipoua guide (p110). Then it's back to Opononi for your choice of a crayfish lunch ($65) or a picnic ($17). Rawene and Kohukohu follow, heading back to Paihia by 4pm.

## RUSSELL

pop 820

Although it was once known prosaically as 'the hellhole of the Pacific', those coming to Russell for debauchery will be sadly disappointed: they've missed the orgies on the beach by 170 years. Instead they'll find a sweetly historic town that is a bastion of cafes, gift shops and B&Bs.

### INFORMATION

**Russell Booking & Information Centre** ( ☎ 09-403 8020; www.russellinfo.co.nz; ☻ 8.30am-4.30pm Apr-Sep, 8am-7pm Oct-Mar) Located on the pier.

Cape Reinga (p108)

DAVID WALL

## SIGHTS & ACTIVITIES

The small but modern **Russell Museum** ( ☎ 09-403 7701; www.russellmuseum.org.nz; 2 York St; adult/child $7.50/2; ⏰ 10am-4pm) has a well-presented Maori section, a large 1:5-scale model of Captain Cook's *Endeavour* and a 10-minute video on the town's history.

Russell lays claim to some of NZ's oldest buildings, including **Christ Church** (1836), the country's oldest church.

## SLEEPING & EATING

**ourpick Wainui** ( ☎ 09-403 8278; stocken@xtra.co.nz; 92d Te Wahapu Rd; dm/d/tr $30/60/90) Hard to find but well worth the effort, this modern bush retreat with direct beach access has only two rooms sharing a pleasant communal space. It's 5km from Russell on the way to the car ferry. Take Te Wahapu Rd and then turn right into Waiaruhe Way.

**Seaport Village** ( ☎ 09-403 7833; www.seaportvillage.co.nz; 10 Chapel St; dm $30, d $130-195, apt $150-390) This central 'village' spans all price brackets, with comfortable B&B rooms with polished wooden floors and self-contained multiroom apartments. The two linked dorms have proper mattresses, an en suite and a kitchen – and they're just over the fence from the pub.

**Commodore's Lodge** ( ☎ 09-403 7899; www.commodoreslodgemotel.co.nz; 28 The Strand; units $150-650; 🏊 ) Being the envy of every passer-by makes up for the lack of privacy in the front apartments facing the waterfront promenade. Spacious, nicely presented units are the order of the day here, along with a great pool and free kayaks, dinghies and bikes.

**Tuk Tuk** ( ☎ 09-403 7111; 19 York St; mains $15-24; ⏰ 10am-11pm; Ⓥ ) Thai fabrics adorn the tables and Thai favourites fill the menu. In clement weather grab a table out front and watch Russell's little world go by.

**ourpick Kamakura** ( ☎ 09-403 7771; 29 The Strand; lunch $15-30, dinner $29-33; ⏰ breakfast Sat & Sun, lunch & dinner daily) The flashest option in Russell by a long way, this restaurant has a breezy beach-house feel. The Pacific Rim menu gainfully plunders Asian and French styles to produce beautifully presented, delicious meals. In summer it hosts a monthly artisan market (www.artisanmarket.co.nz).

## GETTING THERE & AWAY

The quickest way to reach Russell by car is via the car ferry (car and driver $10, motorcycle and rider $5, passenger adult/child $1/50c), which runs every 10 minutes from Opua (5km from Paihia) to Okiato (8km from Russell), between 6.50am and 10pm. Buy your tickets on board.

On foot, the quickest and easiest way to reach Russell is on the regular passenger ferry (adult/child one way $6/3, return $10/5) from Paihia. It runs from 7am to 7pm (until 10pm October to May), generally every 20 minutes but hourly in the evenings. Buy your tickets on board or at the i-SITE in Paihia.

## PAIHIA & WAITANGI

pop 1800 & 800

The birthplace of NZ (as opposed to Aotearoa), Waitangi inhabits a special, somewhat complex place in the national psyche – aptly demonstrated by the mixture of celebration, commemoration, protest and apathy that accompanies the nation's birthday (Waitangi Day, 6 February).

It was here that the long-neglected and much-contested Treaty of Waitangi was first signed between Maori chiefs and the British Crown, establishing British sovereignty or something a bit like it, depending on whether you're reading the English or Maori version of the document.

Joined to Waitangi by a bridge, Paihia would be a fairly nondescript coastal town if it wasn't the main entry point to the Bay of Islands.

## INFORMATION

**Bay of Islands i-SITE** ( ☎ 09-402 7345; www.visitnorthland.co.nz; Marsden Rd; ⏲ 8am–5pm Mar–mid-Dec, to 8pm mid-Dec–Feb; 🖳 🛜 ) Information and internet access ($4 per hour).

## SIGHTS & ACTIVITIES

### WAITANGI TREATY GROUNDS

A visit to the **Waitangi Treaty Grounds** ( ☎ 09-402 7437; www.waitangi.net.nz; 1 Tau Henare Dr; adult/child $20/10; ⏲ 9am-5pm mid-Apr–Oct, 9am-7pm Nov–mid-Apr) is a must for every itinerary. It's full of cultural icons – the colonial-style Treaty House with its manicured garden and lawns, the surrounding bush full of native birds, the spiritual *whare* (house) and the warlike *waka* (canoe), the three flags (UK, NZ and Maori) and the hillside views of a still-beautiful land.

A 30-minute **cultural performance** (adult/child $15/8; ⏲ check website or call) demonstrates traditional Maori song and dance, including *poi* (a women's formation dance that involves manipulating a ball of woven flax) and *haka* (war dance). There are various **guided tours** (adult/child $15/8; ⏲ check website or call) available. The **Ultimate Waitangi Experience** (adult/child $25/14) is a combined ticket including a tour and a performance. In summer, the 45-minute twilight show **Land of Plenty** (adult/child $25/8; ⏲ 6pm) is staged and can be combined with a drinks or meal package at the cafe.

### WAKA JOURNEY

For a hands-on experience of Maori culture, **Waka Tai-a-Mai** ( ☎ 09-405 9990; www.taiamaitours.co.nz; 2hr trip $75; ⏲ 10am & 1pm Oct-Apr) gives you the opportunity to paddle a traditional 50ft carved *waka*. Leaving from the Waitangi bridge, the journey heads up to the Haruru Falls before visiting a replica Maori village. The Ngapuhi hosts wear traditional garb and perform the proper *karakia* (incantations), as well as some excellent storytelling.

## SLEEPING

**Saltwater Lodge** ( ☎ 09-402 7075; www.saltwaterlodge.co.nz; 14 Kings Rd; dm $27-33, d/tr/q $115/135/155; 🖳 🛜 ) Even the dorms at this excellent, large, purpose-built backpackers have en suites, bedding and lockers. Cow-print and red-leather couches make for a cool communal lounge. There are large balconies, a bar and free bicycles, movies and racquets.

**Baystay B&B** ( ☎ 09-402 7511; www.baystay.co.nz; 93a Yorke Rd, Haruru Falls; r $115-145; 🖳 🛜 ) Probably the only accommodation in NZ to have a Johnny Mnemonic pinball machine in the lounge room, this isn't your average B&B. Enjoy valley views from the spa pool of this slick, gay-friendly establishment.

**our pick** **Tarlton's Lodge** ( ☎ 09-402 6711; www.tarltonslodge.co.nz; 11 Sullivans Rd; r $150-240) Striking architecture combines with up-to-the-minute decor in this hilltop B&B with expansive bay views. Of the three luxurious suites in the main building, two have their own outdoor spas. The mid-priced rooms are in an older building across the lane but they share the same aesthetic, views and breakfast.

**Decks of Paihia** ( ☎ 09-402 6146; www.decksofpaihia.com; 69 School Rd; d $195-245; 🖳 🐾 ) Architecturally impressive, this place offers light, modern bedrooms, granite bathrooms and a big deck with bay views. The elegant pool, set between house and bush, is irresistible.

PAUL KENNEDY

Waitangi Day *kapa haka* performance

## EATING

**our pick** **Waikokopu Cafe** ( ☎ 09-402 6275; Waitangi Treaty Grounds; mains $14-20; ☺ 9am-5pm) The setting is a cracking start – by a pond, backed by bush and overlooking the Treaty Grounds. The locale is matched by Kiwi icons on the menu – the ever popular 'fush and chups', and the Rainbow Warrior – 'French toast sunk in maple syrup, bacon and banana'.

**Only Seafood** ( ☎ 09-402 6066; 40 Marsden Rd; mains $29-33; ☺ dinner) A superb place for local seafood, with dishes ranging from the simple (catch-of-the-day with lemon and parsley) to all manner of creamy, spicy concoctions. The fat Pacific oysters served with soy, wasabi and pickled ginger are sublime.

## GETTING THERE & AROUND

**InterCity** ( ☎ 09-583 5780; www.intercity.co.nz) and associated buses head daily to Auckland ($25, four hours), Whangarei ($23, 70 minutes), Kerikeri ($17, 25 minutes), Mangonui ($30, 80 minutes) and Kaitaia ($37, two hours). **Naked Bus** ( ☎ 0900 62533 per min $1.80; www.nakedbus.com; advance fares from $1) departs at 7.20am for Whangarei (95 minutes) and Auckland (four hours), carrying on to Rotorua (8½ hours), Taupo (10 hours) and Napier (12 hours).

Ferries depart regularly for Russell. If you've more money to spend and less time to wait, **Ocean Blue Water Taxis** ( ☎ 021 273 1655; fishcatcher@xtra.co.nz) and **Paihia Island Shuttle** ( ☎ 0800 387 892; www.islandshuttle.co.nz) will take you anywhere.

For bikes, visit **Bay Beach Hire** ( ☎ 09-402 6078; www.baybeachhire.co.nz; Marsden Rd; ☺ 9am-5.30pm).

## THE FAR NORTH

If it sounds remote, that's because it is. The far-flung Far North is always playing second fiddle to the Bay of Islands for attention and funding, yet the subtropical tip of the North Island has more breathtaking coastline per square kilometre than anywhere but the offshore islands.

## CAPE REINGA & NINETY MILE BEACH

Maori consider Cape Reinga (Te Rerenga-Wairua) the jumping-off point for souls as they depart on the journey to their spiritual homeland. On its west coast Ninety Mile Beach (Ninety Kilometre Beach would be more accurate) is a continuous stretch lined with high sand dunes, flanked by the Aupouri Forest.

### SIGHTS

Standing at windswept **Cape Reinga lighthouse** and looking out over the ocean gives a real end-of-the-world feeling. This is where the waters of the Tasman Sea and Pacific Ocean meet, breaking together into waves up to 10m high in stormy weather. Visible on a promontory slightly to the east is a spiritually significant 800-year-old **pohutukawa tree**; souls are believed to slide down its roots. Out of respect to the most sacred site in Maoridom, don't go near the tree and refrain from eating or drinking anywhere in the area.

A walk along Te Werahi Beach to **Cape Maria van Diemen** (five hours loop) takes you to the westernmost point. This is one of many sections of the three- to four-day, 53km **Cape Reinga Coastal Walkway** (from Kapowairua to Te Paki Stream) that can be tackled individually. Beautiful **Tapotupotu Bay** is a two-hour walk east of Cape Reinga, via Sandy Bay and the cliffs.

A large chunk of the land around Cape Reinga is part of the **Te Paki Recreation Reserve** managed by DOC. There are 7 sq km of giant sand dunes on either side of the mouth of Te Paki Stream. Clamber up to take flying leaps off the dunes or toboggan down them.

### TOURS

Bus tours go to Cape Reinga from Kaitaia, Ahipara, Doubtless Bay and the Bay of Islands (see p104).

**Cape Reinga Adventures** ( ☎ 09-409 8445; www.capereingaadventures.co.nz; half-/full-day 4WD trips $75/135) Real action men who offer 4WD tours (including sunset visits to the cape after the crowds have

Cape Reinga lighthouse

PAUL KENNEDY

gone), fishing, kayaking, sandboarding and dune-surfing as day activities or as overnight camping trips ($150 to $220). They also hire kayaks ($60 for 24 hours) and sandboards ($20).

**Far North Outback Adventures** ( ☎ 09-408 0927; www.farnorthtours.co.nz) Flexible, day-long tours from Kaitaia/Ahipara from $600 (one to three people) to $650 (four or five people), including morning tea and lunch. You can visit remote areas such as Great Exhibition Bay ($10 per person access fee).

**Paradise 4x4** ( ☎ 0800 494 392; www.paradisenz.co.nz; 2 people $600, per additional person $50) Operates flexible, exclusive 4WD tours from Doubtless Bay up Ninety Mile Beach to Cape Reinga, including Devonshire tea and gourmet lunch with local wine. Hokianga tours also available.

## SLEEPING & EATING

**Ninety Mile Beach Top 10 Holiday Park** ( ☎ 09-406 7298; www.ninetymilebeach.co.nz; 6 Matai St, Waipapakauri; sites per person $16, cabins $80-110; 🖳 ) Rows of tidy units line the sunburnt grass at this well-positioned holiday park, within earshot of Ninety Mile Beach's roaring surf.

**Pukenui Lodge Motel** ( ☎ 09-409 8837; www.pukenuilodge.co.nz; cnr SH1 & Wharf Rd, Pukenui; dm/r $25/65, units $115-170; 🖳 🐾 ) This clean, welcoming backpackers occupies a historic villa (1891) filled with mismatched furniture and an ancient TV. It's a more charming prospect than the bog-standard motel units.

**North Wind Lodge Backpackers** ( ☎ 09-409 8515; www.northwind.co.nz; 88 Otaipango Rd, Henderson Bay; dm/tw/d/tr $27/58/64/84) Six kilometres down an unsealed road on the peninsula's east side, this unusual turreted house offers a homely environment and plenty of quiet spots on the lawn to sit with a beer and a book.

## GETTING THERE & AROUND

Apart from numerous tours, there's no public transport past Pukenui, which is linked to Kaitaia ($5, 45 minutes) by **Busabout Kaitaia** ( ☎ 09-408 1092; www.cbec.co.nz).

Far North Rd (SH1F) is sealed as far as Waitiki Landing. The final 7km are currently being sealed, starting from Cape Reinga and heading backwards.

Fill up with petrol before hitting the Aupouri Peninsula. The petrol station at Waitiki Landing has been known to run out.

# KAURI COAST

The main reason for coming here is to marvel at the kauri forests, one of the great natural highlights of NZ.

## WAIPOUA KAURI FOREST

The highlight of Northland's west coast, this superb forest sanctuary – proclaimed in 1952 after much public pressure – is the largest remnant of the once-extensive kauri forests of northern NZ. The forest road (SH12) stretches for 18km and passes some huge trees – a kauri can reach 60m in height and have a trunk 5m in diameter.

Control of the forest has recently been returned to Te Roroa, the local *iwi* (tribe), as part of a settlement for Crown breaches of the Treaty of Waitangi. Te Roroa runs the **visitor centre** ( ☎ 09-439 6445; www.teroroa.iwi.nz; 1 Waipoua River Rd; ⏰ 9am-6.30pm summer, 9am-4.30pm winter) and camping ground near the south end of the park.

## SIGHTS & ACTIVITIES

Near the north end of the park, not far from the road, stands mighty **Tane Mahuta**, named for the Maori forest god. At 51m, with a 13.8m girth and wood mass of 244.5 cubic metres, he's the largest kauri alive. You don't so much look at Tane Mahuta; it's as if you're granted an audience to his hushed presence. He's been holding court here for somewhere between 1200 and 2000 years.

A little further south a short road leads to the Kauri Walks car park. From here, a 20-minute (each way) walk leads to **Te Matua Ngahere** (the Father of the Forest). At 30m he's shorter than Tane Mahuta, but he has the same noble presence, reinforced by his substantial girth – he's the widest living kauri (16.4m).

Close by are the **Four Sisters**, a graceful stand of four tall trees that have fused together at the base. A 40-minute walk leads to **Yakas**, the seventh-largest kauri.

**Footprints Waipoua** ( ☎ 0800 687 836; www.footprintswaipoua.co.nz; adult/child $95/35) is a four-hour twilight tour led by Maori guides into Waipoua Kauri Forest

### SLEEPING & EATING

**Waipoua Forest Campground** ( ☎ 09-439 6445; www.teroroa.iwi.nz; 1 Waipoua River Rd; sites per adult/child $14/7, cabin s/tw/tr/q $15/50/60/80, house $175) Situated next to the Waipoua

River and the visitor centre, this peaceful camping ground offers hot showers, flush toilets and a kitchen. The cabins are DOC-style – spartan, with unmade swab beds (bring your own linen or hire it).

**Waipoua Lodge B&B** ( ☎ 09-439 0422; www.waipoualodge.co.nz; SH12; r incl breakfast $570-590; 🛜 ) This fine old villa at the southern edge of the forest has four luxurious, spacious suites, which were originally the stables, the woolshed and the calf-rearing pen! Decadent dinners ($90) are available.

**Morrell's Cafe** ( ☎ 09-405 4545; 7235 SH12, Waimamaku; mains $8-14; 🕙 9am-4pm) Perhaps this is where Hokianga's hippies ended up. This bright-yellow cafe and craft shop serves up tasty snacks in a former cheese factory near the north end of the forest.

# COROMANDEL REGION

## GETTING THERE & AROUND

Daily buses on the Auckland-to-Tauranga route pass through Thames and Waihi,

Thames

CAROL WILEY

while others loop through Coromandel Town, Whitianga and Tairua.

It's definitely worth considering the beautiful ferry ride from Auckland via Waiheke Island to Coromandel Town (see p114).

# THAMES

pop 10,000

Thames dates from a time when gold-digging had a much different connotation to what it does today. Dinky 19th-century wooden buildings still dominate the town centre, but grizzly prospectors have been replaced by alternative lifestylers.

**Thames i-SITE** ( ☎ 07-868 7284; www. thamesinfo.co.nz; 206 Pollen St; ❂ 8.30am-5pm Mon-Fri, 9am-4pm Sat & Sun) has information and internet access.

## SIGHTS & ACTIVITIES

The **Goldmine Experience** ( ☎ 07-868 8514; www.goldmine-experience.co.nz; cnr Moanataiari Rd & SH25; adult/child $15/5; ❂ 10am-4pm Jan-Mar, 10am-1pm Apr-Sep) allows you to walk through a gold-mine tunnel, watch a stamper battery crush rock, learn about the history of the Cornish miners and try your hand panning for gold ($2 extra).

**Eyez Open** ( ☎ 07-868 9018; www.eyez open.co.nz; per day $30, 1- to 4-day tours $110-750) rents out bikes and organises small-group cycling tours of the peninsula (minimum four to six people).

## SLEEPING & EATING

our pick **Brunton House B&B** ( ☎ 07-868 5160; www.bruntonhouse.co.nz; 210 Parawai Rd; r $160-180, tr $195; 🖥 🛜 🐾 ) Recent renovations of this impressive two-storey kauri villa (1875) have upgraded the kitchen and bathrooms, while staying true to the building's historic credentials (there are no en suites). Guests can relax in the grounds, by the pool, in the designated lounge or on the upstairs terrace.

**Cotswold Cottage** ( ☎ 07-868 6306; www. cotswoldcottage.co.nz; 36 Maramarahi Rd; r $165-200) Looking over the river and racecourse, this pretty villa has had a modern makeover with luxurious linen and an outdoor spa pool. The comfy rooms all open onto a deck.

our pick **Rocco** ( ☎ 07-868 8641; 109 Sealey St; mains $24-25; ❂ lunch daily, dinner Tue-Sun) Housed in one of Thames' gorgeous kauri villas, Rocco serves a lively tapas selection and more substantial mains, making good use of local ingredients (mussels, fish) and high-quality Spanish imports (chorizo, cheese, olives). In clement weather take a seat among the crushed-shell and swirling brick paths outside.

## GETTING THERE & AROUND

Thames is the transport hub of the Coromandel. **InterCity** ( ☎ 09-583 5780; www.intercity.co.nz) and its associates have daily buses to/from Auckland ($28, two hours), Coromandel Town ($16, 72 minutes), Whitianga ($34, 90 minutes), Tairua ($17, 44 minutes), Waihi ($20, 45 minutes), Hamilton ($24, 1¾ hours) and Tauranga ($28, 1¾ hours), stopping outside the i-SITE and Sunkist Backpackers.

**Naked Bus** (www.nakedbus.com) operates in conjunction with **Tairua Bus Company** ( ☎ 07-864 7770; www.tairuabus.co.nz) for daily services between Thames and Tairua (from $1, 50 minutes), stopping at Ngatea for connections to Auckland, Tauranga and Rotorua.

**Go Kiwi** ( ☎ 0800 446 549; www.go-kiwi. co.nz) has daily shuttles to/from Auckland ($42, two hours), Auckland airport ($54, 90 minutes), Whitianga ($36, 1¾ hours), Tairua ($26, 70 minutes) and Whangamata ($64, 75 minutes).

# COROMANDEL REGION

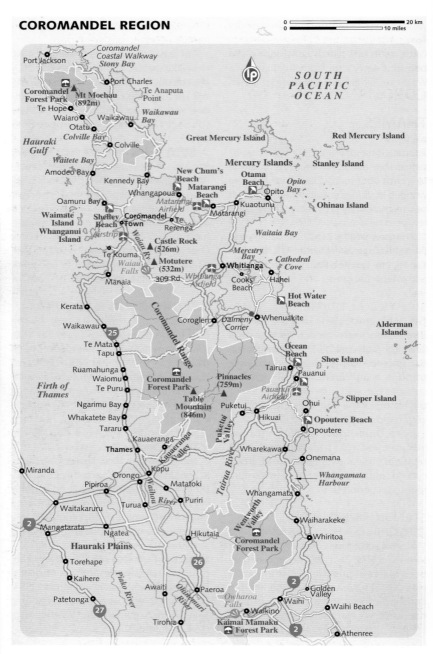

**Paki Paki Bike Shop** (☎ 07-867 9026; www.pakipakibikeshop.co.nz; Goldfields Shopping Centre) rents out bikes for $25 a day and performs repairs.

# COROMANDEL TOWN

pop 1620

Even more crammed with heritage buildings than Thames, Coromandel Town is a thoroughly quaint little place. Its natty cafes, interesting art stores, excellent sleeping options and delicious smoked mussels could keep you here longer than you expected.

**Coromandel Town i-SITE** (☎ 07-866 8598; www.coromandeltown.co.nz; 355 Kapanga Rd; ☺ 9am-5pm Mon-Fri, 9am-4pm Sat & Sun Apr-Oct, 9am-5pm daily Nov-Mar) has internet access ($6 per hour) and maps of local walks ($1).

## SIGHTS & ACTIVITIES

The **Coromandel Goldfield Centre & Stamper Battery** (☎ 07-866 7933; 410 Buffalo Rd; adult/child $10/5; ☺ tours 2pm & 3pm Tue, Thu, Sat & Sun) is an 1899 rock-crushing plant with informative one-hour tours. You can also try panning for gold ($5).

The amazing **Driving Creek Railway & Potteries** (☎ 07-866 8703; www.drivingcreekrailway.co.nz; 380 Driving Creek Rd; adult/child $20/11; ☺ departures 10.15am & 2pm) is 3km north of Coromandel Town. The unique train runs up steep grades, across four trestle bridges, along two spirals and a double switchback, and through two tunnels, finishing at the 'Eye-full Tower'. The hour-long trip passes artworks and regenerating native forest – more than 17,000 natives have been planted, including 9000 kauri.

**Coromandel Kayak Adventures** (☎ 07-866 7466; www.kayakadventures.co.nz) offers paddle-powered tours ranging from half-day ecotours (for 1/2/3/4/5/6 paddlers $200/200/267/356/425/474) to fishing trips (half-/full day $195/375).

## SLEEPING & EATING

**Coromandel Holiday Park** (☎ 07-866 8830; www.coromandelholidaypark.co.nz; 636 Rings Rd; sites per person $20, dm $30, cabins $77-137, units

Heritage building, Coromandel Town

$137-177; 🖥 📶 🐾 ) Well-kept and welcoming, with nicely painted cabins and manicured lawns, this large park includes the semi-separate Coromandel Town Backpackers. It gets busy in summer, so book ahead.

**Lions' Den** ( ☎ 07-866 8157; www.lionsden hostel.co.nz; 126 Te Tiki St; dm/r $24/55; 📶 ) Chill out to the hippy vibe in this magical place. A tranquil garden with fish pond, fairy lights and wisteria vines, and a relaxed collection of comfy rooms (dotted with African and North American bits and bobs) make for a soothing spot to rest up.

**Anchor Lodge** ( ☎ 07-866 7992; www. anchorlodgecoromandel.co.nz; 448 Wharf Rd; dm $25, d $60-65, unit $125-275; 📶 🐾 ) Not many places can boast their own goldmine and glowworm cave but this upmarket backpacker/motel combo has them, and a heated swimming pool and spa to boot. The 2nd-floor units look over the nikau palms and agaves to the harbour.

**our pick** **Driving Creek Cafe** ( ☎ 07-866 7066; 180 Driving Creek Rd; mains $8-16; ⏲ 9.30am-5pm; 🖥 V ) A large selection of vegetarian, vegan, gluten-free, organic and fair-trade delights awaits at this funky mud-brick cafe. The food is wonderful – beautifully presented, fresh and healthy. Once sated, the kids can play in the sandpit while the adults check their email ($6 per hour).

**Pepper Tree Restaurant & Bar** ( ☎ 07-866 8211; 31 Kapanga Rd; lunch $17-25, dinner $23-33; ⏲ lunch & dinner daily; 📶 ) C-Town's most upmarket option, Pepper Tree dishes up generously proportioned French-style cooking with a particular emphasis on local seafood. On a summer's evening, the courtyard tables under the shady tree are the place to be.

## GETTING THERE & AWAY

By far the nicest way to travel from Auckland is by ferry. Operator **360** Discovery ( ☎ 0800 888 006; www.360discovery. co.nz) has five boats weekly to/from Auckland (one way/return $49/79, two hours) via Orapiu on Waiheke Island (one way/return $39/69, 70 minutes). It makes a great day trip, and there's a guided-tour option (adult/child $136/78) that includes Driving Creek Railway and the Goldfield Centre. The boats dock at Hannafords Wharf, Te Kouma, where free buses shuttle passengers 10km into town.

**InterCity** ( ☎ 09-583 5780; www.intercity. co.nz) and its partners have daily buses to/from Whitianga ($18, 80 minutes), Thames ($16, 72 minutes), Te Aroha ($20, 2¾ hours) and Hamilton ($40, 3¾ hours).

**Naked Bus** (www.nakedbus.com) operates in conjunction with **Tairua Bus Company** ( ☎ 07-864 7770; www.tairuabus.co.nz; advance fares from $1) for daily services to Tairua (two hours), via Whitianga (one hour), Hahei (90 minutes) and Hot Water Beach (95 minutes).

**Go Kiwi** ( ☎ 0800 446 549; www.go-kiwi. co.nz) runs shuttles from late October to Easter to/from Auckland ($50, 3¾ hours), Auckland airport ($66, 3¼ hours) and Whitianga ($23, 50 minutes).

# WHITIANGA

pop 3800

If you come to Whitianga you'd better want to get wet. The big attractions are the sandy beaches of Mercury Bay and the diving, boating and kayaking opportunities afforded by the craggy coast and nearby Te Whanganui-A-Hei Marine Reserve.

**Whitianga i-SITE** ( ☎ 07-866 5555; www. whitianga.co.nz; 66 Albert St; ⏲ 9am-5pm Mon-Fri, 9am-4pm Sat & Sun, extended in summer) has information and internet access ($9 per hour).

## SIGHTS & ACTIVITIES

**Buffalo Beach** stretches along Mercury Bay, north of the harbour. A five-minute passenger ferry ride (adult/child/bicycle $2/1/50c; ☺ 7.30am-2.15am Christmas-Jan, 7.30am-6.30pm & 7.30-8.30pm & 9.30-11pm Feb-Christmas) will take you across the harbour to **Whitianga Rock Scenic & Historical Reserve**, **Flaxmill Bay**, **Shakespeare's Lookout**, **Captain Cook's Memorial**, **Lonely Bay** and **Cooks Bay**, all within walking distance.

**Seafari Windsurfing** ( ☎ 07-866 0677; Brophy's Beach), 4km north of Whitianga, hires out sailboards (from $25 per hour) and kayaks (from $15 per hour), and provides windsurfing lessons (from $40 including gear).

## SLEEPING & EATING

**On the Beach Backpackers Lodge** ( ☎ 07-866 5380; www.coromandelbackpackers.com; 46 Buffalo Beach Rd; dm $24-26, s $49-53, d $66-96; 🖳 ) Brightly painted, beachside and brilliant, this well-run YHA has a large choice of sleeping options, including some with sea views and en suites. It provides free kayaks, boogie boards and spades (for Hot Water Beach).

**our pick** **Pipi Dune B&B** ( ☎ 07-869 5375; www.pipidune.co.nz; 5 Pipi Dune; s/d $85/125; 🛜 ) You'll be as snug as a pipi in its shell in this attractive B&B in a quiet cul-de-sac, and you'll have a lot more room to move: pipi shells don't tend to accommodate guest lounges with kitchenettes, laundries and free wi-fi.

**Cafe Nina** ( ☎ 07-866 5440; 20 Victoria St; mains $8-18; ☺ breakfast & lunch) Barbecue for breakfast? Why the hell not. Too cool to be constrained to four walls, the kitchen grills bacon and eggs on an outdoor hotplate while the punters spill out onto tables in the park.

**our pick** **18sixtyfive** ( ☎ 07-866 0456; 121a Cook Dr; lunch $14-17, dinner $32-35; ☺ lunch & dinner) A fitting indulgence after a hot-water soak, the Lost Spring's restaurant offers smart fusion dining in the elegant surrounds of a converted 1865 schoolhouse.

## GETTING THERE & AROUND

**InterCity** ( ☎ 0508 353 947; www.intercity.co.nz) has a daily bus to/from Thames ($34, 90 minutes) via Tairua ($17, 44 minutes),

RICHARD CUMMINS

Mercury Bay, Whitianga

DAVID WALL

Cathedral Cove, Hot Water Beach

## ➘ HOT WATER BEACH

Justifiably famous, Hot Water Beach is quite extraordinary. For two hours either side of low tide, you can access an area of sand in front of a rocky outcrop at the middle of the beach where hot water oozes up from beneath the surface. Bring a spade, dig a hole and *voila,* you've got a personal spa pool. Surfers stop off before the main beach to access some decent breaks.

Spades ($5) can be hired from the **Hot Water Beach Store**, which has a cafe attached. The wonderful **Hot Waves Café** also rents spades ($5) and serves excellent food in cool surroundings. In summer there are queues out the door.

A nice hillside pad, **Hot Water Beach B&B** has priceless views, a spa bath on the deck and attractive living quarters.

The Hahei bus services stop here, but only on pre-booked requests.

**Things you need to know: Hot Water Beach Store** ( ☎ 07-866 3006; Pye Pl; 9am-7pm summer, low tide winter); **Hot Waves Café** ( ☎ 07-866 3887; 8 Pye Pl; meals $10-17; 8.30am-4pm); **Hot Water Beach B&B** ( ☎ 07-866 3991; www.hotwaterbedandbreakfast. co.nz; 48 Pye Pl; r $250)

stopping at the i-SITE, Cat's Pyjamas and On The Beach.

**Naked Bus** (www.nakedbus.com) partners with **Tairua Bus Company** ( ☎ 07-864 7770; www.tairuabus.co.nz; advance fares from $1) for daily services to Coromandel Town (one hour), Hahei (30 minutes), Hot Water Beach (40 minutes) and Tairua (one hour).

**Go Kiwi** ( ☎ 0800 446 549; www.go-kiwi.co.nz) shuttles head to Tairua ($24, one hour), Thames ($36, 1¾ hours) and Auckland ($65, four hours) daily, with services to Waihi ($42, 2¼ hours) and Tauranga ($60, three hours) from December to Easter.

## HAHEI

pop 270 (7000 in summer)

A legendary Kiwi beach town, little Hahei balloons to bursting in summer but is nearly abandoned otherwise – apart from the busloads of tourists doing the obligatory stop-off at Cathedral Cove.

## SIGHTS & ACTIVITIES

Beautiful **Cathedral Cove**, with its famous gigantic stone arch and natural waterfall shower, is best enjoyed early or late in the day – avoiding the worst of the hordes. On the way there's rocky **Gemstone Bay** (which has a snorkelling trail where you're likely to see big snapper, crayfish and stingrays) and sandy **Stingray Bay**.

**Cathedral Cove Sea Kayaking** ( ☎ 07-866 3877; www.seakayaktours.co.nz; 88 Hahei Beach Rd; half-/full day $85/145) runs guided kayaking trips around the rock arches, caves and islands in the Cathedral Cove area. The Remote Coast Tour heads the other way when conditions permit, visiting caves, blowholes and a long tunnel.

**Cathedral Cove Dive & Snorkel** ( ☎ 07-866 3955; www.hahei.co.nz/diving; Hahei Beach Rd; dives $69-105) runs daily dive trips and rents out scuba gear ($60), snorkelling gear ($20), bikes ($20) and boogie boards ($20).

## SLEEPING & EATING

**ourpick** **Tatahi Lodge** ( ☎ 07-866 3992; www.tatahilodge.co.nz; Grange Rd; dm/d $30/80, units $140-310; 🖳 🛜 ) A wonderful place where backpackers are treated with at least as much care and respect as the bromeliad-filled garden. The dorm rooms and excellent communal facilities are just as attractive as the pricier self-contained units. Gifts of free fruit in season provide much-needed vitamin replenishment to those hardcore bag-of-rice-a-week types.

**Church** ( ☎ 07-866 3533; www.thechurch hahei.co.nz; 87 Hahei Beach Rd; cottages $130-220; 🖳 ) These beautifully kitted-out, rustic timber cottages have stylish, modern but natural interiors in a photogenic garden setting. Housed in the ultracharming wooden church at the top of the drive is Hahei's swankiest eatery (mains cost from $30 to $37).

## GETTING THERE & AROUND

**Tairua Bus Company** ( ☎ 07-864 7770; www.tairuabus.co.nz; advance fares from $1), in association with **Naked Bus** (www.nakedbus.com), has daily services to Coromandel Town (90 minutes) via Whitianga (30 minutes) and Tairua (30 minutes) via Hot Water Beach (10 minutes).

From Boxing Day to Waitangi Day the council runs buses from the Cooks Beach side of the Ferry Landing to Hot Water Beach, stopping at Hahei (adult/child $2/1).

# WAIKATO & THE KING COUNTRY

## GETTING THERE & AROUND

Hamilton is the transport hub, with its airport servicing extensive domestic routes and some international ones. Buses link the city to everywhere in the North Island.

Trains are an option, but are infrequent and surprisingly expensive on short legs. The main trunk-line between Auckland and Wellington stops at Hamilton, Otorohanga, Te Kuiti and Taumarunui.

## HAMILTON

pop 140,700

Landlocked cities in an island nation are never going to have the glamorous appeal of their coastal sisters. But something strange has happened in Hamilton recently. Perhaps it's a sign of the rising fortunes of Waikato farmers that the city has sprouted a sophisticated and vibrant stretch of bars and eateries around Hood and Victoria Sts that – on the weekend at least – leave Auckland's Viaduct Harbour for dead in the boozy fun stakes.

### INFORMATION

**Hamilton i-SITE** ( ☎ 07-839 3580; www.visithamilton.co.nz; 5 Garden Pl; ⏱ 9am-5.30pm Mon-Fri, 9.30am-3.30pm Sat & Sun)

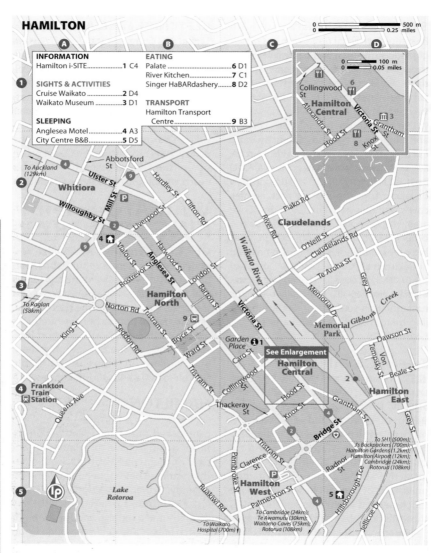

**HAMILTON**

| | | |
|---|---|---|
| **INFORMATION** | | |
| Hamilton i-SITE | **1** C4 | |
| | | |
| **SIGHTS & ACTIVITIES** | | |
| Cruise Waikato | **2** D4 | |
| Waikato Museum | **3** D1 | |
| | | |
| **SLEEPING** | | |
| Anglesea Motel | **4** A3 | |
| City Centre B&B | **5** D5 | |

| | | |
|---|---|---|
| **EATING** | | |
| Palate | **6** D1 | |
| River Kitchen | **7** C1 | |
| Singer HaBARdashery | **8** D2 | |
| | | |
| **TRANSPORT** | | |
| Hamilton Transport | | |
| Centre | **9** B3 | |

## SIGHTS & ACTIVITIES

The excellent **Waikato Museum** ( ☎ 07-838 6606; www.waikatomuseum.co.nz; 1 Grantham St; admission by donation, charge for touring exhibitions; ◷ 10am-4.30pm) has five main areas: an art gallery; interactive science galleries; Tainui galleries housing Maori treasures, including the magnificently carved *waka taua* (war canoe) *Te Winika*; a Hamilton history exhibition entitled Never a Dull Moment; and a Waikato River exhibition.

Stretching over 50 hectares of riverbank southeast of the centre, **Hamilton Gardens** ( ☎ 07-838 6782; www.hamilton gardens.co.nz; Cobham Dr; admission free; enclosed section ☻ 7.30am-sunset) incorporates a large park, cafe, restaurant and extravagantly themed enclosed gardens.

The strong-flowing Waikato River is well worth investigating. **Cruise Waikato** ( ☎ 0508 426 458; www.cruise-waikato.co.nz; Memorial Park Jetty; cruises from adult/child $20/10) runs a range of cruises, focused variously on sightseeing, history or your belly (coffee and muffins, sausage sizzles or picnics).

Another river option is the **City Bridges River Tour** ( ☎ 07-847 5565; www.canoeand kayak.co.nz; 2hr trip adult/child $50/30), a guided kayak ride through the city. **Wiseway Canoe Adventures** ( ☎ 021 988 335; www. wisewayadventures.com; 2hr trip adult/child $50/20) runs a similar trip, and offers freedom hire.

## SLEEPING

**J's Backpackers** ( ☎ 07-856 8934; www.jsback packers.co.nz; 8 Grey St; dm/s/d/tr $28/60/66/82; 🖳 🛜 ) A homely hostel occupying a char-acterful house near Hamilton Gardens, friendly J's offers good security, a smallish kitchen and bright, tidy rooms with new mattresses. There's also a barbecue out the back.

**City Centre B&B** ( ☎ 07-838 1671; www.city centrebnb.co.nz; 3 Anglesea St; s/d/tr $80/99/130; 🖳 🛜 ) At the quiet riverside end of a central city street (five-minutes walk to the Victoria/Hood St action), this sparkling self-contained apartment opens on to a swimming pool. Self-catering breakfast provided.

**Anglesea Motel** ( ☎ 0800 4264 5732, 07-834 0010; www.angleseamotel.co.nz; 36 Liverpool St; d/2-bedroom unit/3-bedroom unit from $135/260/305; 🛜 🛜 ) A far preferable option to anything on Ulster St's 'motel row', the Anglesea has plenty of space, friendly managers, free wi-fi, pool, squash and tennis courts, and not un-stylish decor. Hard to beat.

## EATING

**River Kitchen** ( ☎ 07-839 2906; 237 Victoria St; mains $7-16; ☻ 7am-4pm Mon-Fri, 8am-4pm Sat &

Greenhouse and pond, Hamilton Gardens

DAVID WALL

**Sun)** Heralded as Waikato's 'Best New Cafe' by *Cafe* magazine, hip River Kitchen does things with simple style: cakes, gourmet breakfasts and fresh seasonal lunches (angle for a slice of the Spanish duck pie); and there's a barista who knows his beans.

**our pick Singer HaBARdashery** (☎ 07-839 1537; 15 Hood St; brunch $11-19, tapas $9-19; ☯ lunch & dinner) A classy operator on the Hood St strip, Singer is a moody tapas and wine bar occupying the oldest stone building in Hamilton – a former haberdashery. Expect a dizzying selection of wines and beers, great coffee, satisfying brunches and zingy tapas (try the Needle: eye fillet, mushroom, scallop, chorizo, and haloumi skewered on a knitting needle).

**Palate** (☎ 07-834 2921; 170 Victoria St; mains $25-33; ☯ dinner Tue-Sat) Given this restaurant's deserved status as the best in the central North Island, it's surprisingly reasonably priced. Chef/owner Mat McLean delivers an innovative mod-NZ menu and free tasters between courses.

## GETTING THERE & AWAY

**Air New Zealand** (☎ 0800 737 000; www.airnewzealand.co.nz) has regular direct flights from **Hamilton Airport** (☎ 07-848 9027; www.hamiltonairport.co.nz; Airport Rd) to Auckland, Christchurch, Gisborne, Napier, New Plymouth, Palmerston North, Rotorua, Tauranga, Wellington and Whakatane.

Internationally, **Pacific Blue** (☎ 0800 670 000; www.pacificblue.com.au) flies from Hamilton to Sydney and Brisbane.

All buses arrive and depart from the **Hamilton Transport Centre** (☎ 07-834 3457; cnr Anglesea & Bryce Sts). Environment Waikato's **Busit!** (☎ 0800 4287 5463; www.busit.co.nz) has numerous services throughout the region, including Ngaruawahia ($3.70, 25 minutes), Cambridge ($6, 40

minutes), Te Awamutu ($6, 30 minutes) and Raglan ($7.30, one hour).

**Raglan Shuttle Co** (☎ 0800 8873 27873, 0212 612 563; www.solscape.co.nz/shuttle.html) links Hamilton with Raglan (one-way $60). Auckland connections also available.

**InterCity** (☎ 09-583 5780; www.intercity.co.nz) services numerous destinations including the following:

| TO | PRICE | HOW LONG | HOW OFTEN |
|---|---|---|---|
| Auckland | $21 | 2hr | 10 daily |
| Cambridge | $19 | 25min | 5 daily |
| Rotorua | $34 | 1½hr | 6 daily |
| Wellington | $75 | 9hr | 4 daily |

**Naked Bus** (☎ 0900 62533; www.nakedbus.com) services run to the following destinations (among many others):

| TO | PRICE | HOW LONG | HOW OFTEN |
|---|---|---|---|
| Auckland | $21 | 2¼hr | 3-5 daily |
| Cambridge | $14 | 30min | 3-4 daily |
| Rotorua | $24 | 2hr | 2-3 daily |
| Wellington | $49 | 10hr | 1-3 daily |

Hamilton is on the **Overlander** (☎ 0800 872 467; www.tranzscenic.co.nz; daily Oct-Apr, Fri-Sun May-Sep) route between Auckland ($53, 2½ hours) and Wellington ($107, 9½ hours) via Otorohanga ($53, 45 minutes). Trains stop at Hamilton's **Frankton Train Station** (Queens Ave), 1km west of the city centre; note that there are no ticket sales here.

## GETTING AROUND
### TO/FROM THE AIRPORT

Hamilton Airport is 12km south of the city. International departure tax is $25 for those 12 years and over; $10 for kids. The **Super Shuttle** (☎ 0800 748 885, 07-843 7778; www.supershuttle.co.nz; one-way $21) offers a door-to-door service into the city. A taxi costs around $40.

## BUS

Hamilton's **Busit!** ( ☎ 0800 4287 5463; www.busit.co.nz; tickets adult/child $2.90/1.30) network services the city-centre and suburbs daily from around 7am to 7.30pm (later on Friday). Busit! also runs a free **CBD shuttle** ( 🕒 7am-6pm Mon-Fri, 9am-1pm Sat), looping around Victoria, Liverpool, Anglesea and Bridge Sts every 10 minutes.

# RAGLAN

pop 2700

Laid-back Raglan may well be NZ's perfect surfing town. It's small enough to have escaped mass development – perhaps due to a mainstream Kiwi preference for the safer white-sand east-coast beaches – yet it's big enough for a bit of bustle.

The nearby surf spots – Indicators, Whale Bay and Manu Bay – are internationally famous for their point breaks, attracting surfers from around the world.

## INFORMATION

**Visitor Information Centre** ( ☎ 07-825 0556; www.raglan.org.nz; 2 Wainui Rd; 🕒 9.30am-5pm Mon-Fri, 10am-5pm Sat, 10am-4pm Sun) DOC brochures plus information about local accommodation and activities. Reduced hours in winter.

## SIGHTS & ACTIVITIES

The instructors at **Raglan Surf School** ( ☎ 07-825 7873; www.raglansurfingschool.co.nz; 5b Whaanga Rd, Whale Bay; 3hr lesson incl transport $89) pride themselves on getting 95% of first-timers standing during their first lesson. Experienced wave hounds can hire surfboards (from $15 per hour), boogie boards ($5 per hour) and wetsuits ($5 per hour).

**Solscape** ( ☎ 07-825 8268; www.solscape.co.nz; 611 Wainui Rd, Manu Bay; lessons $85)

offers 2½-hour lessons, as well as board and wetsuit hire (per half-day $40).

If you would rather spend more time above the water than in it, **Raglan Kite Surf School** ( ☎ 07-825 8702, 0212 524 117; lessons per hr $60) runs one-on-one lessons wherever the wind's blowing.

Raglan Harbour is great for kayaking. Raglan Backpackers (below) has single/double ocean kayaks for hire (per half-day $30/40).

## SLEEPING

**ourpick** **Raglan Backpackers** ( ☎ 07-825 0515; www.raglanbackpackers.co.nz; 6 Wi Neera St; dm/s $25/52, d $66-76; 🖳 ) This welcoming, purpose-built hostel has a laid-back holiday-house vibe. It's right on the water's edge, and some rooms have sea views; the rest are arranged around a garden courtyard. For small groups there is a separate self-contained wing sleeping up to eight. There are kayaks for hire (from $15), or if that's too strenuous you can take a yoga class, swan about in a hammock, strum a guitar or drip in the sauna. Can we stay another night?

**Raglan Sunset Motel** ( ☎ 07-825 0500; www.raglansunsetmotel.co.nz; 7 Bankart St; d $140; 🛜 ) A block or so back from the action, this two-storey motel with faux shutters randomly adhered to the facade is barely seven years old. As you'd expect, everything's in good nick. The owners also have self-contained apartments (doubles from $150) and beach houses (four people from $250) available around town.

**Journey's End B&B** ( ☎ 07-825 6727; www.raglanaccommodation.co.nz; 49 Lily St; s/d $90/140, exclusive use 2/4 people $180/240) No it's not Mt Doom; quite the opposite, in fact. These two attractive en-suite rooms share a central modern lounge with a kitchenette and a deck overlooking the wharf and harbour.

## EATING

**Vinnie's** ( ☎ 07-825 7273; 7 Wainui Rd; meals $8-23; �” 10am-late Tue-Sun; �ᗑ ) Run by a long-lost New Yorker, Vinnie's looks like a truck stop from the outside, but inside it's all Hawaiian prints, reggae tunes and surf movies flickering on the walls. On the food front it's burgers, salads, wraps, cheese-steaks, pizzas and their 'famous' meatloaf. Free wi-fi is available, too.

**Tongue & Groove** ( ☎ 07-825 0027; 19 Bow St; mains $9-18; �” 8.30am-3pm Mon-Thu, 8.30am-8.30pm Fri & Sat, 8.30am-8pm Sun; Ⓥ ) There are plenty of streetside seats and retro couches for wine sipping in this funky corner cafe, with surf mags strewn about and lots of local art. The delicious vegetarian roti is a bargain ($14).

## GETTING THERE & AROUND

From Hamilton, Raglan is 48km west along SH23.

Environment Waikato's **Busit!** ( ☎ 0800 4287 5463; www.busit.co.nz, adult/child $7.30/3.70) heads between Hamilton and Raglan (one hour) three times daily on weekdays and twice daily on weekends.

**Raglan Shuttle Co** ( ☎ 0800 8873 27873, 0212 612 563; www.solscape.co.nz/shuttle.html) links Raglan with Hamilton (one-way $60) and Auckland ($100).

**Bike2Bay** ( ☎ 07-825 0309; www.bike2bay. com; 24b Stewart St; hire per hr/half-/full day $8/22/33; �” 9.30am-5pm) has mountain bikes for hire, and does repairs.

# SOUTH OF RAGLAN
## NGARUNUI BEACH

Less than a kilometre further south, this is a great beach for grommets learning to surf. On the clifftop is the club for the volunteer lifeguards who patrol part of the black-sand beach from late October until April. This is the only beach with lifeguards and the best ocean beach for swimming.

## MANU BAY

Another 2.5km journey will bring you to this legendary surfing spot, said to have the longest left-hand break in the world. The elongated uniform waves are created by the angle at which the Tasman Sea swell meets the coastline (it works best in a southwesterly swell).

**our pick** **Solscape** ( ☎ 07-825 8268; www. solscape.co.nz; 611 Wainui Rd; sites per person $15, cabooses dm/d $25/60, tepees s/d/q $50/68/136, cottages d $110-180; ⌨ ⸞ ) offers backpacker accommodation in recycled train carriages with a homely communal lounge/kitchen. The ultimate greenie experience could well be chilling out in a surprisingly comfortable tepee, surrounded by native bush, knowing that you're completely 'off the grid' – while not sacrificing hot showers (solar) and decent toilets (composting). Self-contained sea-view cottages, surf lessons (p121) and massage therapy ($65 per hour) complete the bewildering array of services available here.

## WHALE BAY

This renowned surfing spot is a kilometre further west from Manu Bay and is usually less crowded, but from the bottom of Calvert St you do have to clamber 600m over the rocks to get here.

Deep in native bush, **Karioi Lodge** ( ☎ 07-825 7873; www.karioilodge.co.nz; 5b Whaanga Rd; dm/d $27/69; ⌨ ) offers a sauna, a flying fox, mountain bikes, bush and beach walks, sustainable gardening, tree planting and the Raglan Surf School (p121). There are no en suites but the rooms are clean and cosy.

These friendly folks also run nearby **Sleeping Lady Lodging** ( ☎ 07-825 7873; www.sleepinglady.co.nz; 5b Whaanga Rd; lodges $125-240), a collection of luxury self-contained lodges.

# WAITOMO CAVES

Even if damp, dark tunnels sound like your idea of hell, take a chill pill and head to Waitomo anyway. In the midst of the King Country, NZ's rural heartland, these limestone caves, with accompanying geological formations and glowing bugs, are deservedly one of the premier attractions of the North Island.

## INFORMATION

**Waitomo i-SITE** ( ☎ 07-878 7640; www.waitomo caves.com; 21 Waitomo Caves Rd; ⏱ 8am-8pm Jan & Feb, 8.45am-5pm Mar-Dec; 🖳 ) has internet access and acts as a post office and booking agent.

## SIGHTS & ACTIVITIES

Adjoining the i-SITE, the **Waitomo Caves Discovery Centre** ( ☎ 07-878 7640; www.waito mo-museum.co.nz; 21 Waitomo Caves Rd; admission adult/child $5/3; ⏱ 8am-8pm Jan & Feb, 8.45am-5pm Mar-Dec) has excellent exhibits explaining how caves are formed, the flora and fauna that thrive in them and the history of Waitomo's caves and cave exploration.

## UNDERGROUND

**Legendary Black Water Rafting Company** ( ☎ 0800 228 464; 585 Waitomo Caves Rd; www.waitomo.com) claims to have invented black-water rafting! Its Black Labyrinth tour ($110, three hours, minimum age 12) involves floating in a wetsuit on an inner tube down a river that flows through Ruakuri Cave. The Black Abyss tour ($215, five hours, minimum age 16) is more adventurous and includes a 30m abseil into Ruakuri Cave, plus more glowworms, tubing and cave climbing.

**Spellbound** ( ☎ 0800 773 552, 07-878 7622; www.glow-worm.co.nz; 10 Waitomo Caves Rd; tours adult/child $66/24) is a good option if you don't want to get wet and want to avoid the big groups in the main caves. This three-hour tour and raft ride departs from the pyramid-like booking office in the middle of town (usually 10am, 11am, 2pm and 3pm, varying seasonally) and goes through parts of the glowworm-filled Mangawhitiakau cave system, 12km south of Waitomo.

PAUL KENNEDY

Surfers at Manu Bay, south of Raglan

Stalactites and stalagmites, Waitomo Caves

# ⭷ WAITOMO CAVES

The big-three caves are all operated by the same company, based at the new **Waitomo Caves Visitor Centre**. Various combo deals are available, including the Triple Cave Combo (adult/child $105/44).

The 45-minute guided tour of the **Glowworm Cave**, which is behind the visitor centre, leads past impressive stalactites and stalagmites into a large cavern known as the Cathedral. The highlight comes at the tour's end when you board a boat and swing off onto the river. As your eyes grow accustomed to the dark, you'll see a Milky Way of little lights surrounding you – these are the glowworms.

Three kilometres west from the Glowworm Cave is **Aranui Cave**. This cave is dry (hence no glowworms) but compensates with an incredible array of limestone formations. Thousands of tiny 'straw' stalactites hang from the ceiling. It's an hour's walk to the caves, otherwise the visitors centre can arrange transport.

Culturally significant **Ruakuri Cave** has an impressive 15m-high spiral staircase, removing the need to trample through the Maori burial site at the cave entrance (as tourists did for 84 years). Tours lead through 1.6km of the 7.5km system, taking in vast caverns with glowworms, subterranean streams and waterfalls, and intricate limestone structures. Tours depart from the Legendary Black Water Rafting Company (p123).

**Things you need to know: Waitomo Caves Visitor Centre** (☎ 0800 456 922; www.waitomo.com; Waitomo Caves Rd; 🕙 9am-5pm); **Glowworm Cave** (Waitomo Caves Rd; tours adult/child $39/18; 🕙 tours every 30min 9am-5pm); **Aranui Cave** (Tumutumu Rd; tours adult/child $39/18; 🕙 45min tours 10am, 11am, 1pm, 2pm, 3pm); **Ruakuri Cave** (☎ 0800 228 464; Tumutumu Rd; tours adult/child $60/24; 🕙 2hr tours 9am, 10am, 11.30am, 12.30pm, 1.30pm, 2.30pm & 3pm).

**Waitomo Adventures** ( ☎ 0800 924 866, 07-878 7788; www.waitomo.co.nz; 654 Waitomo Caves Rd) offers five different cave adventures, with discounts for various combos and for advance bookings. The Lost World (four-/seven-hour trip $270/395) trip starts with a 100m abseil down into the cave, then – by a combination of walking, climbing, spider-walking, inching along narrow rock ledges, wading and swimming through a river – you take a three-hour journey through a 30m-high cave to get back out, passing glowworms, amazing rock formations, waterfalls and more.

Haggas Honking Holes ($215 , four hours) includes professional abseiling instruction followed by three abseils, rock climbing and travelling along a subterranean river with waterfalls, traversing narrow passageways and huge caverns.

TumuTumu Toobing ($150 , four hour) is a walking, wading, swimming and tubing trip. St Benedict's Cavern ($145, three hours) includes abseiling and a subterranean flying fox in an attractive cave with straw stalagmites.

Readers recommend **Green Glow Eco-Adventures** ( ☎ 0800 476 459; www.greenglow. co.nz; 6hr tour per person for 2-4 people $100, for 1 person $200), which runs customised, small-group Waitomo tours, putting a caving, abseiling, rock-climbing, photographic or glowworm spin on your day (or all of the above!). It's based in Te Kuiti, 20 minutes from Waitomo.

## WALKING
The i-SITE has free pamphlets on walks in the area. The walk from the Aranui Cave to the Ruakuri Cave is an excellent short path. From the Glowworm Cave ticket office, there's a 10-minute walk to a lookout. Also from here, the 5km, three-hour-return **Waitomo Walkway** takes off through

farmland, following Waitomo Stream to the **Ruakuri Scenic Reserve**, where a 30-minute return walk passes by a natural limestone tunnel. There are glowworms here at night – drive to the car park and bring a torch to find your way.

## SLEEPING
**Juno Hall Backpackers** ( ☎ 07-878 7649; www.junowaitomo.co.nz; 600 Waitomo Caves Rd; sites per person $15, dm $27, d with/without bathroom $76/66, tr $95/85, q $120; ☐ ☎ ⊠ ) A slick purpose-built hostel 1km from the village, offering a warm welcome, a warmer wood fire in the woody lounge area, and an outdoor pool and tennis court.

**Waitomo Top 10 Holiday Park** ( ☎ 0508 498 666, 07-878 7639; www.waitomopark.co.nz; 12 Waitomo Caves Rd; sites from $20, cabins $65-110, units $130-170; ☐ ☎ ⊠ ) This superb camping ground in the heart of the village has spotless facilities, beaut new cabins and plenty of outdoor action to keep the kids busy (pool, spa, playground and neighbouring rugby pitch…).

**Waitomo Caves Guest Lodge** ( ☎ 07-878 7641; www.waitomocavesguestlodge.co.nz; 7 Waitomo Caves Rd; s $80, d $100-120, extra person $25, all incl breakfast; ☎ ) Bags your own cosy little en suite cabin at this central lodge with a sweet garden setting. The top ones have valley views. Large continental breakfast and resident dog included.

**Abseil Inn** ( ☎ 07-878 7815; www.abseilinn. co.nz; 709 Waitomo Caves Rd; d incl breakfast $135-165; ☎ ) A veeery steep driveway (abseiling in from a helicopter might be an easier approach) takes you to this delightful B&B with four themed rooms, great breakfasts and witty hosts. The biggest room has a double bath and valley views.

## EATING
**Morepork Pizzeria & Cafe** ( ☎ 07-878 3395; Kiwi Paka, Hotel Access Rd; breakfast & lunch $7-15,

Redwoods – Whakarewarewa Forest (p130)

dinner $13-27; ☻ 8am-8pm) At the Kiwi Paka backpackers, this cheery joint is a jack-of-all-trades eatery serving breakfast, lunch and dinner either inside or out on the deck. The 'Caveman' pizza is a winner (the first person to ask for more pork will be shown the door).

**our pick** **Huhu** ( ☎ 07-878 6674; 10 Waitomo Caves Rd; lunch $12-19, dinner $23-35; ☻ 10.30am-9pm; ☏ Ⓥ ) Easily the best choice, you won't be disappointed if you come here twice a day. Slick and modern with charming service, it has great views from the afternoon-tipple-friendly terrace and sublime contemporary NZ food. Graze from a seasonal tapas-style menu (large or small plates) of kiwi specialities such as *rewana* bread and beetroot-coloured *urenika* potatoes.

## GETTING THERE & AWAY
**Naked Bus** ( ☎ 0900 62533; www.nakedbus. com) runs around five buses weekly to/

Hamilton ($29, one hour) and New Plymouth ($39, three hours).

The **Waitomo Shuttle** ( ☎ 07-873 8279; waikiwi@ihug.co.nz; one-way adult/child $10/5) heads to the caves five times daily from Otorohanga (15 minutes away), coordinating with bus and train arrivals.

**Waitomo Wanderer** ( ☎ 0508 926 337; www.waitomotours.co.nz, day tour incl Glowworm Cave $119) operates a daily return service from Rotorua or Taupo, with optional caving and tubing add-ons (packages from $188 to $288). Shuttle-only services cost $45 each way.

# ROTORUA & THE BAY OF PLENTY
## GETTING THERE & AROUND
Air New Zealand has flights from Tauranga and Whakatane to Auckland and Wellington; and from Rotorua to Sydney (every Tuesday and Saturday), Auckland,

links Auckland with Tauranga, Whakatane and Rotorua.

InterCity and Naked Bus services connect Tauranga, Rotorua and Whakatane with most other main cities in NZ.

# ROTORUA

pop 70,400

Catch a whiff of Rotorua's sulphur-rich, asthmatic airs and you've already got a taste of NZ's most dynamic thermal area, home to spurting geysers, steaming hot springs and exploding mud pools. The Maori revered this place, naming one of the most spectacular springs Wai-O-Tapu (Sacred Waters). Today 35% of the population is Maori, with their cultural performances and traditional *hangi* as big an attraction as the landscape itself.

## INFORMATION

**Rotorua i-SITE** (Map p127; ☎ 0800 768 678, 07-348 5179; www.rotoruanz.com; 1167 Fenton St; ◷ 8am-6pm) is the hub for all travel information and bookings including DOC walks. Also has an exchange bureau, cafe, showers and lockers.

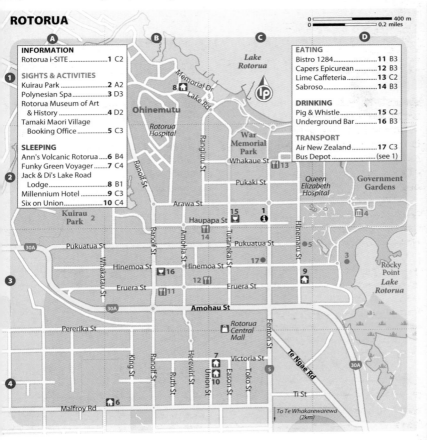

**ROTORUA**

| INFORMATION | |
|---|---|
| Rotorua i-SITE | 1 C2 |
| **SIGHTS & ACTIVITIES** | |
| Kuirau Park | 2 A2 |
| Polynesian Spa | 3 D3 |
| Rotorua Museum of Art & History | 4 D2 |
| Tamaki Maori Village Booking Office | 5 C3 |
| **SLEEPING** | |
| Ann's Volcanic Rotorua | 6 B4 |
| Funky Green Voyager | 7 C4 |
| Jack & Di's Lake Road Lodge | 8 B1 |
| Millennium Hotel | 9 C3 |
| Six on Union | 10 C4 |
| **EATING** | |
| Bistro 1284 | 11 B3 |
| Capers Epicurean | 12 B3 |
| Lime Caffeteria | 13 C2 |
| Sabroso | 14 B3 |
| **DRINKING** | |
| Pig & Whistle | 15 C2 |
| Underground Bar | 16 B3 |
| **TRANSPORT** | |
| Air New Zealand | 17 C3 |
| Bus Depot | (see 1) |

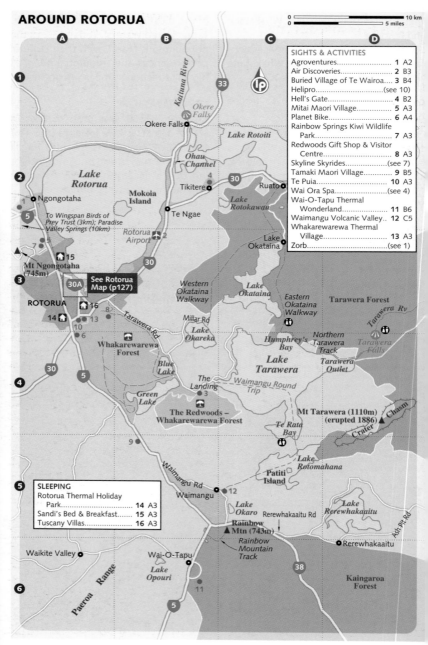

# AROUND ROTORUA

0 — 10 km
0 — 5 miles

See Rotorua Map (p127)

Map labels: Kaituna River, Okere Falls, Lake Rotoiti, Ohau Channel, Lake Rotokawau, Ruato, Lake Rotokawau, Lake Okataina, Lake Okataina, Eastern Okataina Walkway, Tarawera Forest, Tarawera Rv, Tarawera Falls, Tarawera Outlet, Northern Tarawera Track, Humphrey's Bay, Lake Tarawera, Mt Tarawera (1110m) (erupted 1886), Crater, Chasm, Lake Rotomahana, Patiti Island, Lake Rerewhakaaitu, Rerewhakaaitu, Ash Pit Rd, Kaingaroa Forest, Lake Okaro, Rerewhakaaitu Rd, Rainbow Mtn (743m), Rainbow Mountain Track, Wai-O-Tapu, Lake Opouri, Paeroa Range, Waikite Valley, Te Rata Bay, Waimangu, Waimangu Rd, Green Lake, The Landing, Waimangu Round Trip, Blue Lake, The Redwoods – Whakarewarewa Forest, Lake Okareka, Millar Rd, Western Okataina Walkway, Whakarewarewa Forest, Tarawera Rd, ROTORUA, Mt Ngongotaha (745m), To Wingspan Birds of Prey Trust (3km); Paradise Valley Springs (10km), Ngongotaha, Lake Rotorua, Mokoia Island, Tikitere, Te Ngae, Rotorua Airport, Okere Falls

## SIGHTS
### GEOTHERMAL ATTRACTIONS

Rotorua's main drawcard is **Te Whakarewarewa** (pronounced 'Fa-ka-re-wa-re-wa'), a thermal reserve 3km from the city centre at the south end of Fenton Street. This area's full name is Te Whakarewarewatanga o te Ope Taua a Wahiao, meaning 'The Gathering Together of the War Party of Wahiao', although many people just call it 'Whaka'. There are more than 500 springs here, varying from cold to boiling cauldrons. The most famous spring is **Pohutu** ('Big Splash' or 'Explosion'), a geyser which erupts up to 20 times a day, spurting hot water up to 30m skyward. You'll know when it's about to blow because the **Prince of Wales' Feathers** geyser will start up shortly before.

There are two main tourist operations here: Te Puia and Whakarewarewa Thermal Village. Pohutu and the Prince of Wales' Feathers geyser are part of **Te Puia** (Map p128; ☎ 0800 837 842, 07-348 9047; www.tepuia.com; Hemo Rd; admission incl tour &

daytime cultural performance adult/child $50/25, tour & Te Po evening concert & hangi $99/50, combination $130/65; ☺ 8am-6pm summer, 8am-5pm winter), the most polished of NZ's Maori cultural attractions.

Tours of Te Puia take 90 minutes and depart on the hour from 9am (last tour 4pm in winter, 5pm in summer). Daytime cultural performances (lasting 45 minutes) start at 10.15am, 12.15pm and 3.15pm, while nightly **Te Po Indigenous Experience** *hangi* concerts are held in the evenings at 6.15pm.

**Whakarewarewa Thermal Village** (Map p128; ☎ 07-349 3463; www.whakarewarewa.com; 17 Tryon St; admission incl tours & concerts adult/child/family $28/12.50/68.50; ☺ 8.30am-5pm, tours 9am-4pm, concerts 11.15am & 2pm), on the eastern side of Whaka, is a living village, where *tangata whenua* (the locals) still reside, as they and their ancestors have for centuries. It's these local villagers who show you around and tell you the stories of their way of life and the significance of the steamy bubbling pools, silica terraces and the geysers that, although inaccessible

DESTINATION ROTORUA TOURISM MARKETING

**Rotorua Museum of Art & History (p130)**

from the village, are easily viewed from vantage points (the view of Pohutu is just as good from here as it is from Te Puia, and is considerably cheaper).

There are cultural performances at 11.15am and 2pm, and guided tours at 9.30am, 10.30am, 11.45am, 12.30pm, 1.30pm and 3.30pm.

Close to the centre of Rotorua is **Kuirau Park** (Map p127), a volcanic area that you can wander around for free. It has a crater lake, pools of boiling mud and plenty of huffing steam.

## ROTORUA MUSEUM OF ART & HISTORY

This impressive museum (Map p127; ☎ 07-350 1814; www.rotoruamuseum.co.nz; Government Gardens; admission adult/child/family $12/5.50/28; ☼ 9am-5pm Apr-Sep, 9am-8pm Oct-Mar, tours hourly 10am-4pm plus 5pm Dec-Feb) is housed in a grand mock-Tudor building originally constructed as a spa retreat in 1908.

A gripping 20-minute film on the history of Rotorua, including the Tarawera eruption, runs every 20 minutes from 9am (not for small kids – the seats vibrate and the eruption noises are authentic!).

## ACTIVITIES
### MOUNTAIN BIKING

On the edge of town, **The Redwoods – Whakarewarewa Forest** (see p138) is home to some of the best **mountain-bike trails** in the country. There is close to 100km of tracks to keep bikers of all skill levels happy for days on end.

At the Waipa Mill car park entrance to the forest, the starting point for the bike trails, you can hire bikes from **Planet Bike** (Map p128; ☎ 07-346 1717; 027-280 2817; www.planetbike.co.nz; Waipa State Mill Rd; bikes per 2hr/

day $35/55, 2hr guided rides from $65; ☼ 10am-3pm daily Nov-Apr, Sat & Sun only May-Oct). It can also arrange shuttles to get you to the park.

## THERMAL POOLS & MASSAGE

The **Polynesian Spa** (Map p127; ☎ 07-348 1328; www.polynesianspa.co.nz; Government Gardens, off Hinemoa St; main pool adults-only $20, private pools per 30min adult/child $25/4, family pool adult/child/family $13/6/32, spa therapies from $80; ☼ 8am-11pm, spa therapies 9am-8pm) is in the Government Gardens. A bathhouse was opened at these springs in 1882 and people have been swearing by the waters ever since.

Also housed in the modern complex are several more commercial activities such as luxury therapies (massage, mud and beauty treatments) as well as a cafe and gift shop.

## WHITE-WATER RAFTING & SLEDGING

Thrill seekers can find plenty of white-water action around Rotorua with the chance to take on the Grade V Kaituna River, complete with a startling 7m drop at Okere Falls. Sledging (in case you didn't know) is zooming downriver on a highly manoeuvrable body board.

**Kaitiaki Adventures** (☎ 0800 338 736, 07-357 2236; www.kaitiaki.co.nz) Offers white-water rafting trips on the Kaituna ($85) and Wairoa ($99), and sledging on the Kaituna ($99) and Wairoa (one guide per person, $299).

**River Rats** (☎ 0800 333 900, 07-345 6543; www.riverrats.co.nz) Takes on the Wairoa ($110), Kaituna ($90) and Rangitaiki ($120); also runs a scenic trip on the Rangitaiki, which is good for youngsters (adult/child $120/80).

UPPER NORTH ISLAND

Maori performers, Te Puia (p129), Rotorua

ROTORUA & THE BAY OF PLENTY

## ◥ MAORI CONCERTS & HANGI

Maori culture is a major drawcard in Rotorua and, although some find it heavily commercialised, it's a great opportunity to learn more about the indigenous culture of NZ. The two big activities are concerts and *hangi* meals, often packaged together in an evening's entertainment that features the famous *hongi* (greeting), *haka*, and *poi* dances.

Tamaki Maori Village is an established favourite, and does an excellent twilight tour to a *marae* (meeting house) and Maori village 15km south of Rotorua. The concert is followed by a meat-heavy *hangi*.

A similar package is offered by Mitai Maori Village. This family-run outfit offers a popular three-hour evening event of concert performance, *hangi* and glowworm bushwalk, which can be combined with a tour of Rainbow Springs Kiwi Wildlife Park (p136) next door, where you can enjoy the coloured nightlights and walk through the open Kiwi enclosure (adult/child under 9/child under 15 $116/31.50/63, four hours). Pick-ups are available.

Te Puia (p129) puts on three day-time shows (10.15am, 12.15pm & 3.15pm) and one nightly show (6.15pm), while Whakarewarewa Thermal Village (p129) has two daylight shows (11.15am & 2pm; included with admission), great for busy people.

Things you need to know: Tamaki Maori Village (Map p128; ☎ 07-349 2999; www.maoriculture.co.nz; booking office 1220 Hinemaru St; admission adult/child $100/58; ✆ tours depart 5pm, 6pm & 7pm summer, 5pm & 7pm winter); Mitai Maori Village (Map p128; ☎ 07-343 9132; www.mitai.co.nz; 196 Fairy Springs Rd; concert & hangi adult/child 5-9yr/child 10-15yr/family $99/19/49/259; ✆ 6.30pm).

MICHAEL GEBICKI

Champagne Pool, Wai-O-Tapu Thermal Wonderland

## ⟩ IF YOU LIKE...

If you like Te Whakarewarewa (p129), we think you'll like these other hot spots around Rotorua:

- Hell's Gate & Wai Ora Spa (Map p128; ☎ 07-345 3151; www.hellsgate.co.nz; SH30, Rotorua; admission adult/child/family $30/15/75; ⏰ 8.30am-8.30pm) A 10-hectare geothermal reserve with a huge thermal waterfall, Maori carvers and weavers, and the indulgent Wai Ora Spa.
- Waimangu Volcanic Valley (off Map p128; ☎ 07-366 6137; www.waimangu.com; 587 Waimangu Rd, Rotorua; walking tour adult/child $32.50/10, boat cruise $40/10; ⏰ 8.30am-5pm daily, to 6pm Jan) Spectacular geothermal features including the 80°C Inferno Crater Lake, and Frying Pan Lake, the largest hot spring in the world.
- Wai-O-Tapu Thermal Wonderland (Map p128; ☎ 07-366 6333; www.waiotapu. co.nz; 201 Loop Rd, off SH5; admission adult/child/family $30/10/75; ⏰ 8.30am-5pm) The boiling, multi-hued Champagne Pool, bubbling mud pool, stunning mineral terraces and the Lady Knox Geyser.

Wet 'n' Wild ( ☎ 0800 462 7238, 07-348 3191; www.wetnwildrafting.co.nz) Runs trips on the Kaituna ($95), Wairoa ($99) and the Mokau ($145), as well as easy-going Rangitaiki trips (adult/child $120/80) and longer, helicopter-access trips to remote parts of the Motu and Mohaka (two to five days $550 to $925).

### KAYAKING

Adventure Kayaking ( ☎ 027 499 7402; www.adventurekayaking.co.nz; hire per day $40, trips per half-/full day from $70/110) Takes trips on Lakes Rotorua, Rotoiti, Tarawera and Okataina; also offers freedom hire.

Kaituna Kayaks ( ☎ 07-362 4486; www. kaitunakayaks.com; half-day trip $149, lessons half-/full day $149/290) Guided tandem trips and kayaking lessons on the Kaituna.

River Rats ( ☎ 0800 333 900, 07-345 6543; www.riverrats.co.nz; hire per half-/full day from $25/45, 2/4hr trip $40/95) Freedom hire plus two-hour self-guided trips down the Ohau Channel and four-hour guided paddles to Manupirua Springs Hot Pools on Lake Rotoiti.

## SCENIC FLIGHTS

**Air Discovery (Map p128; ☎ 0800 247 347, 07-575 7584; www.airdiscovery.co.nz; Rotorua airport; 90min/half-day flights $399/599)** Volcanic explorations over White Island and the Taupo region (including Mt Ruapehu, Mt Ngarahoe and Mt Tongariro).

**Helipro (Map p128; ☎ 0800 435 4776, 07-357 2512; www.helipro.co.nz; 8min–3½hr $89-855)** Based at Te Puia, Helipro runs a variety of helicopter trips including city flights, and Mt Tarawera and White Island landings.

## TOURS

**Elite Adventures ( ☎ 07-347 8282; www. eliteadventures.co.nz)** Half-day (adult/child from $75/55) and full-day (adult/child from $200/110) tours covering a selection of Rotorua's major cultural and natural attractions.

**Indigenous Trails ( ☎ 07-542 1074; www. itrails.co.nz; day trip $338)** Full-day Maori-guided tours around Rotorua, with a bungy jump, river cruise, kiwi-meeting, cultural show and *hangi*.

**Rotorua Duck Tours ( ☎ 07-345 6522; www.rotoruaducktours.co.nz; adult/child/family $62/35/145; ⏰ 11am, 1pm & 3.30pm summer, 11am & 2.15pm winter)** Ninety-minute trips in an amphibious, bio-fuelled vehicle taking in the major sites around town and heading out onto three lakes (Rotorua, Okareka and Tikitapu).

## SLEEPING

**our pick Funky Green Voyager (Map p127; ☎ 07-346 1754; www.funkygreenvoyager.com; 4 Union St; dm from $24, d with/without bathroom $65/57; 🖥 📶 )** Green on the outside and on the inside – due to several cans of paint and a dedicated environmental policy – the Funky GV features laid-back tunes and plenty of sociable chat among a spunky bunch of guests and worldly wise owners, who know what you want when you travel. The best doubles have en suites; dorms are roomy with quality mattresses.

River Rats rafting down Tutea Falls, Rotorua

DESTINATION ROTORUA TOURISM MARKETING

**Rotorua Thermal Holiday Park** (Map p128; ☎ 07-346 3140; www.rotoruathermal.co.nz; Old Taupo Rd; unpowered/powered sites $30/34, dm from $21, d cabins/motel from $54/95; 🖳 🛜 🛄 ) This epic holiday park on the edge of town has a real holiday resort feel, with rows of cabins and tourist flats, a 100-bed lodge, tent sites galore and convenience facilities such as a shop and cafe. There's plenty of room to move with lots of open grassy areas, plus hot mineral pools for the soakers.

**Six on Union** (Map p127; ☎ 0800 100 062, 07-347 8062; www.sixonunion.co.nz; 6 Union St; d/f from $95/150; 🛜 🛄 ) Hanging baskets ahoy! This modest place is a budget bonanza with pool, spa and small kitchenettes. Rooms are functional and freshly painted, and the swimming pool area is in good nick. The location is away from traffic noise, but still an easy walk to the city centre.

**Ann's Volcanic Rotorua** (Map p127; ☎ 0800 768 683, 07-347 1007; www.rotorua motel.co.nz; 107 Malfroy Rd; d $99-149, 2bedroom ste & house $159-179; 🛜 ) Ann's is a basic and affordable motel that has family charm and an ever-friendly host with loads of advice on things to see and do. Larger rooms feature courtyard spas and facilities for travellers with disabilities, and there's a house available for big groups. Rooms close to the street are a tad noisy.

**Jack & Di's Lake Road Lodge** (Map p127; ☎ 0800 522 526; www.jackanddis.co.nz; 21 Lake Rd; s/d/apt $99/119/250; 🛜 ) Lakeside views and a central-but-secluded location make this boutique hotel a persuasive option. The upstairs penthouse is ideal for couples, while downstairs is better for families or groups. A spa pool, lazy lounge areas and full kitchens add to the appeal.

**Sandi's Bed & Breakfast** (Map p128; ☎ 0800 726 3422, 07-348 0884; www.sandisbedand breakfast.co.nz; 103 Fairy Springs Rd; d/f incl breakfast $120/150; 🛜 🛄 ) A friendly, family B&B run by the well-humoured Sandi who offers helpful tourist tips and a ready smile. The best bets are the two chalets with TV and plenty of room to move. Thoughtful extras including fresh fruit with brekkie and the sun deck gets rave reviews from former guests. A couple of kilometres north of town.

HOLGER LEUE

Maori wood carving, Te Puia (p129)

**Tuscany Villas (Map p128; ☎ 0800 802 050, 07-348 3500; www.tuscanyvillasrotorua.co.nz; 280 Fenton St; d from $140)** With its Italian-inspired architecture, this family-owned hotel is a real eye-catcher from the road. It pitches itself perfectly at both the corporate and leisure traveller, both of whom will appreciate the lavish furnishings, multiple TVs, DVD players and huge, deep spa baths.

**Millennium Hotel (Map p127; ☎ 07-347 1234; www.millenniumrotorua.co.nz; cnr Eruera & Hinemaru Sts; d from $340; )** The slick Maori-inspired lobby sets the scene for this elegant five-storey motel. Lakefront rooms afford excellent views as does the club room, a laid-back lounge available exclusively to guests. The poolside *hangi* is one of the better ones in town.

## EATING

**Capers Epicurean (Map p127; ☎ 07-348 8818; 1181 Eruera St; breakfast & lunch mains $6-20, dinner $13-28; 7.30am-late; V)** This slick, barnlike deli is always busy with diners showing up for cabinets crammed full of delicious gourmet sandwiches, pastries, salads and cakes, and an excellent blackboard menu of brekkies and other tasty hot foods (try the carrot, leek and fetta lasagne). There's also a deli section stocked with olive oils, marinades, relish, jams and chocolates.

our pick **Lime Caffeteria (Map p127; ☎ 07-350 2033; cnr Fenton & Whakaue Sts; mains $13-24; 7.30am-4.30pm; V)** Sitting on a quiet, leafy corner near the lake, this refreshing cafe is especially good for alfresco breakfasts and dishes with a welcome twist: try the chicken-and-chorizo salad or prawn-and-salmon risotto in lime sauce. Classy counter snacks, excellent coffee and outdoor tables, too. 'This is the best lunch I've had in ages', says one happy punter.

**Sabroso (Map p127; ☎ 07-349 0591; 1184 Haupapa St; mains $15-36; 5-10pm Thu-Tue)** What a surprise! This modest Latin American cantina – adorned with sombreros, guitars, hessian tablecloths and salt-and-pepper shakers made from Corona bottles – serves adventurous south-of-the-border fare to spice up bland Kiwi palates. The black-bean chilli is a knock-out (as are the margaritas).

**Bistro 1284 (Map p127; ☎ 07-346 1284; 1284 Eruera St; mains $30-35; 6pm-late)** Definitely one of RotoVegas' hot dining spots, this intimate place (all chocolate and mushroom colours) serves stylish NZ cuisine with an Asian influence. It's an excellent place to sample great local ingredients, and be sure to leave room for some delectable desserts.

## DRINKING

our pick **Underground Bar (Map p127; ☎ 07-348 3612; www.croucherbrewing.co.nz; basement, 1282 Hinemoa St; 4-8pm Wed & Thu, 4-11pm Fri & Sat, 2-6pm Sun)** 'It's all about the beer' at this crafty underground bunker, run by the lads from Croucher Brewing Co, Rotorua's best microbrewers. Down a pint of fruity pale ale, aromatic Drunken Hop Bitter or malty pilsener and wonder how you'll manage a sleep-in tomorrow morning.

**Pig & Whistle (Map p127; ☎ 07-347 3025; www.pigandwhistle.co.nz; cnr Haupapa & Tutanekai Sts; 11.30am-late)** This excellent microbrewery pub in a former police station offers a conducive atmosphere in which to enjoy the Swine lager (big-screen TV, beer garden, live music Thursday to Saturday), while serving up some of the best simple grub in town (mains from $19 to $30). Its menu runs the gamut from spare-ribs to a gluten-free vegetarian toastie.

## GETTING THERE & AROUND

**Air New Zealand (Map p127; ☎ 07-343 1100; www.airnewzealand.co.nz; 1103 Hinemoa St; 9am-5pm Mon-Fri)** offers daily direct flights to Auckland, Christchurch and Wellington, with onward connections to other destinations. Air New Zealand also links Rotorua with Sydney every Tuesday and Saturday.

All the major bus companies stop outside the i-SITE (see p127), from where you can arrange bookings.

**InterCity** (☎ 09-583 5780; www.intercity.co.nz) runs buses to various destinations:

| TO | PRICE | HOW LONG | HOW OFTEN |
|---|---|---|---|
| Auckland | $50 | 4hr | 8 daily |
| Hamilton | $35 | 1½hr | 6 daily |
| Taupo | $32 | 1hr | 5 daily |
| Tauranga | $25 | 1½hr | 4 daily |
| Wellington | $57 | 8hr | 4 daily |

**Naked Bus** (☎ 0900 62533; www.nakedbus.com) services run to the same destinations, as listed following:

| TO | PRICE | HOW LONG | HOW OFTEN |
|---|---|---|---|
| Auckland | $35 | 4hr | 3 daily |
| Hamilton | $24 | 1½hr | 3 daily |
| Taupo | $19 | 1hr | 2 daily |
| Tauranga | $11 | 1½-4hr | 2-3 daily |
| Wellington | $39 | 8hr | 1 daily |

**Twin City Express** (☎ 0800 422 9287; www.baybus.co.nz) buses run twice daily Monday to Friday between Rotorua and Tauranga/Mt Maunganui via Te Puke ($11, 1½ hours).

### TAXI
**Fast Taxis** (☎ 07-348 2444)
**Rotorua Taxis** (☎ 07-348 1111)

### TO/FROM THE AIRPORT
The airport is about 10km out of town to the east. **Super Shuttle** (☎ 0800 748 885, 07-345 7790; www.supershuttle.co.nz) offers a door-to-door airport service for $20 for the first person and $6 for each additional passenger. A taxi from the city centre costs about $25.

# AROUND ROTORUA
## RAINBOW SPRINGS
**Rainbow Springs Kiwi Wildlife Park** (Map p128; ☎ 0800 724 626, 07-350 0440; www.rainbowsprings.co.nz; 192 Fairy Springs Rd; 24hr pass adult/child/family $26/15/69; ⏱ 8am-10pm) is a must-do for nature lovers. At the heart of the park are the natural springs, home to wild trout and eels, which you can see from the underwater viewer. Animals abound, both introduced species such wallabies, emus and rainbow lorikeets and interesting native birds such as kea, kaka and pukeko.

The highlight of the park is **Kiwi Encounter** (www.kiwiencounter.co.nz; admission family/adult/child $27.50/17.50/75; ⏱ tours on the hr 10am-4pm), home to NZ's largest kiwi recovery program – a nationally significant nonprofit conservation project. Be prepared for an emotional rollercoaster on the excellent 45-minute tour that has you tiptoeing through the actual incubator and hatchery areas. A combo Kiwi Encounter/Wildlife Park ticket costs adult/child/family $42/23/110.

Rainbow Springs is 3km north of central Rotorua on SH5 towards Hamilton and Auckland.

## SKYLINE SKYRIDES
Swinging up Mt Ngongotaha is **Skyline Skyrides** (Map p128; ☎ 07-347 0027; www.skylineskyrides.co.nz; Fairy Springs Rd; gondola adult/child/family $24/12/60, 5 luge rides $30, sky swing adult/child $30/20; ⏱ 9am-11pm). This gondola cruises up to a hilltop of fun which features panoramic views of the lake and a speedy luge on which you can scoot part way back down on three different tracks before coming back up on a chairlift (to do it all over again). For even speedier antics, try the sky swing, a screaming swoosh through the air at speeds of up to 160km/h.

Kea, New Zealand native parrot

DAVID WALL

## ⬎ IF YOU LIKE...

If you like Rainbow Springs (left) we think you'll like these other wildlife encounters:

- **Paradise Valley Springs** (off Map p128; ☎ 07-348 9667; 467 Paradise Valley Rd, Rotorua; www.paradisevalleysprings.co.nz; adult/child $26/13; ⌚ 8am-5pm) A six-hectare park with trout, big slippery eels, deer, alpaca, possums and lions.
- **Wingspan Birds of Prey Trust** (off Map p128; ☎ 07-357 4469; www.wingspan.co.nz; 1164 Paradise Valley Rd, Rotorua; adult/child $15/5; ⌚ 9am-3pm) This organisation is dedicated to conserving three threatened NZ birds: the falcon, hawk and owl. Go in time to see the 2pm flying display.
- **Altura Gardens & Wildlife Park** (☎ 07-878 5278; www.alturapark.co.nz; 477 Fullerton Rd, Waitomo Caves; admission adult/child $12/5; ⌚ 9am-5pm) Chat with a cockatoo, outstare a morepork or pat a blue-tongue lizard (who once bit Tom Cruise on the nose...not a difficult target, some might suggest). Horse treks also available.

## AGROVENTURES & AGRODOME

**Agroventures** (Map p128; ☎ 0800 949 888, 07-357 4747; www.agroventures.co.nz; Western Rd, Ngongotaha; ⌚ 9am-5pm) is a veritable hive of entertaining activities, 9km north of Rotorua on SH5 (courtesy shuttle available).

Start off with the 43m **bungy** (www.rotoruabungy.co.nz; adult/child $95/80) and the **Swoop** (www.swoop.co.nz; adult/child $49/35), a 130km/h swing that can be enjoyed alone or with friends. If that's not enough, try

**Freefall Xtreme** (www.freefallxtreme.co.nz; 3min per adult/child $85/49), which simulates skydiving by blasting you 5m into the air on a column of wind.

Also here, the **Shweeb** (www.shweeb.co.nz; adult/child $49/35) is a monorail velodrome from which you hang in a clear capsule and pedal along recumbently at speeds of up to 60km/h. Alongside is the **Agrojet** (www.agrojet.co.nz; adult/child $49/35), allegedly NZ's fastest jetboat, speeding and splashing around a 1km artificial course.

Across the road is the **Zorb** (Map p128; ☎ 0800 227 474; www.zorb.co.nz; rides from $49; ◷ 9am-5pm Apr-Nov, to 7pm Dec-Mar) – look for the grassy track down the hill with what looks like large, clear, people-filled spheres bouncing and rolling down at some speed.

## THE REDWOODS – WHAKAREWAREWA FOREST

This **forest park** (www.redwoods.co.nz; admission free) is 3km southeast of town on Tarawera Rd. It was originally home to more than 170 tree species (a few less now), planted from 1899 to see which could be grown successfully for timber.

Clearly signposted walking tracks range from a half-hour wander through the **Redwood Grove** to an enjoyable whole-day route to the Blue and Green Lakes. Most walks start from the **Redwoods Gift Shop & Visitor Centre** (Map p128; ☎ 07-350 0110; Long Mile Rd; ◷ 8.30am-5.30pm Mon-Fri & 10am-5pm Sat & Sun Oct-Mar, 8.30am-4.30pm Mon-Fri & 10am-4pm Sat & Sun Apr-Sep), where you can get maps and view displays about the forest.

Aside from walking, the park is great for picnics, and is acclaimed well beyond the town for its enjoyable and accessible mountain biking (see p130).

## BURIED VILLAGE OF TE WAIROA

Fifteen kilometres from Rotorua on the Tarawera Rd, which passes the pretty Blue and Green Lakes, is the **buried village** (Map p128; ☎ 07-362 8287; www.buried village.co.nz; Tarawera Rd; admission adult/child/ family $30/8/68; ◷ 9am-5pm Nov-Mar, to 4.30pm Apr-Oct), the site of one of the most dramatic natural events to occur in NZ in the last 150 years – the 1886 eruption of Mt Tarawera. Here you can see the buildings that were submerged by the eruption,

creating an odd time capsule of NZ in the 19th century, with highlights such as the Rotomahana Hotel, a blacksmith's shop and several *whare*.

# THE BAY OF PLENTY

This is where New Zealanders have come on holiday for generations, lapping up salt-licked activities and lashings of sunshine.

## TAURANGA

pop 118,200

Tauranga (pronounced Tao-wronger) has been booming since the 1990s and remains one of NZ's fastest-growing cities.

Tauranga is the place to fulfil all your watery dreams: with marinas chock-a-block with beautiful boats, sandy surf beaches and water sports aplenty, this is about as Riviera as NZ gets.

### INFORMATION

**Tauranga i-SITE** ( ☎ 07-578 8103; www.bay ofplentynz.com; 95 Willow St; ◷ 8.30am-5.30pm Mon-Fri, 9am-5pm Sat & Sun) Local tourist information, bookings and InterCity bus tickets, and DOC maps.

### SIGHTS & ACTIVITIES

The **Tauranga Art Gallery** ( ☎ 07-578 7933; www.artgallery.org.nz; cnr Wharf & Willow Sts; admission by donation; ◷ 10am-4.30pm) presents historic and contemporary art, and houses a permanent collection along with frequently changing local and visiting exhibitions. The building itself is a former bank, although you'd hardly know it – it's an altogether excellent space with no obvious compromise (cue: applause!).

### SWIMMING WITH DOLPHINS

**Butler's Swim With Dolphins** ( ☎ 0508 288 537, 07-578 3197; www.swimwithdolphins.

TOURISM BAY OF PLENTY

Dolphins swimming

co.nz; full-day trips adult/child $125/100; 🕒 leaves Tauranga 9am, Mt Maunganui 9.30am) Even without dolphins, the trips are always entertaining, particularly with Cap'n Butler, a real old salt who protested against nuclear testing at Mururoa Atoll.

**Dolphin Seafaris** ( ☎ 0800 326 8747, 07-577 0105; www.nzdolphin.com; half-day trip adult/ child $140/90; 🕒 8am) Eco-attuned trips departing Tauranga and Mt Maunganui.

### KAYAKING

The Wairoa River is great for kayaking, offering something for paddlers at all levels. **Waimarino Adventure Park** ( ☎ 07-576 4233; www.waimarino.com; 36 Taniwha Pl, Bethlehem; kayak tours from $55, park day-pass adult/child $39/30), on the banks of the river, offers freedom kayak hire for leisurely paddles along 12km of flat water, runs self-guided tours further up the river, and offers sea kayaking trips.

### SKYDIVING

**Tauranga Tandem Skydiving** ( ☎ 07-576 7990; www.tandemskydive.co.nz; Tauranga Airport; jumps 8000/10,000/12,000ft $245/275/345) offers various jumps with views of White Island, Mt Ruapehu and the East Cape.

### SCENIC FLIGHTS

**Aerius Helicopters** ( ☎ 0800 864 354; www.aerius.co.nz; flights from $59) Local flights and excursions as far as Waitomo and Whakaari/White Island.

**Air Discovery** ( ☎ 0800 247 347, 07-575 7588; www.airdiscovery.co.nz; flights from $299) Offers one- to two-hour fixed-wing flights over Whakaari/White Island and Mt Tarawera.

### SLEEPING

**Harbourside City Backpackers** ( ☎ 07-579 4066; www.backpacktauranga.co.nz; upstairs, 105 The Strand; dm/d from $28/72; 🖥 🛜 ) Enjoy sea views from this sociable hostel, handy to The Strand's bars. Rooms are smallish but clean, and you'll spend more time on the roof terrace anyway. There's no car park, but there is a public car park down the road that's empty at the right time.

**Roselands Motel** ( ☎ 07-578 2294; www.roselands.co.nz; 21 Brown St; d/ste from $115/135; 🛜 ) Tarted up with splashes of orange paint and new linen, this sweet, old-style motel is in a quiet but central location. Expect roomy units (all with kitchens), highchairs for the kids and yoga lessons by arrangement. Don't mess with the resident cat…

**Harbour City Motor Inn** ( ☎ 07-571 1435; www.taurangaharbourcity.co.nz; 50 Wharf St; d from $150; ⊚ ) In the middle of town, with plenty of parking, this newish motor inn has all the mod cons such as a spa bath, TV and a business desk in every room. Friendly staff offers sound local advice on your itinerary.

**Hotel on Devonport** ( ☎ 0800 322 85687, 07-578 2668; www.hotelondevonport.net.nz; 72 Devonport Rd; d/ste $160/200) City-centre Devonport is top of the town, with bay-view rooms, noise-reducing glass, slick interiors and sassy staff, all of which appeals to business travellers and luxury weekenders.

## EATING

**Fresh Fish Market** ( ☎ 07-578 1789; 1 Dive Cres; meals from $5; ☽ lunch & dinner) A local legend serving up fresh fish and chips right on the water's edge.

**Naked Grape** ( ☎ 07-579 5555; 97 The Strand; breakfast & lunch $7-21, dinner mains $28-32; ☽ 7am-late) With cheery staff, lilting jazz and wine-coloured rugs, this hip Strand wine bar draws the daytime crowds with pastas, pizzas, salads, good coffee and beaut breakfasts. At night it's moodier, with mains such as honey-braised lamb and lemon-marinated chicken breast.

**Zeytin** ( ☎ 07-579 0099; 83 The Strand; mains $19-27; ☽ lunch & dinner Tue-Sun) Ask the locals to name their favourite restaurant, and odds-on they'll name Zeytin – a real Turkish delight. Real food, real cheap, with something for everyone along the lines of kebabs, delicious homemade breads, dips

and healthy salads, wood-fired pizza and a few exotic surprises.

## GETTING THERE & AROUND

**Air New Zealand** ( ☎ 07-577 7300; www.airnewzealand.co.nz; cnr Devonport Rd & Elizabeth St; ☽ 9am-5pm Mon-Fri) has daily direct flights to Auckland, Wellington and Christchurch, with connections to other centres.

**InterCity** ( ☎ 09-583 5780; www.intercity.co.nz) tickets and timetables are available at the i-SITE. It runs buses to destinations including the following:

| TO | PRICE | HOW LONG | HOW OFTEN |
|---|---|---|---|
| Auckland | $45 | 4¼hr | 6 daily |
| Hamilton | $31 | 2-3hr | 5 daily |
| Rotorua | $25 | 1½hr | 4 daily |
| Taupo | $40 | 3hr | 4 daily |
| Wellington | $96 | 9hr | 3 daily |

**Naked Bus** ( ☎ 0900 62533; www.nakedbus.com) services connect Tauranga with destinations including those listed below:

| TO | PRICE | HOW LONG? | HOW OFTEN? |
|---|---|---|---|
| Auckland | $25 | 4¼hr | 2 daily |
| Hamilton | $22 | 2hr | 2 daily |
| Rotorua | $11 | 1½hr | 3 daily |
| Taupo | $29 | 6hr | 3 daily |
| Wellington | $41 | 12½hr | 1 daily |

**Bay Hopper** ( ☎ 0800 422 928; www.baybus.co.nz) runs the Twin City Express bus twice daily between Tauranga/Mt Maunganui and Rotorua via Te Puke ($11, 1½ hours).

**Luxury & Coastline Shuttles** ( ☎ 0800 454 678, 07-574 9600; www.coastlineshuttles.co.nz) runs airport transfers to Auckland ($90), Hamilton ($75) and Rotorua ($90), and runs from Tauranga Airport into Central Tauranga ($15).

The **Mt Maunganui Ferry** ( ☎ 07-579 1325 www.kiwicoastcruises.co.nz; tickets one-way adult/child $8/5; ⊗ Dec-Mar) to/from Mt Maunganui departs The Strand; ask the i-SITE for a schedule.

## MT MAUNGANUI
pop 18,600

Named after the hulking 232m hill that punctuates the sandy peninsula occupied by the township, up-tempo Mt Maunganui is often just called 'the Mount', or Mauao, which translates as 'caught by the light of day'. It's considered part of greater Tauranga, but really is an enclave unto itself, with lots of great cafes and restaurants, hip bars and fabulous beaches.

### INFORMATION

The friendly **Mt Maunganui i-SITE** ( ☎ 07-575 5099; www.bayofplentynz.com; Salisbury Ave; ⊗ 9am-5pm) staff will assist you with information and bookings.

### SIGHTS & ACTIVITIES

The Mount lays claim to being NZ's premier surf city (they teach surfing at high school!). Carve up the waves at **Mount Beach**, which has an 100m artificial surf reef not far offshore, or there's sheltered-beach swimming on the western side of the peninsula. To learn to surf, try the following operators:

**Hibiscus** ( ☎ 07-575 3792; www.surfschool. co.nz; lessons per 2hr/2 days $80/150) Run by experienced surfer Rebecca Taylor.

**Mount Surfshop** ( ☎ 07-575 9133; www. mountsurfshop.co.nz; 96 Maunganui Rd; rental per day wetsuit/surfboard $15/40, lessons per 2hr $60)

**New Zealand Surf School** ( ☎ 021 477 873; www.nzsurfschools.co.nz; 1/2hr lesson $50/80)

Mauao itself can be explored via **walking trails** winding around it and leading up to the summit. The summit walk takes about an hour and gets steep near the top. You can also climb around the rocks on **Moturiki Island**, which adjoins the peninsula. The island and the base of Mauao also make up the **Mauao Base Track** (3½km, 45 minutes), which wanders through magical groves of pohutukawa trees that bloom between November and January.

PAUL KENNEDY

Mount Beach, Mt Maunganui

## SLEEPING & EATING

**Pacific Coast Lodge & Backpackers**
( ☎ 0800 666 622; www.pacificcoastlodge.co.nz;
432 Maunganui Rd; dm/d from $24/70; 💻 ) Not
far from the action, this efficiently run,
clean hostel is the pick of the bunch for
those who want a good night's sleep,
with drinkers encouraged to go into town
after 10pm. Purpose-built bunkrooms are
roomy and spangled with jungle murals.

**Mission Belle Motel** ( ☎ 0800 202 434;
www.missionbellemotel.co.nz; cnr Victoria Rd &
Pacific Ave; d/f $120/180; 🛜 ) With a distinctly
Tex-Mex exterior (like something out of an
old Clint Eastwood movie), this family-run
motel goes all modern inside, with especially good two-storey family rooms with
large bathtubs, plus sheltered barbecue
and courtyard areas.

**Belle Mer** ( ☎ 0800 100 235, 07-575 0011;
www.bellemer.co.nz; 53 Marine Pde; apt $190-
450; 🛜 🐶 ) A classy beachside complex
of two- and three-bedroom apartments,
some with sea-view balconies and others
opening onto private courtyards (though
you'll more likely head for the resort-style
pool terrace). Rooms are tastefully decorated in warm tones, and have everything
you need for longer stays, with proper
working kitchens and laundries.

**our pick** **Providores Urban Food Stor**
( ☎ 07-572 1300; 19a Pacific Ave; meals $5-18
🕐 7.30am-5pm; 🅥 ) Surf videos set the
mood as your eyes peruse fresh-baked
breads, buttery croissants, home-smoked
meats and cheeses, organic jams and
free-range eggs – perfect ingredients for
a bang-up breakfast or a hamper-filling
picnic on the beach. Superb!

**Slow Fish** ( ☎ 07-574 2949; Shop 5, Twin
Towers, Marine Pde; meals $6-19; 🕐 7am-4.30pm
There's no slacking about in the kitchen
of this award-winning, eco-aware café,
which promotes the art of savouring fine
locally sourced food. It's so popular you'll
have to crow-bar yourself in the door or
pounce on any available alfresco seat, but
it's absolutely worth it for its free-range
eggs and ham, Greek salads and divine
counter selection.

## GETTING THERE & AWAY

Mt Maunganui is across the harbour
bridge from Tauranga, or accessible from
the south via Te Maunga on SH2.

The **Tauranga Ferry** ( ☎ 07-579 1325; www.
kiwicoastcruises.co.nz; tickets one-way adult/child
$8/5; 🕐 Dec-Mar) to/from Tauranga departs
Salisbury Wharf; ask at the i-SITE (p141)
for a schedule.

# ↘ LOWER NORTH ISLAND

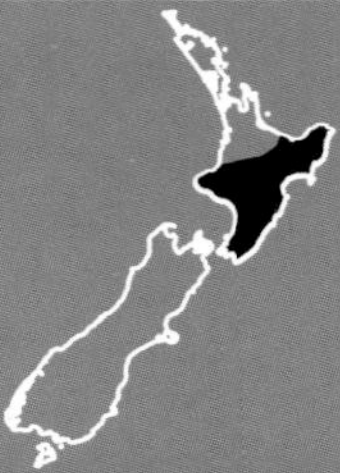

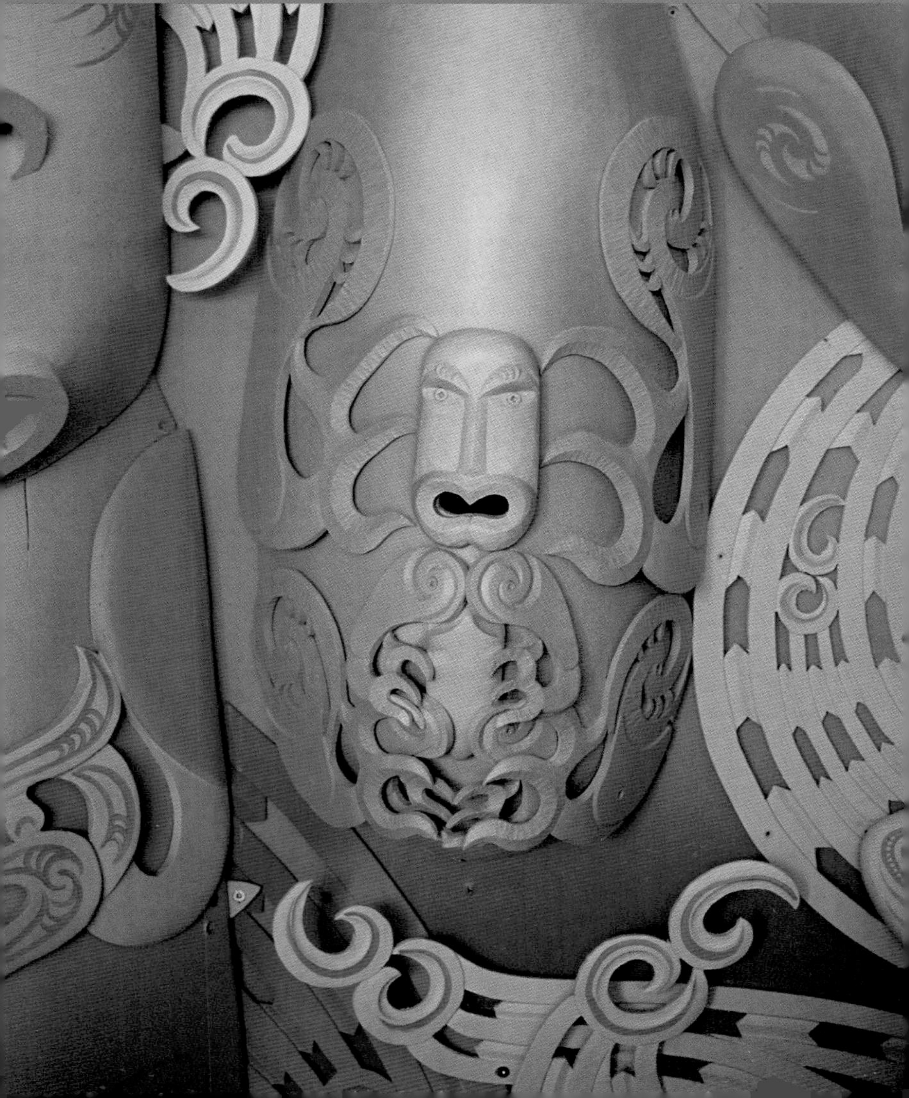

# LOWER NORTH ISLAND

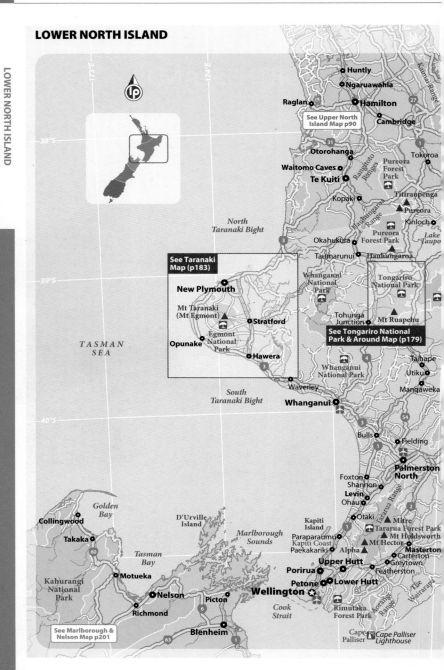

See Upper North Island Map p90

See Taranaki Map (p183)

See Tongariro National Park & Around Map (p179)

See Marlborough & Nelson Map p201

Huntly
Ngaruawahia
Raglan
Hamilton
Cambridge
Tokoroa
Otorohanga
Waitomo Caves
Te Kuiti
Pureora Forest Park
Titiraupenga
Pureora
Kinloch
Kopaki
Rangitoto Ranges
Hauhungaroa Range
Okahukura
Lake Taupo
North Taranaki Bight
Pureora Forest Park
Taumarunui
Hauhungaroa
Whanganui National Park
Tongariro National Park
New Plymouth
Mt Taranaki (Mt Egmont)
Stratford
Tohunga Junction
Mt Ruapehu
Egmont National Park
Opunake
Hawera
TASMAN SEA
Whanganui National Park
Taihape
Utiku
South Taranaki Bight
Waverley
Mangaweka
Whanganui
Bulls
Fielding
Palmerston North
Foxton
Shannon
Levin
Ohau
Collingwood
Golden Bay
D'Urville Island
Kapiti Island
Otaki
Tararua Range
Mitre
Takaka
Marlborough Sounds
Paraparaumu
Kapiti Coast
Paekakariki
Alpha
Mt Hector
Tararua Forest Park
Mt Holdsworth
Masterton
Carterton
Greytown
Featherston
Tasman Bay
Motueka
Upper Hutt
Porirua
Petone
Lower Hutt
Kahurangi National Park
Nelson
Picton
Wellington
Cook Strait
Richmond
Rimutaka Forest Park
The Wairarapa
Cape Palliser
Cape Palliser Lighthouse
Blenheim

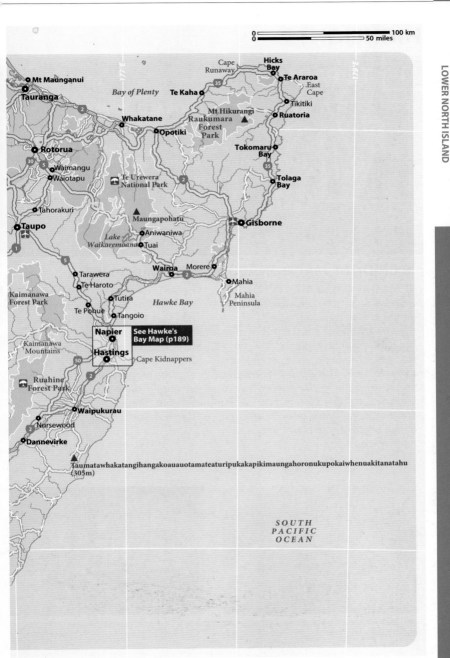

# HIGHLIGHTS

## 1   TE PAPA

### BY BRIDGET MACDONALD, TE PAPA

Te Papa translates into 'container of treasures' – that's what we are, a giant six-storey treasure box! Admission is free, which really encourages people to come in and learn a bit more about New Zealand. Obviously we showcase Maori culture, which is unique to NZ – we really celebrate that. It's an intense, interactive NZ focus.

## ⬎ BRIDGET MACDONALD'S DON'T MISS LIST

### ❶ MAORI GALLERIES & TOURS

On level 4 you can see a beautiful example of a traditionally carved *marae* (meeting house), contrasting with a big contemporary *marae*. We have many Maori guides, and special Maori tours as well. The Bush City exhibit covers everything from wetlands to volcanic regions, forests and caves: you can learn about how Maori used to live and see how plants are used in modern-day life.

### ❷ NATIONAL ART COLLECTION

On upper level 5 we have an exhibition called Toi Te Papa: Art of the Nation – a chronological story of NZ's art history. It takes you right through from traditional woodcarving to big contemporary works that change regularly – there's always something fresh and new.

Clockwise from top: Moa, Awesome Forces; Maori carving, National Art Collection; The Wall, Our Space; Traditional *marae*

### ❸ GOLDEN DAYS, LEVEL 4

See some nostalgic footage covering 80 years of iconic moments in NZ history. The film explores the good and the bad in NZ – people from all over find a connection with it. It runs every 20 minutes.

### ❹ OUR SPACE, LEVEL 2

Our Space has a 14m satellite map of NZ. When you stand on it, imagery and video clips from that region light up on the wall beside you. People can look and see where they've been and where they're going. The Wall is where people can upload their own images to our database before they arrive. Using interactive wand technology, you can look for your images and manipulate them on giant screens.

### ❺ AWESOME FORCES, LEVEL 2

The Earthquake House here is extremely popular. It gives people an understanding of our geological landscape. When they're moving through the country they can understand how the forces of the tectonic plates have actually created the landscape right throughout NZ.

## ➘ THINGS YOU NEED TO KNOW

**When to visit** If people want to come in and feel like they have a bit more space to themselves, we're open to 9pm on Thursdays **Best photo op** Up on level 6 there's a view out over the entire harbour; it's quite spectacular **For full details, see our author's review, p157**

# HIGHLIGHTS

## 2 NAPIER ART DECO

### BY ROBERT MCGREGOR, NAPIER ART DECO TRUST

Napier's 1931 earthquake (7.8 on the Richter scale) caused 261 casualties regionally – 157 in Napier. The town was subsequently rebuilt in architectural styles fashionable at the time: art deco, Spanish Mission, Prairie-style…The Art Deco Trust helps people value this architecture, which many were once not aware of, or even actively disliked. Now they're proud of it.

## ⇘ ROBERT MCGREGOR'S DON'T MISS LIST

### ❶ ART-DECO HIGHLIGHTS

My favourite individual buildings are the National Tobacco Company (p193), the Daily Telegraph (p191) and the Municipal Theatre. Also the landscaped gardens and architectural features along the waterfront – these were the final touches when they finished rebuilding the city. The plaza here provides a setting for civic events, which most towns don't have.

### ❷ HOUSES IN MAREWA

Marewa, Napier's art-deco suburb, has a real concentration of art-deco houses. Most of them are well preserved – some have had pitched roofs put on them, but many of them look as they always did. The council now enforces regulations to preserve the architectural qualities here.

### ❸ TAKE A GUIDED TOUR

You can do a self-guided tour around the main buildings (you could easily

Clockwise from top: The Daily Telegraph Building (p191); Art-deco streetscape; Dressed up for Art Deco Weekend; Art-deco building detail

CLOCKWISE FROM TOP: JOHN HAY; JOHN ELK III; MICHAEL COYNE; JOHN ELK III

spend a couple of hours), or take a guided tour (p193). There's a one-hour morning walk, which is good for people who don't have much time or who are leaving town that day; a two-hour afternoon walk; and evening walks (summer only) that take 90 minutes.

## ❹ ART DECO WEEKEND

This year we had perfect weather for Art Deco Weekend (www.artdeconapier. com/art_deco_weekend_87.aspx), and despite the recession ticket sales were good. New Zealanders aren't traditionally into dressing up, but we see a lot of period costumes and vintage Packard cars driving around this weekend. There's lots of great Hawke's Bay wine and food, and jazz and dancing in the street. It's great fun.

## ❺ A VISIT TO HASTINGS

Hastings (p195) is about 20km down the road. It was less damaged than Napier in the earthquake, but there are some lovely art-deco buildings there, too. There's always been a rivalry between the two cities – it's unusual to have two such towns in close proximity.

## ↘ THINGS YOU NEED TO KNOW

Best time to visit Summer for festivals; spring or autumn for fewer crowds
Best photo op Summer-morning sunshine illuminating south-facing facades
Architectural surprises The National Tobacco Company and AMP buildings, inspired by Frank Lloyd Wright's Prairie style See the Napier section, p191

# HIGHLIGHTS

**3**

## ⬈ NOCTURNAL WELLINGTON

Everyone in Wellington (p156) seems to be in a band and looks a tad depleted, as if they party hard and spend their time daubing canvasses and scribbling poetry…It follows that there's a lot going on here at night! Wellington's pubs, live-music rooms and coffee shops are kickin' after the sun goes down. Go bar-hopping around Cuba St and Courtenay Pl and see what kind of fun comes your way.

**4**

## ⬈ TONGARIRO NATIONAL PARK

Want some alpine time? Make a beeline for Tongariro (p178), New Zealand's oldest national park. Crowned by three snowy volcanic peaks, the park is the North Island's best ski spot, and is also home to the country's best day walk, the Tongariro Alpine Crossing. If you have a bit more time up your sleeve (or in your boots), tackle the longer Tongariro Northern Circuit, which is dotted with volcanic craters and lakes.

### ⬊ SPORTY TAUPO

The main urban hub on the Central Plateau, Taupo (p170) is the North Island's version of Queenstown – a place to challenge your sense of self-preservation with skydiving, bungy jumping, white-water rafting, snow sports, mountain biking... It's a progressive, upbeat sort of town, the adrenaline generated by outdoor activities infusing both culture and commerce.

### ⬊ HAWKE'S BAY WINERIES

Welcome to the sunny East Coast! The Hawke's Bay area enjoys the perfect climate for growing grapes. The wineries (p190) around Napier and Hastings are getting a serious rep for bordeaux, chardonnay and syrah; tour the cellar doors and see what the fuss is about.

### ⬊ MT TARANAKI

You'll be forgiven for not quite believing your eyes as you approach Mt Taranaki (p185); the symmetrical flanks of this gorgeous volcanic cone rise up from the plains like the curl of a breaking wave, arcing up to a snowy summit. With brilliant walks and New Plymouth's cafes not far away, Mt Taranaki is well worth a detour.

3 DAVID WALL; 4 GARETH MCCORMACK; 5 ROSS BARNETT; 6 JOHN HAY; 7 PAUL KENNEDY

3 Oriental Bay, Wellington (p156); 4 Emerald Lakes, Tongariro National Park (p178); 5 Boating on Lake Taupo (p168); 6 Grapes on the vine; 7 Mt Taranaki (Egmont National Park; p185)

# BEST...

## ↘ ADRENALINE RUSHES

- **Skydiving, Taupo** (p171) The skydiving capital of the known universe!
- **Jetboating, Waikato River** (p175) Scoot along NZ's longest river.
- **Makara Peak Mountain Bike Park** (p161) Bone-jarring trails near Wellington.
- **Surf Highway 45** (p187) Gnarly breaks south of New Plymouth.

## ↘ SHORT WALKS

- **Tongariro Alpine Crossing** (p180) Legendary one-day tramp across volcanic mountainscapes.
- **Napier art-deco walking tour** (p193) Explore Napier's architectural gems on foot.
- **Huka Falls Walkway** (p172) From Taupo along the great, grey-green, greasy Waikato River.
- **Red Rocks Coastal Walk** (p161) Explore Wellington's craggy coastline.

## ↘ PLACES TO GET LOST

- **Te Urewera National Park** (p190) Virgin forests and lakes in the North Island's biggest national park.
- **Cape Palliser** (p197) Seal colonies and surf breaks near Wellington.
- **Lake Taupo** (p168) Take a cruise or fishing trip far from shore.
- **Mt Ngauruhoe** (p180) The spooky stand-in for Mt Doom in *Lord of the Rings*.

## ↘ PLACES TO GET BOOZY

- **Wairarapa Wine Country** (p168) Over the hills (and not so far away) from Wellington.
- **Hawke's Bay Wine Region** (p190) Sunny days and classy tastings around Napier.
- **Wellington's Pubs & Bars** (p164) Get down-and-dirty with Wellington's thirsty throngs.
- **Taupo** (p170) Backpackers and beer: it's a symbiotic relationship.

Outdoor drinking scene, Wellington (p164)

NICK SERVIAN / WELLINGTONNZ.COM

# THINGS YOU NEED TO KNOW

## ⬏ VITAL STATISTICS

- **Population** Wellington 164,000; Taupo 21,040; New Plymouth 45,230
- **Telephone code** ☎ 04 Wellington; ☎ 07 Taupo; ☎ 06 Taranaki & East Coast
- **Best time to visit** March to May (autumn)

## ⬏ LOCALITIES IN A NUTSHELL

- **Wellington** (p156) NZ's capital is flush with culture, coffee and crazy nightlife.
- **Taupo & the Central Plateau** (p168) Skiing, skydiving and volcanic mountain wilderness.
- **Taranaki** (p182) Enjoy New Plymouth's cafes and beaches and photogenic Mt Taranaki.
- **East Coast & Hawke's Bay** (p188) Laid-back and sunny, with wine tasting, beach-bumming and art-deco architecture.

## ⬏ ADVANCE PLANNING

- **One month before** Organise domestic flights, train trips and car hire.
- **Two weeks before** Book a South Island ferry crossing (p166) and accommodation across the region.
- **One week before** Book a Hawke's Bay winery tour (p190), and reserve a table at one of Wellington's top restaurants (p163).

## ⬏ RESOURCES

For bookings and information on regional accommodation, transport and activities, plus DOC info and contacts:

- **Napier i-SITE** (www.visitus.co.nz)
- **New Plymouth i-SITE** (www.newplymouthnz.com)
- **Taupo i-SITE** (www.laketauponz.com)
- **Wellington i-SITE** (www.wellingtonnz.com)

## ⬏ EMERGENCY NUMBERS

- **Ambulance, fire service & police** (☎ 111)

## ⬏ GETTING AROUND

- **Bus** (p167) around downtown Wellington.
- **Ferry** (p166) from Wellington to the South Island.
- **Hire a car** (p167) across the Central Plateau, Taranaki and the East Coast.
- **Mini-bus** around the Hawke's Bay (p190) and Wairarapa (p168) wineries.
- **Train** (p167) from Wellington to Auckland.
- **Walk** the Tongariro Alpine Crossing (p180).

# LOWER NORTH ISLAND ITINERARIES

## WINDY WELLINGTON Three Days

To get the lay of the (1) Wellington (p156) land, drive up Mt Victoria (p160), or ride the cable car up to the Wellington Botanic Gardens (p160). After lunch on cool Cuba St (p163), immerse yourself in all things Kiwi at Te Papa (p157) or the Museum of Wellington (p157). Drink beer by the jug at Mighty Mighty (p164).

The next day, fuel-up with coffee and eggs at Cafe L'Affare (p163) then head to Zealandia (p160) to meet the birds and learn about NZ conservation. For dinner try Chow (p163) or Pravda (p163), then spend your evening watching a movie at the Embassy Theatre (p165), bar-hopping along Courtenay Pl, or munching a midnight snack at a late-closing cafe (p163)… or all three!

On day three hightail it out of Wellington for some wine tasting around (2) Martinborough (p168), followed by seal-spotting along the wild (3) Cape Palliser (p197).

## ACTION STATIONS Five Days

Explore the active side of (1) Wellington (p156): storm the trails at Makara Peak Mountain Bike Park (p161), kayak or kiteboard on the harbour (p161), or check out some cricket memorabilia at the New Zealand Cricket Museum (p160). After all that activity, reward yourself with a drink at Matterhorn (p164).

Get ready for some white-knuckle action around (2) Taupo (p170) on the Central Plateau: try your hand at skydiving, bungy jumping, parasailing or white-water rafting (p171). Not far out of town you can try jetboating on the Waikato River (p175).

Next stop is (3) Tongariro National Park (p178). If it's ski season you can hit the slopes at NZ's largest ski area, centred on the twin resorts of Whakapapa and Turoa (p181); if not, tackle the awesome Tongariro Alpine Crossing day walk (p180).

To complete exhausting yourself, hop on a flight over to Taranaki and spend a day rampaging through the breaks along (4) Surf Highway 45 (p187), the highlight of which is the wicked reef break at Stent Road.

## TAKE A WALK ON THE WILD SIDE One Week

Take some time to appreciate the wild fringes of the Lower North Island.

On the northern side of the Hawke's Bay region, hook out onto the strangely barren (1) Mahia Peninsula (p189), with its painterly palette of azure waters, black-sand beaches and chalk-white cliffs. Continuing south, a remote pocket of the East Coast protects NZ's

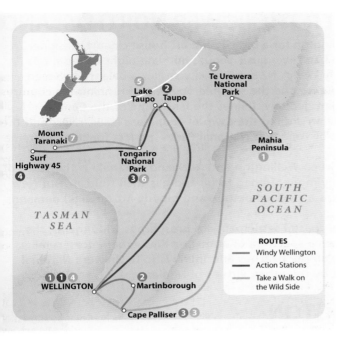

largest national park, (2) Te Urewera (p190), with its shimmering lakes and steep, forested hillsides.

East of Wellington, (3) Cape Palliser (p197), has seal colonies, a lonesome lighthouse and end-of-the-world vibes. Experience the wild side of (4) Wellington (p156) along the Red Rocks Coastal Walk (p161) or with a less-strenuous trip to Zealandia (p160), a great place to see native wildlife (including kiwi and tuatara).

The Central Plateau is the wild volcanic heart of the North Island – spend a few days exploring vast (5) Lake Taupo (p168) and the eerie wilderness of (6) Tongariro National Park (p178).

If you have time, trek over to (7) Mt Taranaki (p185), in Egmont National park, a peak of extraordinary beauty.

# DISCOVER THE LOWER NORTH ISLAND

Rock into Wellington for a big-city hit: art-house cinema, designer boutiques, hip bars, live-music venues and late-night coffee shops – it's all in 'Windy Welly'. NZ's capital city strikes a balance between creative exuberance and the sensible business of running the country.

NZ's exuberant geology defines the landscape of the Central Plateau. Revolving around the town of Taupo are lakes, rivers and the volcanic peaks of Tongariro National Park – perfect for some extreme outdoor action!

Halfway between Wellington and Auckland, Taranaki is the Texas of NZ, its economy more attuned to oil and gas than tourism. But New Plymouth makes a civilised detour, and moody Mt Taranaki demands to be visited.

From remote coastal settlements to prosperous wine towns, the East Coast offers a spectrum of authentic Kiwi experiences: rural Maori villages, empty beaches and the mystic Te Urewera National Park are offset by the urban virtues of Napier.

# WELLINGTON

pop 164,000

A small city with a relatively big reputation, Wellington is most famous for being NZ's capital. It is *infamous* for its weather, particularly the gale-force winds wont to barrel through, wrecking umbrellas and obliterating hairdos.

Downtown, the city is compact and vibrant, buoyed by a surprising number of museums, theatres, galleries and shops. A caffeine- and cocktail-fuelled hospitality scene fizzes and pops among the throng.

## ORIENTATION

The city congregates in the western corner of Wellington harbour, with the city suburbs clinging to the steep valleys and hills on all sides. Cuba St (literate, arty types) and Courtenay Pl (young larrikins) are the main nightlife hot spots, while Willis St, Queens Wharf and Lambton Quay are peppered with eating, drinking and shopping opportunities.

The airport is located 8km southeast of the city centre.

## INFORMATION

**DOC visitor centre** (Department of Conservation; ☎ 04-384 7770; www.doc.govt.nz; 18 Manners St; 🕙 9am-5pm Mon-Fri, 10am-3.30pm Sat) Bookings, passes and information for national and local walks, parks, huts and camping, plus permits for Kapiti Island.

**Post office** (www.nzpost.co.nz; 2 Manners St)

**Wellington Accident & Urgent Medical Centre** (☎ 04-384 4944; 17 Adelaide Rd, Newtown; 🕙 8am-11pm) No appointment necessary; also home to the after-hours pharmacy (open from 8am to 11pm).

**Wellington i-SITE** (☎ 04-802 4860; www.wellingtonnz.com; Civic Sq, cnr Wakefield & Victoria Sts; 🕙 8.30am-5pm Mon-Fri, 9.30am-4.30pm Sat & Sun; 🖳 ) The staff books almost everything, and cheerfully distributes the *Official Visitor Guide to Wellington*. Internet access and cafe also on-site.

## SIGHTS
### MUSEUMS & GALLERIES

For an imaginative, interactive experience of Wellington's social and salty maritime history, swing into the **Museum of Wellington** ( ☎ 04-472 8904; www.museum ofwellington.co.nz; Queens Wharf; admission free; ⊙ 10am-5pm).

The much-loved **City Gallery** ( ☎ 04-801 3021; www.citygallery.org.nz; Civic Sq, Wakefield St; admission by donation, charges may apply for major exhibits; ⊙ 10am-5pm) reopened late in 2009 after renovations and the addition of a new wing. Expect surprises: the gallery's a little cracker that secures acclaimed contemporary international artists as well as unearthing and supporting

COURTESY OF TE PAPA

Te Papa

## ⟩ TE PAPA

**Te Papa**, the 'Museum of New Zealand', is an inspiring, interactive repository of historical and cultural artefacts. 'Te Papa Tongarewa' loosely translates as 'treasure box'. The building dominates the Wellington waterfront and has become a national icon – an innovative celebration of the essence of NZ.

Among Te Papa's treasures is a huge Maori collection and its own *marae* (meeting house); dedicated hands-on 'discovery centres' for children; natural history and environment exhibitions; Pacific and NZ history galleries; and traditional and contemporary art and culture. Exhibitions occupy impressive gallery spaces with a touch of hi-tech (eg motion-simulator rides and a house shaking through an earthquake). Big-name, temporary exhibitions incur an admission fee.

You could spend a day exploring Te Papa's six floors but still not see it all. To target your areas of interest head to the information desk at level 2. To get your bearings, the one-hour Introducing Te Papa tour ($12) is a good idea; tours leave from the information desk at 10.15am and 2pm daily. Two cafes and two excellent gift shops round out the Te Papa experience.

**Things you need to know:** Map p158; ☎ 04-381 7000; www.tepapa.govt.nz; 55 Cable St; admission free; ⊙ 10am-6pm Mon-Wed & Fri-Sun, to 9pm Thu; Ⓟ

# WELLINGTON

**INFORMATION**

| | |
|---|---|
| Australian High Commission | 1 C2 |
| Canadian Embassy | 2 B5 |
| DOC Visitor Centre | 3 B6 |
| Fijian High Commission | 4 C3 |
| French Embassy | 5 B6 |
| German Embassy | 6 C2 |
| Israeli Embassy | 7 B4 |
| Japanese Embassy | 8 B6 |
| Netherlands Embassy | 9 B4 |
| Post Office | 10 B6 |
| UK High Commission | 11 B3 |
| US Embassy | 12 C2 |
| Wellington Accident & Urgent Medical Centre | 13 C8 |
| Wellington I-SITE | 14 B6 |

**SIGHTS & ACTIVITIES**

| | |
|---|---|
| Cable Car Lower Terminal | 15 B5 |
| Cable Car Upper Terminal | 16 A5 |
| City Gallery | 17 B6 |
| Ferg's Kayaks | 18 C5 |
| Museum of Wellington | 19 C5 |
| New Zealand Cricket Museum | 20 C8 |
| Te Papa | 21 C6 |
| Wellington Botanic Gardens | 22 A5 |
| Wild Winds | 23 D6 |

**SLEEPING**

| | |
|---|---|
| Booklovers B&B | 24 D8 |
| Cambridge Hotel | 25 C7 |
| Comfort & Quality Hotels | 26 B7 |
| Copthorne Hotel | 27 D6 |
| Mermaid | 28 A7 |
| Museum Hotel | 29 C6 |
| Tinakori Lodge | 30 B3 |
| Victoria Court | 31 B7 |
| YHA Wellington City | 32 C7 |

**EATING**

| | |
|---|---|
| Cafe L'Affare | 33 C7 |
| Chow | 34 C7 |
| Commonsense Organics | 35 C6 |
| Fidel's | 36 B7 |
| Midnight Espresso | 37 B7 |
| Moore Wilson Fresh | 38 C7 |
| Pravda | 39 B5 |
| Scopa | 40 B7 |

**DRINKING**

| | |
|---|---|
| Good Luck | 41 B7 |
| Hummingbird | 42 C7 |
| Mac's Brewery Bar | 43 C6 |
| Malthouse | 44 C7 |
| Matterhorn | 45 B6 |
| Mighty Mighty | 46 B6 |
| Vivo | 47 B6 |

500 m
0.25 miles

LOWER NORTH ISLAND

WADESTOWN

THORNDON

Town Belt

Northern Walkway

Tinakori Rd

Grant Rd

Glenmore St

Bolton St

Bowen St

Aurora Tce

The Terrace

Hawkestone St

Molesworth St

Hill St

Murphy St

Pipitea St

Aitken St

Sydney St

Ballance St

Lambton Quay

Wellington Urban Mwy

Thorndon Quay

Tinakori Rd

Hobson St

Mulgrave St

Featherston St

Customhouse Quay

Wellington

Thorndon Quay

Waterloo Quay

Aotea Quay

Westpac Trust Stadium

Port of Wellington Container Terminal

Pipitea Quay

Wellington-Picton Ferry (Bluebridge Services)

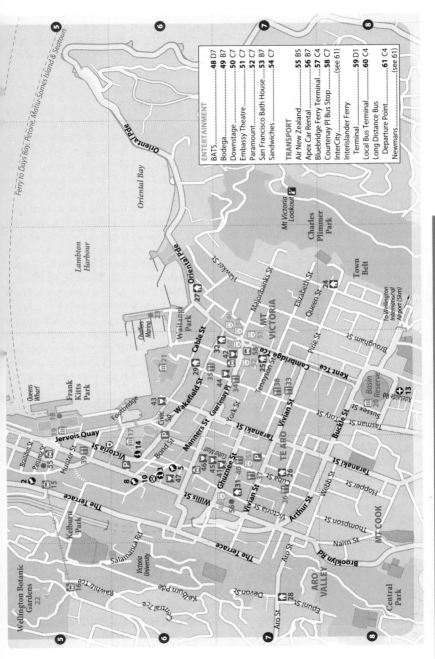

Ferry to Days Bay, Petone Matiu-Somes Island & Seatoun

Oriental Pde

Oriental Bay

Lambton Harbour

Mt Victoria Lookout

Charles Plimmer Park

Town Belt

To Wellington International Airport (5km)

MT VICTORIA

Majoribanks St

Elizabeth St

Queen St

Pirie St

Kent Tce

Cambridge Tce

Broughan St

Hawker St

Tennyson St

Cable St

Wakefield St

Courtenay Pl

York St

Taranaki St

Vivian St

Webb St

Hopper St

Tory St

Sussex St

Tasman St

Buckle St

Basin Reserve

Adelaide Rd

TE ARO

MT COOK

ARO VALLEY

Central Park

Brooklyn Rd

Aro St

Nairn St

Thompson St

Devon St

Epuni St

The Terrace

Salamanca Rd

Victoria University

Kelburn Pde

Rawhiti Tce

Central Tce

Wellington Botanic Gardens

Kelburn Park

Queens Wharf

Frank Kitts Park

Jervois Quay

Victoria St

Willis St

Manners St

Cuba Mall

Cuba St

Ghuznee St

Dixon St

Bond St

Hunter St

Brandon St

Panama St

The Terrace

Waitangi Park

Chaffers Marina

Civic Sq

Footbridge

those at the forefront of New Zealand's scene.

Cricket boffins will be bowled over by the historical memorabilia at the **New Zealand Cricket Museum** (☎ 04-385 6602; www.nzcricket.co.nz; Old Grandstand, Basin Reserve; adult/child $5/2; ☒ 10.30am-3.30pm daily Nov-Apr, Sat & Sun May-Oct).

### GARDENS & LOOKOUTS

The expansive, hilltop **Wellington Botanic Gardens** (☎ 04-499 1400; www .wellington.govt.nz; admission free; ☒ dawn-dusk; Ⓟ) can be conveniently visited via a cable-car ride (nice bit of planning, eh?). The hilly 25-hectare gardens boast a tract of original native forest along with varied collections including a beaut rose garden and international plant collections.

One of Wellington's most famous attractions is the little red **cable car** (☎ 04-472 2199; www.wellingtoncablecar.co.nz; one-way adult/child $3/1, return $5/2; ☒ every 10min, 7am-10pm Mon-Fri, 8.30am-10pm Sat, 9am-10pm Sun) that clanks up the steep slope from Lambton Quay to Kelburn.

For the best view of the city, harbour and surrounds, venture up to the lookout atop the 196m **Mt Victoria**, east of the city centre.

### WILDLIFE

The groundbreaking wildlife sanctuary **Zealandia** (☎ 04-920 9200; www.visitzealandia .com; Waiapu Rd; adult/child/family $15/7/37; ☒ 9am-5pm, last entry 4pm; Ⓟ) is tucked in the hills about 2km west of town (buses 3, 18, 21, 22 and 23 trundle nearby). The fenced mainland 'conservation island' is home to more than 30 native bird species including kiwi, saddleback, kaka and hihi, as well as the most accessible wild population of tuatara.

**Wellington Zoo** (☎ 04-381 6755; www. wellingtonzoo.com; 200 Daniell St; adult/concession/child $15/10/7.50; ☒ 9.30am-5pm, last entry 4.15pm; Ⓟ) has a commitment to conservation and research. There's a plethora of native and non-native wildlife here, including the residents of the outdoor lion and chimpanzee parks; and the nocturnal kiwi house, which also houses tuatara. The

Cable car, with views across Wellington

OLIVER STREWE

zoo is located 4km south of the city; catch bus 10 or 23.

## ACTIVITIES
### MOUNTAIN BIKING
Wellington's good for cycling, if you don't mind hills. The excellent Makara Peak Mountain Bike Park (www.makarapeak. org.nz) in the hills of Karori is 4km west of the city centre. The main entrance is on South Karori Rd – catch bus 3 or 18. Mud Cycles ( ☎ 04-476 4961; www.mudcycles.co.nz; 338 Karori Rd, Karori; half-day/full day/weekend bike hire $30/45/70; ⏰ 9.30am-6pm Mon-Fri) has mountain bikes for hire, is close to the park, and also runs guided tours catering for all levels.

### WALKING
The wild-and-woolly Red Rocks Coastal Walk (two to three hours, 8km return), 7km south of the city, follows the tumultuous volcanic coast from Owhiro Bay through Te Kopahou Reserve to Red Rocks and Sinclair Head, where there's a seal colony. Take bus 4 to Owhiro Bay Pde, then it's 1km to the quarry gate where the walk starts.

### OTHER ACTIVITIES
With all this wind and water, Wellington was made for sailboarding and kiteboarding, and there are plenty of good launching points within 30-minutes' drive of the city. Wild Winds ( ☎ 04-384 1010; www.wildwinds.co.nz; Chaffers Marina, Oriental Bay; ⏰ 10am-6pm Mon-Fri, to 3pm Sat, 11am-3pm Sun) runs two-hour windsurfing lessons for beginners ($110), and three-hour kiteboarding lessons from $195.

At the long-running Ferg's Kayaks ( ☎ 04-449 8898; www.fergskayaks.co.nz; Shed 6, Queens Wharf; ⏰ 10am-8pm Mon-Fri, 9am-6pm Sat & Sun) you can punish your tendons with indoor rock climbing (adult/child

$15/9), cruise the waterfront on a pair of inline skates ($15 for two hours) or paddle around the harbour in a kayak (from $15 for one hour).

## TOURS
Walk Wellington ( ☎ 04-802 4860; www. walk.wellington.net.nz; adult/child $20/10; ⏰ tours 10am daily year-round, plus 5.30pm Mon, Wed & Fri Nov-Mar) Informative two-hour walking tours focusing on the city and waterfront, departing the i-SITE. Book online or just turn up.
Wellington Rover ( ☎ 0800 426 211, 04-471 0044; www.wellingtonrover.co.nz; adult/child $40/25; ⏰ departs i-SITE 9am, 11.30am & 2.30pm) The 2½-hour Explorer Tour with a hop-on/hop-off option visits places that are tricky to reach without a car (Mt Victoria, South Coast beaches, Red Rocks seal colony). Also runs customised tours, and half-/full day LOTR trips ($90/150) complete with Hobbit ears.
Zest Food Tours ( ☎ 04-801 9198; www. zestfoodtours.co.nz; tours from $125) Runs 2½- to four-hour small-group city sightseeing tours; longer tours include lunch with matched wines at a top restaurant. Also runs Wairarapa food and wine tours (part- and full day from $230).

## SLEEPING
### BUDGET
Cambridge Hotel ( ☎ 0800 375 021, 04-385 8829; www.cambridgehotel.co.nz; 28 Cambridge Tce; dm $23-25, s/d/tw $61/80/85, s/d/tw/tr/f with bathroom $90/99/109/130/140; 🖳 🛜 ) Top-quality pub accommodation at affordable prices in a heritage hotel. En suite rooms have Sky TV, phone and fridge (try for a room at the back if you're a light sleeper). The backpacker wing has a well-stocked kitchen, flash bathrooms, and dorms with no natural light but sky-high ceilings. Cheap bar meals are a plus.

**YHA Wellington City** ( ☎ 04-801 7280; www.yha.co.nz; cnr Cambridge Tce & Wakefield St; dm $30-33, d with/without bathroom $108/88; 🖳 🛜 ) YHA Welly wins points for the biggest and best communal areas: superior kitchens, huge dining areas (group dinner nights are a blast), games room, reading room and dedicated movie room with hi-tech projector. Sustainable initiatives (recycling, composting and energy-efficient hot water) impress, and there's a comprehensive booking service at reception.

## MIDRANGE & TOP END

**Mermaid** ( ☎ 04-384 4511; www.mermaid.co.nz; 1 Epuni St; s $90-150, d $100-145; 🛜 ) In the ubercool Aro Valley 'hood, Mermaid is a small women-only guest house in a colourfully restored villa. Each room is individually themed with artistic flair (one with private bathroom, three with shared facilities). Great cafe, bakery and deli on your doorstep.

**Tinakori Lodge** ( ☎ 0800 939 347, 04-939 3478; www.tinakorilodge.co.nz; 182 Tinakori Rd; s $99-120, d $140-170; 🅿 🛜 ) Built in 1868 from native timbers, this lodge is in the thick of historic Thorndon, but a bit too close to the motorway for utter tranquillity. It's still a good option, with its rooms (five with en suites, four with shared facilities) decorated in refined, motherly style.

**Comfort & Quality Hotels** ( ☎ 0800 873 553, 04-385 2156; www.hotelwellington.co.nz; 223 Cuba St; d $100-170; 🖳 🎦 ) Two hotels in one: the sympathetically renovated historic Trekkers building with its smaller, cheaper rooms (Comfort); and the recently built, snazzier high-rise Quality with modern styling and a swimming pool. Both share in-house bar and dining room (meals available, $14 to $28).

**Booklovers B&B** ( ☎ 04-384 2714; www.booklovers.co.nz; 123 Pirie St; s/d from $150/180; 🅿 🖳 🛜 ) Booklovers is a gracious B&B run by award-winning author Jane Tolerton (her books are among the thousands shelved around the house). Four guest rooms have TV, CDs and CD/DVD player; three have en suites, one has a private bathroom. Bus 2 runs from the front gate to Courtenay Pl and the train station, and the city's 'green belt' begins next door.

**Victoria Court** ( ☎ 04-472 4297; www.victoria court.co.nz; 201 Victoria St; r $145-200; 🅿 🛜 ) Our top motel choice, right in the city centre, with plenty of parking. The affable owners offer spotless, stylish studios and apartments with spas, cooking facilities, suede couches, slick blond-wood joinery and new TVs. Two disabled-access units; larger units sleep six.

**Copthorne Hotel** ( ☎ 0800 782 548, 04-385 0279; www.millenniumhotels.co.nz/cophorne orientalbay; 100 Oriental Pde; d $160-290; 🅿 🖳 🛜 🎦 ) A tasteful refurb has this upmarket operation on ritzy Oriental Pde looking as good as gold, from the polished reception, through a seemingly endless maze of corridors, to the fancy bar and dining room. Handsome rooms are spread over two wings: the Bay wing has larger rooms with harbour views; the Roxburgh has smaller rooms, some with harbour views and some without. Parking costs $20 per day.

**Museum Hotel** ( ☎ 0800 994 335, 04-802 8900; www.museumhotel.co.nz; 90 Cable St; r & apt Mon-Thu $190-325, Fri-Sun $150-325; 🅿 🖳 🛜 🎦 ) Sometimes called 'Museum Hotel de Wheels' (to make way for Te Papa, it was rolled here from its original location 120m away), the Museum is a quirky, boutique affair. Eclectic decor (chandeliers, edgy modern art), sassy staff, a decent restaurant and groovy tunes piped into the lobby make a refreshing change from homogenised business hotels. Tasty weekend/weekly rates.

Cafe L'Affare

## EATING
### RESTAURANTS
**Scopa** ( ☎ 04-384 6020; cnr Cuba & Ghuznee Sts; mains $14-30; 🕙 9am-late Mon-Sun) Perfect pizza, proper pasta and other authentic Italian treats. Opened in 2006, this modern *cucina* (kitchen) is already a Wellington institution. Slick, friendly service and consistently good food make it deservedly so. Watch the groovy 'Cubans' from a seat in the window. Lunchtime specials; sexy evenings complete with cocktails.

**Chow** ( ☎ 04-382 8585; Level 1, 45 Tory St; meals $18-30; 🕙 noon-midnight) Home of the legendary blue cheese and peanut wonton, Chow is a stylish pan-Asian restaurant-cum-bar: a must for people who love exciting food, interesting decor and the odd cocktail. The perfect place to share food and conversation. The hip Motel bar is adjacent.

**Pravda** ( ☎ 04-499 5570; 107 Customhouse Quay; mains $25-35; 🕙 7.30am-late Mon-Fri, 9am-late Sat) A classy downtown cafe (more a chic restaurant by Wellington standards), scoring well with readers and folks that hand out culinary excellence awards. The opulent space (styled in quasi-USSR mode) is a formal backdrop for enjoying well-assembled duck, chicken, fish and NZ lamb mains. Fantastic desserts and coffee.

### CAFES
**Midnight Espresso** ( ☎ 04-384 7014; 178 Cuba St; meals $6-16; 🕙 7.30am-3am Mon-Fri, 8am-3am Sat & Sun; Ⓥ ) The city's original late-night cafe, with food that's hearty, tasty and inexpensive – heavy on the wholesome and vegetarian. Sit in the window with Havana coffee and cake; it's the quintessential Wellington cafe experience.

**Cafe L'Affare** ( ☎ 04-385 9748; 27 College St; meals $6-18; 🕙 8am-4pm) Cafe L'Affare is the centre of a small empire, from which its own beans are roasted and distributed. Its Professor Brainstorm–emporium interior is a hive of activity, with speedy baristas, crowded communal tables and a disco ball. At weekends, kids aplenty add to the cacophony, but everyone adds their cheery thanks to snappy service and wicked brekkies of eggie excellence.

**Fidel's** ( ☎ 04-801 6868; 234 Cuba St; meals $6-18; ⌚ 7.30am-midnight Mon-Fri, 9am-midnight Sat & Sun; Ⓥ ) A Cuba St institution for caffeine-craving, upbeat left-wing subversives. Eggs any-which-way, pizza and salads are pumped out of the itsy kitchen, along with Welly's best milkshakes. Revolutionary memorabilia adorn the walls of the interior; decent outdoor areas, too. A super-busy crew cope with the chaos admirably.

### SELF-CATERING

**Commonsense Organics** ( ☎ 04-384 3314; 260 Wakefield St; ⌚ 9am-7pm Mon-Fri, 9am-6pm Sat & Sun) Organic produce (wine, fruit, vegies, nuts, tea, herbs etc), and food for the intolerant.

**Moore Wilson Fresh** ( ☎ 04-384 9906; cnr College & Tory Sts; ⌚ 7.30am-7pm Mon-Fri, 7.30am-6pm Sat, 9am-5pm Sun) An unsurpassed array of (predominantly NZ) produce, baking, mountains of cheese… just endless goodies. Go.

## DRINKING

**Mighty Mighty** ( ☎ 04-384 9085; 104 Cuba St; ⌚ 4pm-late Wed-Sat) Possibly the hippest of the capital's drinking establishments and music venues. 'Inside-a-pinball-machine' decor, pink velvet curtains, kitsch gew-gaws and Wellington's best barstaff make this an essential port of call for those wanting to experience the best of NZ's bar scene. Get dancing.

**Matterhorn** ( ☎ 04-384 3359; 106 Cuba St; ⌚ 10am-late) Perennially popular bar, with a clientele as interesting as its drinks list. Worthy winner of numerous accolades including NZ's best bar and restaurant. Slick and ultracool, with great attention to detail. Occasional live music provided by some of Aotearoa's freshest bands and musicians.

**Malthouse** ( ☎ 04-802 5484; 48 Courtenay Pl; ⌚ lunch-late Mon-Sat) Beervana. An immense array of beers (both local and international) that would make even the most fervent of hop-heads quiver at the knees. NZ *does* brew great beer, and this is the place to quaff them.

**Vivo** ( ☎ 04-384 6400; 19 Edward St; ⌚ 3pm-late Mon-Fri, 5pm-late Sat) A tomelike list of approximately 700 wines from around the world, with more than 50 available by the glass. Exposed bricks and timber beams give Vivo an earthy cellarlike feel, while the fairy lights look like stars set against the dark ceiling.

## ENTERTAINMENT
### LIVE MUSIC & CLUBS

**San Francisco Bath House** ( ☎ 04-801 6797; www.sfbh.co.nz; 171 Cuba St; ⌚ 5pm-late Wed-Fri, 8pm-late Sat) Wellington's best mid-sized live-music venue, playing host to the cream of NZ artists, as well as quality acts from abroad (Fleet Foxes, Gomez…) Somewhat debauched balcony action, five deep at the bar, but otherwise well run and usually lots of fun.

**Bodega** ( ☎ 04-384 8212; www.bodega.co.nz; 101 Ghuznee St; ⌚ 4pm-late) A trailblazer of the city's modern live-music scene, and still considered an institution despite its move from a derelict heritage building to a concrete cavern. 'The Bodge' offers a full and varied program of gigs in a pleasant space with a respectable dance floor and filler-up food.

**Sandwiches** ( ☎ 04-385 7698; www.sandwiches.co.nz; 8 Kent Tce; ⌚ 4pm-late Tue-Sat) Get yourself a slice of NZ's electronic artists and DJs, regular multiflavoured international acts and the capital's best sound system.

### THEATRES

**BATS** ( ☎ 04-802 4175; www.bats.co.nz; 1 Kent Tce; tickets $15-20; ⌚ box office open 2hr before each show) Wildly alternative BATS presents cutting-edge and experimental NZ theatre – varied, cheap, and intimate.

**Downstage** ( ☎ 04-801 6946; www.down stage.co.nz; cnr Courtenay Pl & Cambridge Tce; tickets $25-45; ⊗ box office 9am-5.30pm Mon, 9am-show time Tue-Sat) NZ's most enduring professional theatre company has a strong presence in Wellington (established 1964). Original NZ plays, dance, comedy and musicals in a 250-seat auditorium.

## CINEMAS

**Embassy Theatre** ( ☎ 04-384 7656; www. deluxe.co.nz; 10 Kent Tce; tickets adult/child $15/9; ⊗ 11am-midnight) Wellywood's cinema mothership: built in the 1920s, restored in 2003. Screens mainstream films; bar and cafe on-site.

**Paramount** ( ☎ 04-384 4080; www.paramount .co.nz; 25 Courtenay Pl; tickets adult/child $14.50/9; ⊗ noon-midnight) A lovely old complex screening largely art-house, documentary and foreign flicks.

## GETTING THERE & AWAY
### AIR
Wellington is an international gateway to NZ. See p373 for information on international flights. **Wellington Airport (WLG;**

Outdoor bar area, Cuba St, Wellington

OLIVER STREWE

## ↘ IF YOU LIKE...

If you like **Mighty Mighty** (p164), we think you'll appreciate the boozy offerings of these other Wellington bars:

- **Mac's Brewery Bar** ( ☎ 04-381 2282; cnr Taranaki & Cable Sts; ⊗ 10.30am-late) Occupying a renovated warehouse on a prime waterfront site, this microbrewery does a great job of looking seriously committed to the craft.
- **Hummingbird** ( ☎ 04-801 6336; 22 Courtenay Pl; ⊗ 9am-late) Popular with the sophisticated set, Hummingbird is usually packed – both inside in the intimate, stylish dining room and bar, and outside on streetside tables.
- **Good Luck** ( ☎ 04-801 9950; basement, 126 Cuba St; ⊗ 5pm-late Tue-Sun) Cuba St's Chinese opium den, without the opium. This is a slickly run, sultry basement bar playing fresh hip-hop and electronica.

☎ 04-385 5100; www.wellington-airport.co.nz; ☽ 4am-1.30am) has touch-screen information kiosks in the luggage hall. If you're in transit or have an early flight, you can't linger overnight inside the terminal. Departure tax on international flights is adult/child $25/10.

**Air New Zealand** (☎ 0800 737 000, 04-474 8950 or 04-388 9900; www.airnewzealand.co.nz; cnr Lambton Quay & Grey St; ☽ 9am-5pm Mon-Fri, 10am-1pm Sat) offers flights between Wellington and most domestic centres, including the following:

| TO | PRICE | FREQUENCY |
| --- | --- | --- |
| Auckland | from $49 | up to 20 daily |
| Christchurch | from $49 | up to 14 daily |
| Dunedin | from $120 | up to 6 daily |
| Queenstown | from $116 | 1 daily |
| Rotorua | from $95 | up to 3 daily |

**Jetstar** (☎ 0800 800 995; www.jetstar.com) flies between Wellington and Auckland (from $49, three daily), and Christchurch (from $50, one daily). **Pacific Blue** (☎ 0800 670 000; www.pacificblue.co.nz) flies between Wellington and Auckland (from $65, three daily), and Christchurch (from $50, two daily).

**Soundsair** (☎ 0800 505 005, 03-520 3080; www.soundsair.com) flies between Wellington and Picton (from $79, up to eight daily), Nelson (from $90, up to three daily) and Blenheim (from $79, one daily).

## BOAT

Wellington is a major transport hub, being the North Island port for the interisland ferries. On a clear day, sailing into Wellington Harbour or through the Marlborough Sounds is magical.

**Bluebridge Ferries** (☎ 0800 844 844, 04-471 6188; www.bluebridge.co.nz; adult/child $50/25) crossing takes three hours, 20 minutes. Departs Wellington at 3am, 8am, 1pm and 9pm daily (no 3am or 9pm services Saturday). Departs Picton at 2am, 8am, 2pm & 7pm daily (no 8am service Saturday; no 2am service Sunday). Cars and campervans up to 4m long cost from $110; campervans under 5.5m from $150; motorbikes $50; bicycles $10.

The **Interislander** (☎ 0800 802 802, 04-498 3302; www.interislander.co.nz; adult/child from $46/23) crossing takes three hours, 10 minutes. Departs Wellington at 2.25am, 8.25am, 2.05pm and 6.25pm; departs Picton at 6.25am, 10.05am, 1.10pm, 6.05pm and 10.25pm. From November through to April there's an extra 10.25am sailing from Wellington and an extra 2.25pm sailing from Picton. Cars are priced from $101; campervans (up to 5.5m) from $126; motorbikes $46; bicycles $15.

Book ferries at hotels, by phone, online, at travel agents and with operators directly (online is the cheapest option). Bluebridge is based at Waterloo Quay, opposite the Wellington train station. The Interislander terminal is about 2km northeast of the city centre; a shuttle bus ($2) runs to the Interislander from platform 9 at Wellington train station (where long-distance buses also depart) at 7.35am, 9.35am (peak season only), 1.15pm and 5.35pm. It also meets arriving ferries, returning passengers to platform 9.

## BUS

Wellington is a bus-travel hub, with connections north to Auckland and all major towns in between. **InterCity** (☎ 04-385 0520; www.intercity.co.nz) is the main North Island bus company, travelling just about everywhere. InterCity and **Newmans** (☎ 04-385 0521; www.newmanscoach.co.nz) buses depart from platform 9 at the train station. Typical fares include: Auckland (from $30, 11 hours, three daily), Palmerston North (from $13, 2¼ hours, six daily), Rotorua (from $30, 7½ hours, twice daily).

**Naked Bus** ( ☎ 0900 62533; www.naked bus.com) runs north from Wellington to all major North Island destinations, including Palmerston North ($1 to $22, 2½ hours, two daily), Napier ($1 to $35, five hours, four times a week), Taupo (from $1 to $43, 6½ hours, one daily) and Auckland (from $1 to $34, 12 hours, one daily), with myriad stops en route. You can buy bus tickets on the ferry to Picton, connecting to the Naked Bus South Island Network. Buses depart from the Bunny St bus stop.

### TRAIN
The long-haul **Tranz Scenic** ( ☎ 0800 872 467; www.tranzscenic.co.nz) routes include the *Overlander* between Wellington and Auckland (from $49, 12 hours, one daily) departing Wellington at 7.25am (Friday, Saturday and Sunday May to September); and the *Capital Connection* between Wellington and Palmerston North ($24, 2¼ hours, one daily Monday to Friday) departing Wellington at 5.17pm.

### GETTING AROUND
### TO/FROM THE AIRPORT
**Super Shuttle** ( ☎ 0800 748 885; www .supershuttle.co.nz; 1/2 passengers $15/21; ☒ 24hr) provides a door-to-door minibus service between the city and airport, 8km southeast of the city.

The **Airport Flyer** ( ☎ 0800 801 700; www. metlink.co.nz; airport-city per adult/child $8/4.50) bus runs between the airport, Wellington and Lower Hutt (reduced service to Upper Hutt), calling at major stops. Buses run from the city to the airport between 5.50am and 8.50pm; and from the airport, between 6.30am and 9.30pm.

A taxi between the city centre and airport costs around $30.

RICHARD CUMMINS
Interisland ferry

### BUS
Frequent and efficient Go Wellington, Valley Flyer, Newlands Coach Services and Mana Coach Services buses run from 7am to 11.30pm on most suburban routes. Buses depart from Wellington train station, or from the main bus stop on Courtenay Pl near the Cambridge Tce intersection.

### CAR
Aside from the major international rental companies (see p379), Wellington has several operators that will negotiate cheap deals, especially for longer-term rental of two weeks or more, but rates generally aren't as competitive as in Auckland. Operators include the following:

**Ace Rental Cars** (☎ 0800 535 500, 04-471 1176; www.acerentalcars.co.nz; 126 Hutt Rd; ⏰ 8am-5pm)

**Apex Car Rental** (☎ 0800 300 110, 04-385 2163; www.apexrentals.co.nz; 186 Victoria St; ⏰ 8am-5pm)

**Omega Rental Cars** (☎ 0800 667 722, 04-472 8465; www.omegarentals.com; 96 Hutt Rd; ⏰ 8am-5pm)

If you plan to explore both the North and South Islands, most companies suggest you leave your car at Wellington and pick up another one in Picton after crossing Cook Strait.

### TAXI

**Green Cabs** (☎ 0508 447 336)
**Wellington City Cabs** (☎ 0800 388 8000)
**Wellington Combined Taxis** (☎ 0800 384 444)

### TRAIN

**Tranz Metro** (☎ 0800 801 700; www.tranzmetro.co.nz) operates four train routes running through Wellington's suburbs to regional destinations. Trains run frequently from around 6am to 11pm, departing Wellington train station. Timetables are available from convenience stores, the train station, Wellington i-SITE and online.

# THE WAIRARAPA

The Wairarapa is the large slab of land east and northeast of Wellington, beyond the craggy Tararua and Rimutaka Ranges. Named after Lake Wairarapa (Shimmering Waters), a shallow 8000-hectare lake, the region has traditionally been a frenzied hotbed of sheep farming. More recently, wineries have sprung up – around Martinborough, most famously – which has turned the region into a decadent weekend retreat.

# MARTINBOROUGH

pop 1360

The most popular visitor spot in the Wairarapa, Martinborough is a pretty town with a leafy town square and some charming old buildings, surrounded by a patchwork of pasture and a pinstripe of grapevines.

The **Martinborough i-SITE** (☎ 06-306 5010; www.wairarapanz.com; 18 Kitchener St; ⏰ 9am-5pm Mon-Fri, 10am-4pm Sat & Sun) is full of brochures and information.

With so many **wineries** (see the boxed text, right) scattered around town, there are no points for guessing what the town's main attraction is.

If overnighting, **Claremont** (☎ 0800 809 162, 06-306 9162; www.theclaremont.co.nz; 38 Regent St; d $125-160, 4-person apt $275; ⌨) is a classy accommodation enclave off Jellicoe St. It has two-storey, self-contained units in great nick, modern studios with spa baths, and sparkling two-bedroom apartments, all at reasonable rates (even cheaper in winter and/or midweek). **Peppers Martinborough Hotel** (☎ 06-306 9350; www.martinboroughhotel.co.nz; The Square; d incl breakfast $300-385; ⌨ 📶) is a grand old hotel on the main square that's been magnificently restored, with 16 spacious, luxury rooms, each individually decorated with pizzazz.

# TAUPO & THE CENTRAL PLATEAU

NZ's largest lake, Lake Taupo, sits in the caldera of a volcano that began erupting roughly 300,000 years ago. Today the 606-sq-km lake and its surrounding waterways are serene enough to attract fishing enthusiasts from all around the world.

OLIVER STREWE

Vineyard, Martinborough

## WAIRARAPA WINE COUNTRY

Martinborough is the undisputed hub of the action, renowned for its gravels that produce particularly remarkable pinot noir and distinctive whites. Our picks of the bunch:

**Ata Rangi** ( ☎ 06-306 9570; www.atarangi.co.nz; Puruatanga Rd) One of the region's pioneering winemakers. Great drops across the board and cute cellar door.

**Coney** ( ☎ 06-306 8345; www.coneywines.co.nz; Dry River Rd) Friendly tastings and lovely restaurant. Winery tours by arrangement.

**Margrain** ( ☎ 06-306 9292; www.margrainvineyard.co.nz; cnr Princess St & Huangarua Rd) Pretty winery and site of the Old Winery Cafe; a good pit stop overlooking the vines.

**Vynfields** ( ☎ 06-306 9901; www.vynfields.com; 22 Omarere Rd) Five-star, spicy pinot noir and a lush lawn on which to enjoy a platter. Organic/biodynamic wines.

Numerous operators run bus tours around Martinborough and the region:

**Dynamic Tours** ( ☎ 04-478 8533; www.dynamictours.co.nz; from $225) Customised wine tours, run from Wellington.

**Hammond's Scenic Tours** ( ☎ 04-472 0869; www.wellingtonsightseeingtours.com; full-day tour adult/child $195/97.50) Full-day winery tours including gourmet lunch.

**Tranzit Coachlines** ( ☎ 0800 471 227, 06-370 6600; www.tranzit.co.nz; 316 Queen St, Masterton) Two daily tours depart from Wellington or the main Wairarapa towns. The Gourmet Wine Escape ($161) visits Martinborough vineyards and includes tastings and lunch.

## GETTING THERE & AROUND

**Air New Zealand** (www.airnz.co.nz) has regular flights from Taupo to Auckland and Wellington. The **Tranz Scenic Overlander** (www.tranzscenic.co.nz) train on the Auckland–Wellington line stops at National Park village, Ohakune and Taihape.

**InterCity** (www.intercity.co.nz) buses travel to all of the region's major towns, connecting with most major destinations around NZ, while **Naked Bus** (www.nakedbus.com) is useful for Taupo and Turangi.

# TAUPO
pop 21,040

The increasingly exciting town of Taupo now rivals Rotorua as the North Island's adrenaline capital, with an abundance of blood-pumping activities.

**Taupo i-SITE** ( ☎ 07-376 0027; www.lake tauponz.com; Tongariro St; ⏰ 8.30am-5pm) handles bookings for accommodation, transport and activities; has a free town map as well

as Department of Conservation (DOC) maps and information.

## SIGHTS

The **Taupo Museum & Art Gallery** ( ☎ 07-376 0414; www.taupomuseum.co.nz; Story Pl; adult/child $5/free; ⏰ 10am-4.30pm) has historical displays covering the local forestry, nautical and trout-fishing industries, a mock-up of a 19th-century shop and a moa skeleton.

There are 10m-high **Maori carvings**, accessible only by boat, at the lake's Mine Bay (see right and p172 for boat-charter operators).

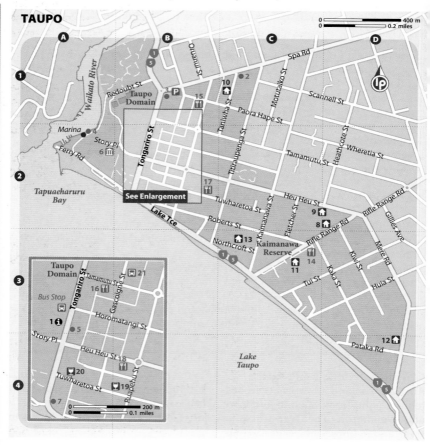

TAUPO

# ACTIVITIES
## BUNGY JUMPING
The picturesque **Taupo Bungy** ( ☎ 07-377 1135; www.taupobungy.co.nz; jump $109; ⏲ 8.30am-5pm) site is the most popular on the North Island. It sits on a cliff edge over the mighty Waikato River, and has plenty of vantage points if you're too chicken to jump.

## FISHING & CRUISING
Anglers are in the right place, because this region is justifiably world famous for trout. You can arrange guided trips or get gear and licences for independent trips at **Greenstone Fishing** ( ☎ 07-378 3714; www. greenstonefishing.co.nz; 147 Tongariro St; gear hire from $10; ⏲ 8.30am-5.30pm Mon-Fri, to 4.30pm Sat & Sun) and **Taupo Rod & Tackle** ( ☎ 07-378 5337; www.tauporodandtackle.co.nz; 7 Tongariro St; gear hire $15-45; ⏲ 8.30am-6pm Mon-Sat, 9.30am-5pm Sun).

The best place to book trips – whether fishing or cruising – is through the **launch office** (Lake Taupo Charter Office; ☎ 07-378 3444; www.fishcruisetaupo.co.nz; Marina; ⏲ 9am-5pm Dec-Mar, 9.30am-3pm Apr-Nov), which books for around 20 boats, catering to individuals or groups.

## MOUNTAIN BIKING
There are good mountain-bike tracks just out of town in the Wairakei and Pureora Forests and along the Waikato River. You can download maps for these from www. biketaupo.org.nz.

Rapid Sensations (p172) runs guided three-hour rides in the Wairakei Forest (guided trips $75, bike hire half-/full day $45/55).

## SKIING
Taupo is tantalisingly close to the ski fields, being 1¼ hours drive to Whakapapa, and two hours to Turoa (see p181). You can hire gear all around and up the mountain, and also at **Pointons Ski Shop** ( ☎ 07-377 0087; 57 Tongariro St; ski/ snowboard hire $30/40; ⏲ 7am-7pm Apr-Sep; 8.30am-5.30pm Mon-Fri, 8.30am-4pm Sat, 10am-3pm Sun Oct-Mar).

## SKYDIVING
More than 30,000 jumps a year are made from Taupo, which makes it the skydiving capital of the world. The following operators sit alongside each other at the airport and offer some of the best rates in NZ:
**Skydive Taupo** ( ☎ 0800 586 766; www.sky divetaupo.co.nz; 12,000ft/15,000ft $250/340)
**Taupo Tandem Skydiving** ( ☎ 07-377 0428; www.tts.net.nz; 12,000ft/15,000ft $249/339)

## SWIMMING
Twenty minutes' walk from town you'll find the **Huka Falls Walkway hot springs**, a pleasant and well-worn spot

Lake Taupo (p168)

JON DAVISON

under a bridge where you can take a dip for free, in natural surrounds.

## TRAMPING

There are some great walks in and around Taupo, ranging from sedate ambles to more gnarly all-dayers. A good place to start is DOC's leaflet *Lake Taupo – A Guide to Walks and Hikes* ($2.50).

The **Huka Falls Walkway** is an enjoyable, easy walk from Taupo to the falls along the east bank of the Waikato River, about a 1½-hour walk from the centre. Carrying on from the falls is the **Huka Falls to Aratiatia Rapids Walking Track**. The rapids are 7km away (another two-plus hours). There are good views of the river, Huka Falls and the power station across the river.

Taupo can also serve as a base from which to walk the Tongariro Alpine Crossing (see p180).

## WATER SPORTS

**Big Sky Parasail** ( ☎ 0800 724 475; www.big skyparasail.co.nz; Lake Tce; ⏲ 8am-6pm summer only) Runs lake parasailing (400ft/800ft $75/85) from the lakefront.

**Canoe & Kayak** ( ☎ 07-378 1003; www. canoeandkayak.co.nz; 77 Spa Rd; ⏲ 9am-5pm Mon-Sat) Instruction and boat hire (from the lake's edge in high summer), as well as guided tours: two-hour trip on the Waikato River ($45) or a half-day to the Maori carvings ($90).

**Rapid Sensations/Kayaking Kiwi** ( ☎ 07-378 7902; www.rapids.co.nz, www.kay akingkiwi.com; 413 Huka Falls Rd) Runs kayak trips to the Maori carvings ($108, 4½ hours) and a gentle paddle along the Waikato ($45, two hours). Also runs six-hour white-water rafting trips on the Tongariro River ($135) and shorter trips along a calmer section ($115, 2½ hours).

## TOURS
### AERIAL SIGHTSEEING

**Air Charter Taupo** ( ☎ 07-378 5467; www. airchartertaupo.co.nz; Taupo Airport; flights $80-250) Scenic flights ranging from 15 minutes to one hour, across Huka Falls, Lake Taupo and Tongariro National Park.

**Helistar Helicopters** ( ☎ 07-374 8405; www.helistar.co.nz; 415 Huka Falls Rd; flights $99-995) Located about 3km northeast of town, Helistar offers a variety of scenic helicopter flights, from 10 minutes to two hours. Combine a Helistar trip with the Huka Falls Jet in the Huka Star combo (from $193).

## OTHER TOURS

**Paradise Tours** ( ☎ 07-378 9955; www. paradisetours.co.nz; tours adult/child $99/45) Three-hour tours to the Aratiatia Rapids, Craters of the Moon and Huka Falls. Also offers tours to Tongariro National Park, Orakei Korako, Rotorua, Hawke's Bay and Waitomo Caves.

**pureORAwalks** ( ☎ 021-715 947; www.pure orawalks.com; adult/child $85/62) Four-hour Nature-Culture walks in Pureora Forest Park, Lake Rotopounamu and Whirinaki Forest Park, offering insight into *Maoritanga* (things Maori) – including traditional uses of flora and fauna, local history and legends.

## SLEEPING

**Blackcurrant Backpackers** ( ☎ 07-378 9292; www.blackcurrentbp.co.nz; 20 Taniwha St; dm $22-25, s/d/tr $50/70/84) Still permeated by that new-paint-and-carpet smell when we visited, this ageing motel has been fitted out with flash en suites and super-comfy beds. The staff rivals the cartoon blackcurrants in the Ribena ads for chirpiness.

**Lake Taupo Top 10 Holiday Resort** ( ☎ 07-378 6860; www.taupotop10.co.nz; 28 Centennial Dr; campsites per adult/child $23/13, cabins $99-128, units $149-365; 🖥 🛜 🏊 ) The slickest of the local camping grounds, this 20-acre park has all the mod cons, including heated swimming pool, tennis courts and a shop. It's 2.5km from the i-SITE.

**Bella Vista** ( ☎ 07-378 9043; www.bellavista motels.co.nz; 143 Heu Heu St; d $110-145, tr $145-165, q $185; 🛜 ) One of the growing number of Bella Vista motels nationwide, this one offers personal service by way of dog-loving owners Aaron and Tracey. Rooms are clean and comfortable, if a little bland.

**Catelli's of Taupo** ( ☎ 0800 88 44 77; www. catellis.co.nz; 23-27 Rifle Range Rd; r $135-145, ste $160-235; 🛜 ) The exterior is all hobbitish '80s curves, sloping roofs and nipple-pink trim, but these orderly motel units have a fresh modern feel inside. In summer it's worth paying the extra $5 for a garden studio with an outside sitting area.

**Suncourt** ( ☎ 07-378 8265; www.suncourt. co.nz; 14 Northcroft St; d $135-170, tr $155-190, q $170-220; 🖥 🛜 🏊 ) This rambling, lake-gazing complex encloses comfortable, well-furnished units with facilities including a spa pool and kids playground. Larger rooms with verandas and full kitchens are ideal for families. Regular conferences can book the place out.

**Beechtree** ( ☎ 07-377 0181; www.beechtree motel.co.nz; 56 Rifle Range Rd; d $140-180, tr $170, apt $220-250; 🖥 🛜 ) The Beechtree, and its sister motel Miro next door, offers classy rooms at a reasonable rate. The decor is fresh and modern, in neutral tones and creates a feeling of light and air, as do the large windows, ground-floor patios and upstairs balconies.

**Lake** ( ☎ 07-378 4222; www.thelakeonline. co.nz; 63 Mere Rd; r $150-195) A reminder that 1960s and '70s design wasn't all Austin Powers–style groovaliciousness and bell-bottoms, this unusual boutique motel is crammed with classic furniture from the likes of Saarenin and Mies Van der Rohe.

**Acacia Cliffs Lodge** ( ☎ 07-378 1551; http://acaciacliffslodge.co.nz; 133 Mapara Rd, Acacia Bay; r $650; 🖥 🛜 ) Pushing the romance switch way past 'rekindle', this luxurious B&B, high in the hills above Acacia Bay, offers four modern suites – three with sumptuous lake views and one that compensates for the lack of them with a curvy bath and a private garden.

## EATING

**Fine Fettle** ( ☎ 07-378 7674; 39 Paora Hape St; mains $6-15; ☺ breakfast & lunch) An airy cafe on a quieter edge of town, serving wholefood, organic, and GE- and gluten-free options. The healthy, satisfying offerings include quiches and fresh salads, plus juices, smoothies and iced chai.

**Replete** ( ☎ 07-378 0606; 45 Heu Heu St; mains $6-16; ☺ breakfast & lunch) Widely regarded as one of Taupo's best cafes, Replete's counter is packed full of delicatessen delights – running the gamut from sandwiches and salads to sweets. Its pastry selection is particularly commendable. A blackboard menu offers inexpensive and interesting light meals.

**Pimentos** ( ☎ 07-377 4549; 17 Tamamutu St; mains $26-29; ☺ dinner Wed-Mon) Such a local favourite that you may well need to book to enjoy some of the town's best food in this convivial environment. Its lamb shanks and mash are legendary, but the relatively short menu offers plenty of well-considered experimentation.

**Plateau** ( ☎ 07-377-2425; 64 Tuwharetoa St; mains $30-34; ☺ lunch & dinner) One of a growing number of brewery-branded gastro-pubs, Plateau is a great place for a drink (Monteith's beer being the main poison), but the food is the key. The menu is predominantly modern NZ (think lamb rump and rib-eye), with plenty of fancy fusion twists.

**Brantry** ( ☎ 07-378 0484; 45 Rifle Range Rd; mains $32-37; ☺ dinner) Chef Prue Campbell and sister Felicity continue to run the best and most consistent restaurant in the region at this 1950s town house, a few minutes from the town centre. Dine in intimate, unobtrusive surrounds, inside or out. The menu makes use of some of NZ's finest ingredients, including top-quality cuts of beef and lamb. The set menu (two/three courses $40/50) is a gift.

## DRINKING

**Bond** ( ☎ 07-377 2434; 40 Tuwharetoa St) Aiming for 007-like sophistication, this is Taupo's most upmarket bar, with European beers, tapas and DJs up late. The drinks cost a pretty Money-Penny, but you may still see a Q at the bar.

**Shed** ( ☎ 07-376 5393; 18 Tuwharetoa St) A lively place to sup a beer and catch the big game, sit outside and watch the world go by, or strut your stuff to DJs at the weekends. Food is punter-pleasing pub fare in man-sized portions.

## GETTING THERE & AWAY
### AIR

**Taupo Airport** ( ☎ 07-378 7771; www.taupo airport.co.nz; Anzac Memorial Dr) is 8km south of town. **Air New Zealand** ( ☎ 0800 737 000; www.airnz.co.nz) has daily direct flights to Auckland (45 minutes) and Wellington (one hour), with onward connections.

### BUS

The main bus stop is at the **Taupo Travel Centre** ( ☎ 07-378 9032; 16 Gascoigne St), which operates as a booking office. **InterCity/ Newmans** ( ☎ 09-583 5780; www.intercity.co.nz) runs several daily buses to Turangi ($25, 44 minutes), Auckland ($57, five hours), Hamilton ($51, three hours), Rotorua ($29, one hour), Tauranga ($47, 2¾ hours), Napier ($35, two hours), Palmerston North ($51, 4¼ hours) and Wellington ($61, six hours).

Budget operator **Naked Bus** ( ☎ 0900 62533 per min $1.80; www.nakedbus.com) has daily services to the same destinations (excluding Tauranga), with super-early-bird prices starting from $1. Buses stop outside the i-SITE.

Shuttle services operate year-round between Taupo, Turangi and Tongariro National Park. In winter, services run to Whakapapa Ski Area (1½ hours) and can include package deals for lift tickets and ski hire. See p182 for details.

## GETTING AROUND

**Taupo's Hotbus** ( ☎ 0508 468 287; www.hotbus.co.nz; 1st stop $15, then per stop $5; ◷ 9am-4pm Oct-Mar, 10am-3pm Apr-Sep) is a hop-on, hop-off bus that does an hourly circuit of all the major attractions in and around Taupo, from the i-SITE.

# AROUND TAUPO

## WAIRAKEI PARK

Crossing the river at Tongariro St and heading north from town on SH1, you'll arrive at the Wairakei Park area, also known as the Huka Falls Tourist Loop.

## HUKA FALLS

These falls mark the spot where NZ's longest river, the Waikato – which, here, has only just been born from Lake Taupo – is slammed into a narrow chasm, making a dramatic 10m drop into a surging pool. The falls are clearly signposted and have a car park and kiosk alongside. You can also take a few short walks around the area or pick up the longer Huka Falls Walkway back to town, or the Aratiatia Rapids Walking Track to the rapids (see p172).

## VOLCANIC ACTIVITY CENTRE

What's the story with all the geothermal activity in this area? The **volcanic activity centre** ( ☎ 07-374 8375; www.volcanoes.co.nz; Karetoto Rd; adult/child $9.50/5; ◷ 9am-5pm Mon-Fri, 10am-4pm Sat & Sun) has all the answers.

## HUKAFALLS JET & PRAWN FARM

Further down the Falls Loop road is the launching site for **Hukafalls Jet** ( ☎ 07-374 8572; www.hukafallsjet.com; trips adult/child $99/59). This 30-minute thrill ride takes you up the river to the spray-filled foot of the Huka Falls and down to the Aratiatia Dam,

DAVID WALL

**Huka Falls**

all the while dodging daringly and doing acrobatic 360-degree turns.

# TURANGI

pop 3900

Once a service town for the nearby hydro-electric power station, Turangi's claim to fame nowadays is undoubtedly its fish. It proclaims itself 'Trout Fishing Capital of the World'.

## INFORMATION

The **Turangi i-SITE** ( ☎ 07-386 8999; www. laketauponz.com; Ngawaka Pl; ☺ 8.30am-5pm) is a good stop for information on Tongariro National Park, Kaimanawa Forest Park, trout fishing, and snow and road conditions. The Turangi–Taupo **DOC visitors**

centre ( ☎ 07-386 8607; Turanga Pl; ☺ 8am-4.30pm Mon-Fri) is near the junction of SH41 and Ohuanga Rd.

## SIGHTS & ACTIVITIES
### TOKAANU THERMAL POOLS

The **Tokaanu Thermal Pools** ( ☎ 07-386 8575; Mangaroa St; public pools adult/child $6/4, private pools per 20min $9/5; ☺ 10am-9pm), 5km northwest of Turangi, is an unpretentious facility with hot pools, a trout stream, a picnic area, displays and a shop.

### TRAMPING

There are several short walks around town, most of which are detailed in DOC's *Lake Taupo – A Guide to Walks and Hikes* ($2.50), along with many others around the district.

A favourite is the **Tongariro River Lookout Track** (one hour loop), a riverside amble affording views of Mt Pihanga. This track joins the **Tongariro River Walkway** (three hours return), which follows the east bank of the river to the Red Hut suspension bridge.

There is another nice lake stroll at **Lake Rotopounamu** (Greenstone Lake), 11km southwest of Turangi on SH47. A favourite for walkers, swimmers, twitchers and tree huggers alike, it's a 30-minute walk to the lake from the car park, and two hours around.

### TROUT FISHING

February and March are the best months for brown trout, but rainbow fishing is good year-round on the river. Licences are available from DOC or the i-SITE. If you're not sure where to start, a fishing guide can give you some local know-how, as well as transport, gear, licence and meals by arrangement.

**Brett Cameron** ( ☎ 07-378 8192; www.cpf. net.nz; half-/full day from $280/580) Also offers

View of Turangi and the Tongariro River
DAVID WALL

boat charters (per hour $100, minimum three hours) and quad-bike adventure fishing in National Park township (one/two people $750/850). Licences extra.

**John Sommervell** ( ☎ 07-386 5931; www.nymphfish.com; half-/full day from $250/500)

**Tightline Charters** ( ☎ 07-386 0033; www.tightlinecharters.co.nz; per hr $85)

There are several companies in town that hire and sell gear, and handle bookings for guides and charters.

**Barry Greig's Sporting World** ( ☎ 07-386 6911; www.greigsport.co.nz; 59 Town Centre; ☼ 9am-5pm)

**Creel Tackle House** ( ☎ 07-386 7929; 183 Taupahi Rd; ☼ 8am-5pm Mon-Fri, 7.30am-3.30pm Sat & Sun)

**Sporting Life** ( ☎ 07-386 8996, www.sportinglife-turangi.co.nz; Town Centre; ☼ 8am-5.30pm) Its website details the latest fishing conditions.

## OTHER ACTIVITIES

The Tongariro River has some superb Grade III rapids for river rafting, as well as Grade I stretches suitable for beginners in the lower reaches during summer. **Tongariro River Rafting** ( ☎ 07-386 6409; www.trr.co.nz; Atirau Rd; adult/child $109/99) can start you off with a three-hour trip on Grade II Tongariro rapids or take you on a full day's raft fishing (summer only, price on enquiry).

**Wai Maori** ( ☎ 07-386 0315; www.waimaori.com; 203 Puanga St, Tokaanu) offers guided white-water kayaking (November to April, per person $129) or trips accompanied only by trout down the gentle Tokaanu Stream to Lake Taupo, passing boiling mud, hot pools and wetlands on the way (90 minutes/half-day/full day $30/40/65).

Rapid Sensations in Taupo also runs white-water trips on the Tongariro River (see p172).

## SLEEPING & EATING

**Extreme Backpackers** ( ☎ 07-386 8949; www.extremebackpackers.co.nz; 22 Ngawaka Pl; dm $23-25, s $43-53, d $56-66; ⌨ ⌚ ) Crafted from pine and corrugated iron, this modern backpackers has the bonus of a climbing wall and cafe. Cheaper dorms have eight bunks and skip the carpet, while pricier doubles have en suites, but all rooms are clean and comfy. A lounge with an open fire, a sunny courtyard with hammocks and a barbecue make this a relaxing budget bet.

**Creel Lodge** ( ☎ 07-386 8081; www.creel.co.nz; 183 Taupahi Rd; s $95-130, d $110-150, tr $130-170, q $150-190; ⌚ ⌦ ) Set in green and peaceful grounds, this heavenly hideaway backs onto a fine stretch of the Tongariro River. All the ground-level suites have their own kitchens and a balcony overlooking attractive gardens.

**Anglers Paradise Motel** ( ☎ 07-386 8980; www.anglersparadise.co.nz; cnr Ohuanga Rd & Raukura St; d $115-160, tr $130-160, q $145-160; ⌨ ⌦ ) Looking like something out of Twin Peaks, this place sits in a 1 hectare leafy pocket where privacy prevails. Rooms are trimmed in dark wood and feature big TVs and superking beds.

**Oreti** ( ☎ 07-386 7070; Mission House Dr, Pukawa Bay; mains $29-34; ☼ lunch Thu-Sun, dinner Tue-Sun) It's hard to imagine a more romantic spot to while away a balmy summer's evening than looking over the lake from Oreti's terrace. As you pick your way through a heavily laden antipasti lunch platter you might have to remind yourself that you're not actually on the Mediterranean.

**Tongariro Lodge** ( ☎ 07-386 7946; Grace Rd; mains $35; ☼ dinner) Some of the world's most famous blokes (Robert Mitchum, Liam Neeson, Larry Hagman, Jimmy Carter, Timothy Dalton) have come to this luxury riverside fishing lodge, set in

LOWER NORTH ISLAND

TAUPO & THE CENTRAL PLATEAU

9 hectares of parkland, to relax in wood-panelled anonymity. Not surprisingly, the menu's oriented around man-sized slabs of meat, but the real squeals of delight come when a lucky lodger is presented with their day's catch, smoked and served to perfection.

## GETTING THERE & AWAY

**InterCity/Newmans** ( ☎ 09-583 5780; www.intercity.co.nz) services stop outside the i-SITE. The Auckland–Wellington and Tauranga–Rotorua–Wellington buses that travel along the eastern side of the lake all stop at Turangi (from Taupo $16, 45 minutes).

**Naked Bus** ( ☎ 0900 62533 per min $1.80; www.nakedbus.com; advance fares from $1) uses the same stop for their daily services to Auckland (6½ hours) via Taupo (one hour) and Rotorua (two hours). Going south, buses run to Wellington (5½ hours) via all major stops, including Palmerston North (three hours).

For information about Tongariro shuttle services, see p182.

# TONGARIRO NATIONAL PARK

With its towering active volcanoes, Tongariro is one of NZ's most spectacular parks, perhaps best known for its cameo as Mordor in Peter Jackson's *Lord of the Rings* trilogy. In summer it offers excellent short walks and longer tramps, most notably the Tongariro Northern Circuit and the Tongariro Alpine Crossing. In winter it's a busy ski area.

## INFORMATION

The **DOC visitor centre** ( ☎ 07-892 3729; www.doc.govt.nz; ☯ 8am-6pm Dec-Mar, to 5pm Apr-Nov) is in Whakapapa (pronounced 'fa-ka-pa-pa') Village, on the northwestern side of the park. It has maps and info on all corners of the park, including walks, huts and current skiing, track and weather conditions. When visiting Tongariro National Park, you must be properly equipped and take safety precautions, including leaving your itinerary with a responsible person.

Mt Ruapehu (p180), Tongariro National Park

MAX PAOLI & RUTH EASTHAM

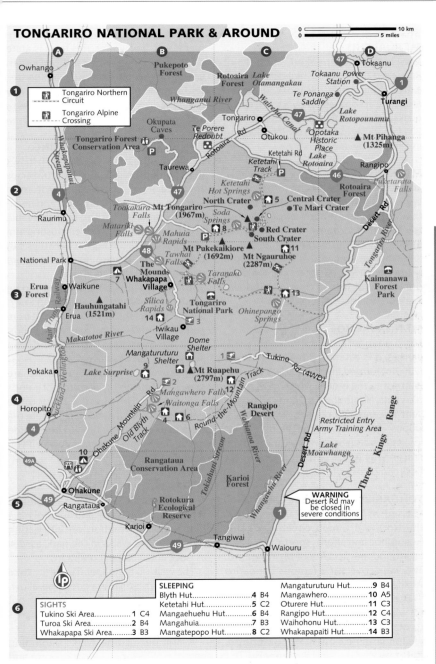

# TONGARIRO NATIONAL PARK & AROUND

## SIGHTS & ACTIVITIES
### MT RUAPEHU
The long, multipeaked summit of Ruapehu (2797m) is the highest and most active of the park's volcanoes. The latest eruption, accompanied by a small earthquake, came out of the blue in September 2007, seriously injuring a climber sleeping in a hut on the mountain.

### MT TONGARIRO
The Red Crater of Mt Tongariro (1968m) last erupted in 1926. This old but still active volcano has a number of coloured lakes dotting its uneven summit as well as hot springs gushing out of its side at Ketetahi. The Tongariro Alpine Crossing, a magnificent walk, passes beside the lakes, right through several craters, and down through lush native forest.

### MT NGAURUHOE
Much younger than the other two volcanoes, it is estimated that Ngauruhoe (2290m) formed in the last 2500 years. In contrast to the others, which have multiple vents, Ngauruhoe is a conical, single-vent volcano with perfectly symmetrical slopes – the only one of the three that looks like a stereotypical volcano and the reason why it was chosen to star as Mt Doom in *Lord of the Rings*.

### TONGARIRO NORTHERN CIRCUIT
Classed as one of NZ's Great Walks, the Northern Circuit circumnavigates Ngauruhoe and affords spectacular views all around, particularly of Mt Tongariro. The walk covers the famous Tongariro Alpine Crossing.

The safest and most popular time to walk the track is from December to March. The track is served by four well-maintained huts: **Mangatepopo**, **Ketetahi**, **Oturere** and **Waihohonu**. The huts have mattresses, gas cookers in summer, toilets and water. This track is quite difficult in winter, when it is covered in snow, and becomes a tough alpine trek requiring ice axes and crampons. You may need to factor in significant extra walking time, or not attempt it at all.

### TONGARIRO ALPINE CROSSING
Reputedly the best one-day walk in NZ, the Tongariro Alpine Crossing traverses spectacular volcanic geography, from an active crater to steaming vents and beautiful coloured lakes. Although achievable in one day, the Crossing is exhausting and shouldn't be taken lightly. Weather can change without warning, so make sure you are adequately equipped.

The Tongariro Alpine Crossing can be reached from Mangatepopo Rd, off SH47, and from Ketetahi Rd, off SH46. Theft from parked vehicles is a problem at both ends: don't leave valuables in the car and keep everything out of sight.

Because of its popularity, there are plenty of shuttle services to both ends of the track. The shuttles need to be booked and you'll need to complete the track in a reasonable time to be assured of your lift home – they won't wait if you dawdle.

### OTHER WALKS
The DOC and i-SITE visitor centres at Whakapapa, Ohakune and Turangi have maps and information on interesting short and long walks in the park, as well as track and weather conditions.

The walk up to Ruapehu's **Crater Lake** (seven hours return) is a good one, allowing you to see the acidic lake up close, but this walk is strictly off limits when there's volcanic activity.

A number of fine walks beginning near the Whakapapa visitor centre and from the road leading up to it are listed in DOC's *Walks in and Around Tongariro National Park* ($3), including the following:

**Ridge Track** A 30-minute return walk that climbs through beech forest to alpine-shrub areas for views of Ruapehu and Ngauruhoe.

**Tama Lakes** A 17km track to the Tama Lakes (five to six hours return), on the Tama Saddle between Ruapehu and Ngauruhoe. The upper lake affords fine views of Ngauruhoe and Tongariro (but beware of winds on the saddle).

**Taranaki Falls** A two-hour, 6km loop track to the 20m Taranaki Falls on Wairere Stream.

## SKIING

Ruapehu's **Whakapapa Ski Area** ( ☎ 07-892 3738; www.mtruapehu.com; lift pass per half-/full day $52/83) and **Turoa Ski Area** ( ☎ 06-385 8456; website & prices as above) offer similar skiing to suit all levels: around 400 hectares of field each, both taking you up to a maximum altitude of around 2300m. You can hire gear in Taupo, National Park, Ohakune, or at Whakapapa's **Edge to Edge** ( ☎ 0800 800 754; www.edgetoedge.co.nz; Skotel Alpine Resort; 1-day full ski gear $35-43, 1-day snowboard gear $43-50), which also stocks a full range of climbing and alpine gear.

The **Tukino Ski Area**, on the eastern side of Ruapehu, is only accessible by a 4WD road.

## SLEEPING

**Skotel Alpine Resort** ( ☎ 07-892 3719; www.skotel.co.nz; Whakapapa Village; s/d/tr/cabin $40/55/80/160, r $135-215; 🖥 🛜 ) NZ's highest hotel offers three-bed backpacker rooms, cabins and regular hotel rooms. With timbered decor, the complex has an alpine feel; it also has a few luxuries, including sauna, spa pool, gym, ski shop, games room, licensed restaurant (dinner

DAVID WALL

Mt Ruapehu

only, mains from $19 to $29) and, most importantly, bar.

**Fergusson Villas** ( ☎ 07-892 3809; www.chateau.co.nz; Whakapapa Village; d/q $155/175) These small, self-contained chalets are good for families or small groups, with kitchens and diminutive decks for relaxing on. Booking and check-in is through the Bayview Chateau Tongariro.

**Bayview Chateau Tongariro** ( ☎ 07-892 3809; www.chateau.co.nz; Whakapapa Village; d $190-280, ste $350-1000; 🖥 🛜 ) The landmark of the village, the 106-room Chateau harks back to a refined era, with classic European mansion-house grandeur. Opened in 1929, its refurbishments have seen it retain an old-world charm and dramatic snooker-room styling.

## GETTING THERE & AROUND

There are numerous shuttle services to Whakapapa Village, the Tongariro Alpine Crossing and other key destinations from Taupo, Turangi, National Park and Ohakune. Book your bus in advance to avoid unexpected strandings.

**Extreme Backpackers** (p177) Provides shuttles from Turangi to the Crossing ($35) and Northern Circuit ($40) and, in winter, Whakapapa Ski Area ($40).

**Mountain Shuttle** (☎ 0800 117 686; mountainman989@hotmail.com) Runs between Turangi and Whakapapa/Tongariro Alpine Crossing daily ($35).

**Tongariro Expeditions** (☎ 0800 828 763; www.tongariroexpeditions.com) Runs shuttles from Turangi ($35, 40 mins), Taupo ($55, 1¼ hours), National Park village ($35, 30 minutes) and Whakapapa ($35, 15 mins) for the Crossing and the Northern Circuit.

# TARANAKI

## GETTING THERE & AROUND

Air New Zealand has domestic flights and onward connections to/from New Plymouth. InterCity and Naked Bus run several bus services connecting to New Plymouth; Dalroy Express and White Star are smaller companies on local routes.

## NEW PLYMOUTH

pop 45,230

The city has a thriving arts scene and an outdoorsy focus, with good beaches both in and around it. Egmont National Park is just a short drive away.

For tourist information, head to **New Plymouth i-SITE** (☎ 0800 639 759, 06-759 6060; www.newplymouthnz.com; 1 Ariki St; ☉ 9am-6pm Mon, Tue, Thu & Fri, to 9pm Wed, to 5pm Sat & Sun; 🖳) in the Puke Ariki building. It also has internet.

### SIGHTS

Translating as 'Hill of Chiefs', **Puke Ariki** (☎ 06-759 6060; www.pukeariki.com; 1 Ariki St; admission free; ☉ 9am-6pm Mon & Tue, Thu & Fri, 9am-9pm Wed, 9am-5pm Sat & Sun) is home to the i-SITE, a museum, library, a cafe and the fabulous Arborio restaurant (p184). The excellent **museum** has an extensive collection of Maori artefacts, plus wildlife and colonial exhibits.

The **Govett-Brewster Art Gallery** (☎ 06-759 6060; www.govettbrewster.com; 42 Queen St; admission free; ☉ 10am-5pm) is arguably the country's best regional art gallery and the crowd-pulling jewel in the town's crown. Presenting contemporary – often experimental – local and international shows, it's most famous for its connec-

Clock tower, New Plymouth
OLIVER STREWE

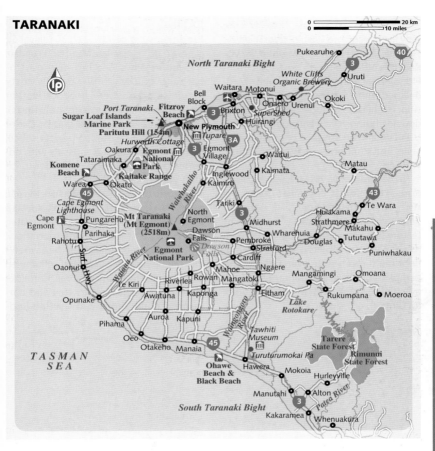

# TARANAKI

*North Taranaki Bight*

tion with NZ sculptor, film-maker and artist Len Lye (1901–1980).

## ACTIVITIES

The black, volcanic-sand beaches of Taranaki are world renowned for surfing and windsurfing. Close to the eastern edge of town are **Fitzroy Beach** (see Map p183) and **East End Beach** (allegedly the cleanest beach in Oceania). There's also decent surf at **Back Beach**, near Paritutu, at the western end of the city. **Beach Street Surf Shop** ( ☎ 06-758 0400; www. taranakisurf.com; 39 Beach St, Fitzroy; 2hr lesson

$75; 🕙 9am-6pm) offers lessons, gear hire and tours.

## SLEEPING

**Seaspray House** ( ☎ 06-759 8934; www. seasprayhouse.co.nz; 13 Weymouth St; dm/s/d $29/45/70; 🖳 ) A big old house with gloriously high ceilings, Seaspray has had a recent makeover inside but remains relaxed and affordable, with well-chosen retro and antique furniture. Fresh and arty, it's a rare bunk-free backpackers (just 14 beds!). Closed June and July.

**Fitzroy Beach Motel** ( ☎ 06-757 2925; www.fitzroybeachmotel.co.nz; 25 Beach St; s/d/2br $120/130/165; ☐ ) Brand-new when we visited, this old-time motel (just 160m from Fitzroy Beach) has been thoroughly redeemed with a major overhaul and extension. Highlights include quality carpets, double glazing, lovely bathrooms, 32 inch LCD TVs, and an absence of poky studio-style units (all one- or two-bedroom). Winner!

**Nice Hotel** ( ☎ 06-758 6423; www.nicehotel. co.nz; 71 Brougham St; d/ste from $230/290; ☐ ) High-class from top to tail, 'nice' is the understatement of the decade. Seven rooms feature luxury furnishings, designer bathrooms and select objets d'art: the ground-floor multi-room suite even has a grand piano! The in-house restaurant, Table, is one for the gourmands (mains $35; open for dinner).

## EATING

**Frederic's** ( ☎ 06-759 1227; 34 Egmont St; plates $7-18; ☺ 2pm-late Mon-Thu, 11am-late Fri-Sun) Freddy's is a fab new gastro-bar with quirky interior design (rusty medieval chandeliers, peacock-feather wallpaper, religious icon paintings), serving generous share-plates. Order some meatballs with bell-pepper sauce, or some green-lipped mussels with coconut cream, chilli and coriander to go with your beer.

**Arborio** ( ☎ 06-759 1241; Puke Ariki, 1 Ariki St; brunch $11-13, dinner $16-32; ☺ breakfast, lunch & dinner) Despite looking like a cheese grater, Arborio is the star of the local food show. It's airy, arty and modern, with sea views and faultless service. The Med-influenced menu ranges from an awesome Moroccan lamb pizza to pastas, risottos and barbecued chilli squid with lychee-and-

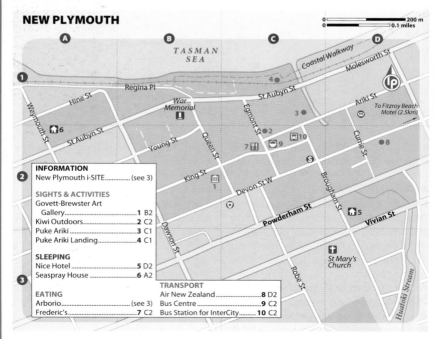

**NEW PLYMOUTH**

0 ——— 200 m
0 ——— 0.1 miles

cucumber noodle salad. Cocktails and NZ wines also available.

## GETTING THERE & AWAY

### AIR

**Air New Zealand** (☎ 0800 737 000, 06-757 3300; www.airnz.co.nz; 12 Devon St E; ☺ 9am-5pm Mon-Wed & Fri, 9.30am-5pm Thu) has daily direct flights to/from Auckland (45 minutes, four daily), Wellington (50 minutes, four daily) and Christchurch (1½ hours, one daily), with onward connections.

**New Plymouth Airport** (☎ 06-755 2250) is 11km east of the centre off SH3. **Scott's Airport Shuttle** (☎ 0800 373 001, 06-769 5974; www.npairportshuttle.co.nz; adult from $22) operates a door-to-door shuttle to/from the airport – you can book online.

### BUS

The **bus centre** is on the corner of Egmont and Ariki Sts.

**InterCity** (☎ 09-583 5780; www.intercity. co.nz) services numerous destinations including the following:

| TO | PRICE | HOW LONG | HOW OFTEN |
|---|---|---|---|
| Auckland | $52 | 6¼hr | 4 daily |
| Hamilton | $45 | 4hr | 2 daily |
| Wellington | $39 | 7hr | 1 daily |

**Naked Bus** (☎ 0900 62533; www.nakedbus. com) services run to the following destinations (among many others). Book in advance for big savings.

| TO | PRICE | HOW LONG | HOW OFTEN |
|---|---|---|---|
| Auckland | $29 | 6¼hr | 1 daily |
| Hamilton | $26 | 3½hr | 1 daily |
| Wellington | $29 | 6hr | 1 daily |

## MT TARANAKI (EGMONT NATIONAL PARK)

A classic 2518m volcanic cone dominating the landscape, Mt Taranaki is a magnet to all who catch its eye. With the last eruption more than 350 years ago (you can see lava flows covering the top 1400m), experts say that the mountain is overdue for another go.

## INFORMATION

**Dawson Falls visitor centre** (☎ 027 443 0248; www.doc.govt.nz; Manaia Rd, Kaponga; ☺ 9am-4pm Thu-Sun Mar-Nov, 9am-4pm daily Dec-Feb) On the southeastern side of the mountain, fronted by an awesome totem pole.

**North Egmont visitor centre** (☎ 06-756 0990; North Egmont; www.doc.govt.nz; ☺ 8am-4.30pm) Current and comprehensive national park info, plus a greasy-spoon cafe (meals from $11 to $19).

HOLGER LEUE

Grazing cattle near Mt Taranaki

## ACTIVITIES

### SCENIC FLIGHTS

To get up above the slopes, try the following operators:

**Beck Helicopters** ( ☎ 0800 336 644, 06-764 7073; www.heli.co.nz) Scenic mountain flights from $225.

**Heliview** ( ☎ 0508 435 484, 06-753 0123; www.heliview.co.nz) Offers a range of sightseeing tours; a 30-minute city-and-mountain flight costs $280.

**New Plymouth Aero Club** ( ☎ 06-755 0500; www.airnewplymouth.co.nz) Standard and customised scenic flights from $66.

### TRAMPING

Due to its accessibility, Mt Taranaki ranks as the 'most climbed' mountain in NZ. Nevertheless, tramping on this mountain is dangerous and should not be undertaken lightly. It's *crucial* to get advice before departing and leave your intentions with a DOC visitor centre or i-SITE.

From North Egmont, the main walk is the scenic **Pouakai Circuit**, a two-day 23km loop through alpine, swamp and tussock areas with awesome mountain views. Short, easy walks from here include the **Ngatoro Loop Track** (one hour), **Veronica Loop** (two hours) and **Connett Loop** (40 minutes return). East Egmont has disabled access on **Potaema Track** (30 minutes return) and **East Egmont Lookout** (30 minutes return); a longer walk is the steep **Enchanted Track** (two to three hours return).

At Dawson Falls you can do several short walks including **Wilkies Pools Loop** (one hour return) or the excellent but challenging **Fanthams Peak Return** (five hours return), which is snowed-in during winter. The **Kapuni Loop Track** (1½ hours) runs to the impressive **Dawson Falls** themselves.

It costs around $300 per day to hire a guide. Some reliable operators:

**Adventure Dynamics** ( ☎ 0800 151 589, 06-751 3589; www.adventuredynamics.co.nz)

**MacAlpine Guides** ( ☎ 06-765 6234, 027 441 7042; www.macalpineguides.com)

**Top Guides** ( ☎ 0800 448 433, 021 838 513; www.topguides.co.nz)

Mt Taranaki viewed from New Plymouth's marina

DAVID WALL

## SLEEPING

**Camphouse** ( ☎ 0800 688 272, 06-756 9093; www.mttaranaki.co.nz/retreat/camphouse; North Egmont; dm/d/f $30/70/160) Bunkhouse-style accommodation behind the North Egmont visitor centre in a historic 1850 corrugated-iron building, complete with bullet holes in the walls (from shots fired at settlers by local Maori during the Taranaki Land Wars). Endless horizon views from the porch.

**Anderson's Alpine lodge** ( ☎ 06-765 6620; www.andersonsalpinelodge.co.nz; 922 Pembroke Rd; d incl breakfast $160-190; 🛜 ) With picture-postcard mountain views, this lovely Swiss-owned lodge is on the Stratford side of the mountain. Inside are three en suite rooms with lots of timberwork; outside are billions of birds and Lady Hookswood-Smith, a rather obstreperous pig.

**Mountain House** ( ☎ 06-765 6100; www.mountainhouse.co.nz; Pembroke Rd; s/d $170/195) This lodge, on the Stratford side of the mountain (15km from the SH3 turn-off and 3km to the Manganui ski area), has recently renovated motel-style rooms and chalets with kitchens.

## GETTING THERE & AWAY

There are three main entrance roads to Egmont National Park, all of which are well signposted and either pass by or end at a DOC visitor centre. Closest to New Plymouth is North Egmont: turn off SH3 at Egmont Village, 12km south of New Plymouth, and follow the road for 14km. From Stratford, turn off at Pembroke Rd and continue for 15km to East Egmont and the Manganui ski area. From the southeast, Upper Manaia Rd leads up to Dawson Falls, 23km from Stratford.

There are no public buses to the national park but numerous shuttle-bus operators will take you there (one-way from $30 to $40; return from $45 to $50): **Cruise NZ Tours** ( ☎ 0800 688 687; kirkstall@xtra.co.nz) Departs New Plymouth 7.30am for North Egmont; returns 4.30pm. Other pick-ups/drop-offs by arrangement.

**Kiwi Outdoors** (Map p184; ☎ 06-758 4152; www.kiwioutdoorsstores.co.nz; 18 Ariki St, New Plymouth; 🕘 8.30am-5pm Mon-Fri, 9am-2.30pm Sat, 10am-2pm Sun) Pick-up points and times to suit; gear hire available.

# SURF HIGHWAY 45

Sweeping south from New Plymouth to Hawera, the 105km-long SH45 is known as Surf Highway 45, and although it does indeed have many good beaches dotted along it, don't expect to see waves crashing ashore the whole way.

## OAKURA

pop 1220

From New Plymouth, first cab off the rank is laid-back Oakura, 15km southwest on SH45. Its broad sweep of beach is hailed by wax heads for its right-hander breaks, but it's also great for families (take sandals – that black sand scorches feet). A surf shop on the main road, **Vertigo** ( ☎ 06-752 7363; vertigosurf@xtra.co.nz; 2hr lessons $75; 🕘 9am-5pm Mon-Fri, 10am-4pm Sat) runs surf lessons.

**Oakura Beach Motel** ( ☎ 06-752 7680; www.oakurabeachmotel.co.nz; 53 Wairau Rd; s/d from $90/100; 🛜 ), a very quiet, seven-unit motel set back from the main road, is just three minutes' walk to the beach. It's a '70s number, but the owners keep things shipshape, and there are 300 DVDs to choose from!

**Ahu Ahu Beach Villas** ( ☎ 06-752 7370; www.ahu.co.nz; 321 Ahu Ahu Rd; s/d/f from $250/250/350; 🖵 ) is pricey, but pretty amazing. Set on a knoll overlooking the big wide ocean, these luxury, architect-designed villas are superbly eccentric, with huge recycled timbers, bottles cast into walls, lichen-covered roofs and polished-concrete floors with inlaid paua. Even rock stars stay here.

## OAKURA TO OPUNAKE

Just after Warea is **Stent Road**, a legendary shallow reef break, suitable for experienced surfers. Newbies will prefer the gentler waves of **Komene Beach**, which at the mouth of Stony River attracts its fair share of interesting bird life, including black swans.

## OPUNAKE

pop 1500

A summer town and the surfie epicentre of the 'Naki, Opunake has a sheltered family beach and plenty of challenging waves further out.

The **Opunake i-SITE** (☎ 0800 111 323, 06-761 8663; opunakeI@stdc.govt.nz; Tasman St; 🕙 9am-5pm Mon-Fri, 9.30am-1pm Sat; 💻 🛜 ) is in the local library and has free internet.

**Dreamtime Surf Shop** ( ☎ 06-761 7570; 102 Tasman St; 🕙 9am-5pm) has internet access and surf-gear hire (surfboards/body-boards/wetsuits per half-day $30/20/10).

**Opunake Motel & Backpackers** ( ☎ 06-761 8330; www.opunakemotel.co.nz; 36 Heaphy Rd; dm $25, cottage & units d $85-100) offers a range of options from old-style motels to a funky dorm lodge on the edge of some sleepy fields (a triumph in genuine retro).

**Sugar Juice Café** ( ☎ 06-761 7062; 42 Tasman St; snacks $4-10, mains $25-29; 🕙 9am-4pm Tue & Sun, to 10pm Wed-Sat) has the best food on SH45. It is buzzy and brimming with delicious, filling things (try the basil-crusted snapper or cranberry lamb shanks). Terrific coffee, salads, wraps, tarts, cakes and big brekkies too – don't pass it by.

# THE EAST COAST & HAWKE'S BAY

Hawke Bay, the name given to the body of water that stretches from the sunburnt Mahia Peninsula to Cape Kidnappers, looks like it's been bitten out of the North

Valley outlook, Te Mata Peak (p196)

DAVID WAL

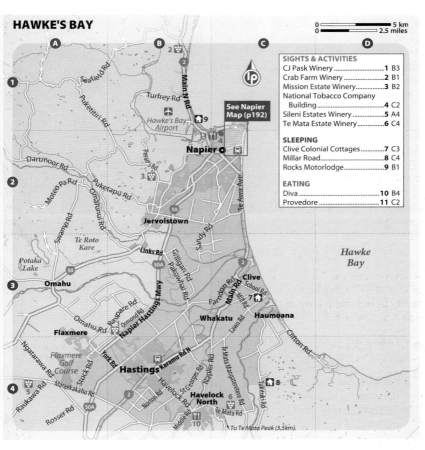

## HAWKE'S BAY

| SIGHTS & ACTIVITIES | |
|---|---|
| CJ Pask Winery | **1** B3 |
| Crab Farm Winery | **2** B1 |
| Mission Estate Winery | **3** B2 |
| National Tobacco Company Building | **4** C2 |
| Sileni Estates Winery | **5** A4 |
| Te Mata Estate Winery | **6** C4 |
| **SLEEPING** | |
| Clive Colonial Cottages | **7** C3 |
| Millar Road | **8** C4 |
| Rocks Motorlodge | **9** B1 |
| **EATING** | |
| Diva | **10** B4 |
| Provedore | **11** C2 |

LOWER NORTH ISLAND

THE EAST COAST & HAWKE'S BAY

Island's eastern flank. Add an apostrophe and an 's' and you've got a region that stretches south and inland to include fertile farmland, surf beaches, mountainous ranges and wild forests.

### GETTING THERE & AROUND

The region's only airports are in Gisborne and Napier. Air New Zealand flies to both from Auckland and Wellington, and also to Napier from Christchurch. Sunair Aviation connects Gisborne and Napier to Hamilton, Palmerston North, Rotorua, Tauranga and Whakatane.

Regular buses ply SH2 and SH5, connecting Gisborne, Wairoa, Napier, Hastings and Waipukurau with the main centres.

## MAHIA PENINSULA

The Mahia Peninsula's eroded hills, sandy beaches and vivid blue sea make it a mini-ringer of the Coromandel, but without the flash tourists and fancy subdivisions, and with the bonus of dramatic Dover-ish cliffs. Mahia has several small settlements, a scenic reserve, and the bird-filled Maungawhio Lagoon, all of which you'll need your own transport to explore.

LOWER NORTH ISLAND

THE EAST COAST & HAWKE'S BAY

ROB BLAKERS

Grapes ready for harvest

## ⤳ HAWKE'S BAY WINERIES

Once upon a time this district was most famous for its orchards. Today its vines have top billing, with Hawke's Bay now New Zealand's second-largest wine producing region.

- **C J Pask** One of the original Hawke's Bay wineries, dedicated to producing great reds.
- **Crab Farm** Decent, reasonably priced wines and a great cafe.
- **Mission Estate** NZ's oldest winery with beautiful grounds, and restaurant housed within a restored, historic seminary.
- **Sileni Estates** Looks like it's been beamed in from space. Tasting room and gourmet food store.
- **Te Mata Estate** Producer of the legendary Coleraine red and Elston chardonnay.

**Things you need to know: C J Pask** (Map p189; ☎ 06-879 7906; www.cjpaskwinery.co.nz; 1133 Omahu Rd; ⏰ 10am-5pm Mon-Sat, 11am-4pm Sun); **Crab Farm** (Map p189; ☎ 06-836 6678; www.crabfarmwinery.co.nz; 511 Main Rd, Bay View; ⏰ 10am-5pm Thu-Mon); **Mission Estate** (Map p189; ☎ 06-845 9350; www.missionestate.co.nz; 198 Church Rd, Napier; ⏰ 9am-5pm Mon-Sat, 10am-4.30pm Sun); **Sileni Estates** (Map p189; ☎ 06-879 8768; www.sileni.co.nz; 2016 Maraekakaho Rd; ⏰ 10am-5pm); **Te Mata Estate** (Map p189; ☎ 06-877 4399; www.temata. co.nz; 349 Te Mata Rd; ⏰ 9am-5pm Mon-Fri, 10am-5pm Sat, 11am-4pm Sun)

## TE UREWERA NATIONAL PARK

Shrouded in mist and mysticism, Te Urewera National Park is the North Island's largest, encompassing 212,673 hectares of virgin forest cut with lakes and rivers. The highlight is Lake Waikaremoana (Sea of Rippling Waters), a deep crucible of water encircled by the Lake Waikaremoana Track, one of NZ's Great Walks (see p325).

**Te Urewera National Park visitor centre** ( ☎ 06-837 3803; www.doc.govt.nz; SH38; ⏰ 8am-4.45pm) at Aniwaniwa is currently limited to one small room in a mouldering building (the future of which was un-decided at the time of research).

## ACTIVITIES

### LAKE WAIKAREMOANA TRACK

The 46km track scales the spectacular Panekiri Bluff, boasting open panoramas interspersed with fern groves and forest. During summer it can get busy, so it pays to book ahead.

There are five huts and campsites spaced along the track, all of which must be pre-booked through DOC as far ahead as possible, regardless of the season. Book at the Aniwaniwa, Gisborne, Wairoa, Whakatane or Napier DOC offices, i-SITEs or online at www.doc.govt.nz.

### OTHER WALKS

There are dozens of walks within the park's vast boundaries, some of which are outlined in DOC's *Lake Waikaremoana Walks* and *Recreation in Northern Te Urewera* pamphlets ($2.50).

Shorter walks and day walks include the **Old Maori Trail** (four hours return) from Rosie Bay to Lake Kaitawa; the **Lake Waikareiti Track** (two hours return; four hours to Sandy Bay Hut one-way) through beech and rimu forest; and the **Lake Ruapani Track** (six hours), including wetland wanderings.

### GETTING THERE & AROUND

Approximately 95km of SH38 between Wairoa and Rotorua remains unsealed and it will take around four bone-rattling hours to do the entire journey (Wairoa to Aniwaniwa 61km; Aniwaniwa to Rotorua 139km).

## NAPIER

pop 55,000

You don't have to be particularly cultured to enjoy Napier but you might find its pas-sion for architecture and fine wine surpris-ingly contagious. The Napier of today is the silver lining of the dark cloud that was NZ's worst natural disaster. Rebuilt after the deadly 1931 earthquake in the popular styles of the time, the city re-tains a unique concentration of art-deco buildings.

**Napier i-SITE** ( ☎ 06-834 1911; www.visit us.co.nz; 100 Marine Pde; ☽ 9am-5pm; ▣ ) has tourist information.

## SIGHTS

### ARCHITECTURE

The 1931 quake demolished most of Napier's brick buildings. Frantic recon-struction between 1931 and 1933 caught architects in the throes of global art-deco mania. A cohesive architectural vision grew from the ruins, giving Napier a new raison d'être.

On the south side of town, on Dickens St, you'll find the deluxe Moorish-Spanish spirals and stucco of the former **Gaiety de Luxe Cinema** and fine sunburst window decorations of the old **State Cinema** – a fine mix of Spanish and art deco.

On Dalton St admire the flamingo hues of the **Hotel Central**, all zigzag swagger and lead-light complexity – it's now a strip club and massage parlour.

At the end of Dalton St is Tennyson St and many striking architectural gems. Two great examples of the Stripped Classical style are the **Scinde Building** with its Mayan botanical flourishes and the **Napier Antique Centre** adorned with *koru* (spiral shape emulating an unfurling fern) patterns – one of only four period buildings in the city to use Maori motifs.

Further along Tennyson is the beau-tifully proportioned **Daily Telegraph Building,** one of Napier's stars, with its superb zigzags, fountain shapes and cen-tral ziggurat aesthetic. If the building is

# NAPIER

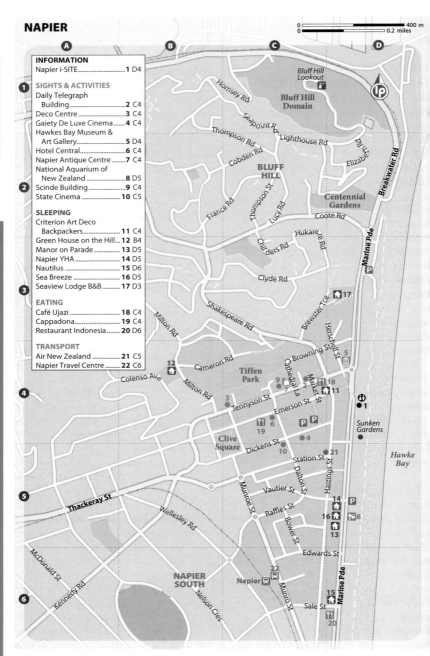

INFORMATION
Napier i-SITE..........................1 D4

SIGHTS & ACTIVITIES
Daily Telegraph
  Building..............................2 C4
Deco Centre...........................3 C4
Gaiety De Luxe Cinema.......4 C4
Hawkes Bay Museum &
  Art Gallery.........................5 D4
Hotel Central.........................6 C4
Napier Antique Centre........7 C4
National Aquarium of
  New Zealand.......................8 D5
Scinde Building.....................9 C4
State Cinema........................10 C5

SLEEPING
Criterion Art Deco
  Backpackers.....................11 C4
Green House on the Hill....12 B4
Manor on Parade.................13 D5
Napier YHA..........................14 D5
Nautilus...............................15 D6
Sea Breeze...........................16 D5
Seaview Lodge B&B...........17 D3

EATING
Café Ujazi.............................18 C4
Cappadona...........................19 C4
Restaurant Indonesia........20 D6

TRANSPORT
Air New Zealand.................21 C5
Napier Travel Centre.........22 C6

open, nip inside and ogle at the painstakingly restored foyer.

The **National Tobacco Company Building** (Map 074; cnr Bridge & Ossian Sts; ☺ 9am-5pm Mon-Fri) is arguably the region's deco masterpiece and is located a short ride from the city centre in Ahuriri.

## MARINE PARADE

Marine Pde is an elegant tree-lined avenue dotted with motels and restored timber earthquake survivors. Along its length are parks, sunken gardens, a minigolf course, a swimming complex, aquarium and museum.

The **Hawke's Bay Museum & Art Gallery** ( ☎ 06-835 7781; www.hbmag.co.nz; 9 Herschell St; adult/child/family $10/5/20; ☺ 10am-6pm) is a repository for a wide range of interesting collections and showcases these in permanent displays of Maori artefacts and a fascinating 1931 earthquake memorial gallery (do watch the deeply moving film).

The **National Aquarium of New Zealand** ( ☎ 06-834 1404; www.national aquarium.co.nz; 546 Marine Pde; adult/child $16/8; ☺ 9am-5pm, feedings 10am & 2pm) is a modern complex with a stingray-inspired roof. Inside you'll find a crocodile, piranhas, turtles, eels, kiwis, tuatara and a whole lotta fish.

## TOURS

Napier's Art Deco Trust promotes and protects the city's architectural heritage. Its one-hour guided deco walk ($14) departs the i-SITE daily at 10am; the two-hour version ($20) leaves the **Deco Centre** ( ☎ 06-835 0022; www.artdeconapier. com; 163 Tennyson St; ☺ 9am-5pm) at 2pm daily. The Deco Centre stocks assorted paraphernalia, including brochures for the excellent self-guided *Art Deco Walk* ($5), *Art Deco Scenic Drive* ($5) and

LOWER NORTH ISLAND

THE EAST COAST & HAWKE'S BAY

JOHN ELK III
Art-deco detail, Napier

*Marewa Meander* ($3). Marewa is a suburb southwest of Napier's city centre, and deco through-and-through.

Numerous operators offer tours of the deco delights and excursions around the local area:

**Absolute de Tours** ( ☎ 06-844 8699; www. absolutedetours.co.nz) runs 'The Deco Tour' of the city, Marewa and Bluff Hill ($38, 75 min) in conjunction with the Deco Centre, as well as half-day tours of Napier and Hastings ($60).

**Deco Affair Tours** ( ☎ 06-835 4492; www. decoaffair.com; tours $20-90) trips the light fantastic in a cherry-red 1934 Buick hosted by the endearingly eccentric Bertie, clad in full period regalia.

For listings of Hawke's Bay winery tours, see p190.

## SLEEPING

**Criterion Art Deco Backpackers** ( ☎ 06-835 2059; www.criterionartdeco.co.nz; 48 Emerson St; incl breakfast dm $20, s $40-75, d $55-80, tr/q $78/87; 🖳 🛜 ) If it is interesting architecture and a central location that you're after, here you have it. The vast communal area showcases the impressive internal features of what is Napier's best Spanish Mission specimen. There is a free continental breakfast and special deals for guests in the restaurant-bar downstairs.

**Napier YHA** ( ☎ 06-835 7039; www.yha. co.nz; 277 Marine Pde; dm $29-33, s/d $40/68; 🖳 🛜 ) Napier's friendly YHA is housed in a beachfront earthquake-survivor with a seemingly endless ramble of rooms; try to book one back from the street. There's a fabulous overhanging reading nook and a sunny rear courtyard.

**Sea Breeze** ( ☎ 06-835 8067; seabreeze. napier@xtra.co.nz; 281 Marine Pde; s $95, d $110-130) Inside this Victorian seafront villa are three coloured themed rooms (Chinese, Indian and Turkish), decorated with a cornucopia of artefacts and exotic flair.

**Green House on the Hill** ( ☎ 06-835 4475; www.the-green-house.co.nz; 18b Milton Oaks, Milton Rd; s/d $110/135; 🖳 🛜 ) This meat-free B&B is up a steep hill and rewards with leafy surrounds and city views. Delicious home-baked goodies and fine herbal teas are most likely to make an appearance.

**Rocks Motorlodge** (Map p189; ☎ 06-835 9626; www.therocksmotel.co.nz; 27 Meeanee Quay, Westshore; unit $110-180; 🖳 🛜 ) Located just 80m from the beach, the Rocks has corrugated stylings and woodcarving that have raised the bar on Westshore's motel row. Interiors are plush with a colour-splash, and some have a spa bath, others a claw-foot. Free internet, free gym, and laundry.

**Seaview Lodge B&B** ( ☎ 06-835 0202; cvulodge@xtra.co.nz; 5 Seaview Tce; s $120-130, d $150-170) This grand Victorian villa (1890) is queen of all she surveys – which is most of the town and a fair bit of ocean. The elegant rooms have tasteful period elements and either private bathrooms or en suites. It's hard to resist a sunset tipple on

Tramping Te Urewera National Park (p190)

OLIVER STREWE

the veranda, which opens off the swanky guest lounge.

**Manor On Parade** ( ☎ 06-834 3885; manor onparade@xtra.co.nz; 283 Marine Pde; d $140-180) Comfortable and friendly, this two-storey wooden villa on the waterfront has proved itself a solid option, both for having survived the earthquake and for its latter day incarnation as a B&B.

**Nautilus** ( ☎ 06-974 6550; www.nautilus napier.co.nz; 387 Marine Pde; studio/ste $175-300; 🖳 🛜 ) Napier's newest hotel, and a relatively good bit of architecture it is, too. Views from every room, decor with spunk, spa baths, private balconies and an in-house restaurant.

## EATING

**Cappadona** ( ☎ 06-835 3368; 189 Emerson St; snacks $2-9, mains $9-16; 🕘 7am-5pm) In a town of good cafes, this is a stand-out, both for its modern, upbeat ambience, and a packed cabinet of downright foxy food. Besides an alluring row of biscuit jars, iced muffins and cakes, there are fresh sandwiches, salads and pastries. The hot menu features brunchy, lunchy dishes.

**Café Ujazi** ( ☎ 06-835 1490; 28 Tennyson St; snacks $4-9, meals $10-19; 🕘 8am-5pm; Ⓥ ) Ujazi folds back its windows and lets the alternative vibe spill out onto the street. The superb coffee, substantial breakfasts and sparkly staff are a great hangover remedy. Try the *rewana* special – a big breakfast on traditional Maori bread.

**Provedore** (Map p189; ☎ 06-834 0189; 60 West Quay; tapas $6-15, mains $27-35; 🕘 5pm-late Tue-Fri, 10am-late Sat & Sun) A chic little number, from the deco facade inwards. Partake in some of the best food in Napier, from generous tapas, to mains, dessert and cheese. With a clutch of good NZ beers and fine wines, Provedore lures the sophisticated barfly, too.

**Restaurant Indonesia** ( ☎ 06-835 8303; 409 Marine Pde; mains $25-29; 🕘 dinner Wed-Sun; Ⓥ ) Crammed with Indonesian curios, this intimate space oozes authenticity. Lip-smacking Indo-Dutch *rijsttafel* smorgasbords are the house speciality (14 dishes, $35).

## GETTING THERE & AWAY
### AIR
**Hawke's Bay Airport** ( ☎ 06-835 3427; www.hawkesbay-airport.co.nz) is 8km north of the city.

**Air New Zealand** ( ☎ 06-833 5400; www.airnewzealand.co.nz; cnr Hastings & Station Sts) Daily direct flights to Auckland (55 minutes), Wellington (50 minutes) and Christchurch (1 hour 40 minutes); check website for prices and discount fares.

### BUS
**InterCity** (www.intercity.co.nz) operates from the **Napier Travel Centre** ( ☎ 06-834 2720; Munroe St; 🕘 8am-5pm Mon-Fri, 8-11.30am & 12.30-1.30pm Sat & Sun). Buses depart daily for Auckland ($89, seven hours) via Taupo ($35, two hours), Gisborne ($44, four hours) via Wairoa ($31, 2½ hours), and Wellington ($37, 5½ hours) via Hastings ($16 to $20, 25 minutes) and Waipukurau ($12 to $27, one hour).

If you're super-organised you can take advantage of $1 advance fares on **Naked Bus** (www.nakedbus.com) on the Auckland/Wellington route via Hastings and Taupo.

**Bay Xpress** ( ☎ 0800 422 997; www.bayxpress.co.nz) has a daily service to/from Wellington ($40, five hours) via Waipukurau ($10, one hour).

# HASTINGS & AROUND
pop 67,440

Positioned at the centre of the Hawke's Bay fruit bowl, Hastings is the commercial hub of the region, 20km south of Napier.

Similarly devastated by the 1931 earthquake, its fine collation of art deco and Spanish Mission buildings also emerged in the aftermath. It's in the surrounding district that epicurean dreams come true.

A few kilometres of orchards still separate Havelock North from Hastings, although these days it's effectively Hastings' ritziest suburb.

**Hastings i-SITE** (☎ 06-873 0080; www.hastings.co.nz; cnr Russell St & Heretaunga St E; ☽ 8.30am-5pm Mon-Fri, 9am-4pm Sat, 9am-3pm Sun) has internet access, free maps, trail brochures and bookings.

## SIGHTS & ACTIVITIES
### ARCHITECTURE
While art deco abounds, Spanish Mission has the upper hand here. Cream of the crop is the **Hawke's Bay Opera House**

Cliffs near Cape Kidnappers

( ☎ 06-873 8962; www.hawkesbayoperahouse.co.nz; Hastings St S, Hastings).

A close second in the glamorous edifice stakes is the **Westerman's Building** (cnr Russell & Heretaunga St E, Hastings). The **Spanish Mission Hastings walking tour** ( ☎ 0800 427 846; $10; ☽ 11am-12.15pm Sat) starts here; book at the i-SITE.

### TE MATA PEAK
Spiking melodramatically from the Heretaunga Plains, **Te Mata Peak**, 16km south of Havelock North, is part of the 98-hectare Te Mata Trust Park. The road to the 399m summit passes sheep trails, rickety fences and vertigo-inducing stone escarpments cowled in a bleak, lunar-meets-Scottish-Highland atmosphere.

### WINE TOURS
Tours are usually by minibus, lasting around four hours and start at $55 per person, with four or five wineries on the agenda.
**Friendly Kiwi Tours** ( ☎ 021 229 6223; www.friendlykiwi.co.nz)
**Grape Escape** ( ☎ 0800 100 489; www.grapeescape.net.nz)
**Odyssey NZ** ( ☎ 0508 639 773; www.odysseynz.com)

### BIKE TOURS
Costing between $35 and $50 for a full day, a self-guided bicycle tour will temper your viticulture with a little exercise.
**Bike About Tours** ( ☎ 06-845 4836; www.bikeabouttours.co.nz)
**Bike D'Vine** ( ☎ 06-833 6697; www.bikedevine.com)
**On Yer Bike** ( ☎ 06-879 8735; www.onyerbikehb.co.nz)

## SLEEPING & EATING
**Hastings Top 10 Holiday Park** ( ☎ 06-878 6692; www.hastingstop10.co.nz; 610 Windsor Ave

JOHN ELK III

DAVID WALL

Te Mata Peak

## ↘ IF YOU LIKE...

If you like **Te Mata Peak** (left), we think you'll like these other windswept lost-worlds around the Lower North Island:

- **Cape Palliser** On the Wairarapa's south coast are seal colonies, wild surf, black-sand beaches, an isolated lighthouse and rusty bulldozers on the beach: post-apocalyptic stuff!
- **Castlepoint** On the coast 68km east of Masterton in the Wairarapa is this awesome, end-of-the-world place, with a surf-battered reef, craggy 162m-high Castle Rock and rugged walking tracks.
- **Cape Kidnappers** Visit this far-flung neck of the woods east of Hastings between November and late February and check out the colony of gaggling gannets.

campsite $30, unit $55-155; 💻 📶 ) Putting the 'park' back into holiday park within its leafy confines there are sycamore hedges, a topiary 'welcome' sign, stream, duck pond, aviary and plenty of serenity.

**Clive Colonial Cottages** (Map p189; ☎ 06-870 1018; m.jstones@xtra.co.nz; 198 School Rd, Clive; d from $150) Two minutes walk from the beach and almost equidistant from Hastings, Napier and Havelock, these four purpose-built character cottages surround a pretty scented garden on a 2-acre woodland property. Pleasant communal areas include barbecue, games room and *pétanque* court. Bike hire is also available.

**Millar Road** (Map p189; ☎ 06-875 1977; www.millarroad.co.nz; 83 Millar Rd; d $400-500; 🐾 ) Set above a young vineyard in the Tuki Tuki Hills, Millar Road is architecturally heaven-sent. Two seriously plush self-contained cottages (separated by a swimming pool and bar) burst with NZ-made furniture and local artworks. Each comfortably sleeps two couples in separate en-suite rooms.

**Diva** (Map p189; ☎ 06-877 5149; Napier Rd, Havelock North; lunch $15-20, dinner $28-33) The most happening place in Havelock, Diva offers good value lunch (from fish and chips to Caesar salad) and a bistro-style menu featuring fresh seafood and seasonal specialities. Designed to within an inch of its life, the Diva's interior is divided into flash dining room and groovy bar (snacks from $5), plus lively pavement tables.

**Opera Kitchen** (☎ **06-870 6020; 312 Eastbourne St E; snacks $5-7, breakfast/lunch $10-22; ⏰ breakfast & lunch Mon-Sat**) This modern and stylish cafe has an interesting menu, including healthy brekkie options such as strawberries with passionfruit curd yoghurt. For the less calorie-conscious the full breakfast is a real winner, too. Heavenly counter food, great coffee and friendly staff round things out nicely. Eat indoors or outside in the suntrap courtyard.

## GETTING THERE & AROUND

Napier's Hawke's Bay Airport (p195) is a 20-minute drive away. Air New Zealand has an office in central Hastings.

**InterCity** (**www.intercity.co.nz**), **Bay Xpress** (**www.bayxpress.co.nz**) and **Naked Bus** (**www.nakedbus.com**) buses service Napier (p195).

**goBay** (☎ **06-878 9250; www.hbrc.govt.nz**) runs the local bus service, covering Napier, Hastings, Havelock North and thereabouts.

# ➘ MARLBOROUGH &
# NELSON

MICHAEL GEBICKI

Woman feeding an eel, Abel Tasman National Park (p230)

# MARLBOROUGH & NELSON

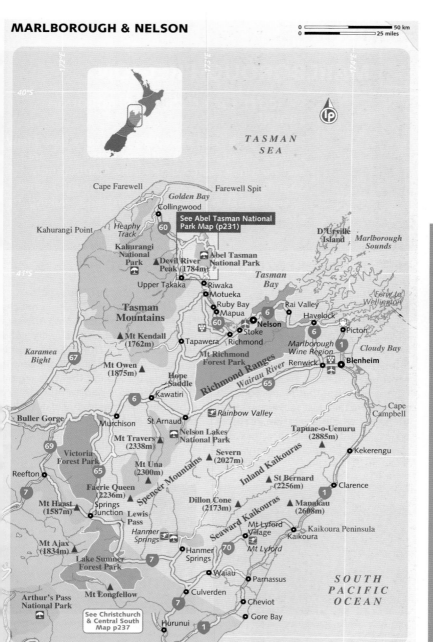

0 — 50 km
0 — 25 miles

*TASMAN
SEA*

Cape Farewell · Farewell Spit

*Golden Bay*
Collingwood

See Abel Tasman National
Park Map (p231)

60

*D'Urville
Island* · *Marlborough
Sounds*

Kahurangi Point · *Heaphy
Track*

Kahurangi
National
Park

Devil River
Peak (1784m)

Abel Tasman
National Park

*Tasman
Bay*

*Ferry to
Wellington*

Upper Takaka · Riwaka
Motueka
Ruby Bay
Mapua

Rai Valley

Havelock

*Tasman
Mountains*

60

Stoke
**Nelson**
Richmond

6

6

Picton

Mt Kendall
(1762m) · Tapawera

Mt Richmond
Forest Park

*Marlborough
Wine Region*

1

*Cloudy Bay*

*Karamea
Bight*

67

Mt Owen
(1875m)

Renwick · **Blenheim**

*Richmond Ranges*

*Wairau River*

Hope
Saddle

55

Buller Gorge

6

Kawatiri

*Rainbow Valley*

*Cape
Campbell*

69

Murchison · St Arnaud

Nelson Lakes
National Park

Tapuae-o-Uenuru
(2885m)

Victoria
Forest Park

Mt Travers
(2338m)

*Inland Kaikouras*

Kekerengu

65

Severn
(2027m)

Reefton

Mt Una
(2300m)

*Spencer Mountains*

St Bernard
(2256m)

Clarence

7

Faerie Queen
(2236m)

Springs
Junction

Dillon Cone
(2173m)

1

Mt Haast
(1587m)

Lewis
Pass

*Seaward Kaikouras*

Manakau
(2608m)

Mt Ajax
(1834m)

Hanmer
Springs

Mt Lyford
Village

Kaikoura Peninsula

Kaikoura

Lake Sumner
Forest Park

70

Mt Lyford

*Arthur's Pass
National Park*

7

Hanmer
Springs

Waiau

Parnassus

*SOUTH
PACIFIC
OCEAN*

Mt Longfellow

7

Culverden

Cheviot

See Christchurch
& Central South
Map p237

Hurunui

1

Gore Bay

MARLBOROUGH & NELSON

HIGHLIGHTS

# HIGHLIGHTS

## 1 MARLBOROUGH REGION

### BY SCOTT MACKENZIE, MARLBOROUGH TRAVEL

Marlborough is an incredibly diverse region. Many visitors spend a couple of days in the wine area, and then have some time in the Marlborough Sounds. There's lots of adventure activities, such as sea kayaking, mountain biking and walking, to provide a really good balance.

## ⬎ SCOTT MACKENZIE'S DON'T MISS LIST

### ❶ MARLBOROUGH WINE

Lots of visitors want to see Cloudy Bay (p221), and that's really worthwhile, but you should also visit a few little boutique wineries where you can taste wines with the owner and the winemaker. Often it's the same person. Remember, also, that Marlborough is about more than just sauvignon blanc: there's a whole spectrum of great wines, including pinot gris, gewürztraminer and chardonnay, to try.

### ❷ MORE THAN JUST WINE

The Marlborough region also produces superb hops. Blenheim's Moa Brewery (p225) is great and offers really good beer tastings. The Renaissance brewery (p225), also in Blenheim, is just fantastic. Around the wine region there are also opportunities to try schnapps, handmade chocolates, olive oil and local cheeses.

Clockwise from top: View from the Queen Charlotte Track (p218); Pier, Marlborough Sounds (p217); Farmers market; Renaissance Brewing (p225); Marlborough vineyard

CLOCKWISE FROM TOP: DESTINATION MARLBOROUGH; DESTINATION MARLBOROUGH; DESTINATION MARLBOROUGH; RENNAISANCE BREWING; DESTINATION MARLBOROUGH

## ❸ MARLBOROUGH FARMERS' MARKET

Blenheim's Marlborough Farmers' Market (www.marketground.co.nz/fmnzmfm; Oct-Jun) is a great way to spend a Sunday morning. It's good for brunch and coffee, and there are wine, beer and cheese tastings. There's usually live music, and you can talk to the people responsible for growing and making all the produce.

## ❹ MARLBOROUGH SOUNDS

Just 25 minutes' drive from the wine region, you're in the Marlborough Sounds (p217). Here you can see the greenshell mussel farms. Visitors get to understand the history of the Sounds and why the mussels grow so well here. Kick back and eat them fresh with a glass of chilled sauvignon blanc.

## ❺ QUEEN CHARLOTTE TRACK

This track (p218) is the region's number-one walkway. A good way to experience it is on a Gourmet Walk with Wilderness Guides (p218) in Picton. Local food and wine and excellent accommodation means visitors can experience the three- to four-day walk in real comfort.

## ⬋ THINGS YOU NEED TO KNOW

Alternative liquid souvenir Kiwi-style liqueurs from the Prenzel distillery at Blenheim's Vines Village (p222) Classiest vineyard dining The degustation menu with wine matches at the Herzog Winery (p221) See the area Take a tour with www.marlboroughtravel.co.nz For full coverage, see p215

MARLBOROUGH & NELSON

HIGHLIGHTS

# HIGHLIGHTS

## 2  ABEL TASMAN NATIONAL PARK

### BY STU HOUSTON, DEPARTMENT OF CONSERVATION

Of all of New Zealand's national parks, Abel Tasman is the most accessible for all ages and fitness levels. The bush meets beautiful golden-sand beaches with amazingly clear water. The Nelson–Tasman region has the highest sunshine hours for NZ and very settled weather, protected all around by mountains.

## STU HOUSTON'S DON'T MISS LIST

### ❶ EXPLORE IN A KAYAK

The best way to see the park is by water, kayaking up the coastline – you see the beaches, the forests, mountains and rocks. The bulk of people do kayaking as a day trip, but to get a real feel for it you should take a three-day kayak trip, I reckon. You can do a quarter-day or half-day, but it's hard to get a feel for the scenery on such a short trip. The kayak operators (p233) can give you all the options: walk a few kilometres, paddle a few…

### ❷ TRAMP THE COAST TRACK

The Abel Tasman is one of those parks where the further into it you go, the better it gets. There are four huts on the track and 19 campsites – the camp spots are primo, with some on the beach, right beside the sea. Most people start at Marahau and head north, tramp for three days and then get a water taxi out at the end.

Clockwise from top: Coastal kayaking (p233); Swing bridge, Abel Tasman Coast Track (p230); Abel Tasman National Park coastline

### ❸ SPOT SOME WILDLIFE

There's a huge seal population here and many little blue penguins within the park (if you don't see them, you'll hear them: they make a lot of noise at night!) We get quite a lot of dolphins travelling through and we see orcas two or three times a year. There are wood pigeons, tuis and bellbirds. A lot of the streams have native fresh water fish – kokopu, inanga – which trout and salmon have forced out in other areas.

### ❹ HAVE A DIP

Swimming here is awesome! There's no glacial run-off and it's one of the few places in the country without any surf. Marahau, where I live, is a swimmer's paradise! The water temperature is around 21°C in summer (even down in Dunedin, which is not much further south, it's around 16°C).

### ↘ THINGS YOU NEED TO KNOW

Best photo op Early morning on the rocks at Marahau Best time to visit Dodge the crowds and visit in March/April, when the water temperature is still OK and there are fewer New Zealanders on holiday See our author's review, p230

# HIGHLIGHTS

## 3   KAIKOURA WILDLIFE

### BY LISA BOND, WHALE-WATCH SEA CAPTAIN

You can watch whales here year-round. We're on the main migratory path for 14 different species of whale and dolphin: it's like being on the main underwater highway. We see humpback whales on their annual migration to Australia, and from June to August sperm whales are feeding closer to land.

## ⌐ LISA BOND'S DON'T MISS LIST

### ❶ WHALE-WATCHING

Take a whale-watching boat or aerial tour (p223) – the better operators can find whales 95% of the time. If you're in luck, you might also see dolphins, seals and marine birds, too.

### ❷ SPY ON SOME SEALS

Visit the colonies either at Point Kean or at Ohau Point. If you get too close to the seals they can be dangerous: the males are very protective around breeding time (September/October). If you stay 6m to 8m away you'll be OK, but they move quite quickly on land – it pays not to get between them and the water. See p223.

### ❸ SWIM WITH DOLPHINS

The dusky dolphins here are sometimes joined by common dolphins. We see Hector's dolphins too, the smallest ocean-going dolphin, and an endangered species found only in NZ. Sometimes we see orcas – they're the main predator to all marine life, so

Clockwise from top: Dusky dolphins (p223); Freshly cooked paua; Fur seal (p223)

obviously we're not swimming with them, we keep people out of the water when they're around! See p223.

### ❸ SAVOUR SOME SEAFOOD

Visit the roadside **Kaikoura Seafood BBQ** (p228) on the way to Point Kean or **Nin's Bin** (p228) and taste some local seafood. You sit outside and they'll cook it up for you. Crayfish is the local specialty, or try whitebait if it's in season; there's also paua, mussels, blue cod and butterfish. Both spots are really popular year-round.

### ❹ GO FISHING OR DIVING

There are half-a-dozen companies that operate in these nutrient-rich waters. You just need to put your line out and you've got a bite within a couple of minutes! You get to keep your catch, and the operators will fillet it and help you prepare it if you want to eat it.

---

### ⬎ THINGS YOU NEED TO KNOW

**Best time to go** Winter (June to August): there's snow on the mountains and you can get the most gorgeous winter days and calm seas. **Best photo op** Whale tails arching out of the sea **Limited time?** Whale, dolphin and albatross trips take only three hours **For more on Kaikoura, see p223**

# HIGHLIGHTS

**4**

## ⬎ NELSON

Anyone here into the arts, good coffee, seafood restaurants, Victorian architecture and careening around the Great Outdoors? The good people of Nelson (p226) deliver it all, lashed with equal measures of eco-awareness and urban bohemia. This funky town offers 'liveability' to its residents and plenty of enticements to keep the itinerant population (you and me) here for a day or three.

**5**

## ⬎ ACTION APLENTY

With all this sunshine, there's no reason not to go outside and run around. Or go sea kayaking, jump out of a plane, try paragliding, sailing, hang gliding, horse riding, kiteboarding, rock climbing, surfing… Nelson (p228) is ground zero for outdoor activities in this region, but you can also get busy around Abel Tasman National Park (p232), Kaikoura (p223) and Marlborough Sounds (p217).

## ⬎ TRAMPING

We hope you've packed your hiking boots! This region is the place to propel yourself onto a wonderfully wild walkway, whether it's a short stretch of the Abel Tasman Coast Track (p233) or a couple of days stomping along the Queen Charlotte Track (p218), here's your chance to get some sun on your skin and some miles into your calf muscles.

## ⬎ SEAFOOD

'I'm on a see-food diet... I see food, then I eat it!' But seriously, if you're partial to fish fillets and molluscs, then you're in the right culinary ocean here. Kaikoura (p225) is the place to try crayfish ('Kai' is Maori for food, and 'koura' means crayfish), while the Marlborough Sounds (p217) area is famous for greenshell mussels.

## ⬎ PICTON

No doubt, Picton (p214) is underrated. Too many people just jump on/off the ferry here and continue on to wherever they're bound... but why not take a day to chill out? Picton is a photogenic wee town on one of the prettiest waterways you could imagine, with plenty of quality places to eat, sleep and drink.

4 DAVID WALL; 5 DAVID WALL; 6 MICHAEL GEBICKI; 7 PAUL KENNEDY; 8 RICHARD BRIGGS / DESTINATION MARLBOROUGH

4 Trafalgar St, Nelson (p226); 5 Seaward Kaikoura Range (p222); 6 Views from the Queen Charlotte Track (p218); 7 Whitebait fritters; 8 Harbour at sunset, Picton (p214)

# BEST...

## ⇖ WILDLIFE, UP CLOSE

- **Kaikoura whales** (p223) Famous whale-watching tours off the Kaikoura coast.
- **Marlborough Sounds dolphins** See them chase the ferry or get close-up on a guided tour (p217).
- **Abel Tasman National Park seals** (p232) A plethora of grunting mammals.
- **Albatross encounters** (p224) Check out the big birds on a tour from Kaikoura.

## ⇖ SCENIC DRIVES

- **Picton–Havelock** Wiggly tarmac along the Marlborough Sounds' southern reaches.
- **Kaikoura–Blenheim** Rte 1 passes surf beaches and lonesome coastlines.
- **Rapaura Rd** The Marlborough wine region's vine-lined 'Golden Mile'.
- **Motueka–Takaka** Over the hills south of Abel Tasman National Park.

## ⇖ PLACES TO GET WET

- **Abel Tasman National Park** (p230) Kayak around this spectacular coastline.
- **Marahau** (p232) Clear, clean waters on the doorstep of Abel Tasman National Park.
- **Tahunanui Beach** Popular sandy stretch 5km south of Nelson.
- **Queen Charlotte Track** (p218) Dunk a toe in the chilly, mirror-flat Marlborough Sounds.

## ⇖ EXCUSES FOR A DRINK

- **Marlborough Wine Region** (p221) We all know why you're here... now get sipping!
- **Blenheim Breweries** (p225) Escape the sav blanc with some microbrewed delights.
- **Nocturnal Nelson** (p229) When the sun goes down Nelson's bars light up.

Left: Albatrosses (p224); Right: Fur seal (p223)

LEFT: DAVID WALL; RIGHT: PAUL KENNEDY

# THINGS YOU NEED TO KNOW

## ⊾ VITAL STATISTICS

- **Population** Picton 4000; Blenheim 26,500; Nelson 43,500
- **Telephone code** ☎ 03
- **Best time to visit** February to May

## ⊾ LOCALITIES IN A NUTSHELL

- **Marlborough Region** (p214) Wine, whale-watching and wilderness from Kaikoura to Blenheim.
- **Marlborough Sounds** (p217) Intricate landscape of bays, inlets, headlands and ridgelines.
- **Marlborough Wine Region** (p221) Superb sauvignon-blanc vineyards behind Blenheim.
- **Nelson Region** (p226) National parks, groovy Nelson and boundless sunshine.

## ⊾ ADVANCE PLANNING

- **One month before** Is it summer? Book your kayak/hike in Abel Tasman National Park (p233)
- **Two weeks before** Book a ferry to/from the North Island (p217) and accommodation across the region.
- **One week before** Book a Marlborough Wine Region winery tour (p219) and a whale-watching trip in Kaikoura (p223).

## ⊾ RESOURCES

For bookings and information on regional accommodation, transport and activities, plus DOC info and contacts:

- **Blenheim i-SITE** (**www.destination marlborough.com**)
- **Kaikoura i-SITE** (**www.kaikoura.co.nz**)
- **Nelson i-SITE** (**www.nelsonnz.com**)
- **Picton i-SITE** (**www.destination marlborough.com**)

## ⊾ EMERGENCY NUMBERS

- **Ambulance, fire service & police** (☎ 111)

## ⊾ GETTING AROUND

- **Ferry** (p217) between Picton and the North Island.
- **Hike** along the Queen Charlotte Track (p218).
- **Kayak** (p233) through Abel Tasman National Park.
- **Minibus** (p219) around the Marlborough Wine Region wineries.
- **Train** between Picton and Kaikoura on the *TranzCoastal* (p217).

MARLBOROUGH & NELSON

THINGS YOU NEED TO KNOW

# MARLBOROUGH & NELSON ITINERARIES

## FOODIE MARLBOROUGH & NELSON Three Days

With only three days around the top of the South Island, don't try and do too much. Relax and focus on some of life's basics: food and wine done the Marlborough & Nelson way.

Don't waste time, head straight to the **(1) Marlborough Wine region** (p221) and get stuck into sampling gewürztraminer, pinot gris, chardonnay and, of course, the region's world-famous sauvignon blanc. If you're more of a beer fan, there are some ace microbreweries (p225) in the area, too.

Back in the calm, clean backwaters of the **(2) Marlborough Sounds** (p217), greenshell mussels find it impossible not to breed, and grow in preposterous numbers. You'll find them on most menus in Picton – a generous bowl steamed with fennel, shallots, white wine and butter will cure what ails you.

Heading southeast to **(3) Kaikoura** (p222) get ready for a seafood frenzy. This is the town to try crayfish (aka lobster), paua (abalone), scallops and all manner of fresh ocean fish. Whip out one of those bottles you've been lugging around since Blenheim and crack into some crustaceans.

## GET BUSY Five Days

Enough sitting around eating and swilling wine! Time to get active.

The main lure for trampers around here is the stellar **(1) Abel Tasman Coast Track** (p230) in Abel Tasman National Park. Tailor your adventure to include hiking along the track and kayaking along the coastline, maybe saving yourself some time with a water-taxi ride or two.

Defy gravity with a paragliding, kiteboarding or hang-gliding lesson in **(2) Nelson** (p228), or succumb to its pull with some skydiving. Ask at the i-SITE about rock-climbing, horse-riding and kayaking operators in the area.

The hills around Nelson are also great for mountain biking, as is the superbly scenic **(3) Queen Charlotte Track** (p218) in the Marlborough Sounds. Traditionally a tramping route, the advent of water taxis now permits bikers to access remote sections of the track, and gives hikers the chance to offload their packs and have them transported to the next campsite. Weightless walking!

Other places where you can try sea kayaking include the **(4) Marlborough Sounds** (p218) and **(5) Kaikoura** (p223).

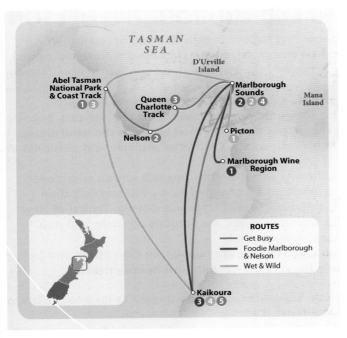

## WET & WILD One Week

If you have a week to burn, the Marlborough and Nelson region offers plenty of opportunities to interact with wild, uninhibited Kiwi critters (no, we're not talking about denizens of the Marlborough Wine region).

As you're pulling into (1) Picton (p217) on the ferry from Wellington, lean over the railings and you'll often see dolphins cascading around in the wake. If not, check them out on a guided tour of the (2) Marlborough Sounds (p217).

There are plenty more dolphins further west in (3) Abel Tasman National Park (p233), where you'll also have the chance to see New Zealand fur seals, little blue penguins, native birds (such as tuis) and the occasional orca.

Tracking back to top of the South Island's east coast, (4) Kaikoura (p223) is a veritable wonderland of wild beasts. The richly-stocked ocean here ensures a steady population of sperm whales, plus an incredible 14(!) species of dolphin swimming past. Tour operators can speed you out onto (or over) the water to see them, plus there are seals mooching about on the point south of town, and albatross and shearwater colonies for the bird nerds.

# DISCOVER MARLBOROUGH & NELSON

These two neighbouring regions in New Zealand have much in common beyond an amenable climate: both boast renowned coastal holiday spots, particularly the Marlborough Sounds and Abel Tasman National Park.

That superb climate means that these two regions have an abundance of luscious produce: summer cherries for starters, but most famously the grapes that work their way into the wine glasses of the world's finest restaurants. Keep your penknife and picnic set at the ready.

A host of small towns and a few big 'uns will service your needs. Most attempt to exude an air of experience, even sophistication. There will be splendid coffee and art-house cinema. Typical of New Zealand, though, beyond the veil are hotdogs on sticks and pub bands so bad they're good.

In high season, these regions are popular, so plan ahead and be prepared to jostle for your gelato with Kiwi holidaymakers.

## GETTING THERE & AROUND

**Soundsair** (www.soundsair.com) is a local airline connecting Wellington with Blenheim, Nelson and Picton. **Air New Zealand** (www.airnewzealand.com) offers domestic flights.

Interisland Cook Strait ferries pull into Picton, which is often the starting point for South Island explorations. From here you can connect to almost anywhere in the South Island by bus; InterCity is the major operator, but there are also local shuttle buses. Tranz Scenic's *TranzCoastal* train takes the scenic route from Picton to Christchurch, via Blenheim and Kaikoura.

# MARLBOROUGH REGION

## PICTON

pop 4000

Half asleep in winter but hyperactive in summer (with up to eight fully-laden ferry arrivals per day), Picton clusters around a deep gulch at the head of Queen Charlotte Sound.

**Picton i-SITE** (☎ 03-520 3113; www.destinationmarlborough.com; Foreshore; ☼ 9am-5pm Mon-Fri, 9am-4pm Sat & Sun) All vital tourist guff including maps and QC Track information. Internet (per hr $6). DOC counter staffed during summer.

Above the foreshore, the **Picton Museum** (☎ 03-573 8283; pictonmuseum@xtra.co.nz; London Quay; adult/child $4/1; ☼ 9am-4pm Mar-Nov, to 5pm Dec-Feb) has a collection of whale bones, shells and model ships, and displays on local history and Maori lore.

A free i-SITE map details several walks around town, including an easy 1km track along Picton Harbour's eastern side to Bob's Bay. The **Snout Walkway** (three hours return) continues along the ridge from Bob's Bay offering superb Queen Charlotte Sound views.

## SLEEPING & EATING

**Tombstone Backpackers** (☎ 0800 573 7116, 03-573 7116; www.tombstonebp.co.nz; 16

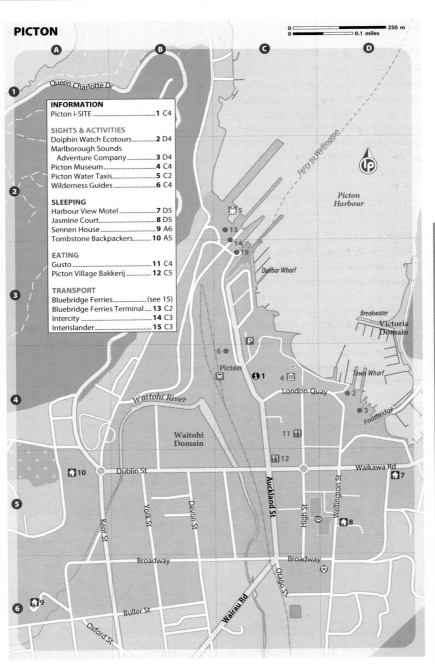

# PICTON

0 _____ 250 m
0 _____ 0.1 miles

**INFORMATION**
Picton i-SITE .........................................**1** C4

**SIGHTS & ACTIVITIES**
Dolphin Watch Ecotours..............**2** D4
Marlborough Sounds
  Adventure Company ..................**3** D4
Picton Museum...............................**4** C4
Picton Water Taxis.........................**5** C2
Wilderness Guides .........................**6** C4

**SLEEPING**
Harbour View Motel ......................**7** D5
Jasmine Court..................................**8** D5
Sennen House ..................................**9** A6
Tombstone Backpackers...............**10** A5

**EATING**
Gusto .................................................**11** C4
Picton Village Bakkerij .................**12** C5

**TRANSPORT**
Bluebridge Ferries....................(see 15)
Bluebridge Ferries Terminal ....**13** C2
Intercity ...........................................**14** C3
Interislander...................................**15** C3

Gravesend Pl; dm $25, d with/without bathroom $75/70; 🖳 🛜) Picton cemetery is across the street – a fact these hosts have turned into a marketing masterstroke. Beyond a coffin-lid door is one of the best hostels we've seen, catering to the new breed of 'flashpackers'. Hotel-worthy doubles, immaculate dorms, spa overlooking the harbour, free breakfast, sunny reading room, pool table, DVD library, free ferry pick-up and drop-off… the list goes on.

**Harbour View Motel** ( ☎ 0800 101 133, 03-573 6259; www.harbourviewpicton.co.nz; 30 Waikawa Rd; d $120-170; 🛜) This tastefully decorated motel enjoys an elevated position, affording views of Picton's mast-filled harbour from its self-contained studios with timber decks.

**Jasmine Court** ( ☎ 0800 421 999, 03-573 7110; www.jasminecourt.co.nz; 78 Wellington St; d $130-210, f $185-225; 🖳 🛜) Top-notch, spacious motel with plush interiors, kitchenettes, free DVD and plunger coffee. Some rooms have a spa; upstairs balconies have harbour views.

**Sennen House** ( ☎ 03-573 5216; www.sennen house.co.nz; 9 Oxford St; d $269-479; 🖳 🛜) Tucked against a steep hillside of regenerating native bush (the odd black-faced sheep in its midst), Sennen House is an exquisitely restored, 1886 weatherboard homestead. Inside are five plush apartments and suites, each with its own entrance and kitchenette facilities, as well as sunny verandas and private lounge/dining areas. A gourmet breakfast hamper is included in the rate.

**our pick** **Picton Village Bakkerij** ( ☎ 03-573 7082; 46 Auckland St; items $2-7; ⏰ 6am-3.30pm; V ) Dutch owners bake trays of European goodies here, including interesting breads, scrumptious pies, super sandwiches, cakes and custardy, tarty treats. Look for the cut-out Amsterdam roofline stapled to the eaves.

**Gusto** ( ☎ 03-573 7171; 33 High St; meals $12-19; ⏰ 7.30am-2.30pm) This workaday joint, with friendly staff and outdoor tables, injects some class into Picton's cafe scene. Beaut breakfasts (French toast with bacon, maple syrup and berry coulis), fan-

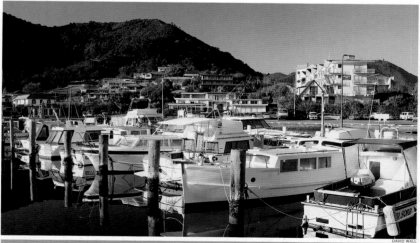

Wharfside, Picton

DAVID WALL

tastic coffee, and locally sourced mains (mussels, lamb and venison).

## GETTING THERE & AWAY
### AIR
Soundsair ( ☎ 0800 505 005, 03-520 3080; www.soundsair.com) flies between Picton and Wellington (adult/child $89/77, up to eight daily). There are discounts for online bookings, and a courtesy shuttle bus ($3) to/from the airstrip at Koromiko, 8km south.

### BOAT
Bluebridge Ferries ( ☎ 0800 844 844, in Wellington 04-471 6188; www.bluebridge.co.nz; adult/child $50/25) Crossing takes three hours, 20 minutes. Departs Wellington at 3am, 8am, 1pm and 9pm daily (no 3am or 9pm services on Saturdays). Departs Picton at 2am, 8am, 2pm and 7pm daily (no 8am service on Saturdays; no 2am service on Sundays). Cars and campervans up to 4m long from $110; campervans under 5.5m from $150; motorbikes $50; bicycles $10.

Interislander ( ☎ 0800 802 802, in Wellington 04-498 3302; www.interislander.co.nz; adult/child from $46/23) Crossing takes three hours, 10 minutes. Departs Wellington at 2.25am, 8.25am, 2.05pm and 6.25pm. Departs Picton at 6.25am, 10.05am, 1.10pm, 6.05pm and 10.25pm. From November through to April there's an extra 10.25am sailing from Wellington and an extra 2.25pm sailing from Picton. Cars are priced from $101; campervans (up to 5.5m) from $126; motorbikes $46; bicycles $15.

### BUS
InterCity ( ☎ 03-365 1113; www.intercitycoach.co.nz; Picton Ferry Terminal) runs services south to Christchurch ($55, 5½ hours, two daily), via Kaikoura ($35, 2½ hours,

two daily) with connections to Dunedin, Queenstown and Invercargill. Services also run to/from Nelson ($34, 2¼ hours, three daily), with connections to Motueka and the West Coast; and to/from Blenheim ($15, 30 minutes, five daily).

Smaller shuttle buses running from Picton to Christchurch (around $40, door to door) include:
Atomic Shuttles ( ☎ 03-349 0697; www.atomictravel.co.nz)
Naked Bus ( ☎ 0900 625 33; www.nakedbus.com)
Southern Link ( ☎ 0508 458 835, 03-358 8355; www.southernlinkcoaches.co.nz)

### TRAIN
Tranz Scenic ( ☎ 0800 872 467, 04-495 0775; www.tranzscenic.co.nz) runs the *TranzCoastal* service daily each way between Picton and Christchurch via Blenheim and Kaikoura (and 22 tunnels and 175 bridges!), departing Christchurch at 7am, Picton at 1pm. The standard adult one-way Picton–Christchurch fare is $104, but discounted fares can be as low as $39. The service connects with the *Interislander* ferry (included in Wellington to Christchurch fares).

## MARLBOROUGH SOUNDS
The Marlborough Sounds are a geographic maze of inlets, headlands, peaks, beaches and watery reaches, formed when the sea flooded into deep valleys after the last ice age. With your own wheels, the wiggly, verdant 35km drive along Queen Charlotte Dr from Picton to Havelock is a great Sounds snapshot (even on a rainy day).

### TOURS
Dolphin Watch Ecotours (Map p215; ☎ 0800 9453 5433, 03-573 8040; www.naturetours.co.nz; Town Wharf; swimming/viewing

$150/100) Half-day 'swim with dolphins' and wildlife tours around Queen Charlotte Sound and Motuara Island bird sanctuary. QC Track cruise/walk options also available.

**Marlborough Sounds Adventure Company** (Map p215; ☎ 0800 283 283, 03-573 6078; www.marlboroughsounds.co.nz; Town Wharf; half- to 3-day tours $75-245) Bike-kayak-walk trips, with options to suit every inclination. The '1-day multi' guided kayak trip followed by QC Track hike ($135) or bike ($155) is a brilliant Sounds sampler.

**Picton Water Taxis** (Map p215; ☎ 03-573 7853, 027 227 0284; www.pictonwatertaxis.co.nz; Town Wharf; ⏱ 24hr)

**Sea Kayak Adventure Tours** (☎ 0800 262 5492, 03-574 2765; www.nzseakayaking.com; Anakiwa Rd, Anakiwa; half-/1-day guided tours $65/95) Guided and independent kayaking trips around Queen Charlotte and Kenepuru Sounds. Also one-day paddle and walk ($85) or paddle and bike ($120) freedom options. Kayak and mountain-bike hire from $50 per day.

**Wilderness Guides** (Map p215; ☎ 0800 266 266, 03-520 3095; www.wildernessguidesnz.com; Picton Railway Station, 3 Auckland St; 1- to 4-day trips incl lunch $90-570) Guided and independent kayak/walk or kayak/bike tours on the QC Track or Nydia Track. Bike hire $50 per day.

## SLEEPING & EATING

**Queen Charlotte Wilderness Park** ( ☎ 03-579 9025; www.truenz.co.nz/wilderness; Cape Jackson; per person 2 nights/3 days $329 or 3 nights/4 days $429) This private nature reserve allows you to venture on to the Outer Queen Charlotte Track, north of Ship Cove up to Cape Jackson. Inclusive packages includes accommodation in en-suite twins or doubles, meals and Picton transfers.

**Hopewell** ( ☎ 03-573 4341; www.hopewell.co.nz; Kenepuru Sound; dm from $30, d with/without bathroom from $120/98, 4-person cottage $160 (for 2 adults); ⏱ closed Jun-Aug; 🖥 🛜 ) One of NZ's best-loved backpackers, Hopewell occupies a remote corner of Kenepuru Sound, surrounded by native bush opening onto the sea. Road access is possible, but the long, bumpy drive makes a water taxi from Te Mahia far preferable.

### GETTING THERE & AROUND

The best way to get around the Sounds is by boat, and fortunately there are a plethora of operators who will oblige either to schedule or on-demand.

Much of the area is accessible by car. The road is sealed to the head of Kenepuru Sound, but beyond that it's nothing but narrow gravel roads with more twists than a hurricane. To drive to Punga Cove from Picton takes two to three hours (45 minutes by boat).

# QUEEN CHARLOTTE TRACK

The hugely popular, meandering Queen Charlotte Track offers gorgeous coastal scenery, isolated coves, diverse accommodation and back-to-nature campsites. The 71km track connects historic Ship Cove with Anakiwa, passing through privately owned land (40% of the track) and DOC reserves.

You can do the walk in sections using local water-taxi transport, or walk the whole three- to five-day journey. Sleeping options are only half a day's walk apart; boat operators will transport your pack along the track for you.

Mountain biking is a viable alternative for fit, competent off-roaders; it's possible to ride the track in two or three days, guided or self-guided.

The Picton i-SITE (p214) stocks the *Queen Charlotte Track Visitor Guide* pamphlet and DOC's *Queen Charlotte Track* brochure, and is the best spot for information.

# BLENHEIM
pop 26,500

Blenheim (pronounced 'Blenum') is a dead-flat, agricultural town 29km south of Picton on the Wairau Plain between the Wither Hills and the Richmond Ranges. The town offers little to enthral or distract except for the brilliant Aviation Heritage Centre and the world-famous wineries just over Blenheim's back fence.

**Blenheim i-SITE** ( ☎ 03-577 8080; www.destinationmarlborough.com; Railway Station, Sinclair St; ☷ 8.30am-5pm Mon-Fri, 9am-3pm Sat & Sun) Information on Marlborough and beyond. Wine trail maps and bookings for everything under the sun.

## SIGHTS

Blenheim's 'big attraction' has always been its wineries, but the **Omaka Aviation Heritage Centre** (Map p222; ☎ 03-579 1305; www.omaka.org.nz; Aerodrome Rd; adult/child/family $20/8/48; ☷ 10am-4pm) has blown the wine out of the water. Aided by the creative geniuses that brought us *Lord of the Rings* (Peter Jackson, Wingnut Films and Weta Workshop), this amazing collection of original and replica Great War aircraft is brought to life with a series of dioramas depicting dramatic wartime scenes such as the death of Manfred von Richthofen, the Red Baron.

## TOURS
### WINE TOURS

Wine tours are generally conducted in a minibus, last between three and seven hours, take in four to seven wineries, and range in price from $45 to $90 (with a few grand tours up to $200 for the day).
**Bubbly Grape Wine Tours** ( ☎ 0800 228 2253; www.bubblygrape.co.nz)
**Highlight Wine Tours** ( ☎ 03-577-9046; www.highlight-tours.co.nz)
**Marlborough Wine Tours** ( ☎ 03-578 9515; www.marlboroughwinetours.co.nz)
Bike hire is available all over town, or take a self-guided tour with **Wine Tours**

Mountain biking, Queen Charlotte Track

ANDREW BAIN

by Bike ( ☎ 03-577 6954; www.winetoursbybike.
co.nz; half-/full-day bike hire $40/55) which in-
cludes pick-up/drop-off, winery map, bot-
tled water, panniers and support vehicle
(if you buy too many bottles!).

## SLEEPING
### IN TOWN

Grapevine Backpackers ( ☎ 03-578 6062;
www.thegrapevine.co.nz; 29 Park Tce; tent sites
$17, dm $24, d $52-66, tr $78; 🖳 🛜 ) Inside an
old maternity home just out of the centre,
Grapevine is a worker-focused hostel with a
brilliant sunset deck by Opawa River. There
are free canoes, and bike hire is $15 per day.

171 On High ( ☎ 0800 587 856, 03-579 5098;
www.171onhighmotel.co.nz; cnr High & Percy Sts; d
$125-185; 🖳 🛜 ) A welcoming option close
to town, these tasteful splash-o-purple
studios and apartments are bright and
breezy in the daytime, warm and shim-
mery in the evening. A wide complement
of facilities include full kitchen, Sky TV and
guest laundry; staff are well-known for
'extra mile' service.

Hotel D'Urville ( ☎ 03-577 9945; www.
durville.com; 52 Queen St; d $185-300; 🖳 🛜 )
Injecting some chutzpah into Blenheim's
old Public Trust buildings, the 11 dazzling
rooms in this boutique hotel are lavishly
decorated and individually themed.
Downstairs is a classy lounge bar and
high-end restaurant (dinner only, mains
around $38), while outside the new deck
bar traps great afternoon sun.

### WINE REGION ACCOMMODATION

**our pick** Vintners Hotel (Map p222; ☎ 03-572
5094; www.mvh.co.nz; 190 Rapaura Rd; d $150-260;
🛜 🍽 ) One of the best among the vines:
16 architecturally designed suites boasting picture windows both sides making
the most of vine and valley views, while
inside the rooms are truly stylish boasting
wet-room bathrooms and abstract art.

Stonehaven (Map p222; ☎ 03-572 9730;
www.stonehavenhomestay.co.nz; 414 Rapaura Rd;
d incl breakfast $185-280; 🖳 🛜 🍽 ) A stella
stone-and-timber B&B among the vines
with three commodious guest rooms
Beds are piled high with pillows; prope
continental breakfast is served in the sum
merhouse; dinner is offered by reques
with rare wines from the cellar; and bike
hire is available on site.

## EATING

Café le Cupp ( ☎ 03-577 7311; 30 Market St
snacks $2-5, meals $6-18; ⏲ 8am-3.30pm Mon
Fri, 9am-1pm Sat) The best tearoom in town
by a country mile. Ogle your way along
the counter (egg sandwiches, mince sa
vouries, lamingtons, carrot cake) or ge
yourself a brekkie such as the full fry-up
French toast or muesli.

Raupo ( ☎ 03-577 8822; 2 Symons St; lunch
$12-18, dinner $22-28; ⏲ 7am-late) An airy
high-ceilinged timber-and-stone build
ing alongside the Opawa River. During
the day there's a satisfying cafe menu
(brekkies, burgers, mussels, lamb shanks
and sweet treats, segueing into slightly
more sophisticated fare of an evening
Sheltered outdoor seating and soft-jazz
grooves on the stereo.

## GETTING THERE & AROUND
### AIR

Air New Zealand ( ☎ 0800 747 000
03-577 2200; www.airnewzealand.co.nz; 29
Queen St; ⏲ 9am-5pm Mon-Fri) has direc
flights to/from Wellington (from $75
12 daily), Auckland ($109, 5 daily) and
Christchurch ($89, 3 daily) with onward
connections.

### BICYCLE

Spokesman ( ☎ 03-578 0433; www.bike
marlborough.co.nz; 61 Queen St; hire per half-/full
day incl helmet $25/40; ⏲ 8am-5.30pm Mon-Fri

Riding through the wine region

IAN TRAFFORD / DESTINATION MARLBOROUGH

10am-1pm Sat) rents bikes; longer hire and delivery by arrangement.

## BUS

**InterCity** ( ☎ 03-365 1113; www.intercitycoach. co.nz) buses run daily from the Blenheim i-SITE to Picton ($15, 30 minutes, five daily) continuing through to Nelson ($31, 1¾ hours, three daily). Buses also head down south to Christchurch ($54, five hours, two daily) via Kaikoura ($33, 1¾ hours).

**Naked Bus** ( ☎ 0900 625 33; www.nakedbus. com) runs from Blenheim to many South Island destinations, including Kaikoura ($20, two hours, two daily), Nelson (from $13, 1¾ hours, one to two daily) and Motueka ($27, 3¾ hours, one daily).

## TRAIN

**Tranz Scenic** ( ☎ 0800 872 467, 04-495 0775; www.tranzscenic.co.nz) runs the *TranzCoastal* service, stopping daily at Blenheim en route to Picton ($27, 27 minutes, departing 11.46am) heading north, and Christchurch ($95, five hours, departing 1.33pm) via Kaikoura ($48, two hours) heading south.

## MARLBOROUGH WINE REGION

Marlborough is NZ's vinous colossus, producing around three quarters of the country's wine. Sunny days and cool nights create the perfect microclimate for cool-climate grapes: world famous sauvignon blanc, top-notch pinot noir, and notable gewürztraminer, riesling, pinot gris and bubbly.

For wine tours, see p219. Also pick up a copy of *The Marlborough Wine Trail* map from Blenheim i-SITE, available online at www.wine-marlborough.co.nz.

**Cloudy Bay** (Map p222; ☎ 03-520 9147; www.cloudybay.co.nz; Jacksons Rd; 🕙 10am-5pm) An understated exterior belies the classy interior of this blue ribbon winery and cellar door. Globally coveted sauvignon blanc, bubbly and pinot noir.

**Herzog Winery** (Map p222; ☎ 03-572 8770; www.herzog.co.nz; 81 Jeffries Rd; 🕙 9am-5pm Mon-Fri, 11am-4pm Sat & Sun) Boutique family-owned winery and acclaimed restaurant. Try the full-bodied montepulciano, a rare grape in these parts.

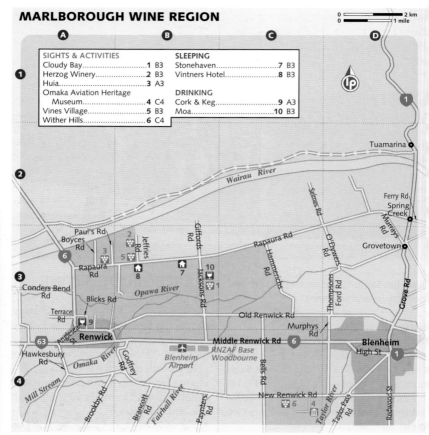

# MARLBOROUGH WINE REGION

| SIGHTS & ACTIVITIES | | | SLEEPING | | |
|---|---|---|---|---|---|
| Cloudy Bay | **1** | B3 | Stonehaven | **7** | B3 |
| Herzog Winery | **2** | B3 | Vintners Hotel | **8** | B3 |
| Huia | **3** | A3 | | | |
| Omaka Aviation Heritage | | | DRINKING | | |
| Museum | **4** | C4 | Cork & Keg | **9** | A3 |
| Vines Village | **5** | B3 | Moa | **10** | B3 |
| Wither Hills | **6** | C4 | | | |

**Huia** (Map p222; ☎ 03-572 8326; www.huia.
net.nz; Boyces Rd; ☒ 10.30am-5pm) Sustainable, small-scale winegrowing and the
cutest yellow tasting room in town. De-
lectable dry-style gewürztraminer.

**Vines Village** (Map p222; ☎ 03-572 8444;
www.thevinesvillage.co.nz; 193 Rapaura Rd;
☒ 9am-5pm) Site of the Bouldevines cellar
door (www.bouldevineswine.co.nz) and
much more: Prenzel Distillery Company,
olive oils, acres of quilts and a reliable
cafe serving affordable home-made fare.

**Wither Hills** (Map p222; ☎ 03-578 4036;
www.witherhills.co.nz; 211 New Renwick Rd;

☒ 10am-4.30pm) One of the region's flag-
ship wineries and an architectural gem.
Premium wines and an excellent lunch
(see below).

# KAIKOURA

pop 3850

Take SH1 132km southeast from
Blenheim (or 183km north from
Christchurch) and you'll wind around the
coast to Kaikoura, a picture-perfect peninsula town backed by the snowcapped
peaks of the Seaward Kaikoura Range.
There are few places in the world with

such awesome mountains so close to the sea, and such a proliferation of wildlife so close at hand: whales, dolphins, seals, penguins, shearwaters, petrels and albatross.

**Kaikoura i-SITE** ( ☎ 03-319 5641; www.kaikoura.co.nz; West End; ☺ 9am-5pm Mon-Fri, to 4pm Sat & Sun, extended hr in summer) Helpful staff make tour, accommodation and transport bookings, and help with DOC-related matters.

## SIGHTS & ACTIVITIES

Near the Point Kean car park is the smelly **seal colony**. The seals laze around in the grass and on the rocks, wondering why everyone is looking at them.

The **Kaikoura Peninsula Walkway** is a must-do if humanly possible. Starting from the town, this three- to four-hour loop heads out to Point Kean, along the cliffs to South Bay, then back to town over the isthmus. En route you'll see fur seals, and red-billed seagull and shearwater (aka mutton bird) colonies. Collect a map at the i-SITE or follow your nose.

## TOURS
### WHALE-WATCHING

**Kaikoura Helicopters** ( ☎ 03-319 6609; www.worldofwhales.co.nz; Railway Station; 15-60min flight from $100-455) Reliable whale-spotting flights (standard tour 30 minutes $195 for 3 or more people), plus jaunts around the peninsula, Mt Fyffe, and peaks beyond.

**Whale Watch Kaikoura** ( ☎ 0800 655 121, 03-319 6767; www.whalewatch.co.nz; Whaleway Station; 3hr tour adult/child $145/60) With knowledgeable guides and fascinating 'world of whales' onboard animation, Kaikoura's biggest operator heads out (with admirable frequency) in boats equipped with hydrophones (under-

water microphones) to pick up whale soundings.

## DOLPHIN & SEAL SPOTTING

**Dolphin Encounter** ( ☎ 0800 733 365, 03-319 6777; www.dolphin.co.nz; 96 The Esplanade; swim adult/child $165/150, observation $80/40; ☺ 8.30am & 12.30pm year-round, plus 5.30am in summer) Here's your chance to rub shoulders with pods of dusky dolphins on three-hour tours; wet suits, masks and snorkels are provided.

**Kaikoura Kayaks** ( ☎ 0800 452 456, 03-319 7118; www.kaikourakayaks.co.nz; 19 Killarney St; seal tours adult/child $85/70; ☺ 8.30am, 12.30pm & 4.30pm Nov-Apr, 9am & 1pm May-Oct) Guided sea-kayak tours to view fur seals and explore the peninsula's coastline.

DAVID WALL

Whale tail, Kaikoura

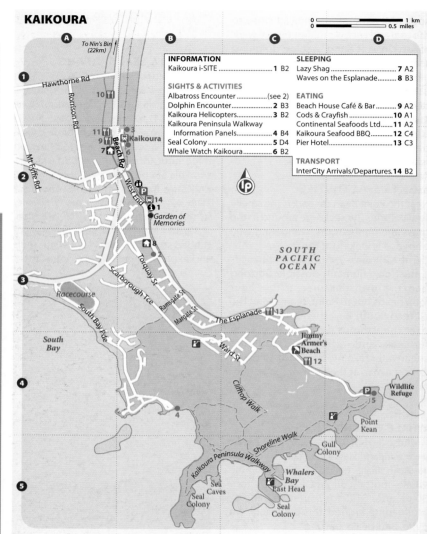

**KAIKOURA**

0 ____ 1 km
0 ____ 0.5 miles

**INFORMATION**
Kaikoura i-SITE .......................... **1** B2

**SIGHTS & ACTIVITIES**
Albatross Encounter ..................(see 2)
Dolphin Encounter......................... **2** B3
Kaikoura Helicopters...................... **3** B2
Kaikoura Peninsula Walkway
   Information Panels..................... **4** B4
Seal Colony .................................. **5** D4
Whale Watch Kaikoura.................. **6** B2

**SLEEPING**
Lazy Shag ..................................... **7** A2
Waves on the Esplanade........... **8** B3

**EATING**
Beach House Café & Bar ............. **9** A2
Cods & Crayfish .......................... **10** A1
Continental Seafoods Ltd....... **11** A2
Kaikoura Seafood BBQ........... **12** C4
Pier Hotel................................... **13** C3

**TRANSPORT**
InterCity Arrivals/Departures.**14** B2

To Nin's Bin
(22km)

Hawthorne Rd
Rorrison Rd
Mt Fyffe Rd
Beach Rd
Kaikoura
West End
Torquay St
Scarborough Tce
Ramsgate St
Margate St
South Bay Pde
Racecourse
South Bay
Ward St
The Esplanade
Clifftop Walk
Cliffside Walk
Shoreline Walk
Kaikoura Peninsula Walkway
Garden of Memories
Jimmy Armer's Beach
Whalers Bay
East Head
Sea Caves
Seal Colony
Seal Colony
Gull Colony
Point Kean
Wildlife Refuge

SOUTH PACIFIC OCEAN

## BIRDWATCHING

**Albatross Encounter** ( ☎ 0800 733 365, 03-319 6777; www.oceanwings.co.nz; 96 The Esplanade; adult/child $110/55; ⏱ 9am & 1pm year-round, plus 6am in summer) is run by the same folks as Dolphin Encounter.

## SLEEPING & EATING

**Lazy Shag** ( ☎ 03-319 6662; lazy-shag@hotmail. com; 37 Beach Rd; dm/s/d $25/50/65; 🖳 🛜 ) The name refers to a local bird species, not the behaviour of guests (but don't rule it out…). This smart lodge occupies a prime spot, with cafes left and right and a party-prone deck taking in mountain views. All rooms have bathrooms; there's a separate TV lounge and pleasant back yard.

**Kaikoura Cottage Motels** ( ☎ 0800 526 882, 03-319 5599; www.kaikouracottagemotels. co.nz; cnr Old Beach & Mill Rds; d $95-140; 🛜 ) This enclave of eight modern tourist flats is looking mighty fine, surrounded by attractive native plantings now in full flourish. Orientated for mountain views, the self-contained units sleep four between an open plan studio-style living room and one private bedroom. Soothing sand-and-sky colour scheme and quality chattels.

**Waves on the Esplanade** ( ☎ 0800 319 589, 03-319 5890; www.kaikouraapartments. co.nz; 78 The Esplanade; apt $190-325; 🛜 ) Can't do without the comforts of home? Here you go: luxury two-bedroom apartments with Sky TV, DVD player, two bathrooms, laundry facilities and full kitchen. Oh, and superb ocean views from the balcony.

**Beach House Café & Bar** ( ☎ 03-319 6030; 39 Beach Rd; mains $8-20; 🕙 9am-4pm) Serving the best brunch and coffee in town, this

Moa beer

MOA BREWERY

## 🔖 IF YOU LIKE...

If you like (or perhaps, if you don't like) the Marlborough wineries (p221), check out the local lager scene at these quality beer barns:

- Moa (Map p222; ☎ 03-572 5146; www.moabeer.co.nz; Jacksons Rd; 🕙 noon-late summer, noon-late Fri-Sun winter) Winemaker's son Josh Scott brews an excellent range of bottle-fermented beers and thirst-quenching ciders at his tasting room-cum-bar in the thick of Marlborough's wineries.
- Renaissance ( ☎ 03-579 3400; www.renaissancebrewing.co.nz; 1 Dodson St, Blenheim; 🕙 11am-late Tue-Fri, 10am-late Sat & Sun) Sample quality Renaissance ales at the Dodson Street Bistro & Ale House, next door to the brewery. The malty Stonecutter Scotch Ale is fulsome and delicious.
- Cork & Keg (Map p222; ☎ 03-572 9328; Inkerman St, Renwick; 🕙 noon-late) English-style country boozer with a pleasant beer patio and pub grub. Moa, West Coast and Benger Gold Cider on tap.

chipper roadside cafe garners more than its fair share of the passing trade. Sit on the front terrace or back deck and reconstitute with green eggs and ham, fish and chips or seafood chowder.

**our pick** **Pier Hotel** ( ☎ 03-319 5037; 1 Avoca St; lunch $14-22, dinner $25-36; ☺ noon-3pm & 5pm-late) Wide views of bay and mountains beyond make this the grandest dining room in town. A cheerful crew serve up generous portions of honest food, such as fresh local fish, venison medallions and crayfish for those with fat wallets. The enticing public bar has reasonably priced beer and bar snacks, historical photos, and a garden bar. What more could you want?

### GETTING THERE & AWAY

#### BUS

**InterCity** ( ☎ 03-365 1113; www.intercity.co.nz) buses run between Kaikoura and Nelson ($64, 3½ hours, one daily), Picton ($35, 2¼ hours, two daily) and Christchurch ($31, 23/4 hours, two daily).

**Naked Bus** ( ☎ 0900 625 33; www.nakedbus. com) also runs to/from Kaikoura to most South Island destinations, departing from the i-SITE.

#### TRAIN

**Tranz Scenic** ( ☎ 0800 872 467, 04-495 0775; www.tranzscenic.co.nz) runs the *TranzCoastal* service, stopping at Kaikoura on its daily run between Picton ($58, two hours 20 minutes) and Christchurch ($60, three hours). The northbound train departs Kaikoura at 9.54am; the southbound at 3.28pm.

## NELSON REGION
### NELSON

pop 43,500

Dishing up a winning combination of great weather, beautiful surroundings, and a high number of charming wooden houses, Nelson is hailed as one of New Zealand's most 'liveable' cities.

**Nelson i-SITE** ( ☎ 03-548 2304; www.nelson nz.com; cnr Trafalgar & Halifax Sts; ☺ 8.30am-5pm

JENNY & TONY ENDERBY

Kitesurfing (p228), Tasman Bay, Nelson

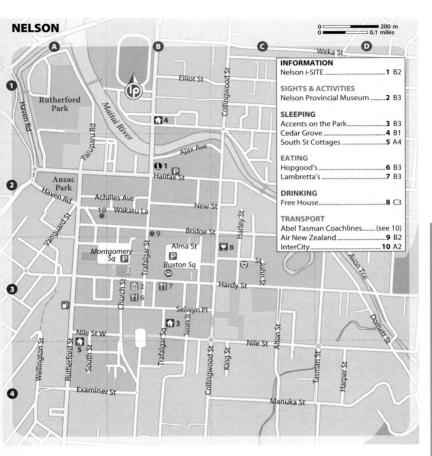

**NELSON**

**Mon-Fri, 9am-5pm Sat & Sun)** Pick up a copy of the *Nelson/Tasman Region Visitor Guide*. The DOC information desk has the lowdown on national parks and walks (including the Abel Tasman and Heaphy tracks).

## SIGHTS

Nelson exudes creativity: it's hardly surprising that NZ's most inspiring fashion show was born here. The concept was to create a piece of art that could be worn and modelled. The idea caught on, and the World of WearableArt Awards Show became an annual event. The awards show has been transplanted to Wellington (p48), but you can ogle entries at Nelson's World of WearableArt & Classic Cars Museum (WOW; ☎ 03-547 4573; www.wowcars.co.nz; 1 Cadillac Wy; adult/child $20/8; ☉ 10am-5pm).

The Nelson Provincial Museum (☎ 03-548 9588; www.nelsonmuseum.co.nz; cnr Hardy & Trafalgar Sts; admission by donation; ☉ 9am-5pm Mon-Fri, 10am-4.30pm Sat & Sun) is one of Nelson's showpieces. The modern space is filled with cultural heritage and natural history exhibits with a regional bias, and there's a great rooftop garden.

MARLBOROUGH & NELSON

NELSON REGION

Caravan selling crayfish, Kaikoura

JOHN ELK III

## ⅃ IF YOU LIKE...

If you like the seafood at the **Pier Hotel** (p226) here are a few less-formal ways to get some *koura* (crayfish) on your plate in Kaikoura:

- **Kaikoura Seafood BBQ** (☎ 027 376 3619; Fyffe Quay; ☼ 10.30am-dark) Alfresco roadside stall near the seal colony – try a fish or scallop sandwich if crayfish doesn't float your boat.
- **Nin's Bin** (☎ 03-319 6454; SH1; ☼ 8am-6pm) An iconic surf-side caravan 23km north of town. Upwards of $35 should get you a decent specimen.
- **Cods & Crayfish** (☎ 03-319 7899; 81 Beach Rd; ☼ 8am-6pm) The place for fresh cooked or uncooked crays.
- **Continental Seafoods** (☎ 03-319 5509; 47 Beach Rd; ☼ 7am-9pm) Fish-and-chipper usually offering a half-cray with salad and chips.

## ACTIVITIES

Tandem paragliding costs around $180, while introductory courses are around $250. Some good operators include the following:

**Adventure Paragliding & Kiteboarding** (☎ 0800 212 359, 03-540 2183; www.skyout.co.nz)

**Cumulus Paragliding** (☎ 03-929 5515; www.cumulus-tandems.co.nz)

**Nelson Paragliding** (☎ 0508 359 669, 03-544 1182; www.nelsonparagliding.co.nz)

An introduction to kiteboarding will cost you around $170:

**Kitescool** (☎ 021 354 837; www.kitescool.co.nz)

**Kite Surf Nelson** (☎ 0800 548 363; www.kitesurfnelson.co.nz)

Hang gliding is arranged through one of two operators:

**Nelson Hang Gliding Adventures** (☎ 03-548 9151; www.flynelson.co.nz; flight $165)

**Hang Gliding New Zealand** (☎ 0800 212 359, 03-540 2183; www.hanggliding.co.nz; flight $180).

Hit the hillside mountain bike trails with **Biking Nelson** (☎ 021 861 725; www.bikingnelson.co.nz), which runs three-hour guided rides including equipment for $99, and hire half-/full-day $40/60.

## SLEEPING

**our pick** **Accents on the Park** ( ☎ 0800 888 335, 03-548 4335; www.accentsonthepark.com; 335 Trafalgar Sq; tent sites $30, dm $20-28, d with/ without bathroom $92/60; 🖳 🛜 ) Prepare to be dazzled. This perfectly positioned hostel has a hotel feel with its professional staff, balconies, on-site cafe-bar (with Mother's home cooking and movie nights with free popcorn), soundproofed rooms, quality linen, superclean bathrooms and bikes for hire. Bravo! (Book early.)

**Cedar Grove** ( ☎ 0800 233 274, 03-545 1133; www.cedargrove.co.nz; cnr Trafalgar & Grove Sts; studio $130-180, d $170-220; 🖳 ) A big old cedar landmarks this smart, modern block of spacious apartments just three minutes' walk to town. Their range of studios and doubles are plush and elegant, with cooking facilities and all the business trimmings (phone, fax, internet jack).

**South Street Cottages** ( ☎ 03-540 2769; www.cottageaccommodation.co.nz; 1, 3 & 12 South St; d $215, apt $240) Stay on NZ's oldest pre-served street in one of three endearing, two-bedroom self-contained cottages built in the 1860s. Each has all the com-forts of home, including kitchen, laundry, log fire and courtyard garden; breakfast provisions supplied. There is a two-night minimum stay. The owners also have a modern two-bedroom apartment on the same street.

## EATING & DRINKING

**Lambretta's** ( ☎ 03-545 8555; 204 Hardy St; mains $16-28; 🕙 7.30am-10pm Mon-Sat, to 5pm in winter, 8.30am-3pm Sun) Feeding what seems like half of Nelson, Lambretta's is a con-tinually busy diner-style joint with ample seating inside and out. Family friendly, the big-eatin' offerings include breakfast, lunch and dinner (pizza, pasta, salad) and hearty counter food along the lines of hu-mungous muffins, pies, filled croissants and sandwiches. Good coffee too.

**Hopgood's** ( ☎ 03-545 7191; 284 Trafalgar St; lunch $14-20, dinner $33-36; 🕙 11am-2pm Thu & Fri, 5.30-late Mon-Sat) Tongue-and-groove–lined Hopgood's is perfect for a romantic dinner or holiday treat. The food is deca-dent and skilfully prepared but unfussy, allowing quality local ingredients to shine. The Asian crispy duck followed by pork belly with watercress and apple purée is a knockout. Desirous, predominantly Kiwi wine list.

**our pick** **Free House** ( ☎ 03-548 9391; 95 Collingwood St; 🕙 4pm-late Mon-Fri, 12pm-late Sat, 12-6pm Sun) Come rejoice at this church of ales. Tastefully converted from its origi-nal, more reverent purpose, it's now home to an excellent, oft-changing selection of NZ craft beers. Hallelujah.

## GETTING THERE & AWAY
### AIR

**Air New Zealand** ( ☎ 0800 737 000, 03-546 3100; www.airnewzealand.co.nz; cnr Trafalgar & Bridge Sts; 🕙 9am-5pm Mon-Fri) has direct flights to/from Wellington (from $79, up to 12 daily), Auckland (from $99, up to 10 daily) and Christchurch (from $79, up to six daily).

**Soundsair** ( ☎ 0800 505 005, 03-520 3080; www.soundsair.com) flies daily between Nelson and Wellington (from $90, up to three daily).

### BUS

**Abel Tasman Coachlines** ( ☎ 03-548 0285; www.abeltasmantravel.co.nz; departs SBL Travel Centre, Bridge St) operates services to Motueka ($12, one hour, four daily), Takaka ($32, two hours, two daily), Kaiteriteri ($20, two hours, 4 daily) and Marahau ($20, 2 hours, 4 daily).

**Atomic Shuttles** ( ☎ 03-349 0697; www. atomictravel.co.nz) runs from Picton to

Nelson ($24, 2¼ hours, twice daily) continuing from Nelson to West Coast centres like Greymouth ($40, 5¾ hours, one daily) and Fox Glacier ($65, 9½ hours, one daily).

**Naked Bus** (☎ 0900 625 33; www.nakedbus.com) South Island destinations from Nelson include Blenheim (from $14, 1¾ hours, up to two daily), Motueka ($11, one hour, one daily) and Westport ($34, 3¾ hours, one daily).

**InterCity** (☎ 03-548 1538; www.intercity.co.nz; departs SBL Travel Centre, Bridge St) runs from Nelson to:

| TO | PRICE | HOW LONG | HOW OFTEN |
| --- | --- | --- | --- |
| Christchurch | $71 | 7hr | 1 daily |
| Kaikoura | $64 | 3½hr | 1 daily |
| Picton | $34 | 2hr | 1-3 daily |

# ABEL TASMAN NATIONAL PARK

The accessible, coastal Abel Tasman is NZ's most visited national park. The park blankets the northern end of a range of marble and limestone hills extending from Kahurangi National Park; its interior is honeycombed with caves and potholes. There are various tracks in the park, including an inland route, although the Coast Track is what everyone is here for.

## ABEL TASMAN COAST TRACK

This 51km, three- to five-day track is one of the most scenic in the country, passing through native bush overlooking golden beaches lapped by gleaming azure water. Visitors can walk into the park, catch water taxis to beaches and resorts along the track, or kayak along the coast.

### INFORMATION

The track operates on a **Great Walks Pass** (per person campsites/huts $12/30 Oct-Apr, $12/8 May-Sep) system. Children are free but booking is still required. The **Great Walks Helpdesk** (☎ 03-546 8210; greatwalksbooking@doc.govt.nz) offers information and can make bookings. You can also book online (www.doc.govt.nz) or in person at the Nelson, Motueka and Takaka i-SITES,

Golden Bay, Abel Tasman National Park

MICAH WRIGHT

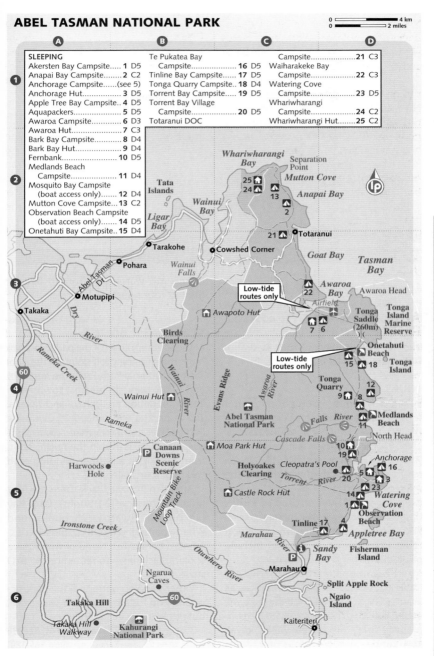

# ABEL TASMAN NATIONAL PARK

**SLEEPING**
Akersten Bay Campsite..... **1** D5
Anapai Bay Campsite........ **2** C2
Anchorage Campsite......(see 5)
Anchorage Hut................. **3** D5
Apple Tree Bay Campsite.. **4** D5
Aquapackers..................... **5** D5
Awaroa Campsite............. **6** D3
Awaroa Hut....................... **7** C3
Bark Bay Campsite............ **8** D4
Bark Bay Hut.................... **9** D4
Fernbank......................... **10** D5
Medlands Beach
 Campsite..................... **11** D4
Mosquito Bay Campsite
 (boat access only)....... **12** D4
Mutton Cove Campsite... **13** C2
Observation Beach Campsite
 (boat access only)....... **14** D5
Onetahuti Bay Campsite.. **15** D4

Te Pukatea Bay
 Campsite.................... **16** D5
Tinline Bay Campsite...... **17** D5
Tonga Quarry Campsite.. **18** D4
Torrent Bay Campsite..... **19** D5
Torrent Bay Village
 Campsite.................... **20** D5
Totaranui DOC

Campsite.................... **21** C3
Waiharakeke Bay
 Campsite.................... **22** C3
Watering Cove
 Campsite.................... **23** D5
Whariwharangi
 Campsite.................... **24** C2
Whariwharangi Hut........ **25** C2

MARLBOROUGH & NELSON

ABEL TASMAN NATIONAL PARK

Azure beaches, Abel Tasman National Park

MICAH WRIGHT

where staff can offer suggestions to tailor the track to your needs and organise transport at each end. Try to book your trip well ahead of time, especially if you're planning on staying in huts between December and March.

## TOURS

See p234 for information about water taxis to the park and scenic flights.

**Abel Tasman Seal Swim** ( ☎ 0800 252 925, 03-527 8383; www.sealswim.com; Aqua Taxi Base, Marahau; 5hr seal swim adult/child $169/130, seal watch $90/70) Tide-scheduled trips to the seal colony.

**Abel Tasman Tours & Guided Walks** ( ☎ 03-528 9602; www.abeltasmantours.co.nz; $195) Small-group, day-long walking tours (minimum two people) include packed lunch and water taxis.

**Abel Tasman Wilson's Experiences** ( ☎ 0800 221 888, 03-528 2027; www.abeltasman .co.nz; 265 High St, Motueka; half-day cruise $70, cruise & walk $55-70, kayak & walk $89-195) Impressive array of cruises, walks, kayak and combo tours. Luxurious beachfront lodges at Awaroa and Torrent Bay for guided-tour guests.

## SLEEPING & EATING

At the southern edge of the park, Marahau is the main jumping-off point for the Abel Tasman National Park. From the northern end of the park, the nearest towns with accommodation are Pohara and Takaka. The whopping **Totaranui DOC Campsite** ( ☎ 03-528 8083; www.doc.govt.nz; unpowered site adult/child $12/6) is also in the north, 32km from Takaka on a narrow, winding road (12km of it unsealed).

Along the Coast Track there are four huts: Anchorage (24 bunks), Bark Bay (34 bunks), Awaroa (26 bunks) and Whariwharangi (20 bunks), plus 19 designated campsites. None of these have cooking facilities – so remember to BYO stove.

Other sleeping options in the park, accessible on foot, by kayak or water taxi, but not by road, include:

**Aquapackers** ( ☎ 0800 430 744, 027 230 7002; www.aquapackers.co.nz; dm/d $65/180)

The *MV Parore* (a former Navy patrol boat) and *Catarac* (a 13m catamaran), moored permanently in Anchorage Bay, provide unusual, but buoyant backpacker options. Facilities are basic but decent; prices include bedding, dinner and breakfast.

**Fernbank** ( ☎ 027 369 9555; www.abeltasman accommodation.co.nz; Torrent Bay; d $160, extra adult/child $15/10) Fernbank comprises two

Sea kayaking, Appletree Bay, Abel Tasman National Park

DAVID WALL

## ❧ PADDLING THE ABEL TASMAN

The Abel Tasman Coast Track has long been trampers' territory, but its main attractions – scenic beaches, isolated coves and rock formations – make it an equally seductive spot for sea kayaking. Fortunately, kayaking can easily be combined with walking and camping.

You can kayak from half a day up to three days, camping ($12 per night) or staying in DOC huts ($30 per night), baches, even a floating backpackers (opposite), either fully catered for or self-catering. You can kayak one day, camp overnight then walk back, or walk further into the park and catch a water taxi back.

Marahau is the main base, but trips also depart Kaiteriteri. A popular choice if time is tight is a half-day guided kayak trip in the south of the park, followed by a walk along the track between Bark Bay and Torrent Bay. This will cost around $160 including water taxis.

Peak season runs from November to Easter, but you can paddle year-round. December to February is the busiest time – it's worth timing your visit earlier or later. In winter you'll see more bird life, and the weather is surprisingly amenable.

**Things you need to know**: Abel Tasman Kayaks ( ☎ 0800 732 529, 03-527 8022; www. abeltasmankayaks.co.nz; Main Rd, Marahau); Kahu Kayaks ( ☎ 0800 300 101, 03-527 8300; www. kahukayaks.co.nz; Sandy Bay Rd, Marahau); Kaiteriteri Kayaks ( ☎ 0800 252 925, 03-527 8383; www.seakayak.co.nz; Kaiteriteri Beach & Marahau Beach Rd, Marahau); Marahau Sea Kayaks ( ☎ 0800 529 257, 03-527 8176; www.msk.net.nz; Abel Tasman Centre, Franklin St, Marahau); Sea Kayak Company ( ☎ 0508 252 925, 03-528 7251; www.seakayaknz.co.nz; 506 High St, Motueka)

MARLBOROUGH & NELSON

NELSON REGION

classic holiday homes at Torrent Bay; each self-contained house can sleep up to seven and are only a minute from the beach. BYO linen (or pay an extra charge) and food.

## GETTING THERE & AWAY
### AIR
**Abel Tasman Air** ( ☎ 0800 304 560, 03-528 8290; www.abeltasmanair.co.nz) Flies to Awaroa from Motueka ($175) or Nelson ($265). Scenic flights available; Heaphy Track connections as well.

**Tasman Helicopters** ( ☎ 03-528 8075; www.tasmanhelicopters.co.nz) Motueka to Awaroa by helicopter costs from $150, one way.

### BUS
**Abel Tasman Coachlines** ( ☎ 03-528 8850; www.abeltasmantravel.co.nz) runs from Nelson to Motueka, then on to:

| TO | PRICE | HOW LONG | HOW OFTEN |
|---|---|---|---|
| Kaiteriteri | $10 | 25min | 3 daily |
| Marahau | $10 | 30min | 3-4 daily |
| Takaka | $23 | 1hr | 2 daily |

**Golden Bay Coachlines** ( ☎ 03-525 8352; www.goldenbaycoachlines.co.nz) run from November to April from Takaka around once daily to Wainui carpark ($16) and Totaranui ($20).

## GETTING AROUND
The beauty of Abel Tasman is that it's easy to get to/from any point on the track by water taxi, either from Kaiteriteri or Marahau. Operators include:

**Abel Tasman Aqua Taxi** ( ☎ 0800 278 282, 03-527 8083; www.aquataxi.co.nz; Kaiteriteri & Marahau)

**Abel Tasman Sea Shuttle** ( ☎ 0800 732 748, 03-527 8688; www.abeltasmanseashuttles.co.nz; Kaiteriteri)

**Marahau Water Taxis** ( ☎ 0800 808 018, 03-527 8176; www.abeltasmancentre.co.nz; Abel Tasman Centre, Franklin St, Marahau)

# CHRISTCHURCH & CENTRAL SOUTH

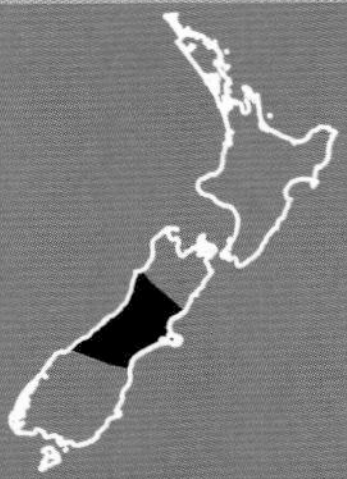

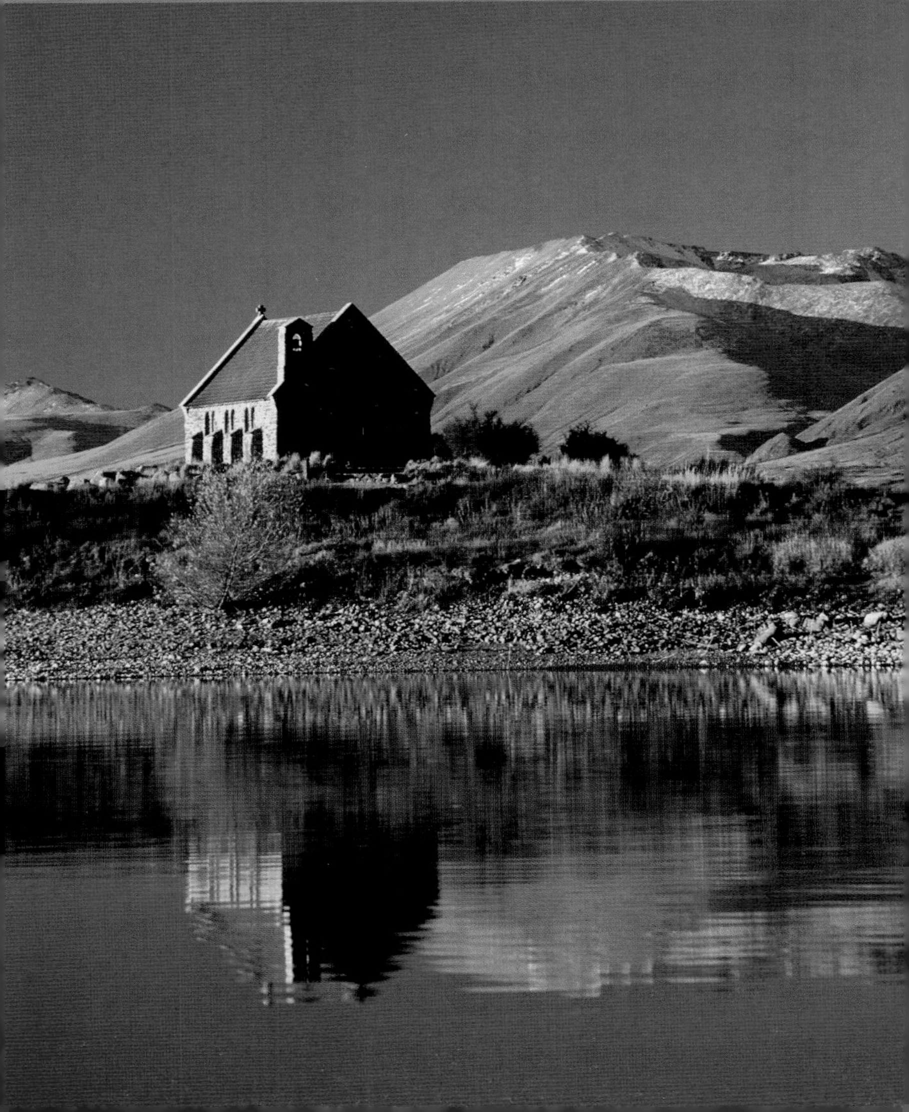

DAVID WALL

ChristChurch Cathedral (p250), Christchurch

# CHRISTCHURCH & CENTRAL SOUTH

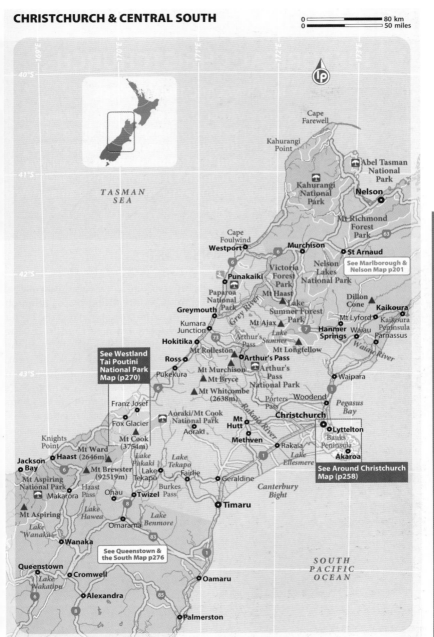

80 km
50 miles

Cape
Farewell

Kahurangi
Point

TASMAN
SEA

Abel Tasman
National
Park

Kahurangi
National
Park

Nelson

Mt Richmond
Forest
Park

Cape
Foulwind

Westport

Murchison

St Arnaud

See Marlborough &
Nelson Map p201

Punakaiki

Victoria
Forest
Park

Nelson
Lakes
National Park

Dillon
Cone

Kaikoura

Paparoa
National
Park

Mt Haast

Lake
Sumner Forest
Park

Mt Lyford

Kaikoura
Peninsula

Greymouth

Grey River

Mt Ajax

Hanmer
Springs

Wiau

Parnassus

Kumara
Junction

Arthur's
Pass

Lake
Sumner

Waiau River

Hokitika

Mt Rolleston

Mt Longfellow

See Westland
Tai Poutini
National Park
Map (p270)

Ross

Mt Murchison

Arthur's
Pass

Waipara

Pukekura

Mt Bryce

Arthur's
Pass
National Park

Mt Whitcombe
(2638m)

Porters
Pass

Woodend

Pegasus
Bay

Franz Josef

Aoraki/Mt Cook
National Park

Mt
Hutt

Christchurch

Fox Glacier

Mt Cook
(3754m)

Aoraki

Methven

Lyttelton

Banks
Peninsula

Knights
Point

Mt Ward
(2646m)

Lake
Pukaki

Lake
Tekapo

Rakaia

Akaroa

See Around Christchurch
Map (p258)

Jackson
Bay

Haast

Mt Brewster
(92519m)

Lake
Tekapo

Fairlie

Lake
Ellesmere

Mt Aspiring
National Park

Haast
Pass

Ohau

Burkes
Pass

Geraldine

Canterbury
Bight

Makarora

Twizel

Mt Aspiring

Lake
Hawea

Lake
Benmore

Timaru

Lake
Wanaka

Omarama

Wanaka

See Queenstown &
the South Map p276

SOUTH
PACIFIC
OCEAN

Queenstown

Cromwell

Oamaru

Lake
Wakatipu

Alexandra

Palmerston

# HIGHLIGHTS

## 1 HISTORICAL CHRISTCHURCH

### BY ROY SINCLAIR, TRAM DRIVER

The preservation of the Gothic-style buildings in central Christchurch is unique, and up to 12% of the city is either park or reserves. Hagley Park, Victoria Sq and the Botanic Gardens are all very central. Christchurch's tramway is also special; apparently a lot of other New Zealand cities now also want a tram.

## ↘ ROY SINCLAIR'S DON'T MISS LIST

### ❶ AVON RIVER

The willow trees around the Avon (p252) apparently came from willows surrounding Napoleon's grave on St Helena. When Mark Twain visited in 1895, he wrote that the willows were the most noble anywhere because of their wonderful ancestry. A plaque commemorating the trees was added near the river in 2001.

### ❷ CHRIST'S COLLEGE

Christ's College (www.christscollege.com) is an interesting place, although I went to the school that had the better rugby team. I was at Christ's College taking photographs once: through the day the buildings all look different, with the stonework standing out in relief in the low light. It's actually NZ's largest collection of heritage buildings owned by a single organisation.

Clockwise from top: Arts Centre (p250); Lunchtime at Christ's College; City trams; Avon River (p252)

### ❸ CHRISTCHURCH CATHEDRAL

I heard in the pulpit of the church once that the reason the cathedral (p250) took forty years to build was because the city fathers of the time were more interested in pubs and brothels than getting the church completed. It's now the most visited church in NZ.

### ❹ ARTS CENTRE

Part of the Arts Centre (p250) is Rutherford's Den, the laboratory of Sir Ernest Rutherford, the first person to split the atom. It's a little ironic that NZ now has an antinuclear foreign policy, as it was a Kiwi that made nuclear energy possible in the first place. Next door is the Great Hall, which has a very photogenic stained-glass window.

### ❺ CHRISTCHURCH TRAMWAY

Drivers on the Christchurch trams (p250) have become ambassadors for the city. I even get to drive past my old workplace at the *Press* newspaper every 25 minutes. An extension is due to open in time for the 2011 Rugby World Cup, and when a second extension is added soon after, it'll be a really comprehensive tram tour.

---

### ↘ THINGS YOU NEED TO KNOW

**Fuel stop** The Dux de Lux (p254), after the Arts Centre's Sunday afternoon market **Recommended tipple** Dux's Nor'wester Strong Ale, named after Canterbury's warm, dry wind **Best modern building** Christchurch Art Gallery (p251) **For full coverage of the city's sights, see p250**

# HIGHLIGHTS

## ⬎ AKAROA & BANKS PENINSULA

Did you know that the South Island almost became a French colony instead of an Anglo outpost? The Brits managed to hoist the Union Jack just two days before 63 French settlers arrived in 1840. **Akaroa** on the **Banks Peninsula** (p258) retains a distinct French influence (good croissants). The picturesque volcanic peninsula also offers hiking, dolphin swimming and sea kayaking.

## ⬎ AORAKI/MT COOK

Standing proud at 3754m, **Aroaki/Mt Cook** (p264) is something to behold. It's quite cloud-covered, but on a clear day the jagged, heaven-high peak is inspiring and humbling. Even when it is cloudy, this mountain's magnitude is undeniable. Walking around the lake-strewn foothills in the crisp alpine air as avalanches rumble on distant slopes, you'll be forgiven for feeling a tad insignificant!

**4**

## GLACIERS

Quick, scoot over to the West Coast and see Franz Josef Glacier (p269) and Fox Glacier (p173) before global warming melts them. You probably don't have to be there in the next 10 minutes – there's a heckuva lot of ice here. Take a hike around the jagged glacial faces, or a scenic flight above or onto these massive rivers of ice.

**5**

## PUNAKAIKI ROCKS

Weird! Piled up like giant-sized flapjacks, the West Coast's Punakaiki Rocks (p266) are worth writing home about – oddball geologic formations will make you wonder if someone/something really did design this lonely planet (and possibly make you hungry). The ocean booms through blowholes nearby.

**6**

## HANMER SPRINGS

Forget your Blackberry, your briefcase, your business...you've come on holiday to *really* de-stress, haven't you? Take a trip 1½ hours north from Christchurch to hassle-free Hanmer Springs (p261), passing rivers, vineyards, mountains and country towns en route. Take a dip in hot mineral springs or have a massage before hitting the restaurants and bars.

2 DAVID WALL; 3 TIM BARKER; 4 DAVID WALL; 5 DOUGLAS STEAKLEY; 6 ROBERT BIRD/ALAMY

2 Akaroa, Banks Peninsula (p258); 3 Aoraki/Mt Cook (p264); 4 Fox Glacier (p273), Westland Tai Poutini National Park; 5 Pancake Rocks (p266), Punakaiki; 6 Hot springs, Hanmer Springs (p261)

# BEST...

## ⭢ NATURAL WONDERS

- **Franz Josef & Fox Glaciers** (p269 and p273) There's only one word that fits…awesome!
- **Aoraki/Mt Cook** (p264) Nobody reached the top until 1894 – it's *really* big.
- **Banks Peninsula** (p258) Spaghetti-like volcanic coastlines.
- **Punakaiki Rocks** (p266) Giant dolomite pancakes…Pass the maple syrup.

## ⭢ SHORT HIKES

- **Christchurch city walks** (p251) Strolls from 1½ hours and up.
- **Hooker Valley** (p264) Glacial streams, swing bridges and pano-ramas.
- **Banks Peninsula Track** (p258) Two- to four-day hop across farm-land by the coast.
- **Mt John** (p263) Three-hour return hike to the summit above Lake Tekapo.

## ⭢ PLACES TO UNWIND

- **Banks of the Avon** (p252) Kick back riverside in downtown Christchurch.
- **Hanmer Springs** (p261) Slip into a hot spa or get a massage.
- **Akaroa** (p258) Sip a coffee, munch a pastry and watch the passers-by.
- **Monteith's Brewing Co** (p268) Big, beery and beautiful on the West Coast.

## ⭢ PLACES TO GET GIDDY

- **Aoraki/Mt Cook** (p264) As high as Kiwis get without wings.
- **Methven** (p262) Everybody sing: '*Up, up and away, my beautiful, my beautiful balloon*'.
- **Franz Josef and Fox Glaciers** (p269 and p273) See them from above with wings or rotorblades.
- **TranzAlpine** (p271) Epic train ride over the Southern Alps.

LEFT: PAUL KENNEDY; RIGHT: GLENN VAN DER KNIJFF

**Left: Akaroa, Banks Peninsula (p258); Punting on the Avon River (p252), Christchurch**

# THINGS YOU NEED TO KNOW

## ⬎ VITAL STATISTICS

- **Population** Christchurch 344,100; Canterbury 559,200; West Coast 32,600
- **Telephone code** ☎ 03
- **Best time to visit** January to March (summer)

## ⬎ LOCALITIES IN A NUTSHELL

- **Christchurch** (p246) The big smoke down south, 'Chch' is an urbane and cultured kind of town.
- **Canterbury** (p261) The region beyond Christchurch offers sky-scraping mountains, convoluted peninsulas and braided rivers.
- **West Coast** (p266) Wild, rainy and eccentric, the West Coast is like nowhere else on Earth.

## ⬎ ADVANCE PLANNING

- **One month before** Book a seat on the *TranzAlpine* train (p271), and your beds from Akaroa to Fox Glacier.
- **Two weeks before** Organise a scenic flight above Mt Cook (p265) or the West Coast glaciers (p272 and p274), or a balloon trip in Methven (p262).
- **One week before** Book a table at a top Christchurch restaurant (p254) and a tour at Monteith's Brewing Co (p268) in Greymouth.

## ⬎ RESOURCES

- **Christchurch i-SITE** (www.christchurch nz.com)
- **DOC Aoraki/Mt Cook visitor information centre** (mtcookvc@doc .govt.nz) Advises on weather conditions, guided tours and tramping.
- **Franz Josef visitor information centre** (www.glaciercountry.co.nz, www .doc.govt.nz) Also the regional DOC office.

## ⬎ EMERGENCY NUMBER

- **Ambulance, fire service & police** (☎ 111)

## ⬎ GETTING AROUND

- **Bus** (p255) from town to town across Canterbury.
- **Hire a car** (p256) to explore beyond the Christchurch city limits.
- **Punt** (p252) along the lazy, languid River Avon.
- **Taxi** (p257) home after a night on the tiles in Lyttelton.
- **Train** across the Southern Alps on the *TranzAlpine* (p271).

# CHRISTCHURCH & CENTRAL SOUTH ITINERARIES

## CHRISTCHURCH EXPLORER Three Days

Hit **(1) Christchurch** (p246) running, with a kick-ass coffee at a central cafe (p254), then a juddery circuit on the city's tramway (p250) to assess the lay of the land. Jump off at the Arts Centre (p250) and have a sticky-beak around the galleries in the area. Other essentials to check off your list include the Canterbury Museum (p251) and the Christchurch Art Gallery (p251). Don't miss an evening session at one of the kooky bars in **(2) Lyttelton** (p257).

The Avon River cuts a lazy, inoffensive ribbon through Christchurch – check the flow on day two in the Botanic Gardens (p250) or push off into the stream on a punt (p252). Close down the day with some boozy wanderings around SOL Sq (p254 and p255).

The next day swarm the shops on High St before lunch at Lunes then dinner at Bodhi Tree (p254).

## GET OUT OF TOWN Five Days

Enough city already? Take a trip out of Christchurch for a ride on the (1) Gondola (p251), then cruise out to the formerly volcanic (2) Banks Peninsula (p258). Explore the very Frenchy (3) Akaroa (p258), with its wildlife-rich harbour, and the peninsula's photogenic outer bays. You can also swim with dolphins here and kayak around the coast.

Spend a few nights on the rambling road: wander west to (4) Lake Tekapo (p263) and the snowy heights of (5) Aoraki/Mt Cook (p264), where you can tramp, ski or take a scenic flight. Also out this way is (6) Methven (p262), a good-time ski-hub for Mt Hutt in winter, and the place to try hot-air ballooning in summer.

Give your compass a twirl: head over to the West Coast and back in a day on the (7) TranzAlpine (p271); or follow the needle north to (8) Hanmer Springs (p261), a low-key hot-springs resort town from which you can launch a wintertime skiing sortie.

## HEADING FOR THE COAST One Week

Trainspotters alert! The **(1) TranzAlpine** (p271), running between Christchurch and Greymouth on the West Coast, is one of the world's classic train rides. The journey through the photogenic Southern Alps is worthwhile in itself (you can head over and back in a day), or use **(2) Greymouth** (p268) as a launch pad to check out the rest of the west.

Before you leave Greymouth, don't miss a tour of Monteith's Brewing Co (p268), a West Coast brewery that started small but now has taps and barrels in pubs and bars across NZ (its Celtic Red ale is a knockout).

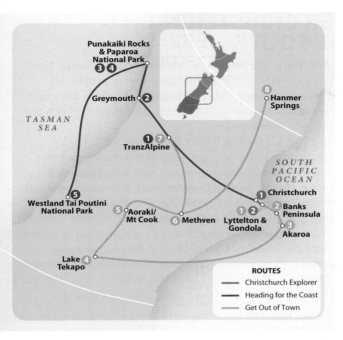

TASMAN SEA

Punakaiki Rocks & Paparoa National Park ❸ ❹

Greymouth ❷

TranzAlpine ❶ ❼

SOUTH PACIFIC OCEAN

Westland Tai Poutini National Park ❺

Aoraki/ ❺ Mt Cook

❻ Methven

Lyttelton & Gondola ❶ ❷

Lake ❹ Tekapo

❶ Christchurch

Banks ❷ Peninsula

Akaroa ❸

❽ Hanmer Springs

**ROUTES**
— Christchurch Explorer
— Heading for the Coast
— Get Out of Town

Heading south you'll bump into the famously globular **(3) Punakaiki Rocks** (p266); you can also take tramp near here in **(4) Paparoa National Park** (p267).

The Big Daddies of West Coast tourism are, however, the momentous Franz Josef Glacier and Fox Glacier, further south in **(5) Westland Tai Poutini National Park** (p267). If you've never seen a glacier before, these two will knock your socks off.

From the West Coast, you can save time with a short flight back to Christchurch from Hokitika.

# DISCOVER CHRISTCHURCH & CENTRAL SOUTH

The jewel of Canterbury, Christchurch is undoubtedly one of New Zealand's must-see cities, combining an easy-going provincial charm with the emerging verve of a metropolis. Modern bars and restaurants complement Gothic architecture, all mixed up with the relaxed ambience of a small town.

Within striking distance lie the Banks Peninsula, with the Francophile attractions of Akaroa, and the take-it-easy spa town of Hanmer Springs. Around Canterbury you can hurl yourself into tramping, mountain biking or skiing at Mt Hutt. Standing sentinel above it all is the country's tallest peak, Aoraki/Mt Cook.

Over the craggy Southern Alps is the West Coast, a truly unique part of NZ. With less than 1% of the country's population scattered amid almost 9% of the country's area, West Coast locals have adapted to become a rugged and individual breed. During summer a phalanx of campervans and tourist buses descends to ogle the kooky Punakaiki Rocks and gargantuan Franz Josef and Fox Glaciers.

## GETTING THERE & AROUND

Christchurch's international airport is serviced by several domestic airlines flying to key destinations around NZ.

Bus and shuttle operators run along the east coast, connecting coastal (and near-coastal) settlements with northern destinations such as Picton and Nelson, and southern towns such as Dunedin.

Rail options for east-coast and coast-to-coast travel are provided by Tranz Scenic; its *TranzAlpine* service connects Christchurch and Greymouth, and its *TranzCoastal* trains chug north to Picton, with connections to the North Island.

# CHRISTCHURCH

pop 344,100

Traditionally the most English of the NZ cities, Christchurch is now embracing the increasingly multicultural nature of urban NZ society. There's still plenty to remind visitors of the city's English past though, with a grand Anglican cathedral rising from a stately square, punts glidin[g] down the sleepy Avon River, and tram[s] rattling contentedly along Worcester St[

## ORIENTATION

Cathedral Sq is the centre of town and i[s] punctuated by the spire of ChristChurc[h] Cathedral. The western inner city is domi-nated by the Botanic Gardens. Colomb[o] St runs north–south through Cathedral S[q] and is the main shopping strip.

## INFORMATION

**24 Hour Surgery** (Bealey Ave Medical Cen-tre; Map p248; ☎ 03-365 7777; cnr Bealey Av[e] & Colombo St; ⏰ 24hr) North of town; n[o] appointment necessary.

**Christchurch Hospital** (Map p248; ☎ 03-364 0640, emergency dept 03-364 0270; 2 Ri[c]carton Ave)

**Christchurch i-SITE** (Map p248; ☎ 03-37[1] 9629; www.christchurchnz.com; Cathedral Sq[; ⏰ 8.30am-5pm, open later in summer) Trans-port, activities and accommodation.

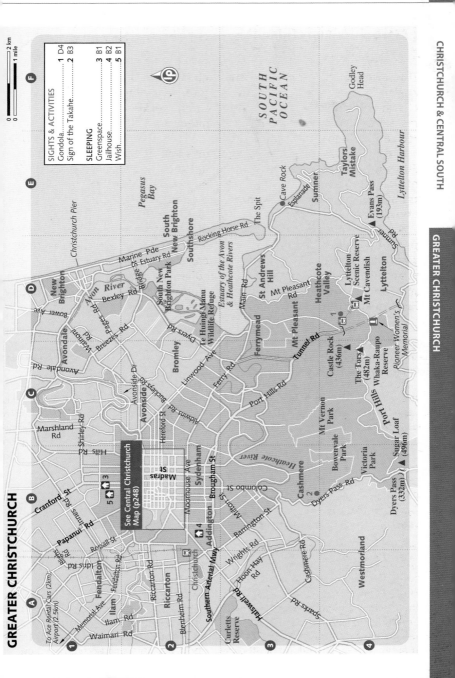

# GREATER CHRISTCHURCH

| SIGHTS & ACTIVITIES | |
|---|---|
| Gondola | **1** D4 |
| Sign of the Takahe | **2** B3 |
| **SLEEPING** | |
| Greenspace | **3** B1 |
| Jailhouse | **4** B2 |
| Wish | **5** B1 |

0 — 2 km
0 — 1 mile

# CENTRAL CHRISTCHURCH

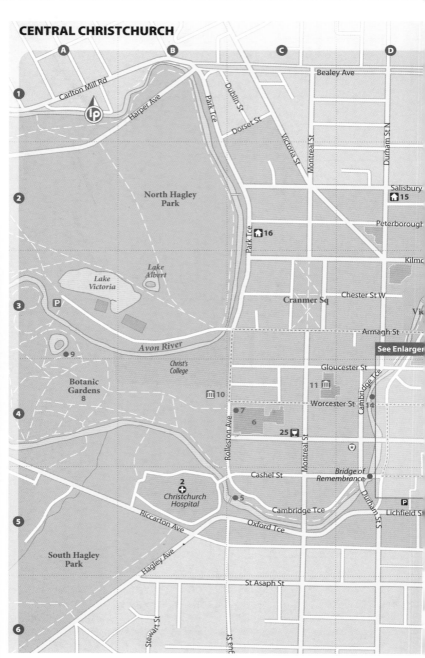

A B C D

1

Bealey Ave

Carlton Mill Rd

Harper Ave

Dublin St

Park Tce

Dorset St

Victoria St

Montreal St

Durham St N

2

North Hagley
Park

Park Tce

Salisbury
15

Peterborough

Kilmo

Lake
Albert

Lake
Victoria

Cranmer Sq

Chester St W

16

3

P

Armagh St

Vic

Avon River

See Enlarger

9

Christ's
College

Gloucester St

Cambridge Tce

Botanic
Gardens
8

11

10

Worcester St

14

4

7

6

25

Rolleston Ave

Montreal St

2
Christchurch
Hospital

Cashel St

Bridge of
Remembrance

5

Riccarton Ave

Cambridge Tce

Durham St S

Lichfield S

P

Oxford Tce

5

South Hagley
Park

Hagley Ave

St Asaph St

6

Stewart St

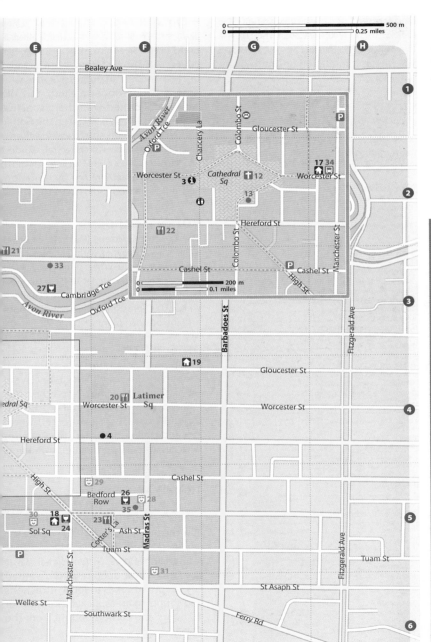

**Department of Conservation (DOC; Map p248; ☎ 03-371 3700; www.doc.govt.nz; Level 4, Torrens House, 195 Hereford St; ☼ 8.30am-5pm Mon-Fri)** Has information on South Island national parks and walkways.

# SIGHTS
## CATHEDRAL SQUARE
Cathedral Sq is where locals and tourists meet, giving the city's flat centrepiece a lively bustle.

**ChristChurch Cathedral (Map p248; ☎ 03-366 0046; www.christchurchcathedral.co.nz; Cathedral Sq; admission free; ☼ 8.30am-7pm Oct-Mar, 9am-5pm Apr-Sep)** was consecrated in 1881 and has an impressive rose window, wooden-ribbed ceiling and tile work emblazoned with the distinctive Fylfot Cross. Climb halfway up the Gothic church's 63m-high **spire (adult/child/family $5/2/10, tokens at the visitors centre)**. Guided 45-minute **tours (☼ 11am & 2pm Mon-Fri, 11am Sat & 11.30am Sun)** are by donation. Self-guided audio tours cost $10.

## BOTANIC GARDENS
The **Botanic Gardens (Map p248; ☎ 03-941 8999; www.ccc.govt.nz/parks/botanicgardens; Rolleston Ave; admission free; ☼ grounds 7am-1hr before sunset, conservatories 10.15am-4pm; ℗ )** comprise 30 riverside hectares planted with 10,000-plus specimens of indigenous and introduced plants.

## ARTS CENTRE
The former Canterbury College site (later Canterbury University), with its enclave of Gothic Revival buildings, is now the excellent **Arts Centre (Map p248; www.artscentre.org.nz; 2 Worcester St; admission free; ℗ )**, where arts and craft outlets share the premises with cinemas, a live theatre, restaurants and cafes.

## TRAMWAY
Trams were introduced to Christchurch streets in 1905 but were discontinued as a means of transport 50 years later. Restored **trams (☎ 03-366 7830; www.tram.co.nz; adult/child $15/5; ☼ 9am-9pm Nov-Mar, to 6pm Apr-Oct)** now operate a 2.5km inner-city loop that takes in local attractions and shopping areas. Tickets are valid for 48 hours and can be bought from the driver.

RICHARD CUMMINS

Curator's house, Botanic Gardens

## CANTERBURY MUSEUM

The absorbing **Canterbury Museum (Map p248; ☎ 03-366 5000; www.canterburymuseum. com; Rolleston Ave; donation $2; ⏰ 9am-5pm Apr-Sep, to 5.30pm Oct-Mar)** has a wonderful collection of items of significance to NZ. Guided tours (donations appreciated) run from 3.30pm to 4.30pm on Tuesday and Thursday. Kids will enjoy the interactive displays at Discovery (admission $2).

## CHRISTCHURCH ART GALLERY

Set in an eye-catching metal-and-glass construction built in 2003, the city's **art gallery (Map p248; ☎ 03-941 7300; www. christchurchartgallery.org.nz; cnr Worcester & Montreal Sts; admission free; ⏰ 10am-5pm Thu-Tue, to 9pm Wed)** has an engrossing permanent collection divided into historical, 20th-century and contemporary galleries, plus temporary exhibitions featuring NZ artists.

## GONDOLA

The **gondola (Map p247; ☎ 03-384 0700; www. gondola.co.nz; 10 Bridle Path Rd; return adult/child/** family $24/10/59; ⏰ 10am-9pm; Ⓟ )** whisks you from the Heathcote Valley terminal to the cafe-restaurant complex on Mt Cavendish (500m) in 10 minutes. Lyttelton bus 28 travels here.

# ACTIVITIES

**City Cycle Hire ( ☎ 0800 424 534, 03-377 5952; www.cyclehire-tours.co.nz; hal-/full day $25/35)** will deliver bikes to where you're staying. Mountain bikes (half-/full day $30/45) will get you nicely off-road.

The i-SITE has information on Christchurch walks. Within the city you'll find the **Riverside Walk** and various historical strolls, while further afield is the excellent cliff-top walk to **Taylors Mistake** (2½ hours).

For great views of the city, take the walkway from the **Sign of the Takahe** (Map p247) on Dyers Pass Rd.

You can walk to Lyttelton on the **Bridle Path** (1½ hours), which starts at Heathcote Valley (take bus 28). The **Godley Head Walkway** (two hours return) begins at Taylors Mistake, crossing and recrossing

Avon River punting

GLENN VAN DER KNI

## ↘ BOATING ON THE AVON

Dating from 1882, the photogenic green-and-white **Antigua Boatsheds** rents out various self-propelled vessels for independent Avon River exploration. The boatsheds are the starting point for **Punting on the Avon**, where someone else does all the work during a half-hour return trip in a flat-bottomed boat. There is another departure point for punting from the landing stage at the Worcester St bridge.

**Things you need to know: Antigua Boatsheds** (Map p248; ☎ 03-366 5885; www .boatsheds.co.nz; 2 Cambridge Tce; kayaks per hr from $10, row boats/paddle boats per 30 min/ hr $20/30; ☺ 9am-5pm); **Punting on the Avon** (Map p248; ☎ 03-366 0337; www.punting .co.nz; 30min trip adult/child $20/10; ☺ 9am-6pm Oct-Apr, 10am-4pm May-Sep)

Summit Rd, and offers beautiful views on a clear day.

From the gondola terminal on Mt Cavendish, walk to **Cavendish Bluff Lookout** (30 minutes return) or the **Pioneer Women's Memorial** (one hour return).

## TOURS

**Christchurch Bike Tours** (☎ 0800 733 257; www.chchbiketours.co.nz; tours from $35) Pedal around on fun, informative, two-hour tours in a city made for biking.
**Christchurch Personal Guiding Service** (Map p248; ☎ 03-379 9629; tours $15; ☺ 10am & 1pm Oct-Apr, 1pm May-Sep) Non-

profit organisation offering informative two-hour city walks. Get tickets from the i-SITE or the red-and-black kiosk in Cathedral Sq.
**Christchurch Sightseeing Tours** (☎ 0508 669 660, 03-366 9660; www.christchurch tours.co.nz; tours $40-46) Offers compre hensive half-day city tours year-round, a 3½-hour circuit of private gardens in spring and summer, and twice-weekly tours of heritage homes.

## SLEEPING

**our pick** **Jailhouse** (Map p247; ☎ 0800 52 546, 03-982 7777; www.jail.co.nz; 338 Lincoln Rd dm/s/d $26/49/70; Ⓟ ▯ ▢) Housed in an old prison that was built in 1874 and only decommissioned in 1999, the Jailhouse is a unique NZ hostel. Twins and doubles are a bit on the small side (remember, it was a prison), but it's still an exceptionally well-run and friendly spot. The city is a pleasant 25-minute walk through Hagley Park, and the upside is that the Jailhouse is quieter than some central hostels.

**Greenspace** (Map p247; ☎ 03-377 8832; www.greenspace.co.nz; 5/48 Trafalgar St, St Albans; d $110, incl breakfast $140; 🅿 🖳 ) This ecofriendly and sunny bed and breakfast – the hosts actually live up the road – oozes privacy with its secluded garden location beside a stream and a stand of native bush.

**Living Space** (Map p248; ☎ 0508 454 846, 03-964 5212; www.livingspace.net; 96 Lichfield St; d $80-120; 🖳 🛜 ) Pitched somewhere between handy central digs for nightlife-loving visitors and compact studios for longer-term visitors, Living Space has minikitchens, high-speed internet and Sky TV.

**ourpick** **Wish** (Map p247; ☎ 03-356 2455; www.wishnz.com; 38 Edgeware Rd, St Albans; s/d incl breakfast $110/140; 🅿 🖳 🛜 ) The rooms and beds at the stylish and modern Wish are supercomfy, but it could be the locally sourced, sustainable and organic breakfasts that you recommend to other travellers. Central Christchurch is a 15-minute walk away, and bus 14 and 16 stop virtually outside.

**Stonehurst** (Map p248; ☎ 0508 786 633, 03-379 4620; www.stonehurst.co.nz; 241 Gloucester St; motel d $110-210, q $260, apt per week $805-1400; 🅿 🖳 🛜 🐾 ) The place to go for great deals on a variety of motel rooms (from studios to two-bedroom units) and fully self-contained tourist flats sleeping up to six (good for groups and not much more expensive than a hostel).

**Hotel off the Square** (Map p248; ☎ 0800 633 843, 03-374 9980; www.offthesquare.com; 115 Worcester St; d $140-180, apt $280; 🖳 🛜 ) This boutique hotel provides a stylish antidote to clinical business hotels. No two rooms are alike, and the place radiates warmth, with vibrant colours and lots of original art and plants. Loft-style apartments provide a self-contained option.

**Focus Motel** (Map p248; ☎ 03-943 0800; www.focusmotel.com; 344 Durham St N; d $140-350; 🅿 🖳 🛜 ) A sleek, centrally located new opening with big-screen TVs and supermodern decor.

**George** (Map p248; ☎ 0800 100 220, 03-379 4560; www.thegeorge.com; 50 Park Tce; r from $350-620; 🅿 🖳 🛜 ) The George has 53 handsomely decorated rooms and suites on the fringe of Christchurch's sweeping

CHRISTCHURCHNZ.COM

SOL Sq

Hagley Park. Discreet staff attend to every whim, there are two excellent restaurants, and ritzy features include plasma TVs, luxury toiletries and glossy magazines.

# EATING

**our pick Lunes** (Map p248; ☎ 03-379 7221; 126 Lichfield St; coffee & cake $6-10; ☺ 8am-5pm) Perhaps the perfect Christchurch cafe, Lunes mixes cool jazz, a professorial approach to making coffee, and perfect mid-afternoon treats such as baked New York cheesecake. Open for just six weeks when we dropped by, and already easily our favourite caffeine haunt in town.

**dose** (Map p248; ☎ 03-374 9907; 90 Hereford St; mains $7-16; ☺ 7am-4pm Mon-Fri, 8am-3pm Sat) Cunningly mismatched furniture, bold local art, and high art-deco ceilings add up to a top place for wickedly strong coffee, superlative bagels, and quite probably Christchurch's best eggs Benedict.

**our pick Bodhi Tree** (Map p248; ☎ 03-377 6808; 808 Colombo St; dishes $11-19; ☺ 6-10pm Tue-Sun; Ⓥ ) Christchurch's only Burmese restaurant is also one of the city's best eateries. Don't come expecting the bold flavours of neighbouring Thailand, but look forward to subtle food crafted from exceptionally fresh ingredients. Dishes are entrée-sized, so drum up a group and sample lots of different flavours.

**Bicycle Thief** (Map p248; ☎ 03-379 2264; 21 Latimer Sq; mains $15-30; ☺ 8am-late Mon-Fri, from 5pm Sat) Tom Waits on the stereo, a corner spot overlooking leafy Latimer Sq, and an excellent wine and beer list. What more could you want? How about great thin-crust pizzas and lovingly prepared rustic Italian cuisine? Cafe, bar or restaurant? You choose.

# DRINKING

**our pick Cartel** (Map p248; ☎ 021 576 857; His Lordships La, SOL Sq; ☺ 4pm-late) Cartel may look like the end result of a garage sale at your quirky uncle's house, but inside the retro interior is a wine list and cocktails to die for. In cooler months, pull up a beanbag in front of the toasty outdoor fire and look forward to music you thought only you knew about.

**Dux de Lux** (Map p248; ☎ 03-366 6919; cnr Hereford & Montreal Sts; ☺ 10.30am-late) Quality microbrewed beers underpin this Christchurch icon. There's good food too, especially seafood and vegetarian, and live music features at least four nights a week.

# ENTERTAINMENT
## LIVE MUSIC

**Southern Blues Bar** (Map p248; ☎ 03-365 1654; 198 Madras St; ☺ 7.30am-late) NZ's oldest blues venue is still going strong; gigs kick off nightly around 10.30pm. Expect a friendly crowd of musos, office workers and the confidently unfashionable.

**Bedford** (Map p248; ☎ 03-374 9988; www.thebedford.co.nz; 46 Bedford Row; ☺ vary by event) The brick building dates back to 1903, but now the sprawling Bedford hosts a thoroughly modern mix of up-and-coming international bands and the best of Kiwi acts with a rocky tinge.

## NIGHTCLUBS

**Double Happy** (Map p248; ☎ 03-374 6463; 182 Cashel St; ☺ 8pm-late Wed-Sun) The city's best bar-club hybrid with great cocktails, Euro beers on tap and an ever-changing diet of dub, house and soul. Perfect for chilled late-night/early-morning denizens.

**Ministry/Propaganda** (Map p248; ☎ 03-379 2910; www.ministry.co.nz; 90 Lichfield St) Two venues in one big space combining an intimate lounge bar and an always-pumping club. House and drum 'n' bass is the usual recipe, but the occasional metal night with live bands ambushes things.

After-dark drinks, Christchurch

## ⌐ IF YOU LIKE...

If you like **Cartel** (left), there's a fair chance you'll dig these other Christchurch booze rooms:

- **Indochine** (Map p248; ☎ 03-365 7323; 209 Cambridge Tce; ☽ 5pm-late Mon-Sat) If you can't score a dinner reservation at this popular eatery, swing by for one of its Asian-inspired cocktails.
- **Cleaners Only** (Map p248; SOL Sq; ☽ 5pm-late Wed-Sun) In a hidden corner of SOL Sq is Christchurch's quirkiest bar, which used to be the lunch room for cleaners at nearby warehouses. Retro ambience endures, complete with old sofas from your first student flat.
- **Foam Bar** (Map p248; ☎ 03-365 2926; 30 Bedford Row; ☽ 5pm-late Wed-Sat) Sophisticated back-alley bar, worth seeking out for its chilled-out crowd, art-bedecked walls and DJ-spun tunes.

## GETTING THERE & AWAY

### AIR

**Christchurch airport** (off Map p247; ☎ 03-358 5029; www.christchurchairport.co.nz) is the South Island's main international gateway. Departure tax on international flights is $25, with children under 12 exempt.

**Air New Zealand** (Map p248; ☎ 0800 737 000, 03-363 0600; www.airnz.co.nz; 549 Colombo St; ☽ 9am-5pm Mon-Fri, 9.30am-1pm Sat) also offers numerous direct domestic flights with connections to other centres.

**Jet Star** (☎ 0800 800 995; www.jetstar.com) offers direct flights to and from Auckland ($49 to $219, six daily), Queenstown ($59 to $189, one daily) and Wellington ($99 to $169, one daily).

**Pacific Blue** (☎ 0800 670 000; www.fly pacificblue.com) flies to and from Auckland (from $90 to $230, two daily) and Wellington (from $60 to $180, two daily).

### BUS

**InterCity** (Map p248; ☎ 03-365 1113; www.intercity.co.nz; 123 Worcester St; ☽ 7am-5.15pm Mon-Sat, to 5.30pm Sun) buses depart from

Worcester St, between the cathedral and Manchester St. Northbound buses go twice daily to Kaikoura (from $14, 2¾ hours), Blenheim (from $24, five hours) and Picton (from $25, 5½ hours), with connections to Nelson ($71, eight hours). One daily bus also goes southwest to Queenstown direct (from $49, eight hours). Heading south, two buses run daily along the coast via the towns along SH1 to Dunedin (from $37, six hours), with connections via Gore to Invercargill (from $53, 9¾ hours) and Te Anau (from $59, 10½ hours).

**Naked Bus** (www.nakedbus.com) heads north to Picton and Nelson, south to Dunedin and southwest to Queenstown. Buses leave from opposite the Holy Grail pub at 88 Worcester St.

Shuttles run to Akaroa, Arthur's Pass, Dunedin, Greymouth, Hanmer Springs, Picton, Queenstown, Twizel, Wanaka, Westport and points in between; see the i-SITE for details (p246).

## TRAIN

**Christchurch railway station** (Map p247; ☎ 0800 872 467, 03-341 2588; Troup Dr, Addington; ☺ ticket office 6.30am-3.30pm Mon-Fri, to 3pm Sat & Sun) is serviced by a free shuttle that picks up from various accommodation; ring the i-SITE (p246) to request pick-up.

The *TranzCoastal* runs daily each way between Christchurch and Picton via Kaikoura and Blenheim, departing from Christchurch at 7am and arriving at Picton at 12.13pm; the standard adult one-way fare to Picton is $83, but fares can be discounted to $59.

The *TranzAlpine* has a daily route between Christchurch and Greymouth via Arthur's Pass (see p271); the standard adult one-way fare is $137, but fares can be discounted to $89. Ask about any current specials.

Contact **Tranz Scenic** (☎ 0800 872 467, www.tranzscenic.co.nz) for more information.

# GETTING AROUND
## TO/FROM THE AIRPORT

The airport is 12km from the city centre.

**Super Shuttle** (☎ 0800 748 885; www.supershuttle.co.nz) operates 24 hours and charges $17 for one person between the city and the airport, plus $4 for each additional person. A cheaper alternative is the **Seven Dollar Bus** (☺ 8am-5pm; one-way $7), which runs every 20 minutes between the airport and Cathedral Sq.

The airport is serviced by the **City Flyer** (☎ 0800 733 287; www.redbus.co.nz; adult/child $7.50/4.50), a bus that runs from Cathedral Sq between 5.30am and 11.30pm Monday to Friday and 7.30am to 11.30pm Saturday and Sunday (departs from the airport 35 minutes later).

A taxi between the city centre and airport costs around $40 to $45.

## CAR & MOTORCYCLE

Major car- and campervan-rental companies all have offices in Christchurch, as do numerous smaller local companies. Some smaller-scale companies:

**Ace Rental Cars** (off Map p247; ☎ 0800 20 029, 03-360 3270; www.acerentalcars.co.nz; 20 Abros Pl)

**First Choice** (Map p248; ☎ 0800 736 822, 03-365 9261; www.firstchoice.co.nz; 132 Kilmore St)

**Omega Rental Cars** (Map p248; ☎ 0800 112 121, 03-377 4558; www.omegarentalcars.com; 20 Lichfield St)

## PUBLIC TRANSPORT

The Christchurch **bus network** (Metro; ☎ 03-366 8855; www.metroinfo.org.nz; ☺ 6.30am-10.30pm Mon-Sat, 9am-9pm Sun) is inexpensive and efficient. A cash fare to anywhere in the city costs $2.80, including one free transfer within two hours.

The **After Midnight Express** (fare $6; ☽ midnight-4am Sat & Sun) operates hourly on five suburban routes, most of them departing Oxford Tce.

## TAXI
**Blue Star** (☎ 0800 379 979)
**First Direct** (☎ 0800 505 555)

# AROUND CHRISTCHURCH

## LYTTELTON
pop 3100

Southeast of Christchurch lie the prominent Port Hills, which slope down to the city's port at Lyttelton Harbour. With attractive heritage architecture and eclectic cafe-bars, Lyttelton is now a popular weekend getaway and dining destination for in-the-know foodies.

The **Lyttelton visitor information centre** (☎ 03-328 9093; www.lytteltonharbour.co.nz; 20 Oxford St; ☽ 9am-5pm Sep-May, to 4pm Jun-Aug) has accommodation and transport information.

The **Lyttelton Museum** (☎ 03-328 8972; Gladstone Quay; admission by donation; ☽ 2-4pm Tue, Thu, Sat & Sun) has interesting maritime exhibits such as wreck-recovered artefacts and ship models, plus Lyttelton memorabilia including a 19th-century pipe organ and an Antarctic gallery (both Scott and Shackleton used the port as a base).

### EATING & DRINKING
**ourpick** **Monster Yakitori** (☎ 03-328 9166; 29 London St; per two skewers $7-11; ☽ 5pm-late Wed-Sun) Classic cocktails and boutique Kiwi beers and wines provide the liquid sustenance for an extended bout of grazing and drinking at this quirky anime-themed yakitori bar. DJs kick in most Saturday nights from 10pm.

**Wunderbar** (☎ 03-328 8818; www.wunderbar.co.nz; 19 London St; ☽ 5pm-late Mon-Fri, 1pm-late Sat & Sun) Wunderbar is a top spot to see NZ's more interesting acts, from raucous rock to late-night/early-morning dub. Look for the sign on London St that says 'Sorry, nice people only' and head down the steps. Be nice.

PAUL KENNEDY

Sumner Rd overlooking Lyttelton Harbour

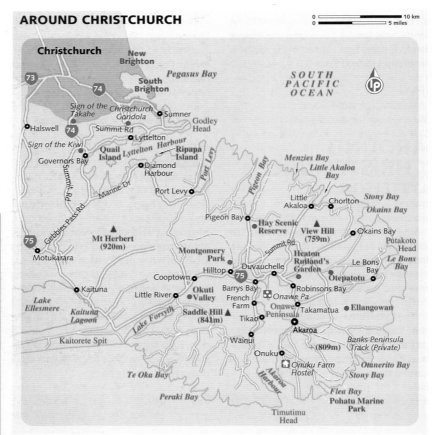

# AROUND CHRISTCHURCH

## GETTING THERE & AWAY

Buses 28 and 35 run from Christchurch to Lyttelton (25 minutes). From Lyttelton by car, you can continue around Lyttelton Harbour on to Akaroa. This winding route is longer and more scenic than the route via SH75 between Christchurch and Akaroa.

## AKAROA & BANKS PENINSULA

Banks Peninsula and its hills were formed by two giant volcanic eruptions. The historic town of Akaroa is a highlight, as is the absurdly beautiful drive along Summit Rd around the edge of the original crater.

Akaroa means 'Long Harbour' in Maori and is the site of the country's first French settlement; descendants of the original French settlers still reside here.

**Akaroa visitor information centre** ( ☎ 03-304 8600; www.akaroa.com; 80 Rue Lavaud; 🕑 9am-5pm) has info on tours, activities and accommodation, including farmstays.

## SIGHTS & ACTIVITIES

The **Banks Peninsula Track** ( ☎ 03-304 7612; www.bankstrack.co.nz; per person $240) is a 35km, four-day walk across private farmland and around the dramatic coastline of Banks Peninsula; cost includes transport from Akaroa and hut accommodation. A two-day option ($160) covers the same ground at twice the speed.

The **Akaroa Adventure Centre** ( ☎ 03-304 8709; Rue Lavaud; **sea kayaks per hr/day $15/55, bikes per hr $15**) rents out sea kayaks, bicycles, golf clubs, fishing rods and windsurfing gear. For $39 (including bike hire) they'll transport you to the top of the volcanic crater around Banks Peninsula from where you can ride downhill all the way to Akaroa.

**Captain Hector's Sea Kayaks** ( ☎ 03-304 7866; Beach Rd; www.akaroaseakayaks.co.nz; **kayak hire per half-/full day $35/60**) is another rental company that offers kayaks, canoes and row boats for self-exploration.

The waters around Akaroa are home to the world's smallest and rarest dolphin, the Hector's dolphin, found only in NZ waters. If viewing the dolphins on a harbour cruise (p260) isn't enough, **Black Cat Cruises** ( ☎ 03-304 7641; www.blackcat.co.nz; **Main Wharf; ☻ five tours daily 6am-3.30pm Oct-April, one tour daily 11.30am May-Sep**) can get you swimming alongside the dolphins (assuming it's not the calving season). Costs are around $130/110 per adult/child for a cruise and swim, and $70/35 per adult/child for a cruise only.

## SLEEPING& EATING

our pick **Onuku Farm Hostel** ( ☎ 03-304 7066; www.onukufarm.com; Onuku Rd; **tent/van sites per person $15, dm/d from $28/66; ☻ closed Jun-Aug; ☐** ) An eco-minded backpackers (with basic huts, tent sites and a comfy house) on a sheep farm near Onuku, 6km south of Akaroa. From November to March the owners organise swimming-with-dolphins tours ($100) and kayaking trips ($45) for guests, and will pick up from

PAUL KENNEDY

Sail boats, Akaroa

Akaroa. The same family has owned the farm since the 1860s, so you should trust them when they say there's some great walks on the 340-hectare spread.

**Oinako Lodge** ( ☎ 03-304 8787; www.oinako .co.nz; 99 Beach Rd; **d incl breakfast $245-285; ☐ ☎** ) This glorious timber mansion was built in 1865 for the then-British magistrate. Almost 15 decades later, it's now a wonderfully upmarket bed and breakfast with six themed rooms, expansive bay windows with sea and garden views, and gourmet breakfasts you'll definitely want to take your time over.

**Bully Hayes** ( ☎ 03-304 7533; 57 Beach Rd; **lunch $13-20, dinner mains $22-30; ☻ 8am-late**) Named after a well-travelled American buccaneer, the menu at this sunny spot kicks off with Akaroa salmon before touching down in New York for gourmet burgers, Italy for pasta, and a leisurely final stop in Spain for tapas. Monteith's beers and a good local wine list make it a worthwhile place to linger.

## GETTING THERE & AWAY

The Akaroa Shuttle ( ☎ 0800 500 929; return $45) departs from outside the Christchurch i-SITE in Cathedral Sq at 8.30am and 2pm,

returning from Akaroa at 10.30am, 3.35pm and 4.30pm. There's an extra departure from Christchurch at 4.30pm on a Friday.

French Connection ( ☎ 0800 800 575; www.akaroabus.co.nz; return from $20) has a year-round daily departure from the Christchurch i-SITE at 8.45am, returning from Akaroa at 2.30pm and 4.30pm. During summer additional services may operate – ask at the Christchurch i-SITE.

New Zealand native kiwi

OLIVER STREWE

## ⬃ IF YOU LIKE...

If you like dolphin swimming with Black Cat Cruises (p159), here are a few other ways to experience the wildlife in this neck of the woods:

- Orana Wildlife Park ( ☎ 03-359 7109; www.oranawildlifepark.co.nz; McLeans Island Rd, Christchurch; adult/child/family $24/8/56) A walk-through native bird aviary, nocturnal kiwi house and a reptile exhibit with wrinkly tuatara. There's Africana, too (lions, rhinos, lemurs, cheetahs…). A shuttle departs Cathedral Sq at 10am and 1pm daily.
- Willowbank Wildlife Reserve ( ☎ 03-359 6226; www.willowbank.co.nz; 60 Hussey Rd, Christchurch; adult/child under 5yr/child 5-15yr/family $25/free/10/65; ☽ 9.30am-dusk) Focuses on native NZ animals and hands-on enclosures with alpacas, wallabies and deer. After-dark tours are a good opportunity to see NZ's national bird, the kiwi. About 6km north of central Christchurch.
- Akaroa Dolphins ( ☎ 0800 990 102, 03-304 7866; www.akaroadolphins.co.nz; 65 Beach Rd, Akaroa; adult/child $68/35; ☽ departures 10.15am, 12.45pm & 3.15pm) Two-hour wildlife cruises, plus evening cruises and birdwatching trips by arrangement. Say 'Hi' to Murphy, wildlife-spotting dog extraordinaire.

Both companies run scenic tours from Christchurch exploring Banks Peninsula ($110).

# CANTERBURY
## HANMER SPRINGS
pop 750

Hanmer Springs, the main thermal resort on the South Island, is located 10km off SH7. It's a pleasantly low-key spot to indulge in pampering in the hot pools and a flash new spa complex. For tourist info, try **Hamner Springs i-SITE** (☎ 0800 733 426, 03-315 7128; www.visithanmersprings.co.nz, www.visithurunui.co.nz; 42 Amuri Ave; ☻ 10am-5pm).

## SIGHTS & ACTIVITIES

Visitors have been soaking in the waters of **Hanmer Springs Thermal Pools** (☎ 0800 442 663, 03-315 7511; www.hanmersprings.co.nz; entry on Jacks Pass Rd; adult/child $18/7; ☻ 10am-9pm) for more than 100 years. In addition to mineral pools, there are landscaped rock pools, a freshwater 25m lap pool, private sauna/steam suites ($24 per half-hour), a restaurant, and a family activity area including a waterslide ($6). The adjacent **Hanmer Springs Spa** (☎ 0800 873 527, 03-315 0029; www.hanmerspa.co.nz; ☻ 10am-7pm) has massage and beauty treatments from $65.

**Hanmer Springs Adventure Centre** (☎ 03-315 7233; www.hanmeradventure.co.nz; 20 Conical Hill Rd; ☻ 9am-5pm) books activities, and rents mountain bikes (per hour/day from $19/45), fishing rods (per day $25) and ski and snowboard gear.

There are two skiing areas nearby. **Hanmer Springs Ski Field** is the closest, 17km (unsealed) from town, and **Mt Lyford Ski Field** is 60km away. They're cheaper than larger resorts.

The *Hanmer Forest Recreation* pamphlet ($2) outlines short walks near town, mostly through picturesque forest.

## SLEEPING & EATING

**Rosie's** (☎ 03-315 7095; roxyrosie@clearnet.nz; 9 Cheltenham St; s $55-90, d $80-130) Rosie was originally from Australia, but she's now offering great Kiwi hospitality at this welcoming reader-recommended spot. Rooms offer either en-suite or shared facilities. Look forward to newly decorated bathrooms and a friendly cat. Rates include breakfast.

**Cheltenham House** (☎ 03-315 7545; www.cheltenham.co.nz; 13 Cheltenham St; s $190-220, d $220-260; ☐ ☏) Centrally located B&B with six snooze-inducing suites, all with private bathroom, and including two in cosy garden cottages. Cooked gourmet breakfasts can be delivered to your room, and there's a billiard table, grand piano and complimentary pre-dinner wine. Avoid the crowds up the road with the private hot tub.

**Monteith's Brewery Bar** (☎ 03-315 5133; 47 Amuri Ave; ☻ 11.30am-late Mon-Fri, from 9am Sat & Sun) The best (and most central) pub in town features lots of different craft beers and tasty tucker from bar snacks ($10 to $15) to full meals ($20 to $30). Platters ($44 to $52) are good value if you've just met some new friends in the hot pools across the road.

**Four Square supermarket** (Conical Hill Rd; ☻ 8.30am-7pm Mon-Sat, 9am-5.30pm Sun).

## GETTING THERE & AWAY

**Hanmer Connection** (☎ 0800 242 663; www.atsnz.com) runs from Hanmer Springs to Christchurch ($33, two daily).

**East West Coach** (☎ 0800 142 622, 03-789 6251) has a service that runs between Christchurch and Westport via the Lewis Pass and also diverts to Hanmer Springs.

DAVID WALL

**Ballooning over the Canterbury Plains, near Methven**

# METHVEN

pop 1140

Methven is busiest in winter, when it fills up with snow-sports fans heading to nearby Mt Hutt. In summer, Methven town is a laid-back option with quieter (and usually cheaper) accommodation than elsewhere in the country, and a 'what shall I do today?' range of warm-weather activities including ballooning, tramping, fishing and skydiving.

**Methven i-SITE** ( ☎ 03-302 8955; www.methveninfo.co.nz; www.amazingspace.co.nz; 160 Main St; ⏰ 8am-6pm daily May-Oct, 9am-5pm Mon-Fri, 11am-4pm Sat & Sun Nov-Apr; 🖳 books accommodation, skiing packages, transport and activities. Internet is available.

## ACTIVITIES

Nearby **Mount Hutt** (www.nzski.com) offers five months of skiing (June to October, weather permitting), often the longest ski season of any resort in NZ.

For mountain bikes, and ski rental and advice, see **Big Al's Snow Sports** ( ☎ 03-302 8003; www.bigals.co.nz; cnr Main St & Forest Dr; mountain bikes per hr/day $12/39).

**Skydiving NZ** ( ☎ 03-302 9143; www.skydivingnz.com; Pudding Hill Airfield) offers tandem jumps from 3600m ($369), and the **NZ Skydiving School** ( ☎ 03-302 9143; www.nzskydivingschool.com) has introductory courses starting at $395.

**Aoraki Balloon Safaris** ( ☎ 0800 256 837, 03-302 8172; www.nzballooning.co.nz; flights $385) offers flights that include snowcapped peaks and a champagne breakfast.

## SLEEPING

**our pick Alpernhorn Chalet** ( ☎ 03-302 8779; www.alpenhorn.co.nz; 44 Allen St; dm $25, d $60-85; 🖳 ) This small, inviting home has a conservatory housing an indoor garden and a spa pool. A log fire, free internet and complimentary espresso coffee seal the deal.

**Breckenridge Lodge** ( ☎ 03-302 8902; www.breckenridgelodge.com; 49-51 South Belt; s/d/tr/q/f incl breakfast $95/115/140/165/185; 🖳 🛜 ) Versatile lodge with a wide array of rooms, warm wooden decor, and a lounge bar. A spa pool, sauna and games room provide plenty of distraction before and after hitting the slopes.

## GETTING THERE & AROUND
**Methven Travel** ( ☎ 03-302 8106; www. methventravel.co.nz; 93 Main St) picks up from Christchurch (adult/child one-way $36/18; ☺ Mon, Wed, Fri, Sat in summer, up to three times daily in winter). Christchurch airport and Cathedral Sq departures are available. Other companies offer this service during winter. Ask at the Christchurch i-SITE (p246) for details.

Shuttles operate from Methven to Mt Hutt ski field in winter for around $35; enquiries and pick-ups are from Methven i-SITE.

# LAKE TEKAPO
pop 315

At the southern end of its namesake lake, this town has unobstructed views across turquoise water, and a backdrop of rolling hills and mountains worthy of a Peter Jackson movie.

**Lake Tekapo i-SITE** ( ☎ 03-680 6579; www.laketekapountouched.co.nz; Godley Hotel, SH8; ☺ 9am-5pm) handles bookings for activities and transport. Also see www.tekapotourism.co.nz.

## SIGHTS & ACTIVITIES
Popular walks include the track to the summit of **Mt John** (three hours return) from just beyond the camping ground.

**Cruise Tekapo** ( ☎ 027 479 7675; www. cruisetekapo.co.nz; 25-/40-min cruise $30/45, fishing per hr $80) can get you out and about on Lake Tekapo.

**Mountain bikes** can be hired out (per hour/half-day $10/25) from both Lakefront Backpackers Lodge and the Lake Tekapo YHA.

In winter, Lake Tekapo is a base for **downhill skiing** at Mt Dobson or Round Hill and **cross-country skiing** on the Two Thumb Range.

## SLEEPING & EATING
**Lake Tekapo Motels & Holiday Park** ( ☎ 0800 853 853, 03-680 6825; www.laketekapo -accommodation.co.nz; Lakeside Dr; unpowered/ powered sites $30/36, cabins & units $70-150; 💻 ☎ ) Has a pretty and peaceful lakeside locale, plus everything from basic cabins to motel units with full kitchen and Sky TV. Newer chalets come with shared picnic tables, barbecues and spectacular lake vistas.

**Glacier Rock Bed and Breakfast** ( ☎ 03-680 6669; www.glacierrock.co.nz; 35 Lochinver Ave; d $195-250; 💻 ☎ ) This architecturally designed home doubles as an art gallery. An artist's – or maybe an architect's – eye is evident in the spacious and airy rooms. Breakfast is served in sunny rooms with huge picture windows.

**ourpick** **Astro Café** (Mt John Observatory; coffee & cake $4-8; ☺ 9am-6pm) This tiny, glass-walled pavilion atop Mt John has insanely spectacular 360-degree views across the entire Mackenzie Basin. Quite possibly one of the best locations on the planet for a cafe, and the coffee and cake is pretty good, too. On our latest visit it had branched out into fresh ham-off-the-bone sandwiches. After dark the cafe becomes the location for astrophotography with local photographer Fraser Gunn.

## GETTING THERE & AWAY
Southbound services to Queenstown and Wanaka, and northbound services to Christchurch, are offered by **Atomic Shuttles** ( ☎ 03-349 0697; www.atomictravel. co.nz), **InterCity** ( ☎ 03-365 1113; www.intercity. co.nz) and **Southern Link Coaches** ( ☎ 0508

458 835; www.southernlinkcoaches.co.nz). One-way fares cost around $30.

**Cook Connection** ( ☎ 0800 266 526; www.cookconnect.co.nz) operates to Mt Cook (one-way $30, one daily) and for an additional $20 you can carry on from Mt Cook to Twizel.

# AORAKI/MT COOK NATIONAL PARK

Mt Cook is a wonderful sight – assuming there's no cloud in the way. Hang around to soak up this awesome peak and the surrounding landscape and try the excellent short walks.

## INFORMATION

The **DOC Aoraki/Mt Cook visitor information centre** ( ☎ 03-435 1186; mtcookvc@doc.govt.nz; 1 Larch Grove; ✆ 8.30am-5pm Oct-Apr, to 4.30pm May-Sep) advises on weather conditions, guided tours and tramping routes, and hires out beacons for trampers ($35).

Stock up on groceries and petrol at Twizel or Lake Tekapo, and note that Mt Cook has no banking facilities.

## SIGHTS & ACTIVITIES

Various easy walks from the Hermitage area are outlined in the brochure *Walks in Aoraki/Mt Cook National Park* ($1), available from the visitor information centre.

The trail to **Kea Point** (two hours return from the village) is lined with native plant life and ends at a platform with excellent views of Mt Cook, the Hooker Valley and the ice faces of Mt Sefton and the Footstool. You'll usually share your walk with a few inquisitive kea.

The walk up the **Hooker Valley** (three hours return) crosses a couple of swing bridges to Stocking Stream and the ter-

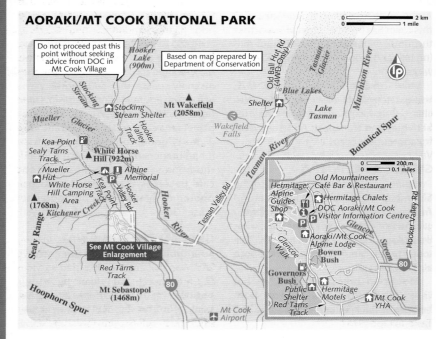

**AORAKI/MT COOK NATIONAL PARK**

JOHN ELK III

Tasman Glacier View track, Aoraki/Mt Cook National Park

minus of the Hooker Glacier. After the second swing bridge, Mt Cook totally dominates the valley.

The **Tasman Glacier View track** (50 minutes return) leads to a viewpoint on the moraine wall, passing the **Blue Lakes** (more green than blue these days) on the way.

From November to March, **Ultimate Hikes** (☎ 0800 686 800, 03-435 1899; www.ultimatehikes.co.nz; full-day walk adult/child $105/65) offers a day-long 8km walk from the Hermitage through the Hooker Valley to the terminal lake of the Hooker Glacier.

## SKI TOURING & HELISKIING

**Alpine Guides** (☎ 03-435 1834; www.alpineguides.co.nz; Sir Edmund Hillary Centre, The Hermitage; ☺ Jul-Sep) does tailored ski-touring trips, and ski-mountaineering and alpine snowboarding courses.

**Southern Alps Guiding** (☎ 027 342 277, 03-435 1890; www.mtcook.com) has a range of heliskiing and boarding options including Tasman Glacier ($775).

## AERIAL SIGHTSEEING

**Mount Cook Ski Planes** (☎ 0800 800 702, 03-430 8034; www.mtcookskiplanes.com), based at Mt Cook airport, offers 40-minute (adult/child $375/275) and 55-minute (adult/child $495/375) flights, both with snow landings. Flightseeing without a landing is a cheaper option; try the 25-minute Mini Tasman trip (adult/child $255/210).

From Glentanner Park, the **Helicopter Line** (☎ 0800 650 651, 03-435 1801; www.helicopter.co.nz) does 20-minute Alpine Vista flights ($210), an exhilarating 30-minute flight over the Ben Ohau Range ($295), and a 45-minute Mountains High flight over the Tasman Glacier and by Mt Cook ($390). All feature snow landings.

## SLEEPING & EATING

**Mt Cook YHA** (☎ 03-435 1820; www.yha.co.nz; mtcook@yha.org.nz; cnr Bowen & Kitchener Dr; dm/d $30/100; ☐ ☎) This excellent hostel has a free sauna, drying room, warming log fires and DVDs. Rooms are clean and spacious; and family rooms and facilities for travellers with disabilities are also available.

**our pick** **Aoraki/Mt Cook Alpine Lodge**
( ☎ 03-435 1860; www.aorakialpinelodge.co.nz;
Bowen Dr; d $159-179, tr/q $164/164, f $200-225;
▣ ☏ ) With colourful Turkish rugs and un-
derfloor heating, the place ensures a warm
welcome. Just a few years old, this cosy
lodge with twin, double and family rooms
is the best place to stay in the village.

**Hermitage** ( ☎ 0800 686 800, 03-435 1809;
www.hermitage.co.nz; Terrace Rd; r $205-560;
▣ ☏ ) A sprawling complex that has long
monopolised accommodation in the village and continues to leverage that position with its room rates. The higher end
rooms are very smart indeed, and include
cinematic views of Mt Cook through huge
picture windows.

**our pick** **Old Mountaineers Café, Bar &
Restaurant** ( ☎ 03-435 1890; Bowen Dr; mains
$20-35; ☏ 11am-late; ▣ ☏ ) Cosy in winter,
with mountain views from outside tables
in summer, this place delivers top-notch
burgers, pizza, pasta and salads, and is a
good-value alternative to the eateries at
the Hermitage. Come for lunch and you
might still be there for happy hour – actually two hours – when it kicks off at 5pm.

## GETTING THERE & AWAY
National bus line **InterCity** ( ☎ 03-365
1113; www.intercitycoach.co.nz) links Mt
Cook to Christchurch ($165, five hours),
Queenstown ($145, four hours) and
Wanaka (with a change in Tarras, 4¼
hours, $195).

InterCity subsidiary **Great Sights**
( ☎ 0800 744 487; www.greatsights.co.nz) runs
a sightseeing dayt rip from Christchurch
($199), and from Christchurch to
Queenstown ($235) via Mt Cook.

The **Cook Connection** ( ☎ 0800 266 526,
021 583 211; www.cookconnect.co.nz) has shuttle services to Glentanner (one-way $15),
Twizel (one-way $22) and Lake Tekapo
(one-way $28).

# THE WEST COAST
## GETTING THERE & AROUND
Air New Zealand flies between Westport
and Wellington, and Hokitika and
Christchurch.

Coaches and shuttles connect to
centres such as Christchurch, Dunedin,
Queenstown and Nelson; major players
are Atomic Shuttles, InterCity and Naked
Bus.

The *TranzAlpine,* one of the world's
great train rides, links Greymouth and
Christchurch; see p291.

# PUNAKAIKI & PAPAROA
# NATIONAL PARK
Located midway between Westport and
Greymouth is Punakaiki, a small settlement beside the rugged 38,000-hectare
Paparoa National Park. For most travellers, it's a quick stop for an ice cream and
a squiz at the Pancake Rocks; a shame
because there's excellent tramping on
offer and some tragically underused char-
ismatic accommodation options.

## INFORMATION
The **Paparoa National Park visitor
information centre** ( ☎ 03-731 1895;
punakaiki@doc.govt.nz; SH6; ☏ 9am-5pm Oct-
Dec, to 6pm Jan-May, to 4.30pm Jun-Sep) has
info-laden displays on the park, and details on activities, accommodation and
trail conditions. Online, see www.puna
kaiki.co.nz.

## SIGHTS
Punakaiki is famous for its fantastic
**Pancake Rocks** and **blowholes**. Through
a layering-weathering process called
stylobedding, the Dolomite Point limestone has formed into what looks like
piles of thick pancakes. When the tide is
right (tide times are posted at the visitor
information centre), the sea surges into

DAVID WALL

Beach on the Truman Track, Paparoa National Park

caverns and booms menacingly through blowholes.

Paparoa National Park is also blessed with sea cliffs, the mountains of the Paparoa Range, rivers, diverse flora and a Westland petrel colony, the world's only nesting site of this rare sea bird.

## ACTIVITIES

**Tramps** in the national park are detailed in the DOC *Paparoa National Park* pamphlet ($1), and include the **Inland Pack Track** (two to three days), a route established by miners in 1867 to dodge difficult coastal terrain.

Shorter options include the **Truman Track** (30 minutes return) and the **Porari River Track** (2½ hours return), which follows a spectacular limestone gorge. The **Fox River Tourist Cave** (three hours return) is open to amateur explorers. BYO torch and wear good walking shoes.

**Punakaiki Canoes** ( ☎ 03-731 1870; www. riverkayaking.co.nz; SH6; canoe hire 2hr/full day $35/55) rents canoes and kayaks near the Pororari River bridge. Guided tours start from $70.

**Green Kiwi Tours** ( ☎ 03 731 1843; www. greenkiwitours.co.nz; guided walking tours from $60, caving from $100) runs information-rich excursions throughout the region with an ecofriendly focus.

## SLEEPING

**Punakaiki Beach Hostel** ( ☎ 03-731 1852; www.punakaikibeachhostel.co.nz; 4 Webb St; tents per person $20, dm/s/d $28/50/70; 🖳 🛜 ) A sandy, beach-bumming hostel with a deep, sea-view veranda and an outdoor spa, just a short stroll from Pancake Rocks and the beach.

**Te Nikau Retreat** ( ☎ 03-731 1111; www. tenikauretreat.co.nz; Hartmount Pl; dm $23, d $60-85, cabins $90; 🖳 ) This unconventional accommodation option is set aesthetically amid the rainforest. From straightforward dorms in a chilled setting all the way through to cabins that take indoor/outdoor flow to a new level (the kitchen is in an attached greenhouse).

## GETTING THERE & AWAY

**InterCity** ( ☎ 03-365 1113; www.intercity.co.nz) links to Westport ($19) and Greymouth ($25). **Naked Bus** (www.nakedbus.com) has a similar service along SH6 to Westport ($22) and Greymouth ($12).

# GREYMOUTH

pop 10,000

On the main road and rail route through Arthur's Pass and across the Southern Alps from Christchurch, Greymouth sees its fair share of travellers taking advantage of outstanding budget accommodation. The **Greymouth i-SITE** ( ☎ 0800 473 966, 03-768 5101; www.greydistrict.co.nz; cnr Herbert & Mackay Sts; ☽ 8.30am-7pm Mon-Fri, 9am-6pm Sat, 10am-5pm Sun Nov-Apr, reduced hours May-Oct; ☐ ) has a very helpful crew with DOC information.

## SIGHTS & ACTIVITIES

The **Point Elizabeth Walkway** (three hours return) heads north of Greymouth into the Rapahoe Range Scenic Reserve. The **Floodwall Walk** from Cobden Bridge towards Blaketown is shorter (30 minutes return).

**Wild West Adventure Co** ( ☎ 0800 147 483, 03-768 6649; www.nzholidayheaven.com; 8 Whall St) runs rafting excursions (priced from $160 to $845), a three-hour river cruise ($145) aboard a Jungle Boat and a 5½-hour Dragons Cave black-water rafting expedition ($160). Inflatable kayak trips start at $225.

## TOURS

**Kea Heritage Tours** ( ☎ 0800 532 868; www.keatours.co.nz; day tours $70-275) Well-informed guides visit West Coast locations such as Blackball and the glaciers. **Monteith's Brewing Co** ( ☎ 03-768 4149; www.monteiths.co.nz; cnr Turumaha & Herbert Sts; admission $15; ☽ tours 11.30am, 2pm, 4pm, 6pm) Finish this excellent 1¼-hour-long tour in the bar by working your way through Monteith's eight brews.

## SLEEPING & EATING

**our pick** **Global Village Backpackers** ( ☎ 03-768 7272; www.globalvillagebackpackers

The West Coast's largest town, Greymouth

PAUL KENNEDY

.co.nz; 42-54 Cowper St; campsite/dm/s/d/tr/q $30/25/60/60/90/108; 🖳 🛜) A collage of African and Asian art is infused with a passionate travellers' vibe here. Free kayaks – the Lake Karoro wetlands reserve is just metres away – and mountain bikes are on tap, and relaxation comes easy with a spa, sauna and riverside barbecue.

**Coleraine Motel** ( ☎ 0800 270 027, 03-768 077; www.coleraicnemotel.co.nz; 61 High St; d $139-200; 🖳 🛜) Rattan furniture, spa baths and king-sized beds add up to the best accommodation in town. We're talking about the luxury units, but the cheaper one- and two-bedroom studios are not far behind.

**ourpick** **Frank's Late Night Lounge** ( ☎ 03-768 9075; 115 Mackay St; mains $13-20; ☽ 5pm-late Thu-Sat; 🅥 ) Effortlessly cool and retro late-night lounge-bar-cafe. A mirrorball hovers blithely above rescued 1950s furniture while Sinatra and Dean Martin bubble away as the soundtrack. An eclectic list of teas and NZ's best boutique beers partner a small global menu, with surprises such as Tibetan *momos* (dumplings) and Moroccan fish. Occasional live gigs complete the picture.

### GETTING THERE & AROUND
The **Greymouth Travel Centre** ( ☎ 03-768 7080; www.westcoasttravel.co.nz; railway station, 164 Mackay St; ☽ 9am-5pm Mon-Fri, 10am-3pm Sat & Sun; 🖳 ) books all forms of transport, including buses, trains and interisland ferries, and has luggage-storage facilities. This is also the bus depot and offers wi-fi access.

**InterCity** ( ☎ 03-365 1113; www.intercity. co.nz) has daily buses (1.30pm) north to Westport ($25, two hours) and Nelson ($60, six hours), and south to Franz Josef ($42, 3½ hours) and Fox Glaciers ($45, 4¼ hours).

**Naked Bus** (www.nakedbus.com) runs north to Nelson and south to Queenstown stopping at Hokitika, Franz Josef and Fox Glaciers, Haast and Wanaka.

**Atomic Shuttles** ( ☎ 03-349 0697; www. atomictravel.co.nz) runs daily to Queenstown ($70, 10½ hours, departs at 7.30am), with daily services to Fox Glacier ($35, 4¼ hours, departing 3.15pm), Picton ($60, 7½ hours, departing 1.15pm) and Hokitika ($15, one hour, departing 2pm).

# WESTLAND TAI POUTINI NATIONAL PARK
Literally the biggest highlights of the Westland Tai Poutini National Park are the Franz Josef and Fox Glaciers. Nowhere else at this latitude do glaciers come so close to the ocean.

Some say Franz Josef is the superior ice experience, and while it's visually more impressive, the walk to Fox is shorter, more interesting and gets you closer to the ice (80m versus 200m).

## FRANZ JOSEF GLACIER
The early Maori knew Franz Joseph as Ka Roimata o Hine Hukatere (Tears of the Avalanche Girl). Legend tells of a girl losing her lover who fell from the local peaks, and her flood of tears freezing into the glacier.

The glacier is 5km from Franz Joseph village; the terminal face is a 40-minute walk from the car park.

### INFORMATION
**Franz Josef visitor information centre** ( ☎ 03-752 0796; www.glaciercountry.co.nz, www. doc.govt.nz; SH6; ☽ 8.30am-6pm Dec-Feb, to 5pm Mar-Nov) Also the regional DOC office; has an excellent display, weather information and tramping-condition updates.

### ACTIVITIES
#### INDEPENDENT WALKS
Several glacier viewing points are accessed from the glacier car park,

# WESTLAND TAI POUTINI NATIONAL PARK

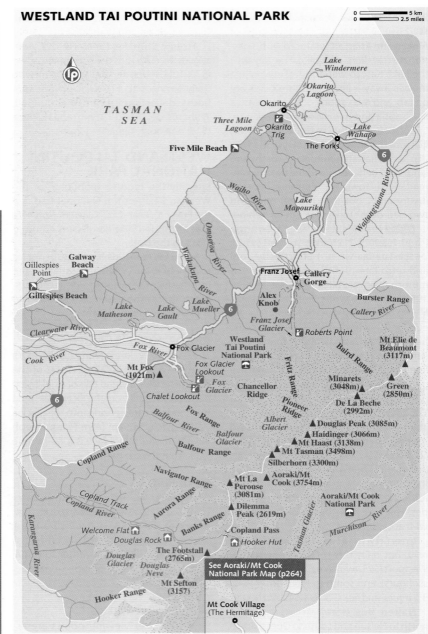

0 — 5 km
0 — 2.5 miles

TASMAN SEA

Lake Windermere

Okarito Lagoon

Okarito

Three Mile Lagoon

Okarito Trig

Lake Wahapo

Five Mile Beach

The Forks

6

Waitangitaona River

Waiho River

Lake Mapourika

Omoeroa River

Gillespies Point

Galway Beach

Waikukupa River

Gillespies Beach

Lake Matheson

Lake Gault

Lake Mueller

6

Clearwater River

Franz Josef

Callery Gorge

Alex Knob

Burster Range

Callery River

Franz Josef Glacier

Fox River

Fox Glacier

Roberts Point

Mt Elie de Beaumont (3117m)

Baird Range

Cook River

Mt Fox (1021m)

Fox Glacier Lookout

Westland Tai Poutini National Park

Fritz Range

Minarets (3048m)

Green (2850m)

6

Chalet Lookout

Fox Glacier

Chancellor Ridge

Pioneer Ridge

De La Beche (2992m)

Fox Range

Albert Glacier

Douglas Peak (3085m)

Balfour River

Balfour Glacier

Haidinger (3066m)

Mt Haast (3138m)

Balfour Range

Mt Tasman (3498m)

Copland Range

Navigator Range

Silberhorn (3300m)

Mt La Perouse (3081m)

Aoraki/Mt Cook (3754m)

Copland Track

Aurora Range

Aoraki/Mt Cook National Park

Copland River

Banks Range

Dilemma Peak (2619m)

Karangarua River

Welcome Flat

Copland Pass

Tasman Glacier

Murchison River

Douglas Rock

Hooker Hut

Douglas Glacier

The Footstall (2765m)

Douglas Neve

Mt Sefton (3157m)

Hooker Range

See Aoraki/Mt Cook National Park Map (p264)

Mt Cook Village (The Hermitage)

including **Sentinel Rock** (20 minutes return) and the **Ka Roimata o Hine Hukatere Walk** (1½ hours return), leading you to the terminal face.

Other longer walks include the **Douglas Walk** (one hour return), off the Glacier Access Rd, which passes moraine from the 1750 advance and Peter's Pool, a small 'kettle lake'. The **Terrace Track** (30 minutes return) is an easy amble over bushy terraces behind the village with Waiho River views. The rough **Callery-Waiho**

The TranzAlpine at Arthur's Pass

## 🡖 THE TRANZALPINE

The *TranzAlpine* is one of the world's great train journeys. Traversing the Southern Alps between Christchurch and Greymouth, and from the Pacific Ocean to the Tasman Sea, the *TranzAlpine* tracks through a sequence of unbelievable landscapes. Leaving Christchurch at 8.15am, it speeds across the flat, alluvial Canterbury Plains to the Alps' foothills. Here it enters a labyrinth of gorges and hills called the Staircase, a climb made possible by three large viaducts and a plethora of tunnels.

The train emerges into the broad Waimakariri and Bealey Valleys and (on a good day) the vistas are stupendous. The beech-forested river valley gives way to the snowcapped peaks of Arthur's Pass National Park. At Arthur's Pass itself (a small alpine village), the train enters the longest tunnel, the 8.5km 'Otira', burrowing under the mountains to the West Coast.

The western side is just as stunning, with the Otira, Taramakau and Grey River valleys, patches of podocarp forest, and the trout-filled Lake Brunner (Moana Kotuku), fringed with cabbage trees. The train rolls into Greymouth at 12.45pm, heading back to Christchurch an hour later, arriving at 6.05pm.

This awesome journey is diminished only when the weather's bad, but if it's raining on one coast, it's probably fine on the other.

**Things you need to know:** ☎ 0800 872 467, 03-768 7080; www.tranzscenic.co.nz; adult/child $118/70, rates vary seasonally.

**Walk** (four hours return) heads off from the village to the Douglas Swing Bridge, optionally extending to Roberts Point.

### GUIDED WALKS & HELIHIKES

Small group walks with experienced guides (boots, jackets and equipment supplied) are offered by **Franz Josef Glacier Guides** ( ☎ 0800 484 337, 03-752 0763; www.franzjosefglacier.com). Half-/full-day walks cost $105/160 per adult (slightly cheaper for children). Full-day trips spend around six hours on the ice, half-day trips up to two hours. Full-day ice-climbing trips ($250 including training) and three-hour helihikes with two hours on the ice ($390) are also available.

**Glacier Valley Eco-Tours** ( ☎ 0800 999 739; www.glaciervalley.co.nz) offers three-hour walks ($65) that are leisurely and packed with local knowledge. Similar walks are offered down at Fox Glacier.

### AERIAL SIGHTSEEING

Most flights also include a snow landing. A 20-minute flight to the head of Franz Josef or Fox Glacier costs around $180. Flights past both of the glaciers and on to Mt Cook cost from $280 to $340.

**Air Safaris** ( ☎ 0800 723 274, 03-752 0716; www.airsafaris.co.nz)

**Fox & Franz Josef Heliservices** ( ☎ 0800 800 793, 03-752 0793; www.scenic-flights.co.nz)

**Mountain Helicopters** ( ☎ 0800 369 432, 03-752 0046; www.mountainhelicopters.co.nz) Also runs shorter 10-minute flights ($105).

## SLEEPING

**Franz Josef Glacier YHA** ( ☎ 03-752 0754; www.yha.co.nz; 2-4 Cron St; dm $28-30, s $55, d $75-96; 🖳 🛜 ) A high-standard, colourful place with more than 100 beds (linen provided) in 36 heated rooms. There are three family rooms, a Kiwi sauna (keep your bathers on, please) and a rainforest at the back door. The needs of travellers with disabilities are well catered for.

**58 on Cron** ( ☎ 0800 662 766, 03-752 0627; www.58oncron.co.nz; 58 Cron St; d $170-225; 🛜 ) No prizes for the name, but with trendy, dark-chocolate decor and flash furniture,

Blue ice, Fox Glacier

OLIVER STREWE

this new bush-side spot is one of FJ's classier motels.

**Punga Grove** ( ☎ 0800 437 269, 03-752 0001; www.pungagrove.co.nz; 40 Cron St; d $190-250) Priding itself on top-notch service, Punga is a quality motel on the rainforest verge. Split-level self-contained family units mix it up with spacious studios. Splurge on a luxury rainforest studio with leather couches.

## EATING & DRINKING

**Full of Beans** ( ☎ 03-752 0139; SH6; mains $5-17; ⏰ 7.30am-late) Cruisy cafe that offers superlative coffee – the best in town – and tasty homemade cakes from go to whoa. Good-value lunch offerings include burgers, Thai curry and chicken pies that are a particular favourite among locals.

**Speights Landing Bar & Restaurant** ( ☎ 03-752 0229; SH6; mains $10-30; ⏰ 7.30am-late) From early to late, the place to be is under the market umbrellas at this cosy pub-cafe. Burgers, soups, pasta and wraps give you plenty of opportunity to overhear other travellers going gaga over the glaciers.

## GETTING THERE & AROUND

**InterCity** ( ☎ 03-365 1113; www.intercity.co.nz) has daily buses south to Fox Glacier ($11, 40 minutes, departing 8am and 5.05pm) and Queenstown ($62, 8 hours, departing 8am); and north to Nelson ($84, 10 hours, departing 9.15am).

**Atomic Shuttles** ( ☎ 03-349 0697; www.atomictravel.co.nz) has daily services south to Queenstown ($50, 7¼ hours, departing 10.15am) via Fox Glacier ($15, 30 minutes), and north to Greymouth ($30, 2½ hours, departing 2.40pm), leaving from the Alpine Adventure Centre.

**Glacier Valley Eco Tours** ( ☎ 03-752 0699; www.glaciervalley.co.nz) runs shuttles to the glacier car park (return trip $12.50).

**Naked Bus** (www.nakedbus.com) runs north to Hokitika and Greymouth, and south to Queenstown stopping at Fox Glacier, Haast and Wanaka.

## FOX GLACIER

Even if you've already been to Franz Josef Glacier, it's still worth checking out Fox. Take a walk around beautiful Lake Matheson, and dive into Fox's array of glacier-related attractions: glacier walks, flights and travellers wearing thermals.

### INFORMATION

**DOC South Westland Area Office** ( ☎ 03-751 0807; SH6; ⏰ 9am-noon & 1-4.30pm Mon-Fri) No longer a general visitor information centre, but has the usual DOC information and weather/track updates.

### ACTIVITIES

#### INDEPENDENT WALKS

It's 1.5km from Fox Village to the glacier turn-off, a further 2km to the car park. The terminal face is 30 to 40 minutes' walk from there, finishing 80m from the ice.

Short walks around the glacier include the **Moraine Walk** (over a major 18th-century advance) and **Minnehaha Walk**. The **River Walk** extends to the **Chalet Lookout Track** (1½ hours return) leading to a glacier lookout.

About 6km down Cook Flat Rd is the turn-off to **Lake Matheson**. It's an hour's walk around the lake, and at the far end (on a clear day) are improbably photogenic views of Mt Tasman and Mt Cook reflected in the water.

#### GLACIER WALKS & HELIHIKES

Guided walks (equipment provided) are organised by **Fox Glacier Guiding** ( ☎ 0800 111 600, 03-751 0825; www.foxguides.co.nz; SH6). Half-day walks cost $95/75 per adult/child; full-day walks cost $145 (over-13s only).

Helihikes cost $395 per person, while a day-long introductory ice-climbing course costs $235 per adult. From October to April, there are also easy-going two-hour interpretive walks to the glacier (adult/child $49/35).

## SKYDIVING & AERIAL SIGHTSEEING

**Skydive Glacier Country** ( ☎ 0800 751 0080, 03-751 0080; www.skydiving.co.nz; Fox Glacier Airfield, SH6, Fox Glacier Village) is a professional outfit that challenges Isaac Newton with thrilling leaps from 12,000ft ($295) or 9000ft ($245).

Aerial sightseeing costs at Fox parallel those at Franz Josef (see p272).

**Helicopter Line** ( ☎ 0800 807 767, 03-751 0767; www.helicopter.co.nz)

**Mount Cook Ski Planes** ( ☎ 0800 368 000, 03-752 0714; www.mtcookskiplanes.com; SH6, Franz Josef Village)

**Southern Lakes Helicopters** ( ☎ 0800 800 732, 03-751 0803; www.heli-flights.co.nz)

## SLEEPING & EATING

**ourpick Lake Matheson Motels** ( ☎ 0800 452 2437, 03-751 0830; www.lakematheson.co.nz; Cook Flat Rd; d $135-190) This unassuming property has been finished off with a real sense of care. From the outside it looks pretty ordinary, but inside the rooms come into their own. The owners have continued to pour profits back into the facilities. You'll find ultra-tidy rooms with up-market amenities that contradict the midrange price.

**Fox Glacier Lodge** ( ☎ 03-751 0888; www.foxglacierlodge.co.nz; Sullivan Rd; d $180-230) Beautiful timber adorns the exterior and interior of this attractive property. It has that mountain chalet vibe that'll look great in your slide show. Top-notch facilities and a home-away-from-home feel seal the deal.

**ourpick Matheson Café** ( ☎ 03-751 0878; Lake Matheson Rd; mains $10-17; ⏲ 7.30am-late) Near the shores of Lake Matheson, this cafe does everything right: slick interior design, inspiring mountain views, strong coffee and up-market Kiwi fare. Get your sketchpad out and while away the afternoon.

## GETTING THERE & AROUND

**InterCity** ( ☎ 03-365 1113; www.intercity.co.nz) runs daily buses north to Franz Josef ($11, 40 minutes, departing 8.30am and 3.25pm); the morning bus continues to Nelson ($85, 11 hours). Daily southbound services run to Queenstown ($58, 7½ hours, departing 8.45am).

**Atomic Shuttles** ( ☎ 03-349 0697; www.atomictravel.co.nz) runs daily to Franz Josef ($15, 30 minutes, departing 9am and 1.55pm), continuing to Greymouth ($35, 3¼ hours). Southbound buses run daily to Queenstown ($45, 6½ hours, departing 11am).

**Fox Glacier Shuttle** ( ☎ 0800 369 287) will drive you to Lake Matheson or Fox Glacier and allow you enough time for a stroll ($12 return, minimum two people).

**Naked Bus** (www.nakedbus.com) runs north to Franz Josef Glacier, Hokitika and Greymouth, and south to Queenstown, stopping at Haast and Wanaka.

# QUEENSTOWN & THE SOUTH

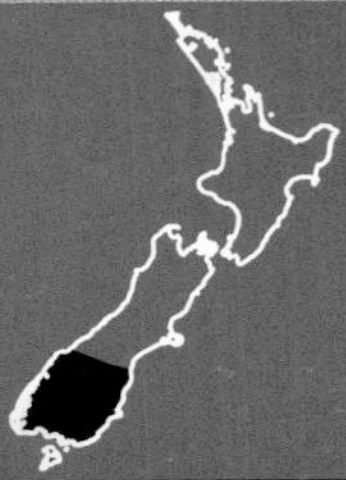

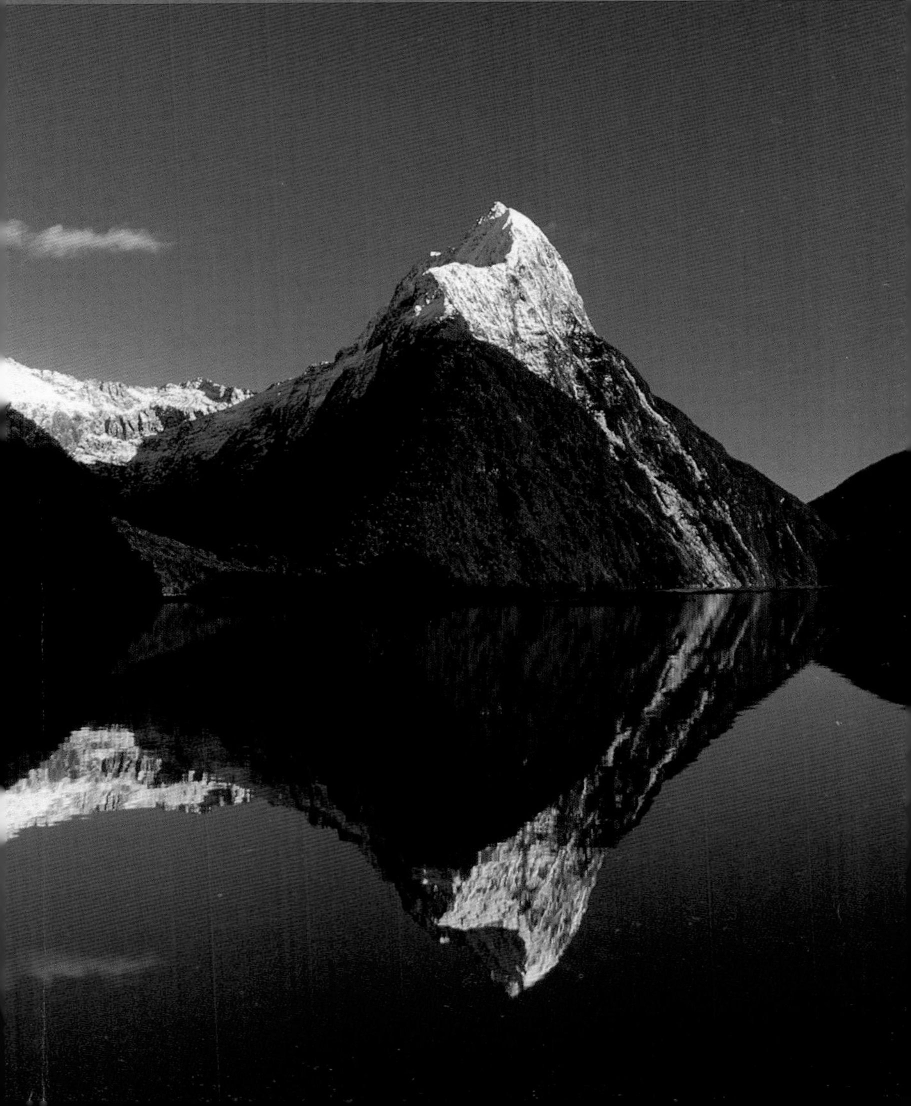

QUEENSTOWN & THE SOUTH

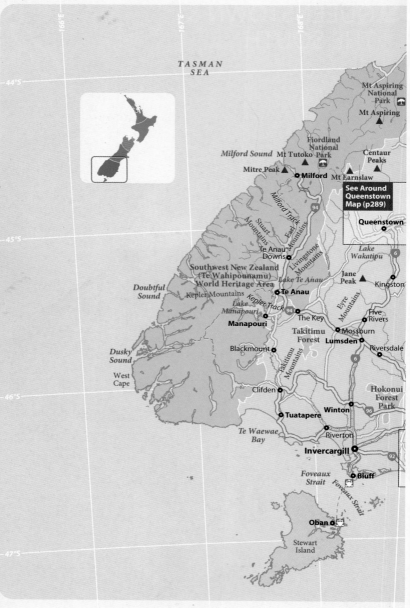

TASMAN
SEA

Mt Aspiring
National
Park
Mt Aspiring

Fiordland
National
Park

Milford Sound  Mt Tutoko
Centaur
Peaks

Mitre Peak   ● Milford   Mt Earnslaw

See Around
Queenstown
Map (p289)

Queenstown

Milford Track

Stuart
Mountains

Earl
Mountains

Lake
Wakatipu

6

Te Anau
Downs

Livingstone
Mountains

Jane
Peak
Kingston

Southwest New Zealand
(Te Wahipounamu)
World Heritage Area

Lake Te Anau

Doubtful
Sound

Kepler Mountains

94  ● Te Anau

Kepler Track

The Key

Eyre
Mountains

Five
Rivers

Lake
Manapouri

94

Mossburn

● Manapouri

Lumsden

6

Dusky
Sound

Blackmount

Takitimu
Forest

Takitimu
Mountains

Riversdale

West
Cape

Hokonui
Forest
Park

Clifden

Winton

96

● Tuatapere

Riverton

Te Waewae
Bay

● Invercargill

92

Foveaux
Strait

● Bluff

Foveaux Strait

● Oban

Stewart
Island

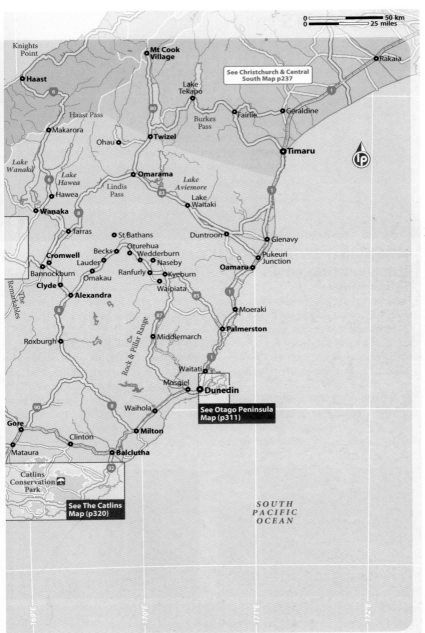

# HIGHLIGHTS

## 1 QUEENSTOWN REGION

### BY ASHLING SWIRTZ, GIBBSTON VALLEY WINES

Queenstown has it all, with a relaxed lifestyle set in spectacular surroundings, and the convenience of a city. Mountain biking, hiking, kayaking, fishing, two great ski fields and adventure activities are all at your fingertips. Afterwards, there are great restaurants and award-winning wines.

### ↘ ASHLING SWIRTZ'S DON'T MISS LIST

#### ❶ DRIVING THE CROWN RANGE ROAD

There are great views on the scenic drive over the **Crown Range Rd** (p284) from Queenstown to Wanaka. Stop at the historic **Cardrona Hotel** (p304), and return to Queenstown via Cromwell. Pick some seasonal fruit at the local orchards.

#### ❷ GIBBSTON VALLEY

Central Otago is renowned for pinot noir; wines produced here rival those of Burgundy. In the **Gibbston Valley** (p296) you can visit six or seven cellar doors within a few kilometres. Most wineries also feature award-winning restaurants for a leisurely lunch.

#### ❸ SKIPPERS CANYON

At **Skippers Canyon** you can see the historic suspension bridge and old township. It's great for an overnight camp or picnic. You can mountain bike, kayak or go jetboating (p290). Getting there takes a bit of effort, but it's worth it: even the drive is worthwhile.

Clockwise from top: Skippers Canyon; Wine cellar, Gibbston Valley Wines; Crown Range Rd

CLOCKWISE FROM TOP: TIM BARKER; DAVID WALL; DAVID WALL

### ❹ SAM SUMMERS HUT TRACK

For a quick day walk you can't beat the **Sam Summers Hut Track** (three hours) in Mt Crichton Scenic Reserve. Sights include native bush, the old hut (still intact) and mining remnants. There's even a glowworm grotto if you go after dark. Ask at DOC (p288) for details.

### ❺ ESCAPING TO GLENORCHY

It's a spectacular drive along Lake Wakatipu to **Glenorchy** (p298), a quaint village with unsurpassed views of snow-capped mountains and the lake head. It's a great spot to unwind, and there's easy access to fly-fishing and tramping. A stop at the local pub is also essential.

❶ Crown Range Rd
❷ Gibbston Valley
❸ Skippers Canyon
❹ Sam Summers Hut Track
❺ Glenorchy

### ↘ THINGS YOU NEED TO KNOW

**Go underground** Descend into NZ's biggest wine cave at Gibbston Valley Wines (p296) **Take a look** Watching from the bridge at Kawarau Bungy (p289) is as exciting as actually jumping… Almost. **Best place to recount your bungy jump** Atlas Beer Café ( ☎ 03-442 5995; Steamers Wharf, Queenstown)

# HIGHLIGHTS

## 2  FIORDLAND

### BY KIM HOLLOWS, HELICOPTER PILOT

Fiordland is a bit like Timbuktu: lots of people know it's there, but they're not sure what it's all about. It's so diverse and across such a large area. If the weather's fine, an aerial overview is the best way to see it, but boat trips, road journeys and tramping are also really good.

## ⬎ KIM HOLLOWS' DON'T MISS LIST

### ❶ DOUBTFUL SOUND

A superb wilderness area, **Doubtful Sound** (p317) is a broad, open water-way. Kayaking on the Sound is a great day out, and the boat operators all do a really good job.

### ❷ MILFORD SOUND

Iconic **Milford Sound** (p318) is better known than Doubtful Sound and it also offers a very different experience – it has a real steepness about it. The boat and kayak operators do an excellent job here, too.

### ❸ ATA WHENUA

The filming of *Ata Whenua* took about two years. I developed a subdivision in Te Anau to fund the movie-making and cinema construction. It was a big undertaking, but the film has become a huge success, seen by tens of thousands of visitors. See p136 for viewing info.

Clockwise from top: Rainbow across Doubtful Sound (p317); Boardwalk on the Hump Ridge Track (p321); View across Fiordland National Park

## ❹ HUMP RIDGE TRACK

It's a very exposed piece of real estate down there, but the **Hump Ridge Track** (p321) is a unique walk. It's really growing in popularity, and is a real credit to the Hump Ridge Trust. What they've achieved with the track is fantastic.

## ❺ FIORDLAND'S UNIQUE WEATHER

In Fiordland, we're at the whim of a large expanse of ocean from the polar cap – we certainly get climatic extremes. However, the mountains actually create two different weather patterns: it can be raining in Milford Sound, but fine in Te Anau, where we actually get less rain than in Auckland.

❶ Doubtful Sound  ❸ Ata Whenua
❷ Milford Sound  ❹ Hump Ridge Track

## ↘ THINGS YOU NEED TO KNOW

**Best spot for a post–Milford Track celebration dinner** The Redcliff Bar & Restaurant (p316) in Te Anau **Meet the locals** The Ranch Bar & Grill (p316) in Te Anau (also the biggest meals in town) **If you don't have a car** Explore Fiordland's nooks and crannies with Trips'n'Tramps (p315)

# HIGHLIGHTS

**3**

## ⬊ SKI THE SOUTH

The Southern Alps jag up high and mighty down here, and with rain-weighty clouds streaming in from the Tasman Sea, expect plenty of winter snow. **Queenstown** (p288) has, of course, long been a hot spot for powder-hounds. Coronet Peak and the Remarkables are the main ski spots near here, but there's also Treble Cone and Cardrona, and great Nordic (cross-country) and snowboarding near Wanaka.

**4**

## ⬊ FIORDLAND NATIONAL PARK

This remote, unpeopled part of NZ is a photographer's dream. Encompassing the iconic **Milford Sound** (p318) and **Doubtful Sound** (p317) and a plethora of less-famed fiords and inlets, Fiordland National Park is seriously photogenic. Take the drive from Te Anau to Milford (p318) and see what we're talking about: all around are mountains, forests and mirror-perfect waterways. It's even beautiful in the rain!

## ⬊ DUNEDIN AFTER DARK

Dunedin's nocturnal **bar, pub and live-music scene** (p308) is much cooler and more progressive than you'd expect in a town of this size at this latitude. Expect lots of grungy pub rock, plus reggae, dub and chilled-out house resonating off the stage, all washed down with quality southern micro- and macro-brewed beers.

## ⬊ WANAKA

Queenstown gets the publicity for its bungy jumps, *aprés-ski* nightlife and ritzy restaurants, but **Wanaka** (p299), about 120km to the northwest, is just as hip without the hype. The extreme activities are all here: jetboating, rafting, skydiving, paragliding, plus there are some cool places to stay, great eateries and even a little art-house cinema. Wanaka rocks!

## ⬊ OTAGO PENINSULA

Like a Jackson Pollock paint spillage on the map, the **Otago Peninsula** (p310) makes a brilliant day trip from Dunedin. Meander around the convoluted bays, headlands and inlets, checking out some southern wildlife en route – royal albatrosses, sea lions and yellow-eyed penguins are all here, happily soaring, grunting and waddling.

3 DAVID WALL; 4 GARETH MCCORMACK; 5 TOURISM DUNEDIN; 6 TIM BARKER; 7 DAVID WALL

3 Treble Cone ski field, near Wanaka; 4 Dusky Track, Fiordland National Park; 5 Bar scene, Dunedin (p308); 6 Mountains beside Lake Wanaka, Wanaka (p299); 7 Otago Peninsula (p310)

# BEST...

## ⇲ WILD RIDES

- **Queenstown bungy jumping** (p289) The original and the best.
- **Wanaka paragliding** (p301) Float down off the top of Treble Cone.
- **Otago Central Rail Trail** (p313) Mountain-bike 150km through the Otago countryside.
- **Helicopter sightseeing** (p316) Sound out Milford Sound from above.

## ⇲ SNOW ZONES

- **Coronet Peak** (www.nzski.com) Queenstown region's oldest ski field...also has night skiing!
- **The Remarkables** (www.nzski.com) Downhill for all comers; tackle the sweeping 'Homeward Bound' run.
- **Snow Park** (www.snowparknz. com) NZ's only dedicated freestyle ski and snowboard area.
- **Snow Farm New Zealand** (www. snowfarmnz.com) Cross-country (Nordic) skiing high above Lake Wanaka.

## ⇲ URBAN MOMENTS

- **Eat out in Queenstown** (p295) From fine dining to perfect pizza.
- **Tune in to Dunedin** (p308) The live-music scene in Dunedin is pumping.
- **Cinema Paradiso** (p303) Art-house flicks in far-flung Wanaka.
- **Caffeine fix** (p307) Dunedin's cafes keep the southern chills away.

## ⇲ NATURAL SPLENDOURS

- **Milford Sound** (p318) Tranquil, reflective, serene...we hope your cruise boat is quiet!
- **Doubtful Sound** (p317) Like Milford, minus the tourists.
- **Otago Peninsula** (p310) Wildlife havens and harbour inlets near Dunedin.
- **The Catlins** (p320) Compact wilderness with waterfalls, forests and wild coast.

LEFT: ANDERS BLOMQVIST; RIGHT: DAVID WALL

**Left:** Bungy jumping (p289), Kawarau Bridge, Queenstown; **Right:** Coronet Peak ski area, Queenstown

# THINGS YOU NEED TO KNOW

## ⬎ VITAL STATISTICS

- **Population** Queenstown 11,000; Dunedin 110,800
- **Telephone code** ☎ 03
- **Best time to visit** December to February (summer) or June to August (ski season)

## ⬎ LOCALITIES IN A NUTSHELL

- **Queenstown & Wanaka** (p288) Savvy ski towns.
- **Dunedin & Otago** (p304) Students, albatrosses, coffee and bike tracks – winning combo!
- **Fiordland & Southland** (p314) Fiordland is a bit like a virginal Norway, while unpretentious Southland has a rich Scottish heritage (listen for the rolling 'r' accent).

## ⬎ ADVANCE PLANNING

- **One month before** Book internal flights, car hire and accommodation (especially in summer and ski season).
- **Two weeks before** Book a cruise on Milford Sound (p318) or Doubtful Sound (p317), or a tour through the Catlins (p320).
- **One week before** Book a bungy in Queenstown (p289), check www.dunedinmusic.co.nz to see who's rocking Dunedin, and book a top-notch dinner in Queenstown (p295).

## ⬎ RESOURCES

- **Dunedin i-SITE** (www.dunedinnz.com) Advice and bookings for accommodation, activities, transport and tours.
- **Queenstown DOC visitor information centre** (queenstownvc@doc.govt.nz)
- **Queenstown i-SITE** (www.queenstown-vacation.com)
- **www.queenstown-nz.co.nz** Official website of Queenstown tourism.

## ⬎ EMERGENCY NUMBERS

- **Ambulance, fire service & police** (☎ 111)

## ⬎ GETTING AROUND

- **Cruise** (p318) on Milford Sound.
- **Drive** along the scenic Te Anau–Milford Highway (p318).
- **Kayak** (p317) on Doubtful Sound.
- **Mini-bus** through the Catlins on a tour (p320).
- **Walk** along the 53.5km Milford Track (p318).

# QUEENSTOWN & THE SOUTH ITINERARIES

## DOWNTOWN QUEENSTOWN Three Days

Kick off your (1) Queenstown (p288) holiday with a breakfast burrito at Halo (p295) before heading to Shotover St to book your adrenaline-charged activities for the next day. Spend the rest of the day visiting the Skyline Gondola and Kiwi Birdlife Park (p289). Hungry again? Go for dinner at The Cow, or Wai Waterfront Restaurant & Wine Bar (p295).

Devote the next day to bungy jumping, hang gliding, white-water rafting or perusing the art galleries in Church La. In the evening, chow down at Winnies (p295) and stay on for the live music or DJs, or head to Bardeaux (p297) for a nocturnal fix.

On day three, kick-start your heart on the (2) Shotover Jet (p290), or take a more leisurely hot-air balloon flight (p294) over the area. Later in the day, explore the cellar doors and tasting rooms at the (3) Gibbston Valley wineries (p296), then toast your good fortune at the Pub on Wharf or Monty's (p297).

## SURF TO SNOW Five Days

Surfing at St Clair and St Kilda beaches in (1) Dunedin (p304) is awesome! Warm up afterwards at one of Dunedin's cafes (p307), then lurch into a night of bar-hopping and live music (p308).

On day two, take a day trip out onto (2) Otago Peninsula (p310) east of Dunedin, exploring little beaches and fishing towns and ogling fur seals, penguins and seabirds up close.

Truck northwest to (3) Queenstown (p288); if you've never tried bungy jumping, paragliding, jetboating or skydiving before, this town's for you. In ski season (p326), the mountains fill with international snow bunnies chasing the dream downhill run.

Heading out of town, check out the local shops and Chinese settlement in (4) Arrowtown (p297). Alternatively, drive around Lake Wakatipu to tiny (5) Glenorchy (p298) for lunch at the Glenorchy Café, then strap on your hiking boots and head into Mt Aspiring National Park to tackle a short tramp in the vicinity of the (6) Routeburn Track (p299).

## THE SOUNDS OF SILENCE One Week

Fiordland National Park is just so darn *pure*…Do places like this really still exist?

After an obligatory night partying in (1) Queenstown (p288), spend a day getting organised (or just eating, drinking and chilling-out) in laid-back (2) Te Anau (p314). The next day take a cruise across the hushed waters of (3) Milford Sound (p318) – an experience that will

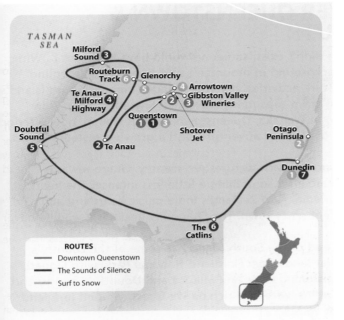

have you reaching for your camera (if you haven't already filled your memory card along the **(4) Te Anau–Milford Highway** (p318).

The Sounds continue to fracture the coastline heading south – **(5) Doubtful Sound** (p317) is one of the biggest and most spectacular, with cascading waterfalls and thick forest rambling down to glassy waters; day cruises, overnight trips and kayaking are all options.

Tracking back east into Southland for a day or two, explore the beautiful **(6) Catlins** (p320) region, either on a tour or under your own steam. From here track back north to **(7) Dunedin** (p304) for an onward flight or some reggae, rock and coffee (the three pillars of modern civilisation).

# DISCOVER QUEENSTOWN & THE SOUTH

If Queenstown didn't exist, someone would have to invent it. With a cinematic background of mountains and lakes and a boggling array of adventure activities, it's little wonder that the South Island's premier tourist town tops many travellers' Kiwi itineraries. Slow down (slightly) in Wanaka, Queenstown's junior sibling, now offering its own menu of outdoor adventure, and a growing restaurant and bar scene.

Unhurried, and rife with picturesque scenery, Otago rewards explorers who are after something a little less intense. The heart of Otago is Dunedin, New Zealand's indie-music heartland and definitive student party town. The Otago Peninsula is a wildlife haven not far away.

The bottom end of the South Island has some of the country's most spectacular landscape: Fiordland National Park, with jagged, misty peaks, glistening lakes and Milford and Doubtful Sounds; and the peaceful Catlins, with bird-rich native forest, verdant farmland and windswept coasts.

# QUEENSTOWN & WANAKA REGION

## GETTING THERE & AROUND

Air New Zealand links Auckland, Wellington and Christchurch to Queenstown, with connections to Wanaka. Jetstar flies to Auckland, Christchurch and Rotorua from Queenstown. Bus and shuttle companies criss-cross Otago from Dunedin to Queenstown and Wanaka. Several divert to Te Anau and Invercargill, and others go north to Christchurch or travel through the Haast Pass and up the West Coast. Major operators include InterCity, Atomic Shuttles, Naked Bus, Tracknet and Wanaka Connexions.

## QUEENSTOWN

pop 11,000

No one has ever visited Queenstown and said, 'I'm bored.' Looking like a small town, but displaying the energy of a small city, Queenstown offers a mountain of activities.

The town's restaurants and bars are regularly packed with a mainly young crowd that really knows how to enjoy themselves on holiday.

### INFORMATION

**Department of Conservation visitor information centre** (DOC; Map p292; ☎ 03-442 7935; queenstownvc@doc.govt.nz; 38 Shotover St; ⊗ 8.30am-5pm May-Nov, to 6pm Dec-Apr) Backcountry Hut Passes and weather and track updates; on the mezzanine floor above Outdoor Sports.

**Queenstown i-SITE** (Map p292; ☎ 0800 668 888, 03-442 4100; www.queenstown-vacation.com; Clocktower Centre, cnr Shotover & Camp Sts; ⊗ 7am-7pm Dec-Apr, to 6pm May-Nov) Also check www.queenstown-nz.co.nz.

# AROUND QUEENSTOWN

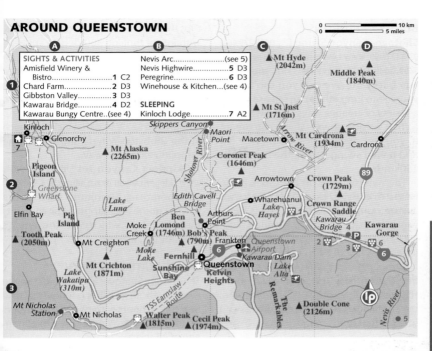

| SIGHTS & ACTIVITIES | | Nevis Arc....................(see 5) |
|---|---|---|
| Amisfield Winery & | | Nevis Highwire...............5 D3 |
| Bistro...........................1 C2 | | Peregrine........................6 D3 |
| Chard Farm.....................2 D3 | | Winehouse & Kitchen...(see 4) |
| Gibbston Valley..............3 D3 | | |
| Kawarau Bridge..............4 D2 | | **SLEEPING** |
| Kawarau Bungy Centre..(see 4) | | Kinloch Lodge................7 A2 |

## SIGHTS & ACTIVITIES

Hop on the **Skyline Gondola** (Map p291; ☎ 03-441 0101; www.skyline.co.nz; Brecon St; adult/child/family return $23/12/59; ☼ 9.30am-6.30pm) for fantastic views of Queenstown, the lake and the mountains. Walking trails include the **loop track** (30 minutes return) or you can try the **Luge** (Map p291).

The **Kiwi Birdlife Park** (Map p292; ☎ 03-442 8059; www.kiwibird.co.nz; Brecon St; adult/child $35/15; ☼ 9am-5pm Oct-Mar, to 6pm Apr-Sep, shows 11am & 3pm) is your best bet to spy a kiwi. Stroll around the sanctuary, watch the conservation show and tiptoe quietly into the darkened kiwi houses.

Combination tickets for a variety of Queenstown's more heart-stopping activities are available from **Queenstown Combos** (☎ 0800 423 836, 03-442 7318; www.combos.co.nz).

## BUNGY JUMPING

Queenstown is famous for bungy jumping, and **AJ Hackett Bungy** (Map p292; ☎ 03-442 7100; www.bungy.co.nz; Station, cnr Camp & Shotover Sts) is the activity's best-known representative. Prices for the following include transport out of town and gondola rides where relevant.

The historic 1880 **Kawarau Bridge** (Map p101; per person $175), 23km from Queenstown, became the world's first commercial bungy site in 1988 and allows you to leap 43m.

Atop Queenstown's gondola, the 47m-high **Ledge Bungy** (Map p291; per person $175) is the only place you can bungy after dark.

The gold-standard jump is the truly awe-inspiring/terrifying/crazy (choose one) 134m-high **Nevis Highwire** (Map p289; per person $250), where you jump from a pod suspended over the Nevis River.

## BUNGY VARIATIONS

**Shotover Canyon Swing** (☎ 0800 279 464, 03-442 6990; www.canyonswing.co.nz; per person $199, additional swings $39) is not your average backyard swing. If you can't force yourself to jump, they can release you in a variety of creative ways – backwards, in a chair, upside down – if you can dream it, you can swing it. It's a 60m free fall and a wild swing across the canyon at 150km/h.

The new swinger on the block is the **Nevis Arc** (Map p289; ☎ 03 442 4007; www.nevisarc.co.nz), at AJ Hackett's Nevis Highwire bungy site. Billed as the world's highest swing (120m), you can fly with a friend in tandem ($300) or go it alone ($170).

Same, same but different is the **Ledge Sky Swing** (Map p291; swing $120), at AJ Hackett's Ledge Bungy site. Shorter swing, but stunning views of Queenstown as you scream your lungs out.

## JETBOATING

**Shotover Jet** (☎ 0800 746 868; www.shotoverjet.co.nz; adult/child $109/69) does half-hour trips through the rocky Shotover Canyons with lots of thrilling 360-degree spins.

**Kawarau Jet** (Map p292; ☎ 0800 529 272, 03-442 6142; www.kjet.co.nz; Queenstown Bay Jetty; adult/child $95/55) does one-hour trips on the Kawarau and Lower Shotover Rivers and a special wine-tasting five-hour trip (adult/child $229/142) that includes lunch at the Gibbston Winery and some wine sampling along the way.

**Skippers Canyon Jet** (☎ 03-442 9434; www.skipperscanyon.co.nz; adult/child $109/69) incorporates a 30-minute blast in the narrow gorges of Skippers Canyon in its three-hour trips, which cover the region's gold-mining history.

## WHITE-WATER RAFTING

The choppy Shotover and calmer Kawarau Rivers are both great for rafting. Trips take four to five hours with two to three hours on the river. There's generally a minimum age of 13 years.

Companies include **Queenstown Rafting** (☎ 0800 723 8464, 03-442 9792; www.rafting.co.nz), **Extreme Green Rafting** (☎ 03

Shotover Jet boat trip, Shotover River Canyons

UROS RAVB

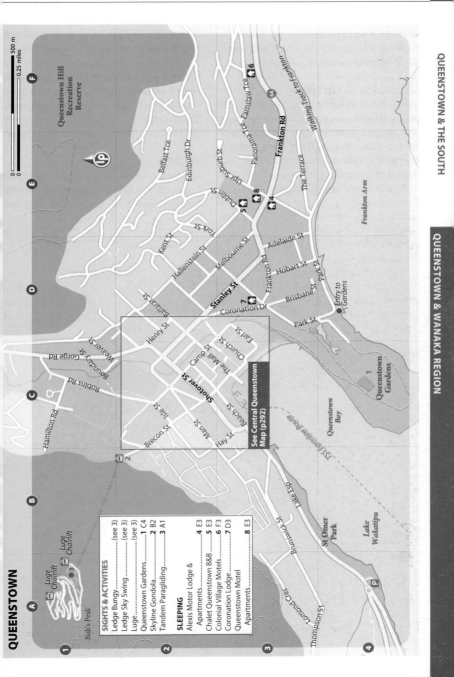

# QUEENSTOWN

**SIGHTS & ACTIVITIES**

| | |
|---|---|
| Ledge Bungy | (see 3) |
| Ledge Sky Swing | (see 3) |
| Luge | (see 3) |
| Queenstown Gardens | 1 C4 |
| Skyline Gondola | 2 B2 |
| Tandem Paragliding | 3 A1 |

**SLEEPING**

| | |
|---|---|
| Alexis Motor Lodge & Apartments | 4 E3 |
| Chalet Queenstown B&B | 5 E3 |
| Colonial Village Motels | 6 F3 |
| Coronation Lodge | 7 D3 |
| Queenstown Motel Apartments | 8 E3 |

See Central Queenstown Map (p292)

QUEENSTOWN & THE SOUTH

QUEENSTOWN & WANAKA REGION

442 8517; www.nzraft.com) and **Challenge Rafting** ( ☎ 0800 423 836, 03-442 7318; www. raft.co.nz); prices start around $175.

### GLIDING & SKYDIVING
**Tandem Paragliding** (Map p291; ☎ 0800 759 688, 03-441 8581; www.paraglide.net.nz; per person $199, if you are on the gondola by 9am $169) takes off from the top of the gondola, while **Flight Park Tandems** ( ☎ 0800 467 325; www.tandemparagliding.com; from 1140m/1620m $179/205) offers spectacular views from Coronet Peak.

Soar with **Skytrek Hang Gliding** ( ☎ 0800 759 873; www.skytrek.co.nz; per person $210) from Coronet Peak or the Remarkables.

The good folks at **NZONE** ( ☎ 0800 376 796, 03-442 5867; www.nzone.biz; from $249) skydiving will toss you out of a perfectly good airplane – attached to somebody who knows how to open the parachute.

### SKIING
The Remarkables (www.nzski.com) and Coronet Peak ski fields (www.nzski.com) are the region's key snow-sport centres.

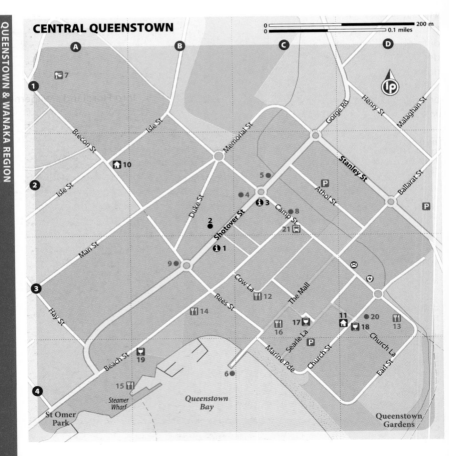

**CENTRAL QUEENSTOWN**

0 ────── 200 m
0 ────── 0.1 miles

For serious skiers, check out **Heli Ski Queenstown** ( ☎ 03-442 7733; www.flynz. co.nz; from $895), **Harris Mountains Heli-Ski** ( ☎ 03-442 6722; www.heliski.co.nz; from $775) or **Southern Lakes Heliski** ( ☎ 03-442 6222; www.southernlakesheliski.co.nz; from $675).

Ski equipment hire companies:
**Gravity Action** (Map p292; ☎ 03-442 5277; 19 Shotover St)
**Snowrental** (Map p292; ☎ 03-442 4187; 39 Camp St)

## MOUNTAIN BIKING

**Fat Tyre Adventures** ( ☎ 0800 328 897; www.fat-tyre.co.nz; from $195) takes small tours off the main trails. Tours cater to different abilities with day tours, multi-day tours, helibiking and singletrack riding.

If you're not keen on strenuous uphill pedalling, chat to the folks at **Vertigo** (Map p292; ☎ 0800 837 8446, 03-442 8378; www.

vertigobikes.co.nz; 4 Brecon St). It runs guided downhill rides into Skippers Canyon and from the top of the gondola. Both options cost $149, and there are helibiking trips on offer, too.

## TRAMPING

Pick up a free copy of *Queenstown Walks and Trails* from the **DOC visitor information centre** (DOC; Map p292; ☎ 03-442 7935; queenstownvc@doc.govt.nz; 38 Shotover St) for local tramping tracks ranging from easy one-hour strolls to tough eight-hour slogs.

The peaceful **Queenstown Gardens** (Map p291) has a number of walking trails to follow. Another short climb is up 900m **Queenstown Hill** (Map p291; two to three hours return); access is from Belfast Tce.

WILL SALTER

**Mountain biker, Lake Wakatipu**

QUEENSTOWN & THE SOUTH

QUEENSTOWN & WANAKA REGION

Helicopter landing near Queenstown

TIM BARKE

**Guided Nature Walks** (☎ 03-442 7126; www.nzwalks.com; adult/child from $103/60) offers excellent walks in the area, including a Walk and Wine option and helihikes.

**Encounter Guided Day Walks** (☎ 03-442 8200; www.ultimatehikes.co.nz; ☯ Oct-Apr) offers day walks on the Routeburn Track (adult/child $145/85), the Milford Track (adult/child $165/95) and near Mt Cook (adult/child $105/65), as well as multiday tramps.

## TOURS

**Nomad Safaris** (☎ 03-442 6699; www.nomadsafaris.co.nz; adult/child $149/75) Runs four-hour tours with a *Lord of the Rings* flavour. If you're 'Bored of the Rings', Nomad has trips on offer that simply take in stunning scenery and hard-to-get-to backcountry vistas.

**Over the Top Helicopters** (☎ 03-442 2233; www.flynz.co.nz; from $225) Heaps of flight options taking in the best of the best views in Queenstown and beyond.

**Sunrise Balloons** (☎ 0800 468 247, 03-442 0781; www.ballooningnz.com; adult/child $375/245) Cruise the lake and mountain breezes in a hot-air balloon.

## SLEEPING

**Nomads** (Map p292; ☎ 03-441-3922; www.nomadshostels.com; 5 Church St; dm $25-34, tw/d $110/130; ☐ ☎) Blessed with stunning exterior architecture and a prime location, this sparkling new hostel is on a fast-track to being the one to beat. Inside, the facilities are top-notch, with en suites aplenty, massive kitchens and other bonuses such as an on-site internet cafe and travel agency.

**Colonial Village Motels** (Map p291; ☎ 03-442 7629; www.colonialvillage.co.nz; 136 Frankton Rd; s/d $115/120) Older-style motel units with gorgeous lake views have been spruced up with classy bed linen and minikitchens. Expect a bit of daytime road noise, but after dark it is considerably quieter.

**Queenstown Motel Apartments** (Map p291; ☎ 0800 661 668, 03-442 6095; www.qma.co.nz; 62 Frankton Rd; d $145) This well-run spot combines newer units, with spa bathrooms, trendy decor and private mini-gardens, with older 1970s-style units that represent good value for larger groups of budget travellers.

**Coronation Lodge** (Map p291; ☎ 0800 420 777, 03-442 0860; www.coronationlodge. co.nz; 10 Coronation Dr; d $170; 🖵 🛜 ) Right beside the Queenstown Gardens, this recently opened lodge has plush bed linen, cosy wooden floors, Turkish rugs, and Sky TV.

**Alexis Motor Lodge & Apartments** (Map p291; ☎ 03-409 0052; www.alexisqueens town.co.nz; 69 Frankton Rd; d $170; 🖵 🛜 ) With energetic family owners, this modern hillside motel with self-contained units is an easy 10-minute walk to town along the lakefront. Ask for an end unit with snap-happy views.

**our pick** **Chalet Queenstown B&B** (Map p291; ☎ 0800 222 457, 03-442 7117; www.chalet. co.nz; 1 Dublin St; d $195; 🛜 ) This recently renovated B&B has become the new standard for boutique accommodation in Queenstown. Perfectly appointed rooms sparkle with modern amenities such as flat-screen TVs, art that stops you in your tracks and bed linen that will leave you laid-up.

**Dairy** (Map p292; ☎ 0800 333 393, 03-442 5164; www.thedairy.co.nz; 10 Isle St; s/d incl breakfast $450/480; 🖵 🛜 ) Once a corner-store, the Dairy's now a luxury guest house with 13 rooms packed with classy touches such as designer bed linen, silk cushions and luxurious mohair rugs. Rates also include freshly baked afternoon tea. From June to September, three-night packages are great value for skiers (double cost from $825 to $945).

## EATING
### RESTAURANTS

**Winnies** (Map p292; ☎ 03-442 8635; 1st fl, 7 The Mall; pizza $15-25; 🕑 noon-late; 🛜 ) Winnies' cool and sassy international team serve up a global array of pizzas with a Thai, Mexican or Moroccan accent. Occasional live music and DJs keep the energy levels up long after you've finished your last slice.

**our pick** **Cow** (Map p292; ☎ 03 442 8588; Cow Lane; mains $18-30; 🕑 noon-midnight) Housed in a former cow shed (hence the name of the restaurant and the street), the Cow hasn't changed its menu since 1976 – and is damn proud of it. Amazing pizzas, simple pasta and stellar garlic bread will leave you satisfied. The atmosphere is cramped with low-slung ceilings, a roaring fire, thick wooden tables and rustic candlelight.

**Wai Waterfront Restaurant & Wine Bar** (Map p292; ☎ 03-442 5969; Steamer Wharf, Beach St; mains $35-50; 🕑 11am-10pm) Small and intimate, Wai (meaning 'water' in Maori) is white-linen classy with lake and mountain views. It's known for lamb and seafood, and the Oyster Bar does the world's favourite bivalve in 17 different ways. The seven-course degustation menu ($115 without wine and $175 with wine) is a splurge-worthy opportunity for a great culinary adventure.

## CAFES & QUICK EATS

**our pick** **Patagonia** (Map p292; ☎ 03-442 9066; 50 Beach St; coffee & chocolate $5-7; 🕑 10am-10pm; 🛜 ) Delicious hot chocolate, homemade choccies and Queenstown's best ice cream. What more do you want? How about a lakefront location and free wi-fi? Patagonia's open until 10pm, so it's your best bet for a late-night coffee.

**Halo** (Map p292; ☎ 03-441 1411; Camp St; mains $12-16; 🕑 7am-10pm) A stylish and sunny place that effortlessly blurs the line between breakfast, lunch and dinner. The breakfast burrito will set you up for a day's adventuring. Come back at night for a Caribbean jerk chicken burger and

QUEENSTOWN & THE SOUTH

QUEENSTOWN & WANAKA REGION

Grape vines, Gibbston Valley

## ⬃ QUEENSTOWN WINERIES

Gung-ho visitors to Queenstown might be happiest dangling off a giant rubber band, but as they are submerged in the icy Kawarau River, they'll be missing out on some of Central Otago's most interesting vineyards just up the road.

On a spectacular river terrace near the Kawarau Bridge, AJ Hackett's original bungy partner Henry van Asch has set up the **Winehouse & Kitchen**. A beautifully restored wooden villa includes a garden cafe and the opportunity to try van Asch's Freefall and Rock Ferry wines, as well as his own van Asch label.

Almost opposite, a winding and scenic road leads to beautiful **Chard Farm**, and a further 700m along is **Gibbston Valley**, the area's largest wine producer.

A further 4km along SH6, **Peregrine** produces excellent sauvignon blanc, pinot noir and pinot gris, and hosts occasional outdoor concerts during summer, sometimes featuring international names.

Further west near the shores of Lake Hayes, the **Amisfield Winery & Bistro** is a regular winner of *Cuisine* magazine's Best NZ Winery Restaurant gong.

Ask at the Queenstown i-SITE for maps and information about touring the Gibbston Valley. Alternatively, visit www.gibbstonvalley.co.nz for more information about this compact wine-growing area with its own unique microclimate. You could also join a wine tour.

**Things you need to know:** Winehouse & Kitchen (Map p289; ☎ 03-442 7310; www.winehouse.co.nz; mains $15-30; ☼ 10am-5pm); Chard Farm (Map p289; ☎ 03-442 6110; www.chardfarm.co.nz; ☼ 11am-5pm); Gibbston Valley (Map p289; ☎ 03-442 6910; www.gvwines.co.nz); Peregrine (Map p289; ☎ 03-442 4000; www.peregrinewines.co.nz; ☼ 10am-5pm); Amisfield Winery & Bistro (Map p289; ☎ 03-442 0556; www.amisfield.co.nz; small plates $16.50; ☼ 11.30am-8pm Tue-Sun)

a glass of local wine. It's beside St James Church.

## DRINKING

**Bardeaux** (Map p292; ☎ 03-442 8284; **Eureka Arcade, 11 The Mall**; ☯ 6pm-4am) Down a narrow alleyway, this small, low-key wine bar is all class. Under a low ceiling await plush leather armchairs and a fireplace made from Central Otago's iconic schist rock. No beanies, rugby jerseys or work boots allowed.

**Monty's** (Map p292; ☎ 03-441 1081; **Church St**; ☯ 11am-late) On warm summer days the patio at Monty's is prime real estate. Same goes for the fire inside when the snow falls. With Monteith's beer on tap, this is a great place for a quiet drink with a predominantly local crowd.

**Pub on Wharf** (Map p292; ☎ 03-441 2155; **Steamer Wharf**; ☯ 10.30am-late) The newest pub in town is also one if its most stylish. Ubercool interior design is shoved to the fore with handsome woodwork, lighting fit for a hipster hideaway and animal heads on the wall to remind you you're still in NZ. Mac's beer on tap, scrummy nibbles and a decent wine list make this a great place to settle in for the evening.

## GETTING THERE & AROUND
### AIR

**Air New Zealand** (Map p292; ☎ 0800 737 000, 03-441 1900; www.airnz.co.nz; 8 Church St) has direct daily flights between Queenstown and Auckland (from $139), Wellington (from $149) and Christchurch (from $89) with connections to Wanaka. **Jetstar** ( ☎ 0800 800 995; www.jetstar.com) has flights to Auckland (from $139), Christchurch (from $100) and Rotorua (from $179).

### BUS

Book seats for **InterCity** (Map p292; ☎ 03-442 4100; www.intercity.co.nz) trips at the i-SITE. It offers daily bus services from Queenstown to Christchurch ($50), Te Anau ($30), Milford Sound ($80), Dunedin ($40) and Invercargill ($45), plus a daily West Coast service to the glaciers ($60) via Wanaka ($17) and Haast Township ($36).

**Naked Bus** (www.nakedbus.com) travels to the West Coast, Te Anau, Christchurch, Dunedin and Invercargill.

The **Bottom Bus** (www.bottombus.co.nz) does a loop service around the south of the South Island (see p321).

Shuttles charge around $20 to $25 to Wanaka, $40 to Dunedin, $30 to Te Anau and $50 to Christchurch. Book at the i-SITE. **Atomic Shuttles** ( ☎ 03-349 0697; www.atomictravel.co.nz) Travels to Wanaka, Christchurch, Dunedin, Greymouth and Invercargill.

**Wanaka Connexions** ( ☎ 03-443 9122; www.time2.co.nz) Offers regular services to Wanaka.

### TO/FROM THE AIRPORT

**Queenstown Airport** (Map p289; ☎ 03-450 9031; www.queenstownairport.co.nz; Frankton) is 8km east of town. **Super Shuttle** ( ☎ 0800 748 885; www.supershuttle.co.nz) picks up and drops off in Queenstown (from $15). **Connectabus** (Map p292; ☎ 03-442 4471; www.connectabus.com; cnr Beach & Camp Sts) runs to the airport ($6) hourly from 6.30am to 10.20pm. **Alpine Taxis** ( ☎ 03-442 6666) and **Queenstown Taxis** ( ☎ 03-442 7788) charge around $25.

# ARROWTOWN

pop 2400

Beloved by day trippers from Queenstown, quaint Arrowtown sprang up in the 1860s following the discovery of gold in the Arrow River. Today the town retains more than 60 of its original wooden and stone buildings, and has pretty, tree-lined avenues, excellent galleries and an expanding array of fashionable shopping opportunities.

## SIGHTS & ACTIVITIES

The **Arrowtown visitor information centre** (☎ 03-442 1824; www.arrowtown.com; 49 Buckingham St; ☯ 8.30am-5pm) shares premises with the **Lake District Museum & Gallery** (www.museumqueenstown.com; adult/child $7/1; ☯ 8.30am-5pm), which has exhibits on the gold-rush era.

Arrowtown has NZ's best example of a gold-era **Chinese settlement** (admission by gold coin donation; ☯ 24hr). Interpretive signs explain the lives of Chinese 'diggers' during and after the gold rush, while restored huts and shops make the story more tangible.

## GETTING THERE & AWAY

From Queenstown, **connectabus** (☎ 03-441 4471; www.connectabus.com) runs regular services (from 7.15am to 10pm) on its green route to Arrowtown (adult/child $8/5). If you're planning a day trip to Arrowtown, a day pass (adult/child $19/9.50) is a little cheaper.

The **Double-Decker Bus Tour** (☎ 03-441 4421; $48) does a three-hour round-trip tour to Arrowtown twice daily. **Arrowtown Scenic Bus** (☎ 03-442 1900; www.arrowtownbus.co.nz) has three services daily (return $25).

# GLENORCHY

pop 220

Set in achingly beautiful surroundings, postage-stamp-sized Glenorchy is the perfect low-key antidote to the hype and bustle of Queenstown. Glenorchy lies at the head of Lake Wakatipu, a scenic 40-minute (68km) drive northwest from Queenstown.

The best place for local information, updated weather and track information,

and hut passes is the **Glenorchy visitor information centre** (☎ 03-409 2049; www.glenorchy-nz.co.nz; Oban St).

**Dart River Safaris** (☎ 0800 327 8538, 03-442 9992; www.dartriver.co.nz; Mull St; adult/child $199/99) journeys by jetboat into the heart of the spectacular Dart River wilderness, followed by a short nature walk and a 4WD trip down a back road to Paradise.

**Kayak Kinloch** (☎ 03-442 4900; www.kayakkinloch.co.nz; adult $40-80, child $35-50) runs excellent guided trips exploring the lake.

## SLEEPING & EATING

**our pick** **Kinloch Lodge** (Map p289; ☎ 03-442 4900; www.kinlochlodge.co.nz; Kinloch Rd; dm $30-33, d $80-120, r $175-195; ▯) Across Lake Wakatipu from Glenorchy, this excellent retreat is a great place to unwind or prepare for a tramp. Rooms in the bunkhouse are comfy and colourful, with an outdoor hot tub and an indoor DVD-packed lounge, both just right for putting your feet up after a long tramp. The 19th-century Heritage Rooms are small but plusher.

**Mt Earnslaw Motels** (☎ 03-442 6993; mtearnslaw@xtra.co.nz; Mull St; d $110; ☎) This cute row of units is older on the outside but redone inside, creating cosy, well-priced rooms with big, comfy recliners, small kitchens and enormous beds.

**our pick** **Glenorchy Café** (GYC; ☎ 03-442 9958; Mull St; breakfast & lunch mains $10-15, pizza $20; ☯ 8am-late May-Oct, dinner Nov-Apr) With a reputation extending beyond little ol' GY, the Glenorchy Café is an institution oozing cool and natural style. Perennial favourites like pizza and breakfast stacks keep locals coming back time after time.

## GETTING THERE & AWAY

With sweeping vistas and gem-coloured waters, the sealed Glenorchy to Queenstown Rd is wonderfully scenic

Backpacker Express at the **Info & Track Centre** (Map p292; ☎ 03-442 9708; www .infotrack.co.nz; 37 Shotover St) provides transport to Glenorchy from Queenstown (adult/child $20/15).

## ROUTEBURN TRACK

The mountainous region at the northern head of Lake Wakatipu has some gorgeous, remote scenery, best viewed while tramping along the famous Routeburn Track. Passing through a huge variety of landscapes with fantastic views, the three- to four-day Routeburn Track is one of the most popular rainforest/subalpine tracks in NZ. Increased pressure on the track has necessitated the introduction of a booking system; reservations are required throughout the main season (October to April), either through DOC visitor information centres, or online via greatwalksbooking@doc.govt.nz or www.doc.govt.nz. There are car parks at the Divide and Glenorchy ends of the Routeburn, but they're unattended, so don't leave any valuables in your car.

The track can be started from either end. Many people travelling from Queenstown try to reach the Divide in time to catch the bus to Milford and connect with a cruise on the sound.

## WANAKA

pop 5000

Beautiful scenery, tramping and skiing opportunities, and an expanding roster of adrenaline-inducing activities have transformed the lakeside town of Wanaka into a year-round tourist destination. The Wanaka region, and especially the activity-filled town itself, is seeing more and more travellers, but it's still a quieter alternative to pumpin' Queenstown.

### INFORMATION

**DOC Wanaka visitor information centre** ( ☎ 03-443 7660; Ardmore St; ☻ 8am-4.30pm Mon-Fri, 9.30am-4pm Sat & Sun, closed noon-12.30pm) In an A-framed building on

CHRISTIAN ASLUND

Aerial skiing, Treble Cone ski field, near Wanaka

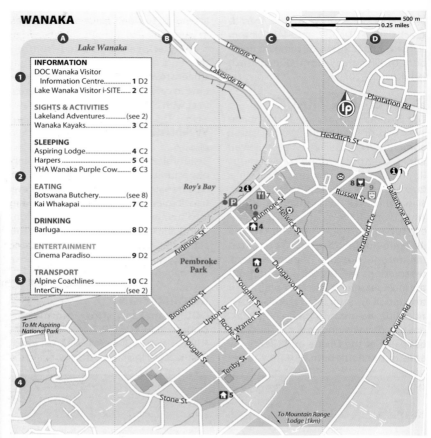

**WANAKA**

**INFORMATION**
DOC Wanaka Visitor
  Information Centre..............**1** D2
Lake Wanaka Visitor i-SITE......**2** C2

**SIGHTS & ACTIVITIES**
Lakeland Adventures............(see 2)
Wanaka Kayaks.......................**3** C2

**SLEEPING**
Aspiring Lodge.......................**4** C2
Harpers...................................**5** C4
YHA Wanaka Purple Cow........**6** C3

**EATING**
Botswana Butchery...............(see 8)
Kai Whakapai .........................**7** C2

**DRINKING**
Barluga...................................**8** D2

**ENTERTAINMENT**
Cinema Paradiso.....................**9** D2

**TRANSPORT**
Alpine Coachlines .................**10** C2
InterCity................................(see 2)

the edge of town, this is the place to en-quire about tramps, and there's a small museum (admission free) on Wanaka geology, flora and fauna.
**Lake Wanaka i-SITE** (☎ 03-443 1233; www.lakewanaka.co.nz; ☽ 8.30am-5.30pm, to 7pm in summer) Off Ardmore St, on the waterfront.

## SIGHTS & ACTIVITIES
Wide valleys, alpine meadows, more than 100 glaciers and sheer mountains make **Mt Aspiring National Park** an outdoor enthusiast's paradise.

## TRAMPING
While the southern end of Mt Aspiring National Park is well trafficked by visitors and includes popular tramps such as the Routeburn Track (p299), there are great short walks and more demanding multi-day tramps in the Matukituki Valley, close to Wanaka; see the DOC leaflet *Matukituki Valley Tracks* ($1). The dramatic **Rob Roy Valley Track** (three to four hours return) takes in glaciers, waterfalls and a swing bridge, yet is a fairly easy route. The **West Matukituki Valley** track goes on to Aspiring Hut (four to five hours return),

a scenic, more difficult walk over mostly grassy flats.

For walks closer to town, pick up the DOC brochure *Wanaka Walks and Trails* ($1).

Many outfits offer guided walking tours around Wanaka, some into Mt Aspiring National Park:

**Alpinism & Ski Wanaka** ( ☎ 03-442 6593; www.alpinismski.co.nz; half-/full day $130/195) Day walks and overnight tramps.

**Eco Wanaka Adventures** ( ☎ 03-443 2869; www.ecowanaka.co.nz; half-/full day from $105/170) Day, half-day and multiday trips.

## JETBOATING & RAFTING

**Lakeland Adventures** ( ☎ 03-443 7495; www.lakelandadventures.co.nz; adult/child $95/45), at the i-SITE, offers one-hour jetboat trips across the lake that include an exciting ride in the winding Clutha River. **Pioneer Rafting** ( ☎ 03-443 1246; www.ecoraft.co.nz; half-day rafts per adult/child $135/75, full-day $185/95) runs eco-rafting on the high-volume Clutha, with Class II to III rapids, gold panning and birdwatching.

## KAYAKING

**Wanaka Kayaks** ( ☎ 0800 926 925; www.wanakakayaks.co.nz; ☀ summer only) is opposite Subway on the beach. It rents kayaks (from $10 to $18) and offers guided lake tours (from $60 per person).

Hire kayaks from **Lakeland Adventures** ( ☎ 03-443 7495; www.lakelandadventures.co.nz), off Ardmore St, on the waterfront, for $15 per hour.

## SKYDIVING & PARAGLIDING

**Skydive Lake Wanaka** ( ☎ 03-443 7207; www.skydivewanaka.com; adult $295-395) does jumps from 12,000 ft and a scary 15,000ft; the latter lets you fall for 60 seconds. **Wanaka Paragliding** ( ☎ 0800 359 754; www.wanakaparagliding.co.nz; adult $180) will take you on tandem flights at 800m from Treble Cone.

## MOUNTAIN BIKING

DOC produces *Mountain-Biking Around Wanaka* (50c), describing mountain-bike rides ranging from 2km (the steep Mt Iron track) to 20km (West Matukituki Valley).

For spectacular guided mountain biking, contact **Freeride NZ** ( ☎ 0800 743 369; www.freeridenz.com), which does full-day trips (from $185), including helibiking options.

Hire bikes from **Lakeland Adventures** ( ☎ 03-443 7495; www.lakelandadventures.co.nz; per hr/full day $10/40).

JOHN ELK III

**Kayakers on the Clutha River**

## AERIAL SIGHTSEEING

**Aspiring Air** ( ☎ 0800 100 943, 03-443 7943; www.aspiringair.com) offers a range of scenic flights, including a 50-minute flight over Mt Aspiring (adult/child $210/120), a Milford Sound fly-past and landing ($375/230) and a sprint around Mt Cook and the glaciers ($395/230).

The following offer 20-minute flights around Wanaka for about $175, and 60-minute tours of Mt Aspiring and the glaciers for about $450.

**Alpine Helicopters** ( ☎ 03-443 4000; www. alpineheli.co.nz)

**Aspiring Helicopters** ( ☎ 03-443 7152; www.aspiringhelicopters.co.nz)

**Wanaka Helicopters** ( ☎ 03-443 1085; www.heliflights.co.nz)

## SLEEPING

**ourpick YHA Wanaka Purple Cow** ( ☎ 03-443 1880; www.yha.co.nz; 94 Brownston St; dm $24-31, d $90-96; 🖥 🛜 ) Warmed by a wood stove, the lounge at this ever-popular hostel holds commanding lake and mountain views; that's if you can tear yourself away from the regular movie nights. There are four-and six-bed dorms and a small array of nice doubles with en suites. Outdoor patios and bike hire will get you breathing in crisp mountain air.

**Harpers** ( ☎ 03-443 8894; www.harpers.co.nz; 95 McDougall St; s/d incl breakfast $100/140) The garden (with pond and waterfall no less) is a labour of love at this friendly B&B, set in a quiet location down a long driveway. Legendary breakfasts are served on a sunny deck with expansive views. You'd be wise to factor a leisurely second cup of breakfast coffee into your day's plans.

**Aspiring Lodge** ( ☎ 03-443 7816; www. aspiringlodge.co.nz; cnr Dunmore & Dungarvon Sts; d $135) Older but well-maintained motel units trimmed with natural wood and with easy access to lakefront bars and restaurants. The motel's helpful team will have plenty of ideas for local activities during your stay.

**ourpick Mountain Range Lodge** ( ☎ 03-443 7400; www.mountainrange.co.nz; Heritage Park, Cardrona Valley Rd; r breakfast incl $280-390; 🖥 🛜 ) This stunning lodge is a vision

Ridge runner near the summit of Mt Roy, overlooking Lake Wanaka

SCOTT DARSNE

of rustic luxury. Seven rooms named for nearby mountain ranges are home to comfy duvets, fluffy robes and views that'll distract you from the nearby skiing and tramping options. Cool touches such as a complimentary glass of wine – from the lodge's own label, no less – and an on-site hot tub complete an already pretty picture.

## EATING

**Kai Whakapai** ( ☎ 03-443 7795; cnr Helwick & Ardmore Sts; meals $10-30; ☺ 7am-late) A Wanaka institution, Kai (the Maori word for food) is the place to be on a sunny day, with perhaps the best patio in all of Aotearoa. Massive sandwiches, great coffee and exceptionally slow service are all a part of the experience.

**Botswana Butchery** ( ☎ 03-443 6745; Post Office Lane; mains $30-45; ☺ 5pm-late) It's a humble name for Wanaka's classiest eatery. In a dining room trimmed with dark wood and leather, Asian-inspired dishes such as seven-spiced big-eye tuna go head to head with Botswana Butchery's signature aged beef steaks. Definitely food for grown-ups, as is the serious Central Otago–skewed wine list.

## DRINKING & ENTERTAINMENT

**Barluga** ( ☎ 03-442 5400; Post Office Lane; ☺ 4pm-late) In the up-and-coming Post Office Lane area, Barluga's leather armchairs and coolly retro wallpaper at first make you think of a refined gentlemen's club. Wicked cocktails and killer back-to-back beats soon break the illusion.

**our pick** **Cinema Paradiso** ( ☎ 03-443 1505; www.paradiso.net.nz; 1 Ardmore St; adult/child $14/9; ☐ ) Playing first-run and classic movies, Cinema Paradiso has got to be the coolest movie theatre around. Forget boring, stiff cinema seats, this theatre is filled with vintage couches to snuggle up on.

Try the homemade ice cream and don't forget to arrive early to get a good couch.

## GETTING THERE & AWAY
### AIR

**Air New Zealand** ( ☎ 0800 737 000; www.airnz.co.nz) has daily flights between Wanaka and Christchurch (from $99). **Aspiring Air** ( ☎ 0800 100 943, 03-443 7943; www.aspiringair.com) has daily flights between Queenstown and Wanaka ($155, 20 minutes) in small, twin-engine planes.

### BUS

The bus stop for **InterCity** ( ☎ 03-443 7885; www.intercity.co.nz) is outside the i-SITE on the lakefront. Wanaka receives daily buses from Queenstown ($17), which motor on to Franz Josef ($46) via Haast Pass ($23). For Christchurch ($79), you'll need to change at Tarras.

**Naked Bus** (www.nakedbus.com) travels to Queenstown, Christchurch, Cromwell and the West Coast.

**Wanaka Connexions** ( ☎ 03-443 9122; www.time2.co.nz) and **Atomic Shuttles** ( ☎ 03-349 0697; www.atomictravel.co.nz) all service Christchurch ($50 to $60) and Queenstown ($20 to $30). Wanaka Connexions and **Catch-a-Bus** ( ☎ 03-479 9960; www.catchabus.co.nz) head to Dunedin ($50); Atomic Shuttles goes to Fox ($40) and Franz Josef ($45) Glaciers and on to Greymouth ($80).

## GETTING AROUND

**Alpine Coachlines** ( ☎ 03-443 7966; www.alpinecoachlines.co.nz; Dunmore St) meets and greets flights at Wanaka Airport ($15), and in summer has twice-daily shuttles for trampers ($35) to Mt Aspiring National Park and Raspberry Creek.

**Wanaka Taxis** ( ☎ 03-443 7999; www.wanakataxis.com) also looks after airport transfers.

# CARDRONA

The sealed **Crown Range Road** from Wanaka to Queenstown via Cardrona is much shorter than the route via Cromwell, but it's a narrow, twisting-and-turning mountain road that needs to be tackled with care, especially in poor weather. In winter it is often snow covered, necessitating chaining up your vehicle's wheels, and is often subject to closure because of the snow – you've been warned.

With views of lush valleys, foothills and countless snowy peaks, this is one of the South Island's most scenic drives. There are plenty of rest stops to drink in the view; particularly good ones are at the Queenstown end of the road, as you switch back down towards Arrowtown.

The unpretentious looking **Cardrona Hotel** ( ☎ 03-443 8153; www.cardronahotel.co.nz; Crown Range Rd; d $135-185) first opened its doors in 1863. There's a deservedly popular pub with a good restaurant (mains from $15 to $20), and a garden bar that just might be NZ's best.

# DUNEDIN & OTAGO

## GETTING THERE & AROUND

**Air New Zealand** (www.airnewzealand.co.nz) flies from Dunedin to Christchurch, Wellington and Auckland. **Pacific Blue** (www.flypacificblue.co.nz) links Dunedin to Auckland and Brisbane, Australia.

Major bus and shuttle operators include InterCity, Atomic Shuttles, Bottom Bus, Catch-A-Bus, Naked Bus and Wanaka Connexions.

## DUNEDIN

pop 110,800

Dunedin's compact town centre blends the historic and the contemporary, reflected in its alluring museums, and tempting bars, cafes and restaurants. The country's oldest university provides loads of student energy to sustain thriving theatre, live-music and after-dark scenes.

### INFORMATION

**Department of Conservation** ( ☎ 03-477 0677; www.doc.govt.nz, dunedinvc@doc.govt.nz; 1st fl, 77 Lower Stuart St; ⏲ 8.30am-5pm Mon-Fri) Information and maps on regional walking tracks and Great Walks bookings.

**Dunedin i-SITE** ( ☎ 03-474 3300; www.dunedinnz.com; 48 The Octagon; ⏲ 8.30am-5pm Mon-Fri, 8.45am-5pm Sat & Sun) Advice and bookings for accommodation, activities, transport and walking tours.

**Urgent Doctors & Accident Centre** ( ☎ 03-479 2900; 95 Hanover St; ⏲ 8am-11.30pm) Deals with emergencies and has a pharmacy open outside normal business hours.

### SIGHTS

The modern and interactive **Otago Museum** ( ☎ 03-474 7474; www.otagomuseum.govt.nz; 419 Great King St; admission by donation, guided tour $10; ⏲ 10am-5pm) explores Otago's cultural and physical past and present, from geology and dinosaurs to the modern day. This is one of the richest repositories of Maori knowledge on the South Island.

Explore NZ's art scene at the expansive and airy **Dunedin Public Art Gallery** ( ☎ 03-474 4000; www.dunedin.art.museum; 30 The Octagon; permanent exhibition free; ⏲ 10am-5pm). Works on permanent show are mainly contemporary, including a big New Zealand collection featuring local kids Ralph Hotere and Frances Hodgkins, Cantabrian Colin McCahon and some old CF Goldie oils.

Baldwin St, Dunedin

DAVID WALL

At the **New Zealand Sports Hall of Fame** (☎ 03-477 7775; www.nzhalloffame.co.nz; Dunedin Railway Station, Anzac Ave; adult/child $5/2; ⊗ 10am-4pm) you can try and match bike-champ Karen Holliday's average speed of 45.629km/h, or check out the high-stepping style of iconic All Black fullback George Nepia.

The world's steepest residential street (or so says the *Guinness Book of World Records*), **Baldwin St** has a clambering gradient of 1 in 1.286 (19 degrees).

## ACTIVITIES

St Clair and St Kilda are both popular swimming beaches (though you need to watch for rips at St Clair). St Clair and St Kilda have consistently good left-hand breaks, and you'll also find good surfing at Blackhead further south, and at Aramoana on Otago Harbour's north shore. **Esplanade Surf School** (☎ 03-455 7728; www.espsurfschool.co.nz; lessons from $45) is based at St Clair beach and provides equipment and lessons.

The **Tunnel Beach Walkway** (45 minutes return; closed August to October) crosses farmland before descending the sea cliffs to Tunnel Beach. Sea stacks, arches and unusual rock shapes have been carved out by the wild Pacific, and a few fossils stud the sandstone cliffs. Catch a Corstorphine bus from the Octagon to Stenhope Cres and walk 1.4km along Blackhead Rd to Tunnel Beach Rd, then 400m to the start of the walkway.

**Cycle Surgery** (☎ 03-477 7473; www.cyclesurgery.co.nz; 67 Lower Stuart St; per day $35) rents out bikes and has mountain-biking info.

## TOURS

**First City Tours** (adult/child $20/10; ⊗ buses depart The Octagon 9am, 10.15am, 1pm, 2.15pm & 3.30pm) Hop-on/hop-off double-decker bus tour that loops around the city.

**Walk Dunedin** (☎ 03-477 5052; 1/2hr walk $12/20; ⊗ 1hr walk 7pm year-round & 9.30am Oct-Apr, 2hr walk 11am year-round) History-themed strolls around the city, organised by the Otago Settlers Museum.

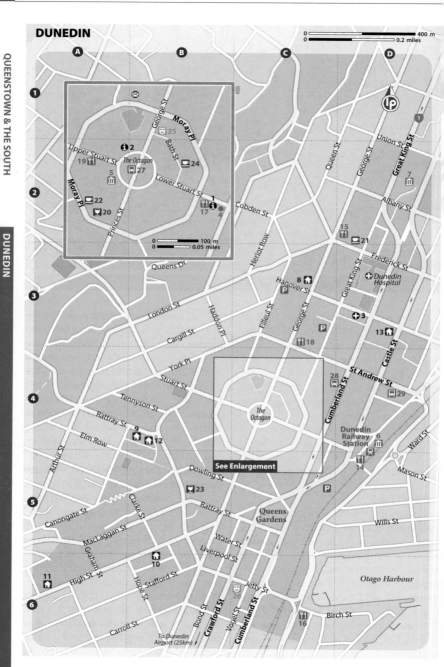

# DUNEDIN

See Enlargement

*The Octagon*

*Queens Gardens*

*Otago Harbour*

To Dunedin Airport (25km)

0        400 m
0        0.2 miles

0        100 m
0        0.05 miles

## SLEEPING

**our pick** **Hogwartz** ( ☎ 03-474 1487; www. hogwartz.co.nz; 277 Rattray St; dm $27-28, s/d/tr $40/64/90; 💻 🛜 ) The Catholic bishop's residence since the 1870s, this beautiful old building has now been converted into a wonderfully complicated warren of comfortable rooms. The five-bed dorm, the bishop's old formal dining room, would almost certainly be the grandest dorm room you have ever stayed in.

**Living Space** ( ☎ 03-951 5000; www.living space.net; 192 Castle St; d $89-149; 💻 🛜 ) Living Space combines kitchenettes in funky colours, whip-smart ergonomic design,

and a central location. There's an onsite laundry and huge shared kitchen, conversation-friendly lounges, and a private DVD cinema. Some rooms are pretty compact, but they're all you need, and represent good value.

**Grandview Bed & Breakfast** ( ☎ 0800 749 472, 03-474 9472; www.grandview.co.nz; 360 High St; d incl breakfast $125-195; 💻 🛜 ) Bold colours, exposed brick walls and snazzy art-deco bathrooms are the highlights at this family-owned B&B on the slopes above town. There are more harbour views from the barbecue and deck, and lots of sunny shared spaces.

**315 Euro** ( ☎ 0800 387 638, 03-477 9929; www.eurodunedin.co.nz; 315 George St; d $150-250; 🛜 ) This sleek new opening is in the absolute heart of George St's daytime retail strip and after-dark eating and drinking hub. Choose from modern studio apartments or larger one-bedroom apartments with full kitchens.

**Dunedin Palms Motel** ( ☎ 0800 782 938, 03-477 8293; www.dunedinpalmsmotel.co.nz; 185-195 High St; d $170-210; 💻 🛜 ) A short stroll from the Speight's Ale House, the art-deco-style Palms has smartly decorated studios and one- and two-bedroom units arranged around a central courtyard.

**Brothers Boutique Hotel** ( ☎ 0800 477 004, 03-477 0043; www.brothershotel.co.nz; 295 Rattray St; d incl breakfast $170-320; 💻 🛜 ) Rooms in this distinctive old 1920s Christian Brothers residence have been refurbished beyond any monk's dreams, while still retaining many unique features. The chapel room ($285) includes the original arched stained-glass windows of its past life.

## EATING
### RESTAURANTS

**Saigon Van** ( ☎ 03-474 1445; 66 St Andrew St; mains $10-15; 🕑 11.30am-2pm Tue-Sun & 5-10pm daily; 🔽 ) The elegant decor looks high-end Asian, but the Vietnamese food is definitely budget-friendly. Try the combination spring rolls ($9 for six) and a bottle of Vietnamese beer to re-create lazy nights in Saigon. The bean-sprout-laden *pho* (noodle soup) and salads are also good.

**Scotia** ( ☎ 03-477 7704; 199 Upper Stuart St; mains $30-32; ☺ 3pm-late) Now relocated from the Dunedin Railway Station to a cosy heritage town house, Scotia toasts all things Scottish with a wall-full of single malt whisky and hearty fare such as smoked salmon and char-grilled venison. The two Scottish Robbies – Burns and Coltrane – look down approvingly on a menu that also includes haggis, and duck and whisky pâté.

**our pick** **Plato** ( ☎ 03-477 4235; 2 Birch St; dinner mains $30-35, brunch mains $15-23; ☺ 6pm-late Mon-Sat & 11am-late Sun) A regular winner in *Cuisine* magazine's Best of NZ's gongs, Plato has a retro-themed location near the harbour and a standout beer and wine list. Plato's spin on seafood is always excellent, and Sunday brunch is worth the shortish trek from the CBD.

## CAFES

**Potpourri** ( ☎ 03-477 9983; 97 Lower Stuart St; snacks $7-10, meals $10-14; ☺ 9.30am-3pm Mon-Fri; Ⓥ ) Funky, homey and very kid-friendly, this small cafe has been fattening up Dunedin's vegetarians and vegans for almost 40 years. Tuck into big, inexpensive portions of quiche, pizza, flatbread melts and spicy samosas.

**Governors** ( ☎ 03-477 6871; 438 George St; mains $9-16; ☺ 7am-9pm Mon-Fri, 8am-9pm Sat & Sun) Popular with students, Governors does a nice line in early morning pancakes and other light meals. If you're feeling a little off the pace after the previous night, a strong coffee and an eggy omelette will be just what the doctor ordered.

## SELF-CATERING

The thriving **Dunedin Farmers Market** (www.otagofarmersmarket.org.nz; ☺ 8am-12.30pm Sat) convenes at the Dunedin Railway Station. It's all local, all eatable (or drinkable) and mostly organic.

## DRINKING & ENTERTAINMENT

Check www.dunedinmusic.co.nz for news and listings of club nights and bands playing around town.

**our pick** **Pequeno** ( ☎ 03-477 7830; www. pequeno.co.nz; alleyway behind 12 Moray Pl; ☺ 5pm-late Mon-Fri, from 7pm Sat) Down the alleyway opposite the Rialto cinema, Pequeno attracts a slightly older, more sophisticated crowd. There are cosy leather couches, a warming fireplace, and an excellent wine selection and interesting tapas menu. Music is generally laid-back and never too loud to intrude on discussions of the latest architectural fashions.

**12 Below** ( ☎ 03-474 5055; alleyway behind 12 Moray Pl; occasional cover charge $5-10; ☺ 8pm-late Tue-Sat) In the same alleyway as Pequeno, 12 Below is a hip and intimate underground bar. There are mismatched comfy seats and couches, and nooks aplenty for chatting to mates; and floor space for those here to listen to live-music acts (a lot of funk and reggae) or wriggle along with the DJ's choice of hip-hop and drum 'n' bass.

**Speight's Ale House** ( ☎ 03-477 9480; 200 Rattray St; ☺ 11am-late) Busy even through the off-months, the Ale House is a favourite of strapping young lads in their cleanest dirty shirts. A good spot to watch the rugby on TV and to try the full range of Speight's beers.

**Bath Street** ( ☎ 03-477 6750; www .myspace.com/bathst; 1 Bath St; ☺ 9pm-late Tue-Sat) When all the other bars are closed, Bath Street's famously good sound system summons Dunedin's unsleeping dance crowd for drum 'n' bass, house and hip-hop.

**Sammy's** (☎ 03-477 2185; www.sammys. co.nz; 65 Crawford St; ☾ vary by event) Dunedin's premier live-music venue draws an eclectic mix from noisy-as-hell punk to reggae and gritty dubstep. It's increasingly the venue of choice for visiting Kiwi bands and up-and-coming international acts.

## GETTING THERE & AWAY
### AIR
There are international flights into Dunedin on **Air New Zealand** (☎ 0800 737 000; www.airnewzealand.co.nz) from Sydney and Melbourne, and flights with **Pacific Blue** (☎ 0800 670 000; www.flypacificblue.co.nz) to and from Brisbane.

Air New Zealand has domestic flights to and from Auckland (from $109), Christchurch (from $59) and Wellington (from $99). Pacific Blue links Dunedin with Christchurch (from $60) and Auckland (from $100).

### BUS
Most buses leave from the Dunedin Railway Station (excluding InterCity buses, which depart from St Andrew St). Check when you make your booking.

Cafes and bars, The Octagon

DAVID WALL

## ⬃ IF YOU LIKE...
If you like the coffee at **Governors** (left), here are a few other spots in Dunedin to kick-start your heart:

- **Fix** (☎ 03-479 2660; 15 Frederick St; ☾ 7.30am-5pm Mon-Fri, 8.30am-3.30pm Sat, 9.30am-late Sun) Wage slaves queue at the pavement window every morning, while students and others with time on their hands relax in the courtyard.
- **Mazagran Espresso Bar** (☎ 03-477 9959; 36 Moray Pl; ☾ 8am-6pm Mon-Fri, 10am-2pm Sat) The godfather of Dunedin's coffee scene, this compact wood-and-brick coffee house is a temple to the magic bean.
- **Strictly Coffee** (☎ 03-479 0017; 23 Bath St; ☾ 8am-4pm Mon-Fri) The second of Dunedin's seriously serious coffee bars, Strictly Coffee is a stylish retro coffee bar hidden down grungy Bath St.

Otago Peninsula

DAVID WALL

**InterCity** ( ☎ 03-471 7143; www.intercity. co.nz; 205 St Andrew St; ⏱ ticket office 7.30am-5pm Mon-Fri, 11am-3pm Sat, 11am-5.15pm Sun, tickets by phone 7am-9pm daily) has direct services to Oamaru ($28, one hour 40 minutes), Christchurch ($50, six hours), Queenstown ($45, 4½ hours), Te Anau ($45, 4½ hours) and Invercargill ($43, four hours).

**Southern Link** ( ☎ 0508 458 835; www. southernlinkcoaches.co.nz) connects Dunedin to Christchurch ($40) and Oamaru ($28). **Naked Bus** ( ☎ 0900 62533; www.nakedbus. com) connects Dunedin with Christchurch ($18), Queenstown ($29) and Invercargill ($29).

The **Bottom Bus** ( ☎ 03-477 9083; www. bottombus.co.nz) does a circuit from Dunedin through the Catlins to Invercargill, Te Anau, Queenstown and back to Dunedin.

Other shuttles departing Dunedin:

**Atomic Shuttles** ( ☎ 03-349 0697; www. atomictravel.co.nz) To and from Christchurch ($35), Oamaru ($20), Invercargill ($35), Queenstown ($40) and Wanaka ($40).

**Wanaka Connexions** ( ☎ 03-443 9122; www.time2.co.nz) Shuttles between Dunedin and Wanaka ($45) and Queenstown ($45).

## GETTING AROUND
### TO/FROM THE AIRPORT

**Dunedin Airport** ( ☎ 03-486 2879; www.dn airport.co.nz) is 27km southwest of the city. The cheapest way to reach it is by a door-to-door shuttle (per person from $15). Try **Kiwi Shuttles** ( ☎ 03-487 9790; www.kiwi shuttles.co.nz), **Super Shuttle** ( ☎ 0800 748 885; www.supershuttle.co.nz) or **Southern Taxis** ( ☎ 03-476 6300; www.southerntaxis.co.nz).

A standard taxi ride between the city and the airport costs around $80. There is no public bus service to the airport.

### BUS

**City buses** ( ☎ 0800 474 082; www.orc.govt.nz) leave from stops in the Octagon, while buses to districts around Dunedin depart a block away from stands along Cumberland St near the Countdown supermarket. View the *Dunedin Bus Timetable* at the Dunedin i-SITE, or see www.orc.govt.nz.

### TAXI

**Dunedin Taxis** ( ☎ 03-477 7777)
**Otago Taxis** ( ☎ 03-477 3333).

# OTAGO PENINSULA

Otago Peninsula has the South Island's most accessible diversity of wildlife. Albatross, penguins, fur seals and sea lions provide a natural background to rugged countryside, wild walks and beaches, and interesting historical sites.

## SIGHTS

### ROYAL ALBATROSS CENTRE

Taiaroa Head, at the peninsula's eastern tip, has the world's only mainland royal albatross colony. The best time to visit is from December to February, when one parent is constantly guarding the young while the other delivers food throughout the day.

The only public access is through the **Royal Albatross Centre** (☎ 03-478 0499; www.albatross.org.nz; Taiaroa Head; ☼ 9am-dusk summer, 10am-4pm winter). One-hour tours (adult/child $45/22.50) include viewing from a glassed-in hut overlooking the nesting sites. There's no viewing from mid-September to late November, and from late November to December the birds are nestbound so it's difficult to see that magnificent wingspan. On Tuesday, the first tour runs at 10.30am.

### YELLOW-EYED PENGUIN RESERVES

One of the world's rarest penguins, the hoiho (yellow-eyed penguin) is found along the Otago coast, and several peninsula beaches are good places to

**OTAGO PENINSULA**

watch them come ashore (any time after 4pm).

The **Yellow-Eyed Penguin Conservation Reserve** ( ☎ 03-478 0286; www.penguinplace.co.nz; McGrouther's Farm, Harington Point Rd; tours adult/child $40/12) has replanted the penguins' breeding grounds, built nesting sites, cared for sick and injured birds and trapped predators. You can see the birds all year round, but summer is best. Between October and March, tours run regularly from 10.15am to 90 minutes before sunset; between April and September they're just from 3.15pm to 4.45pm.

## SEA LIONS

Sea lions are most easily seen on a tour (see right), but are regularly present at **Sandfly Bay**, **Allans** and **Victory Beaches**. Give them plenty of space, as they can really motor over the first 20 metres.

## ACTIVITIES

A popular walking destination is the beautiful **Sandfly Bay**, reached from Seal Point Rd (moderate; 40 minutes) or Ridge Rd (difficult; 40 minutes). From the end of Sandymount Rd, you can follow a trail to the impressive **chasm** (20 minutes). Most trails are closed during September and October for lambing.

**Wild Earth Adventures** ( ☎ 03-489 1951; www.wildearth.co.nz; trips from $95) offers trips in double sea kayaks, with wildlife often sighted en route. Trips run between four hours and a full day, with some starting from Dunedin and some on the peninsula.

**Peninsula Bike & Kayak** ( ☎ 03-478 0724; www.bike-kayak.com) rents bikes ($25/35 per hour/day) and kayaks ($50 for two hours). Guided kayak tours depart from Portobello and run for two or three hours ($120/170 for one/two people).

## TOURS

**Citibus** ( ☎ 03-477 5577; www.transportplace. co.nz; adult/child from $90/30) Tours combining albatross and penguin viewing.

**Elm Wildlife Tours** ( ☎ 0800 356 563, 03-454 4121; www.elmwildlifetours.co.nz; standard tour $89) Small-group tours of up to six

Yellow-eyed penguins

JENNY & TONY ENDERBY

Otago Central Rail Trail, near Hyde

## ↘ OTAGO CENTRAL RAIL TRAIL

Stretching from Dunedin to Clyde, the Central Otago rail branch linked small, inland goldfield towns with the big city from the early 20th century through to the 1990s. After the 150km stretch from Middlemarch to Clyde was permanently closed, the rails were ripped up and the trail resurfaced. The result is a year-round trail that takes cyclists, walkers and horseback riders along a historic route containing old rail bridges, viaducts and tunnels. With excellent trailside facilities (toilets, shelters and information), no steep hills, gobsmacking scenery and profound remoteness, the trail attracts well over 10,000 visitors annually.

The trail can be followed in either direction. The entire trail takes approximately four to five days to complete by bike (or a week on foot), but you can obviously choose to do as short or long a stretch as suits your plans. An evolving highlight of the rail trail is an increasing range of lodging in restored cottages and rural farmhouses.

Zeroing the bike computer at Middlemarch, the towns through which you pass, in order of increasing distance away from Dunedin, are: Hyde (27km), Waipiata (49km), Ranfurly (59km, with a possible detour to Naseby), Wedderburn (63km), Oturehua (75km), Ida Valley (90km), Lauder (107km, with a possible detour to St Bathans), Omakau (117km), Chatto Creek (106km), Alexandra (143km), and finally Clyde (151km).

Mountain bikes can be rented in Dunedin, Middlemarch, Alexandra and Clyde. Any of the area's major i-SITEs or other information centres (including those in Dunedin, Cromwell and Alexandra) can provide you with detailed information on the trail. See www.otagocentralrailtrail.co.nz and www.otagorailtrail.co.nz to get track information, accommodation options and tour company details.

hours. Pick-up and drop-off from Dunedin is included.

## SLEEPING

**our pick** **McFarmers Backpackers** (☎ 03-478 0389; mcfarmers@xtra.co.nz; 774 Portobello Rd; lodge dm/s $27/40, d $55-65, cottage d $90) On a working farm with harbour views, this rustic timber lodge and self-contained cottage are steeped in character and feel instantly like home. Lounge on the window seat or sundeck, barbecue out the back, or get warm in front of the woodburning stove. The cottage is great for families, and there are organic vegies and eggs available.

**Portobello Motels** (☎ 03-478 0155; www.portobellomotels.com; 10 Harington Point Rd, Portobello; d $135-145; 🛜) Sunny, modern, self-contained units just off the main road in Portobello. Studio units have small decks overlooking the bay. One- and two-bedroom units are also available (add $25/15 per extra adult/child), but are viewless.

### GETTING THERE & AROUND

Up to 10 buses travel each weekday between Dunedin's Cumberland St and Portobello Village ($4), with one or two a day continuing on to Harington Point. Weekend services are more limited. Once on the peninsula, it's tough to get around without your own transport. Most tours will pick you up from your accommodation.

There's a petrol station in Portobello, but opening hours are unpredictable. Fill up in Dunedin before driving out.

# CENTRAL OTAGO

Rolling hills, grassy paddocks and a succession of tiny, charming little gold-rush towns make this region worth exploring, though most travellers barely pause for breath as they pass through. However it

rewards a bit of effort: Naseby and Clyde compete for the title of NZ's cutest towns, and rugged and laconic 'Southern Man' types can be seen propping up the bar in backcountry hotels. There are also fantastic opportunities for those on two wheels, whether speeding down old gold-mining trails or taking it easy on the rail trail (see the boxed text, p313). Online see www .centralotagonz.com.

# FIORDLAND & SOUTHLAND

Fiordland is NZ's rawest wilderness area, a jagged, mountainous, forested zone sliced by numerous deeply recessed sounds (which are technically fiords) reaching inland like crooked fingers from the Tasman Sea.

Major bus operators shuttle to Te Anau and Invercargill from Queenstown or Dunedin, and some ply the Southern Scenic Route and take in Milford Sound. These include InterCity, Topline Tours, Atomic Shuttles, the Bottom Bus and Naked Bus.

## TE ANAU

pop 3000
Peaceful, lakeside Te Anau township is a good base for trampers and visitors to Milford Sound, and an ideal place to recharge your batteries.

### INFORMATION
**DOC visitor information centre** (☎ 03-249 0200; www.doc.govt.nz; fiordlandvc@doc. govt.nz; cnr Lakefront Dr & Manapouri Hwy; 🕒 8.30am-6pm) An excellent resource centre for the area, with interesting exhibits.
**Fiordland i-SITE** (☎ 03-249 8900; fiordland -isite@realjourneys.co.nz; 85 Lakefront Dr; 🕒 8.30am-6pm summer, to 5pm winter)

Brochures and info galore along with highway conditions, activities, accommodation and bus bookings.

## ACTIVITIES
### TRAMPING
#### KEPLER TRACK
This 60km circular Great Walk starts less than an hour's walk from Te Anau and heads west into the Kepler Mountains, taking in the lake, rivers, gorges, glacier-carved valleys and beech forest. The walk can be done in four days, or three if you exit at Rainbow Reach.

During the main walking season (October to April), advance bookings must be made by all trampers online at www.booking.doc.govt.nz or at any DOC visitor centre.

#### SHORT WALKS
You can set out along the Kepler Track on free day walks. **Kepler Water Taxi** ( ☎ 03-249 8364; stevsaunders@xtra.co.nz; **one way/return $25/40**) will scoot you over to Brod Bay from where you can walk to Mt Luxmore (seven to eight hours) or along the southern lakeshore back to Te Anau (two to three hours). Regular shuttles leave Te Anau lakefront at 8.30am and 9.30am during summer.

During summer **Trips'n'Tramps** ( ☎ 03-249 7081; www.tripsandtramps.com; ⊙ Oct-Apr) offers small-group, half- to two-day guided hikes on sections of the Routeburn and Kepler and Hollyford Tracks. Some departures incorporate kayaking on Milford Sound. Real Journeys (p318) runs guided day hikes (adult/child $190/123.50, November to mid-April) along an 11km stretch of the Milford Track.

### KAYAKING
Kayaking in the pristine waterways of the World Heritage area is unbeatable. **Fiordland Wilderness Experiences** ( ☎ 0800 200 434; www.fiordlandseakayak.co.nz) runs one-day and multiday kayaking explorations of Lake Te Anau and Lake Manapouri. Prices start at $130 per day. See p318 for kayaking trips on Milford Sound and Doubtful Sound.

ANDREW BAIN

Lake Te Anau

QUEENSTOWN & THE SOUTH

FIORDLAND & SOUTHLAND

## TOURS

**Wings & Water Te Anau** ( ☎ 03-249 7405; www.wingsandwater.co.nz; Lakefront Dr) has sea-plane flights right off Lakefront Dr with a 10-minute zip around the local area (adult/child $95/55) and longer flights over the Kepler Track, and Doubtful and Milford Sounds (from $295). **Air Fiordland** ( ☎ 0800 107 505; www.airfiordland.co.nz) offers similar deals.

**Southern Lakes Helicopters** ( ☎ 03-249 7167; www.southernlakeshelicopters.co.nz; Lakefront Dr) buzzes over Te Anau for 25 minutes ($190) and does longer trips over Doubtful, Dusky and Milford Sounds (from $530) and a chopper/walk/boat option on a part of the Kepler Track ($180).

## SLEEPING

**our pick** **Bob & Maxines** ( ☎ 03-931 3161; bob .anderson@woosh.co.nz; 20 Paton Pl, off Oraka St, dm/tw $30/80; 🖳 ) Only 2.5km out of town, off the Te Anau–Milford Hwy, but feeling a million miles away, this relaxed hostel gets rave reviews for the big mountain views from the communal lounge. Bikes are available to get you back into town.

**Lakeside Motel** ( ☎ 0800 452 537, 03-249 7435; www.lakesideteanau.com; 36 Lakefront Dr; d $130-220; 🖳 🛜 ) With most units directly facing across the grassy lawns to the lake, this motel has excellent views, particularly from the 1st floor. Inside, there's plenty of light from the large windows and good cooking facilities. It's also wheelchair friendly.

**Cosy Kiwi** ( ☎ 0800 249 700, 03-249 7475; www.cosykiwi.com; 186 Milford Rd; s $170-320, d $150-165; 🖳 🛜 ) The sign says B&B, but this friendly spot is actually more of a smart motel with modern well-appointed rooms just a short stroll from bustling downtown Te Anau. Breakfast is included in the rates, and host Eleanor usually offers a couple of cooked options.

**Te Anau Lodge B&B** ( ☎ 03-249 7477; www.teanaulodge.com; 52 Howden St; s $170-320, d $200-350; 🖳 🛜 ) The former 1930s-built Sisters of Mercy Convent, relocated to a grand location just north of town, is a positively decadent accommodation option. Sip your drink in a Chesterfield in front of the fire, retire to your spa before collapsing on a king-sized bed, then awake to a fresh, delicious breakfast in the old chapel.

## EATING & DRINKING

**La Dolce Vita** ( ☎ 03-249 8895; 90 Town Centre; mains $28-32; 🕑 3pm-late) Run by Lombardi, this very stylish, ultramodern-looking restaurant stretches beyond simple Italian fare to include Southland cuisine with fresh seafood, local lamb and big steaks. Freshly made pasta dishes ($22) are also popular.

**Redcliff Bar & Restaurant** ( ☎ 03-249 7431; 12 Mokonui St; mains $30-39; 🕑 5pm-late) Housed in a replica old settler's cottage, Redcliff specialises in a buzzy, convivial atmosphere and locally sourced produce. Try the wild Fiordland venison or tender herby hare. There's occasional live music, a permanent friendly vibe and excellent service.

More raucous is the **Ranch Bar & Grill** ( ☎ 03-249 8801; Town Centre; 🕑 noon-late), with Happy Hour from 8pm to 9pm and good value Sunday-night roast dinners ($13.50).

## ENTERTAINMENT

In between back-to-back showings of the excellent *Ata Whenua* ($10), essentially a 32-minute advertisement for stunning Fiordland scenery, **Fiordland Cinema** ( ☎ 03-249 8812; www.fiordlandcinema.co.nz; 7 The Lane; $15; 🛜 ) shows other flicks, too.

## GETTING THERE & AWAY

**InterCity** ( ☎ 03-249 7559; www.intercity. co.nz) has daily bus services between Te

Kayaker, Doubtful Sound

GARETH MCCORMACK

## ◤ DOUBTFUL SOUND

Massive, magnificent Doubtful Sound is a wilderness area of rugged peaks, dense forest and thundering post-rain waterfalls. It's one of NZ's largest sounds: three times the length and 10 times the area of Milford Sound. Doubtful is also much, *much* less trafficked. If you have the time and the money, it's an essential experience. Fur seals, dolphins, Fiordland crested penguins and seals are all also occasional visitors.

Doubtful Sound is only accessible by tour. **Real Journeys** has a Wilderness Cruise, beginning with a 45-minute boat ride across Lake Manapouri to West Arm power station, followed by a bus ride over Wilmot Pass to the sound, which you explore on a three-hour cruise. There are pickups from Te Anau (adult/child $21/10.50) and Queenstown (adult/child $82/41).

**Adventure Kayak & Cruise** does Doubtful Sound day trips; cruise and kayaking costs $255, while overnight kayak camping trips on the shores of the sound cost $235.

Other cruising options:

**Deep Cove Charters** Intimate overnight cruises with a maximum of 12 passengers. Includes meals, or you can fish for your own dinner.

**Fiordland Explorer Charters** Day cruises with a maximum of 20 people. Free transfers to/from Te Anau.

**Things you need to know:** Real Journeys ( ☎ 0800 656 502; www.realjourneys. co.nz; Pearl Harbour, Manapouri; day trip adult/child $275/60); Adventure Kayak & Cruise ( ☎ 0800 324 966; www.fiordlandadventure.co.nz; ⊗ late Sep-May); Deep Cove Charters ( ☎ 0800 249 682; www.doubtful-sound.com; overnight per person $380); Fiordland Explorer Charters ( ☎ 0800 434 673; www.doubtfulsoundcruise.com; day cruise adult/ child $250/80)

Anau and Queenstown ($38, 2½ hours), Invercargill ($48, 2½ hours) and Dunedin ($45, 4¾ hours).

Other bus services include:

**Bottom Bus** ( ☎ 03-477 9083; http://travel headfirst.com/bottom-bus/) Hop-on, hop-off bus service linking Te Anau to Queenstown, Invercargill and Milford Sound.

**Naked Bus** ( ☎ 0900 62533; www.nakedbus. com) Connects Te Anau with Queenstown ($29), Invercargill ($24) and Milford Sound ($24).

**Topline Tours** ( ☎ 03-249 8059; www.top linetours.co.nz) Daily door-to-door between Te Anau and Queenstown April ($38).

# TE ANAU–MILFORD HIGHWAY

If you don't have the opportunity to hike into Fiordland's wilderness, the 119km road from Te Anau to Milford is the most easily accessible taste of its vastness and beauty. It's a top road trip for sheer scenic wonder. The trip takes two to 2½ hours if you drive straight through, but take time to stop and experience the majestic landscape.

**Milford Sound Lodge** ( ☎ 03-249 8071; www.milfordlodge.com; just off SH94; unpowered/ powered sites per person $16/20, dm/d $30/80; 🖳 🛜 ) is spectacularly located; nestled in forest, surrounded by towering mountains and alongside the Cleddau River. There's a tiny shop-cafe-bar and a free shuttle to Milford Sound, just 1.5km away.

# MILFORD SOUND  ·

pop 170

First sight of Milford Sound is stunning: still, dark waters out of which rise sheer rocky cliffs. Forests clinging to the slopes sometimes relinquish their hold, causing a 'tree avalanche' into the waters. The spectacular, photogenic 1692m-high Mitre Peak rises dead ahead.

## ACTIVITIES
### MILFORD TRACK

The famous Milford Track is a 53.5km walk often described as one of the finest in the world. The number of walkers is limited in the Great Walks season (from late October to late April), and during that period you must follow a one-way, four-day set itinerary. Accommodation is only in huts (camping isn't allowed).

**Ultimate Hikes** ( ☎ 0800 659 255, 03-442 8200; www.milfordtrack.co.nz; Dec to Mar adult/ child $1900/1700, Nov & Apr adult/child $1740/1540) has five-day guided walks that include everything from packs to snacks to raincoats and stays at much flasher accommodation, ending with a celebratory dinner at the last stay, Mitre Peak Lodge at Milford Sound.

**Real Journeys** ( ☎ 0800 656 501; www.real journeys.co.nz; adult/child $190/123.50; 🕙 Nov-mid Apr) runs guided day hikes along an 11km stretch of the Milford Track.

### SEA KAYAKING

**Rosco's Milford Sound Sea Kayaks** ( ☎ 03-249 8500; www.roscosmilfordkayaks. com; tours $115-169) has tours taking in the sound's most breathtaking sights.

**Fiordland Wilderness Experiences** ( ☎ 0800 200 434, 03-249-7700; www.fiordland seakayak.co.nz) also runs guided day paddles on the sound; with/without return transport to Te Anau costs $155/125.

### MILFORD SOUND CRUISES

**Real Journeys** ( ☎ 0800 656 501; www.real journeys.co.nz) does 1¾-hour scenic cruises (adult $62 to $84, child $15). The company also does 2½-hour nature cruises (adult $68 to $88, child $15) with a nature guide for commentary and Q&A.

It also does overnight cruises on two of its boats. You can kayak and take nature tours in tender crafts en route.

**Mitre Peak Cruises** (☎ 0800 744 633; www.mitrepeak.com) runs two-hour tours (adult $64 to $74, child $15) in smallish boats with a maximum capacity of 75. The 4.30pm summer cruise is good because many larger boats are heading back at this time.

**Cruising Milford Sound** (☎ 0800 500 121; www.cruizemilford.co.nz) does 1½-hour trips (adult $55 to $70, child $15) on a smallish, comfortable boat with lots of deck space.

The *Milford Wanderer,* modelled on an old trading scow, accommodates 61 passengers in four-bunk cabins (with shared bathrooms) and costs $230/115 per adult/ child. The *Milford Mariner* sleeps 60 in more up-market, en-suite, twin-share cabins ($470/235 per adult/child).

## SLEEPING & EATING

The excellent **Milford Sound Lodge** (left) is just 1.5km back up the road towards Te Anau. A small cafe is attached.

The **Blue Duck Café & Bar** (☎ 03-249 7931; car park; ☼ 8.30am-late; 💻) serves sandwiches and buffet-type meals. At night the attached bar sees a mix of travellers, trampers and locals.

## GETTING THERE & AWAY
### BUS
**InterCity** (☎ 03-249 7559; www.intercity.co.nz) runs daily bus services from Queenstown ($80) and Te Anau ($39). Trampers' buses also operate from Te Anau and Queenstown and will pick up at the Milford Sound Lodge.

### CAR
It's a magnificent drive from Te Anau to Milford. Fill up with petrol in Te Anau before setting off. Chains must be carried on avalanche-risk days from May to November (there will be signs on the road) and can be hired from most service stations in Te Anau.

UROS RAVBAR

Rainforest near Milford Sound

# THE CATLINS

If you veer off SH1 and head for the coastal route between Invercargill and Dunedin (via SH92), you wind through the enchanting Catlins, a region that combines lush farmland, native forests and rugged bays.

The Catlins is a wonderful place for independent wildlife-watching. Fur seals and sea lions laze along the coast, while elephant seals breed at Nugget Point. In spring, keep your eyes peeled for southern right whales, which are occasionally spotted offshore. Dolphins are also frequent visitors.

## INFORMATION

Contact the main **Catlins information centre** ( ☎ 03-415 8371; catlinsinfo@cluthadc. govt.nz; 20 Ryley St, Owaka; ☼ 9.30am-1pm & 1.30-4.30pm Mon-Fri, 10am-4pm Sat & Sun; 🖳) in Owaka, or the smaller **Waikawa visitors centre** ( ☎ 03-246 8464; waikawa museum@hyper.net.nz; Main Rd, Waikawa; ☼ 10am-5pm; 🖳).

All centres stock the free two-sided *Catlins Highway Guide* map, with comprehensive accommodation phone numbers.

Both www.catlins.org.nz and www.catlins -nz.com are well-maintained websites on the region.

Matai Falls, the Catlins

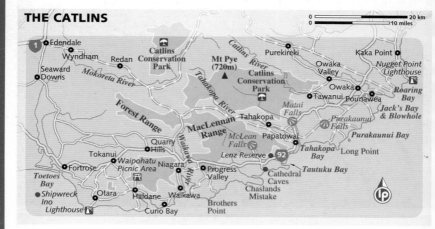

## THE CATLINS

ANDERS BLOMQVIST

Hump Ridge Track

## TOURS

**Bottom Bus** ( ☎ 03-477 9083; www.bottom bus.co.nz) does a regular loop from Queenstown to Dunedin, south through the Catlins to Invercargill, along the Southern Scenic Route to Te Anau, then back to Queenstown.

**Catlins Coaster** ( ☎ 03-477 9083; www.catlins coaster.co.nz), run by Bottom Bus, offers day tours and trips through the Catlins from Dunedin and Invercargill.

**Catlins Natural Wonders** ( ☎ 0800 304 333; www.catlinsnatural.co.nz) also has guided trips focusing on wildlife. One-day trips cost adult/child $130/85 out of Dunedin/ Balclutha, or there's an overnight trip ($200/150, plus accommodation).

## HUMP RIDGE TRACK

The excellent 53km Hump Ridge Track climbs to craggy subalpine heights with views north to Fiordland and south to Stewart Island, and then descends through lush native forests of rimu and beech to the rugged coast. En route the path crosses a number of towering historic wooden viaducts, including NZ's highest. Beginning and ending at Bluecliffs Beach on Te Waewae Bay, 20km from Tuatapere, the track takes three fairly long days to complete.

It's essential to book for this track, which is administered privately rather than by DOC. Contact **Tuatapere Hump Ridge Track** ( ☎ 03-226 6739; www.humpridge track.co.nz). Summer bookings cost from $90 for two nights; winter bookings (May to October) cost $45. There are also guided tour, jetboating and helihiking options.

# ACTIVITIES

Milford Track (p318), Fiordland National Park

New Zealand's astounding natural assets encourage even the laziest lounge lizards to drag themselves outside. Outdoor activities across the nation are accessible and supremely well organised. Commercial operators can hook you up with whatever kind of experience floats your boat – from bungy jumping off a canyon to sea kayaking around a national park – but don't miss the chance to engage with nature one-on-one, a million miles from home, just you and the great void.

## TRAMPING

Tramping (aka hiking) is the perfect vehicle for a close encounter with NZ's natural beauty. There are thousands of kilometres of tracks – some well marked, some barely a line on a map – plus an excellent network of huts enabling trampers to avoid lugging tents and (in some cases) cooking gear.

Before plodding off into the forest, get up-to-date track and weather info and maps from the appropriate authority – usually the **Department of Conservation** (DOC; www. doc.govt.nz), or regional i-SITE visitor information centres. If you've got your heart set on a summer walk along one of the Great Walks, check out the booking requirements and get in early. If you want to avoid the crowds, go in the shoulder season. DOC staff can also help plan tramps on lesser-known tracks.

Online, www.tramper.co.nz is a fantastic website with track descriptions and ratings. For safety tips, see www.mountainsafety.org.nz.

**NEW ZEALAND IN FOCUS**

**ACTIVITIES**

## THE GREAT WALKS

NZ's nine official Great Walks (one of which is actually a river trip!) are the country's most popular tracks. Natural beauty abounds, but prepare yourself for crowds.

On the North Island, the 46km, three-to four-day **Lake Waikaremoana Track** (p191) in Te Urewera National Park is easy-to-medium in difficulty, offering lake views, bush-clad slopes and swimming. Through the volcanic landscape of Tongariro National Park, the **Tongariro Northern Circuit** (p180) is a medium-to-hard three- to four-day tramp over 41km. On remote Stewart Island, the **Raukura Track** (36km over three days) is a medium-difficulty track with bird life (kiwi!), beaches and lush bush. The easy **Whanganui Journey** is a 145km, five-day canoe or kayak down the Whanganui River in Whanganui National Park.

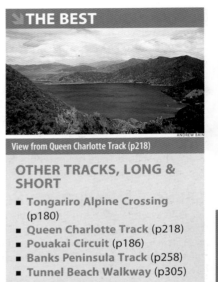

> **THE BEST**

View from Queen Charlotte Track (p218)

ANDREW BAIN

### OTHER TRACKS, LONG & SHORT

- **Tongariro Alpine Crossing** (p180)
- **Queen Charlotte Track** (p218)
- **Pouakai Circuit** (p186)
- **Banks Peninsula Track** (p258)
- **Tunnel Beach Walkway** (p305)

Down south, the hugely popular two- to five-day **Abel Tasman Coast Track** (p230) takes in 51km of beaches and bays of Abel Tasman National Park. The 78km **Heaphy Track** in Kahurangi National Park is a harder walk over four to six days. The easy-to-medium 60km **Kepler Track** (p315) in Fiordland National Park passes lakes, rivers, gorges, glacial valleys and beech forest over three or four days. Also in Fiordland are the easy, four-day **Milford Track** (p318) over 54km, and the medium-difficulty **Routeburn Track** (p299) over three days and 32km.

### PASSES & BOOKINGS

To tramp these tracks you'll need to buy a Great Walk Pass before setting out; these are sold at DOC visitor centres near each walk. These track-specific passes cover you for hut accommodation (from $12 to $45 per person per night, depending on the track and the season) and/or camping (free to $15 per person per night). You can camp only at designated camping grounds; note there's no camping on the Milford Track. In the off-peak season (May to September), Backcountry Hut Passes ($90, valid for 12 months) and pay-as-you-go tickets can be used instead of a Great Walk Pass in many huts – ask DOC for details. Kids under 18 can stay in huts and camp for free on Great Walks.

DOC has introduced a booking system for six of the Great Walks (Lake Waikaremoana, Abel Tasman Coast, Heaphy, Kepler, Milford and Routeburn tracks) to avoid overcrowding and help protect the environment. Trampers must book their chosen hut or campsite and specify dates when they purchase a Great Walk Pass.

Bookings can be made online (www.doc.govt.nz), by email (greatwalksbooking@ doc.govt.nz), by phone, by fax or in person at DOC offices close to the tracks. For full details, see the DOC website. There's no charge to do a day walk on any track, but you have to pay if you're staying overnight.

For other recommended walks, see the boxed text, p325.

## GUIDED WALKS

If you're new to tramping or just want a more comfortable experience, quite a few companies can escort you through the wilds. Usually you'll be staying in comfortable huts with your meals cooked and equipment carried for you.

Places on the North Island where you can sign up for a guided walk include Lake Waikaremoana and Tongariro National Park. On the South Island try the Banks Peninsula Track, the Milford Track or Routeburn Track. Prices for a four-night guided walk start around $1500 and ascend towards $2000 for deluxe guided experiences.

# SKIING & SNOWBOARDING

NZ is an essential southern-hemisphere destination for snow bunnies, with downhill, cross-country and ski mountaineering all passionately pursued. Heliskiing, where choppers lift skiers to the top of long, isolated stretches of virgin snow, also has its fans (see the boxed text, opposite). The NZ ski season is generally from June to October, though it can run as late as November.

Unlike Europe, America or even Australia, NZ's commercial ski areas aren't generally set up as 'resorts' with chalets, lodges or hotels. Rather, accommodation and après-ski carousing are often in surrounding towns that connect with the slopes via daily shuttles.

Some people like to be near Queenstown's party scene or the classic volcanic scenery of Mt Ruapehu; others prefer the high slopes and quality runs of Mt Hutt, uncrowded Rainbow or less-stressed club skiing areas. Club areas are publicly accessible and usually less crowded and cheaper than commercial ski fields, even though nonmembers

The Remarkables ski field, Queenstown

DAVID WALL

pay a slightly higher fee. Many club areas have lodges you can stay at, subject to availability – winter holidays and weekends will be fully booked, but midweek you'll be OK.

Lift passes can cost anywhere from $35 to $90 a day (roughly half for kids). Lesson-and-lift packages are available at most areas. Ski-equipment hire (skis, boots and poles) starts at around $40 a day; snowboard-and-boots hire starts at around $45.

See www.brownbearski.co.nz for online info.

> **HELISKIING**

From July to October, heliski operators cover a wide off-piste (off the beaten slopes) area along the Southern Alps. Costs range from around $750 to $1200 for three to eight runs. **HeliPark New Zealand** (www.helipark.co.nz) at Mt Potts is a dedicated heliski park. Heliskiing is also available at Coronet Peak, Treble Cone, Cardrona, Mt Hutt, Mt Lyford, Ohau and Hanmer Springs.

**NEW ZEALAND IN FOCUS**

**ACTIVITIES**

## NORTH ISLAND

The key North Island ski spots are Whakapapa and Turoa on **Mt Ruapehu** (www.mtru apehu.com) in Tongariro National Park, and **Tukino** (www.tukino.co.nz) on the eastern side of Mt Ruapehu. **Manganui** (www.skitaranaki.co.nz) on Mt Taranaki offers volcano-slope, club-run skiing.

## SOUTH ISLAND

Most of the South Island action revolves around the resort towns of Queenstown and Wanaka. Iconic ski fields near here include **Coronet Peak** (www.nzski.com), the **Remarkables** (www.nzski.com), **Treble Cone** (www.treblecone.com) and **Cardrona** (www.cardrona.com). NZ's only commercial Nordic (cross-country) ski area is **Snow Farm New Zealand** (www.snowfarmnz.com), near Wanaka. **Snow Park** (www.snowparknz.com), also near Wanaka, is NZ's only dedicated freestyle ski and snowboard area.

In South Canterbury there's **Ohau** (www.ohau.co.nz) on Mt Sutton, **Mt Dobson** (www.dobson.co.nz), **Fox Peak** (www.foxpeak.co.nz) and **Round Hill** (www.roundhill.co.nz), which is perfect for beginners and intermediates.

In Central Canterbury, try **Mt Hutt** (www.nzski.com), **Mt Potts** (www.mtpotts.co.nz), **Porters** (www.skiporters.co.nz), **Temple Basin** (www.templebasin.co.nz), **Craigieburn Valley** (www.craigieburn.co.nz), **Broken River** (www.brokenriver.co.nz), **Mt Olympus** (www.mtolympus.co.nz) or the family-friendly **Mt Cheeseman** (www.mtcheeseman.co.nz) near Christchurch.

Northern Canterbury opportunities include **Hanmer Springs** (www.skihanmer.co.nz) and **Mt Lyford** (www.mtlyford.co.nz). In the Nelson region is the low-key **Rainbow** (www.skirainbow.co.nz), with minimal crowds and good cross-country skiing. **Awakino** (www.skiawakino.com) in North Otago is a small player, but good for intermediate skiers.

# EXTREME STUFF

The fact that a pants-wetting, illogical activity such as bungy jumping is now an everyday pursuit in NZ says much about how 'extreme sports' have evolved here. Bungy, skydiving, jetboating and white-water rafting are all well established, all against the laws of nature, and all great fun!

NEW ZEALAND IN FOCUS

ACTIVITIES

Mountain biking, Queen Charlotte Track (p218), Marlborough Sounds

DESTINATION MARLBOROUGH

## BUNGY JUMPING

Bungy jumping (hurtling earthwards from bridges with nothing between you and eternity but a gigantic rubber band strapped to your ankles) has plenty of daredevil panache.

Queenstown is a spider's web of bungy cords, including a 43m jump off the Kawarau Bridge (which also has a bungy theatre and museum), a 47m leap from a ledge at the top of the gondola, and the big daddy – the 134m Nevis Bungy. The 109m-high Shotover Canyon Swing in Queenstown is touted as the world's highest rope swing. See p290 for more.

## SKYDIVING

Ejecting yourself from a plane at high altitude is big business in NZ. There are plenty of professional operators, and at most drop zones the views on the way up (not to mention on the way down) are sublime.

Try tandem skydiving in Auckland, Matamata, Tauranga, the Bay of Islands, Taupo, Kaikoura and Rotorua on the North Island; or in Nelson, Motueka, Christchurch, Fox Glacier, Methven, Wanaka, Queenstown, Te Anau and Kaikoura on the South Island. Check the website of the **New Zealand Parachute Federation** (www.nzpf.org) for info and operator listings.

## JETBOATING

On the South Island, the Shotover and Kawarau Rivers near Queenstown and the Buller River near Westport are renowned jetboating waterways. On the North Island, the Whanganui, Motu, Rangitaiki and Waikato Rivers are excellent for jetboating, and there are sprint jets at the Agrodome in Rotorua. Jetboating around the Bay of Islands in Northland is also de rigueur.

## WHITE-WATER RAFTING

There are almost as many white-water rafting possibilities as there are rivers in the country, and there's no shortage of companies to get you into the rapids. **Whitewater NZ** (www.rivers.org.nz) covers all things white-water. The **New Zealand Rafting Association** (NZRA; www.nz-rafting.co.nz) has an online river guide, and lists registered operators.

# MOUNTAIN BIKING

NZ is laced with quality mountain-biking opportunities. Mountain bikes can be hired in towns such as Queenstown, Wanaka, Nelson, Picton, Taupo and Rotorua, which also have repair shops. Some traditional tramping tracks are open to mountain bikes, but DOC has restricted access in many cases due to track damage and the inconvenience to walkers, especially at busy times.

Various companies will take you up to the tops of mountains and volcanoes (eg Mt Ruapehu, Christchurch's Port Hills, Cardrona and the Remarkables) so you can hurtle back down. Rotorua's Redwood Grove offers famously good mountain biking, as do the 42 Traverse close to Tongariro National Park, the Alexandra goldfield trails in Central Otago, and Twizel near Mt Cook. On the South Island try Waitati Valley and Hayward Point near Dunedin, Canaan Downs near Abel Tasman National Park, Mt Hutt, Methven and the Banks Peninsula.

# AERIAL SIGHTSEEING

Small planes and helicopters circle the skies on sightseeing trips (called 'flightseeing' by the locals) all over NZ, operating from local aerodromes. It's a great (but not particularly environmentally friendly) way to absorb the country's contrasting landscapes, soaring mountains and seldom-viewed terrain deep within national parks. Some of the most photo-worthy trips take place over the Bay of Islands, the Bay of Plenty (especially Whakaari Island), Tongariro National Park (from Taupo; see p172), Mt Taranaki (p186), Aoraki/Mt Cook (p265), the West Coast glaciers (p272 and p274) and Fiordland (from Te Anau; p316).

# SAILING

Surrounded by sea, NZ has a habit of producing some of the world's best mariners. There are plenty of sailing operators who allow you to just laze around on deck or play a more hands-on role. The Bay of Islands (and Whangaroa to the north), the southern lakes (Te Anau and Wakatipu) and the cities of Auckland and Nelson are good places to get some wind in your sails. See www.yachtingnz.org.nz for more details.

## CYCLE TOURING

If you're only in NZ for a short time, you mightn't have considered doing any cycle touring, but with good roads and even better scenery, it's a magical way to see the country. Most towns offer touring-bike hire, at either backpacker hostels or specialist bike shops, and there are repair shops in the bigger towns. Anyone planning a cycling tour (particularly of the South Island) should check out the self-guided tour options at www.cyclehire.co.nz. See also www.cycletour.co.nz for more info.

# SEA KAYAKING

Highly rated sea kayaking areas around NZ include the Hauraki Gulf, the Bay of Islands, Coromandel Peninsula, Marlborough Sounds, Abel Tasman National Park and Fiordland. The **Kiwi Association of Sea Kayakers** (KASK; www.kask.org.nz) is the main NZ organisation. The **Sea Kayak Operators Association of New Zealand** (www.skoanz.org.nz) website has a map of paddling destinations with links to operators.

# SURFING

NZ has a sensational mix of quality waves perfect for both beginners and experienced surfers. Point breaks, reefs, rocky shelves and hollow, sandy beach breaks can all be found.

NZ water temperatures and climate vary greatly from north to south. For comfort while surfing, wear a wet suit. In summer on the North Island you can get away with wearing a spring suit and boardies; on the South Island, a 2mm to 3mm steamer. Steamers are essential in winter.

Top North Island surf spots include Raglan, Mt Maunganui, Taranaki's Surf Highway 45 and the East Coast around Mahia Peninsula. Down south try the Kaikoura Peninsula, Dunedin and the Punakaiki on the West Coast.

Online, www.surfingnz.co.nz lists surf schools, while www.surf.co.nz provides information on many great surf spots.

# HORSE RIDING

Horse riding is commonplace in NZ. Unlike some other parts of the world where beginners get led by the nose around a paddock, here you can really get out into the countryside on a farm, forest or beach. Rides range from one-hour jaunts (from around $50) to week-long, fully catered treks.

For equine info online, see the **Auckland SPCA Horse Welfare Auxiliary Inc** (www.horsetalk.co.nz) website. For trek-operator listings, see www.truenz.co.nz/horsetrekking or www.newzealand.com.

# ⬂ ARTS

DAVID WALL

City Gallery (p157), Civic Sq, Wellington

**Kiwis are a creative bunch, churning out world-class novels, films, TV shows, albums and artworks more regularly than you'd expect from a nation with such humble population stats. Isolation and multiculturalism are key artistic informers: Maori, Polynesian, European and US influences pepper the New Zealand art world. Whether its bold, brutal, watchful, noir or just plain silly, Kiwi art delivers the goods. See also Maori Culture (p351) for information on Maori arts.**

## LITERATURE

A nationalist movement arose in literature in the 1930s, challenging the notion of NZ being an annex of the 'mother country', Britain, and striving for an independent identity. This process continued into the 1950s, a decade historian and poet Keith Sinclair called the time 'when the NZ intellect and imagination came alive'.

Katherine Mansfield's work began a NZ tradition in short fiction, and for years the standard was carried by novelist Janet Frame, whose dramatic life was depicted in Jane Campion's film of her autobiography, *An Angel at My Table*. Her novel *The Carpathians* (1989) won the Commonwealth Writers' Prize. A new era of international recognition began in 1985 when Keri Hulme's haunting *The Bone People* won the Booker Prize (the world is still waiting for the follow-up, *Bait*).

It wasn't until 2007 that another Kiwi looked likely to snag the Booker. Lloyd Jones' *Mister Pip* was pipped at the post, but the nomination rocketed his book up literature charts the world over.

Other notaries to look for on the shelves include Maurice 'gee-I've-won-a-lot-of-awards' Gee, Elizabeth Knox and Emily Perkins. See also Maori Culture (p354) for some Maori literary highlights.

## CINEMA

Peter Jackson's NZ-made *Lord of the Rings* (*LOTR;* 2001–03) trilogy was the best thing to happen to NZ tourism since Captain Cook, but NZ cinema is hardly ever easy-going. Kiwi actor Sam Neill described the country's film industry as 'uniquely strange and dark', producing bleak, haunted work. One need only watch Lee Tamahore's harrowing *Once Were Warriors* (1994) to see what he means.

Critic Philip Matthews goes further: '(Niki Caro's) *Whale Rider,* (Christine Jeffs') *Rain* and *Lord of the Rings* […] all share a kind of land-mysticism, an innately supernatural sensibility.' You could add to this spooky list Jane Campion's *The Piano* (1993), Jackson's *Heavenly Creatures* (1995), Brad McGann's *In My Father's Den* (2004) and James Napier-Roberston's *I'm Not Harry Jenson* (2009).

> ## ⬆ AND THE OSCAR GOES TO…
>
> Other than 2003's winner *Lord of the Rings: Return of the King, The Piano* (1993) is the only NZ movie to be nominated for a Best Picture Oscar. Jane Campion was also the first Kiwi nominated as Best Director; Peter Jackson was the first to win it.
>
> The only Kiwi actors to have won an Oscar are Anna Paquin (*The Piano*) and Russell Crowe (*Gladiator*). Paquin was born in Canada but moved to NZ when she was four, while Crowe moved from NZ to Australia at the same age.

When Kiwis do humour, it's often as black as their rugby jerseys: check out Taika Cohen's oddball loser-palooza *Eagle vs Shark* (2007) and Jonathan King's sickly hilarious *Black Sheep* (2006). Chris Graham's *Sione's Wedding* (2006) is much goofier, and has the second-biggest local takings of any NZ film.

Another *LOTR*-style blockbuster has proved elusive, but the NZ film industry has quietly continued producing well-crafted, affecting movies such as *Dean Spanley* (2008), *The Strength Of Water* (2009), *The Topp Twins: Untouchable Girls* (2009) and *The Lovely Bones* (2009).

## TELEVISION

On the small screen, the HBO-produced musical parody *Flight of the Conchords* – featuring a bumbling Kiwi folk-singing duo trying to make it in New York – has found broad international success. Other local shows worth catching are *Outrageous Fortune,* a rough-edged comedy-drama set in West Auckland, and *bro'Town,* a better-drawn Polynesian version of *South Park.* The long-running soap opera *Shortland St* has been the launch pad for many Kiwi actors.

## MUSIC by Gareth Shute

New Zealand music began with the early forms of singing *(waiata)* developed by Maori following their arrival in the country. The main musical instruments were wind instruments made of bone or wood, with percussion provided by chest- and thigh-slapping. European music steadily developed local variants over the early 1900s.

## ROCK

New Zealand has a kickin' rock scene, its most acclaimed exports being revered indie label Flying Nun and the Finn Brothers. Tim and Neil first came to prominence in late-'70s group Split Enz, who amassed a solid following in Australia, New Zealand, and Canada before disbanding in 1985. Neil then formed Crowded House – one of their early singles, 'Don't Dream It's Over' hit number two on the US charts. Tim later did a brief spell in the band, during which the brothers wrote 'Weather With You', which reached number seven in the UK.

More recently, the NZ music scene has developed new vitality after the government convinced local commercial radio stations to adopt a voluntary quota of 20% local music. Indie rockers such as Shihad, The Feelers, Op-shop, the Datsuns and the D4 have thrived in this environment, as have a set of soulful female solo artists (who all happen to have Maori heritage): Bic Runga, Anika Moa and Brooke Fraser.

For an up-to-date list of gigs, see www.grooveguide.co.nz and www.cheeseontoast. co.nz.

▼**THE BEST**

NICK SERVIAN/WELLINGTONNZ.COM
Live music, Wellington

**LIVE MUSIC VENUES**

- **Bodega, Wellington** (p164)
- **Rising Sun & 4:20, Auckland** (p80)
- **Wunderbar, Lyttleton** (p257)
- **Cassette Number Nine, Auckland** (p79)
- **Sammy's, Dunedin** (p309)
- **Southern Blues Bar, Christchurch** (p254)

## REGGAE & HIP-HOP

The genres of music that have been adopted most enthusiastically by Maori and Polynesian New Zealanders have been reggae (in the 1970s) and hip-hop (in 1980s). In Wellington, a thriving jazz scene took on a reggae influence to create a host of groups that blend dub, roots and funky jazz – most notably Fat Freddy's Drop.

The local hip-hop scene has its heart in the suburbs of South Auckland, which have a high concentration of Maori and Pacific Island residents. Acts to listen out for include Savage (on the iconic label Dawn Raid) Scribe, Che Fu and Smashproof.

## DANCE

Dance music had its strongest following in Christchurch in the 1990s, when it gave rise to the popular dub/electronica outfit Salmonella Dub. Drum 'n' bass remains popular locally and has spawned internationally successful acts such as Concord Dawn and Shapeshifter.

NEW ZEALAND IN FOCUS

## CLASSICAL

In the 1950s Douglas Lilburn became one of the first internationally recognised NZ classical composers. More recent classical luminaries include opera singer Dame Kiri Te Kanawa, pop diva Hayley Westenra, composer John Psathas and composer/percussionist Gareth Farr.

Concerts and classical music recitals can be found at www.eventfinder.co.nz and www.sounz.org.nz.

## VISUAL ARTS

Cultivated by lively tertiary courses, the NZ 'can do' attitude extends to the visual arts. If you're visiting a local's home, don't be surprised to find one of the owner's paintings on the wall or one of their mate's sculptures in the back garden.

Landscape painting constituted the first post-European body of art. John Gully and Petrus van der Velden were among those to paint memorable (if overdramatised) depictions of the land. A little later, Charles Frederick Goldie painted a series of compelling, realist portraits of Maori, who were feared to be a dying race.

From the 1930s NZ art took a more modern direction and produced some of the country's most celebrated artists including Rita Angus, Toss Woollaston and Colin McCahon, whose bleak, brooding landscapes evoke the sheer power of NZ's terrain.

ARTS

# ↘ ENVIRONMENT Vaughan Yarwood

GRANT DIXON

Climber contemplates Aoraki/Mt Cook (p264)

NEW ZEALAND IN FOCUS

ENVIRONMENT

**One of the main reasons travellers come to Aotearoa is to experience the country's superb landscapes. From snowy summits to volcanoes, ocean beaches, glaciers and ancient forests, New Zealand has a wealth of natural assets. But this is also a fragile environment, and the pressures of agriculture, forestry and population growth have all taken a toll.**

## THE LAND

NZ is geologically young – less than 10,000 years old. Straddling two vast tectonic plates, nature's strongest forces are at work here: volcanoes, geothermal geysers, hot springs and mud pools abound…Not to mention earthquakes!

The South Island has the highest mountains – the 650km-long, 3754m-high Southern Alps. Moisture-laden westerly winds blow in, dumping an incredible 15m of rain annually on the Alps' western slopes.

The North Island has a more even rainfall and snares most of the country's volcanic activity – especially around Rotorua and Taupo.

A third of NZ – more than five million hectares – is protected in national parks and reserves, administered by the DOC (www.doc.govt.nz).

## ENVIRONMENTAL ISSUES

The NZ Forest Accord protects native forests, and NZ is also famous for its strong anti-nuclear stance, but to describe NZ as entirely clean-and-green is a misnomer.

European grazing systems have left many hillsides barren and eroded, and despite increasing demand for organic food, most NZ farming still relies on chemical fertilisers, pesticides and herbicides.

NZ's energy consumption has grown phenomenally over the last 20 years – NZ is one of the most inefficient energy users in the developed world. Public transport is often inadequate and ecological values still play little part in urban planning.

Other hot issues include *Didymosphenia geminata* (aka Didymo or 'rock snot') algae in waterways, fixed-net fishing endangering dolphins, and the curse of introduced possums, rats and stoats.

## FLORA & FAUNA

NZ may be geologically young, but its plants and animals are antiques. Tuatara lizards are kin to the dinosaurs, while NZ's distinctive flightless birds (ratites) have distant African and South American cousins.

### BIRDS

The now-extinct, flightless moa was 3.5m tall and weighed more than 200kg; you can see skeletons at Auckland Museum (p63). Rumours of late survivals of this giant bird abound, but none have been authenticated. So if you see a chunky ostrich-like bird in your travels, photograph it – you may have just made the greatest zoological discovery of the last 100 years!

Kiwis are threatened and nocturnal, so it's rare to spot one in the wild.

Other bird-nerd favourites include royal albatrosses, white herons, Fiordland crested and yellow-eyed penguins, Australasian gannets, dotterels and keas. More common are tuis, bellbirds, fantails, pukeko, morepork owls and wekas.

DAVID WALL

Pohutukawa flower

## MARINE MAMMALS

Cruising the waters off NZ are whales, orcas, seals and dolphins. Kaikoura (p206) is the place to see them – sperm whales, fur seals and dusky dolphins are here year-round, and you'll also see migrating humpback, pilot, blue and southern right whales. You can swim with dolphins and seals here, too, and also at Akaroa (p259) and Tauranga (p138).

## TREES

Keep an eye out for yellow-flowering kowhai in spring, and red pohutukawa and rata in summer. Mature, centuries-old kauri are stately emblems of former days: see at Northland's Waipoua Kauri Forest (p109). Also look for rimu (red pine), totara (favoured for Maori war canoes), mamuka (black tree fern) and ponga (silver tree fern).

» **THE BEST**

OLIVER STREWE

Kiwi

### PLACES TO SEE A KIWI

- **Auckland Zoo** (p65)
- **Wellington Zoo** (p160)
- **Willowbank Wildlife Reserve, Christchurch** (p260)
- **Zealandia, Wellington** (p160)
- **National Aquarium of New Zealand, Napier** (p193)
- **Kiwi Birdlife Park, Queenstown** (p289)

NEW ZEALAND IN FOCUS

FAMILY TRAVEL

# FAMILY TRAVEL

DAVID WALL

Moeraki Boulders, Otago

New Zealand is supereasy to tackle with the kids in tow. Accommodation is usually kid-friendly, the public health care system is world-class, and Kiwi food doesn't usually have chilli in it! Baby formula and disposable nappies (diapers) are widely available in cities and towns, most of which have public rooms where mothers (and sometimes fathers) can go to nurse a baby or change a nappy; check with local visitor information centres, city councils, or ask a local – Kiwis are a friendly bunch.

## PRACTICALITIES

For helpful general tips on getting around with the kids, see Lonely Planet's *Travel with Children*. For specialised child care, look under 'babysitters' and 'child-care centres' in the *Yellow Pages* directory, or contact the local council.

### ACCOMMODATION

Many motels and holiday parks have playgrounds, games and DVD players, and occasionally fenced swimming pools and trampolines. Cots, highchairs and baby baths aren't always easy to find at budget and midrange accommodation, but top-end hotels are usually able to supply them. The plushest places have child-minding services, too. B&Bs are not usually amenable to families – many promote themselves as grown-up getaways where peace and quiet are valued above all else! Hostels focussing on the young backpa

of other hostels (including YHA hostels: www.yha.co.nz) offering budget-priced family rooms.

## CAR HIRE

Procuring a kiddie car-seat for your rent-a-car is no problem if you rent through one of the larger companies (Avis, Budget, Europcar etc). Some smaller car-hire companies, however, struggle with the concept. Double-check that the company you choose can supply the right size of seat for your child, and that the seat will be properly fitted. Some companies may legally require you to fit the seat yourself. If your child is under six months of age, they may be too small to fit into a standard car seat, and may require a baby 'capsule' instead. To avoid delays on arrival, make sure you have this conversation with your car-hire company when you're making your reservation.

> ### ⬎ THE NITTY GRITTY
>
> - **Change facilities** At shopping centres and big-ticket attractions
> - **Cots** At many midrange and all top-end hotels
> - **Health** Public medical care is top-notch
> - **High chairs** At most midrange and all top-end eateries
> - **Nappies** Widely available
> - **Strollers** BYO, or buy a cheapie
> - **Transport** Trains, ferries and larger tour buses are kid-friendly

## DISCOUNTS

Child concessions (and family rates) are often available for accommodation, tours, attraction entry fees and air, bus and train transport, with discounts of as much as 50% off the adult rate. Do note, however, that the definition of 'child' can vary from under 12 to under 18 years; toddlers (under four years old) usually get free admission and transport.

## EATING OUT

There are plenty of so-called family restaurants in NZ, where toddlers high chairs are provided and kids can choose from their own menu. Pubs often serve kids' meals and most cafes and restaurants (with the exception of upmarket eateries) can handle the idea of child-sized portions.

## SIGHTS & ACTIVITIES

Fabulous kids' playgrounds (with slides, swings, see-saws etc) proliferate across NZ; local visitor information centres can point you in the right direction.

Some regions produce free information booklets geared towards kids' sights and activities; one example is Kidz Go! (www.kidzgo.co.nz), which details child-friendly activities and restaurants in the larger urban centres.

Other handy websites for families include www.kidspot.co.nz, with lots of kid-centric info from pregnancy through to school-age, and www.kidsnewzealand.com, which has plenty of activities suggestions. Finally, www.kidsfriendlynz.com has extensive links to various facets of NZ kiddie culture.

# FOOD & DRINK Lauraine Jacobs

Bar scene, Vulcan Lane, Auckland

PETER BENNETTS

**Across New Zealand there's an increasing emphasis on fresh, organic food production as the temperate climate, fertile soil and abundant sunshine and rain conspire in farmers' favour. Much large-scale farming is still far from organic, but small-scale farmers markets, organic breweries and wineries, whole-food stores and roadside stalls proliferate.**

Kiwis have also broken free from a long history of stodgy meat-and-three-veg dinners, expanding their tastes into Pacific Rim fusion food. Techniques and ingredients from Southeast Asia, India and around the Pacific have found their way into the local culinary lexicon.

## KIWI DELIGHTS
### MEAT & SEAFOOD

Grass-fed NZ lamb is a must for dedicated carnivores: marinated chops on the barbecue, or a classic roast leg with mint sauce, potatoes and kumara. Kiwis also love their steak – most good restaurants have a fine-grained beef dish on the menu.

With this much ocean to fish, NZ seafood is a must. Look for greenshell mussels, cockles, clams, scallops and wild Bluff oysters. Local crayfish (rock lobster) is rich and succulent, but expensive. Whitebait are a tiny threadlike fish cooked up in fritters during spring.

## FRUIT & VEGETABLES

Scan the roadside farm stalls for kiwifruit and citrus in the Bay of Plenty; avocados near Tauranga; and apples and stone fruit in Hawke's Bay. Fruit-and-veg stalls abound across Nelson and Marlborough, and you can buy freshly dug potatoes direct from Canterbury farmers.

## MAORI & POLYNESIAN SPECIALITIES

Some foods are highly prized by the Maori and Pacific Island population, but won't be found on many menus and isn't to everyone's taste. Mutton bird is fatty and has a fishy flavour; equally fatty is *palusami* – taro leaves or spinach slow-cooked with coconut and corned beef - a traditional favourite with Pacific Islanders.

*Puha* (prickly sow thistle) is popular in Maori cooking: leafy greens are boiled up with pork, mussels or mutton bones. Kina is a sea urchin; the roe is eaten raw from the shell. Paua (abalone) has dark meat that's great grilled or minced for fritters.

On the herbs-and-spices front, horopito (bush pepper), scented kawakawa (bush basil) and kelp salt pop up in speciality food stores.

Buy, beg or wrangle your way to a Maori *hangi* (feast) on your travels. A fire pit is dug, stones placed on the fire, then chicken, lamb, pork, kumara, potatoes, corn and pumpkin are covered with sacks and placed over the hot stones. The pit is covered with earth and the food steams for a few hours. Flavours (usually sans herbs and spices) are earthy and tender. Expect much drinking and conversation!

**▼THE BEST**

JOHN HAY

New Zealand pinot noir

### WINE TOURING

- **Sauvignon blanc in Marlborough** (p221)
- **Syrah and chardonnay in Hawke's Bay** (p190)
- **Pinot noir in the Wairarapa** (p169)
- **Chardonnay on Waiheke Island** (p56)

# CHEERS!

In the wine world, NZ is famous for its Marlborough sauvignon blanc, with fresh, fruity aromas leaping out of the glass. Spend a day meandering between cellar doors in the Marlborough wine region. Other smaller wine regions are dotted around the country.

Kiwi beer is also world-class. There are quality microbreweries in many towns, challenging the big brands (Steinlager, Speight's, Tui) for market share. Keep a taste bud ready for ales, pilseners and stouts from mid-sized brewers such as Monteith's and Mac's, and small operators such as Rotorua's Croucher Brewing Co, Dunedin's Emerson's Brewery, Nelson's Founders Brewery and Auckland's Hallertau.

Coffee is also big business in NZ, and urban caffeine fiends flock to their favourite roasters and baristas. You'll find consistently good espresso across the country.

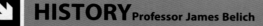

# HISTORY Professor James Belich

Carved wall detail, Maori meeting house, Auckland Museum (p63)

New Zealand's history isn't long, but it is fast. In less than a thousand years these islands have produced two new peoples: the Polynesian Maori and European New Zealanders. The latter are often known by their Maori name, 'Pakeha' (though not all like the term). NZ shares some of its history with the rest of Polynesia, and with some other European settler societies, but has unique features as well. It is the similarities that make the differences so interesting, and vice versa.

## MAKING MAORI

The first settlers of NZ were the Polynesian forebears of today's Maori. But questions remain: where in east Polynesia did they come from – the Cook Islands, Tahiti, the Marquesas? When did they arrive? Did the first settlers come in one group or several?

Prime sites for settlement were warm coastal areas where the food plants brought from Polynesia (kumara or sweet potato, gourd, yam and taro) could grow; sources of workable stone for knives and adzes; and areas with abundant game (such as fur seals

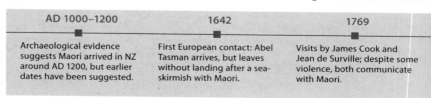

| AD 1000–1200 | 1642 | 1769 |
|---|---|---|
| Archaeological evidence suggests Maori arrived in NZ around AD 1200, but earlier dates have been suggested. | First European contact: Abel Tasman arrives, but leaves without landing after a sea-skirmish with Maori. | Visits by James Cook and Jean de Surville; despite some violence, both communicate with Maori. |

and the now-extinct moa, a huge flightless bird). The first settlers spread from the top of the North Island to the bottom of the South Island within the first 100 years, high-protein diets boosting population growth.

By about 1400, however, with big-game supply dwindling, Maori economics turned from big game to small game (forest birds and rats) and from hunting to gardening and fishing. A good living could still be made, but it required de-

### ⇘ TALK THE TALK

Linguistic similarities between Maori and Tahitian indicate neighbourly relations in the distant past as well as their shared origin. Maori is about as similar to Tahitian as Spanish is to French, despite the 4294km separating these island groups.

tailed local knowledge, steady effort and complex communal organisation, hence the rise of the Maori tribes. As competition for resources increased, so did conflict, leading to the construction of *pa* (fortified villages).

Maori had no metals and no written language (and no alcohol or drugs), but their culture and spiritual life was rich and distinctive. Below Ranginui (sky father) and Papatuanuku (earth mother) were various gods of land, forest and sea, joined by deified ancestors over time. The mischievous demigod Maui, who vanquished the sun and fished the North Island from the sea, was particularly important.

Maori performance, especially group singing and dancing known as *kapa haka,* has real power, even for modern audiences. Visual art, notably woodcarving, is something special – 'like nothing but itself', in the words of 18th-century explorer-scientist Joseph Banks.

For more on Maori Culture, see p351.

## ENTER EUROPE

NZ became a British colony in 1840, but the first authenticated contact between Maori and the outside world took place almost two centuries earlier in 1642, in Golden Bay at the top of the South Island.

Dutchman Abel Tasman sailed from Indonesia, to search for southern land and anything valuable it might contain. Tasman's ships anchored in the bay, and local Maori came out in their canoes to make the traditional challenge: friends or foes? Misunderstanding this, the Dutch challenged back by blowing trumpets. Four crewmen were killed in an ensuing skirmish, and Tasman sailed away and did not come back, nor did any other European for 127 years. But the Dutch did leave a name: 'Nieuw Zeeland' or 'New Sealand'.

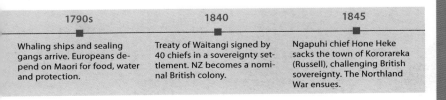

| 1790s | 1840 | 1845 |
|---|---|---|
| Whaling ships and sealing gangs arrive. Europeans depend on Maori for food, water and protection. | Treaty of Waitangi signed by 40 chiefs in a sovereignty settlement. NZ becomes a nominal British colony. | Ngapuhi chief Hone Heke sacks the town of Kororareka (Russell), challenging British sovereignty. The Northland War ensues. |

Contact between Maori and Europeans was renewed in 1769, when English and French explorers arrived, under James Cook and Jean de Surville. Relations were more sympathetic, and exploration continued, motivated by science, profit and empire-building rivalry. Cook made two more visits between 1773 and 1777, and there were further French expeditions.

Unofficial visits, by whaling ships in the north and sealing gangs in the south, began in the 1790s. The first mission station was founded in 1814, in the Bay of Islands, and was followed by dozens of others: Anglican, Methodist and Catholic. Flax and timber trading spawned many small European–Maori settlements by the 1820s. Surprisingly, the most numerous category of European visitor was probably American. New England whaling ships favoured the Bay of Islands for rest and recreation (read: sex and drink); 271 called there between 1833 and 1839 alone. Their favourite haunt was Kororareka (now Russell), known to the missionaries as 'the hellhole of the Pacific'.

One or two dozen clashes dot the history of Maori–European contact before 1840, but given the number of visits, inter-racial conflict was modest. Europeans needed Maori protection, food and labour, and Maori came to need European articles, especially muskets. Whaling stations and mission stations were linked to local Maori groups by intermarriage, which helped keep the peace. In fact, most warfare was between Maori and Maori, notably in the bloody intertribal Musket Wars of 1818–36, which began in Northland and spread south.

Europeans brought such things as pigs and potatoes, which benefited Maori, while muskets and diseases had the opposite effect. The Musket Wars killed perhaps 20,000 Maori, and new diseases did considerable damage too, such that by 1840 the Maori had been reduced to about 70,000, a decline of at least 20%. Maori bent under the weight of European contact, but they certainly did not break.

## MAKING PAKEHA

By 1840 Maori tribes described local Europeans as 'their Pakeha' and valued the profit and prestige they brought enough to want more of them. Accepting nominal British authority seemed the way forward. At the same time, the British government believed that Maori could not handle the increasing scale of unofficial European contact. On 6 February 1840, the two peoples struck a deal, signed at Waitangi. The Treaty of Waitangi now has a standing not dissimilar to that of the Constitution in the US, but is even more contested. The original problem was a discrepancy between British and Maori understandings of this treaty: the English version promised Maori full equality as British subjects, in return for complete rights of government. The Maori version promised that Maori would retain their chieftainship, which implied local rights of governance. The

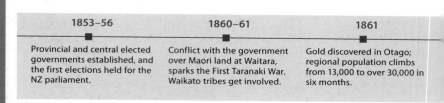

| 1853–56 | 1860–61 | 1861 |
|---|---|---|
| Provincial and central elected governments established, and the first elections held for the NZ parliament. | Conflict with the government over Maori land at Waitara, sparks the First Taranaki War. Waikato tribes get involved. | Gold discovered in Otago; regional population climbs from 13,000 to over 30,000 in six months. |

difference was not great at first, because the Maori version applied outside the small European settlements, but as those settlements grew, conflict brewed.

In 1840, there were only about 2000 Europeans in NZ. The shanty town of Kororareka (Russell), was the capital and biggest settlement. By 1850, six new settlements had formed with 22,000 settlers between them. About half of these had arrived under the auspices of the New Zealand Company, the brainchild of Edward Gibbon Wakefield, who hoped to short-circuit the barbarous frontier phase of settlement with 'instant civilisation'. His success was limited. From the 1850s into the 1880s, his settlers, mostly upper-middle-class gentlefolk, were swamped by the British and Irish diaspora that also populated Australia and North America. In NZ the mix was distinctive: lowland Scots were more prominent in NZ than elsewhere and NZ's Irish, even the Catholics, tended to come from the north of Ireland. NZ's English folk were largely from the counties close to London. Small groups of Germans, Scandinavians and Chinese also arrived, though the Chinese faced increasing racial prejudice from the 1880s, when the Pakeha population reached half a million.

Mass immigration was assisted by the provincial and central governments, which mounted large-scale public works schemes. Government land-grabs of Maori territory continued, but the tribes did not go down without a fight. Indeed, their resistance was one of the most formidable ever mounted against European expansion, comparable

NEW ZEALAND IN FOCUS

HISTORY

PAUL KENNEDY

*The Treaty of Waitangi, the Black and White of It* by Emily Karaka, Auckland Museum (p63)

| 1863–64 | 1865–69 | 1868–72 |
| --- | --- | --- |
| Waikato War. Around 5000 Maori defeated by 20,000 imperial, colonial and 'friendly' Maori troops. | Second Taranaki War. Maori resist First Taranaki War land confiscations and come close to victory. | East Coast War. Escapee Te Kooti leads a holy guerrilla war in the Urewera region. |

NEW ZEALAND IN FOCUS

HISTORY

## ⮌ HISTORY ONLINE

For a thorough overview of NZ history from Gondwanaland to today, visit http://history-nz.org. The Ministry for Culture & Heritage's history website (www.nzhistory.net.nz) is also an excellent source of info on NZ history, including the New Zealand Land Wars.

to that of the Sioux and Seminole in the US. Their struggles became known as the Land Wars.

The first clash took place in 1843 in the Wairau Valley (now a wine region). A posse of settlers set out to enforce British ownership, but encountered the reality of Maori control. Twenty-two settlers and about six Maori were killed. In 1845 more serious fighting broke out in the Bay of Islands, when Ngapuhi chief Hone Heke ransacked Kororareka. Heke confounded three British payback missions, using a modern variant of traditional *pa* fortifications, but Governor Grey claimed victory anyway. Grey fared better in the south, where he arrested influential Ngati Toa chief Te Rauparaha. Pakeha then swamped the few Maori living on the South Island, but the North Island remained a European fringe around an independent Maori heartland.

In the 1850s, settler population and aspirations grew. Fighting broke out again in 1860, continuing sporadically until 1872. In the early years, a Maori nationalist organisation, the King Movement, was the backbone of resistance. In later years, some remarkable prophet-generals, notably Titokowaru and Te Kooti, took over. Most wars were small in scale; the Waikato War of 1863–64 was not. This conflict, fought at the same time as the American Civil War, involved armoured steamships, heavy artillery, telegraph and ten British regiments. Despite the odds, Maori won several battles – including at Gate Pa, near Tauranga, in 1864 – but in the end European numbers and resources ground them down. Maori political (but not cultural) independence ebbed away in the last decades of the 19th century. It finally expired when police invaded a last sanctuary, the Urerewa Mountains, in 1916.

## WELFARE & WARFARE

From the 1850s to the 1880s, despite conflict with Maori, the Pakeha economy boomed on the back of wool exports, gold rushes and massive overseas borrowing. The crash came in the 1880s, when NZ experienced its Long Depression. In 1890 the Liberals came to power, and stayed there until 1912, helped by a recovering economy. The Liberals were NZ's first organised political party, and the first of several governments to give NZ a reputation as 'the world's social laboratory'. NZ became the first country in the world to give women the vote in 1893, and introduced old-age pensions in 1898.

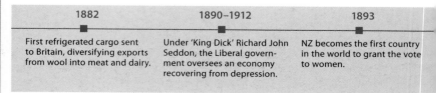

| 1882 | 1890–1912 | 1893 |
| --- | --- | --- |
| First refrigerated cargo sent to Britain, diversifying exports from wool into meat and dairy. | Under 'King Dick' Richard John Seddon, the Liberal government oversees an economy recovering from depression. | NZ becomes the first country in the world to grant the vote to women. |

Bitter industrial unrest flagged the 1912–13 years under the conservative 'Reform' government, which had replaced the Liberals in 1912. Reform remained in power until 1928, and later transformed itself into the National Party. Renewed depression struck in 1929, and NZ's experience of it was as grim. Derelict farmhouses in rural areas often date from this era.

In 1935 a second reforming government took office: the First Labour government, led by Michael Joseph Savage (NZ's favourite Australian). For a time, NZ's Labour was considered the most socialist government outside Soviet Russia. But, when the European chips were down in 1939, Labour had little hesitation in backing Britain.

NZ had also backed Britain in the Boer War (1899–1902) and WWI (1914–18), with dramatic losses in WWI in particular. NZ, a peaceful-seeming country, has spent much of its history at war: in the 19th century it fought at home; in the 20th, overseas.

### ⇘ THE WHITE MOUSE

As far as Kiwi war heroes go, Wellington-born Nancy Wake (code name 'The White Mouse') is right up there. In 1944 she led a guerrilla attack against the Nazis in France with a 7000-strong army, and had the multiple honours of being the Gestapo's most wanted person and being the most decorated Allied servicewoman of WWII.

PAUL KENNEDY

Royal New Zealand Navy at Waitangi Day celebrations, Waitangi (p105), Bay of Islands

| 1914–18 | 1939–45 | 1974 |
| --- | --- | --- |
| NZ's WWI contribution is substantial: 100,000 troops suffer almost 60,000 casualties, mostly in France. | 200,000 NZ troops participate in WWII; 100,000 Americans arrive to defend NZ from the Japanese. | Pacific Island migrants who have outstayed visas subjected to 'Dawn Raids' under the National government. |

# BETTER BRITONS?

British visitors have long found NZ hauntingly familiar. This is not simply a matter of the English, Scottish and Irish origins of most Pakeha. It also stems from the tightening of NZ links with Britain from 1882, when refrigerated cargoes of food were first shipped to London. By the 1930s, 100 giant ships carried frozen meat, cheese and butter, as well as wool, on regular voyages taking about five weeks one way. The NZ economy adapted to the feeding of London and cultural links were also enhanced. This tight relationship has been described as 'recolonial', but it's a mistake to see NZ as an exploited colony. Average living standards in NZ were normally better than in Britain, as were the welfare and lower-level education systems. New Zealanders had access to British markets and culture, and they contributed their share to the latter as equals. The list of 'British' writers, academics, scientists, military leaders, publishers and the like who were actually New Zealanders is long. Indeed, New Zealanders, especially in war and sport, sometimes saw themselves as a superior version of the British – the Better Britons of the south.

'Recolonial' NZ prided itself on its affluence, equality and social harmony, but it was also conformist, even puritanical. Until the 1950s, it was technically illegal for farmers to allow their cattle to mate in fields fronting public roads, for moral reasons. The 1953 American movie *The Wild One* was banned until 1977. Sunday newspapers were illegal until 1969, and full Sunday trading was not allowed until 1989. Licensed restaurants hardly existed in 1960, nor did supermarkets or TV. Notoriously, from 1917 to 1967, pubs were obliged to shut at 6pm (see the boxed text, below).

Despite this Anglo stuffiness, developments in cultural nationalism and free-spirited NZ counterculture began in the 1930s, and really flowered in the 1970s. Writers, artists and film-makers were by no means the only people who 'came out' in that era.

# COMING IN, COMING OUT

The 'recolonial' system was shaken several times after 1935, but managed to survive until 1973, when England joined the EU. By that time, NZ was beginning to develop

## ⬆ THE SIX O'CLOCK SWILL

From 1917 to 1967, NZ liquor laws dictated that pubs shut their doors at 6pm – a puritanical concession aimed at preserving morality in Kiwi society. In the cities, after-work hordes would storm the pubs at 5.05pm, chugging down as many beers as possible before 6pm – the 'Six O'Clock Swill'. In the country, however, the dictum was often ignored, especially on the South Island's marvellously idiosyncratic West Coast.

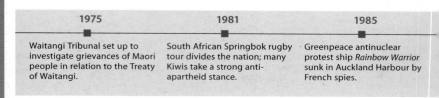

| 1975 | 1981 | 1985 |
| --- | --- | --- |
| Waitangi Tribunal set up to investigate grievances of Maori people in relation to the Treaty of Waitangi. | South African Springbok rugby tour divides the nation; many Kiwis take a strong anti-apartheid stance. | Greenpeace antinuclear protest ship *Rainbow Warrior* sunk in Auckland Harbour by French spies. |

MILLER/GREENPEACE WWW.GREENPEACE.ORG

Greenpeace ship *Rainbow Warrior*, sunk by French secret-service agents in 1985

markets other than Britain and alternative exports to wool, meat and dairy products. Jets were allowing the world and NZ to visit each other more regularly. NZ had only 36,000 tourists in 1960, which has ramped-up to around 2.5 million a year now. Women were beginning to penetrate the upper reaches of the workforce and then the political sphere. Gay people came out, despite the vigorous efforts of moral conservatives. Assertive, university-educated youths were becoming more numerous.

From 1945 Maori experienced both a population explosion and massive urbanisation. In 1936 Maori were 17% urban and 83% rural. Fifty years later, these proportions had reversed. The immigration gates (which had admitted mostly whites until 1960) widened, first to Pacific Islanders, for their labour, and then to Asia.

These transitions would have generated major socioeconomic change regardless of politics, but most New Zealanders associate the country's 'Big Shift' with the politics of 1984, when NZ's third great reforming government was elected. Led by David Lange and Roger Douglas (Minister of Finance), the fourth Labour government adopted an antinuclear foreign policy, exciting the left; and a more open economic policy, delighting the right. NZ's numerous economic controls were dismantled with breakneck speed. Middle NZ was uneasy about the antinuclear policy, which threatened NZ's ANZUS alliance with Australia and the US. But in 1985, French spies sank the antinuclear protest ship *Rainbow Warrior* in Auckland Harbour, killing one crewman. The lukewarm American

| 1987 | 1992 | 2004 |
|---|---|---|
| International stock-market crash hits NZ hard, but the All Blacks win the first Rugby World Cup. | The government begins reparations for land confiscated in the Land Wars and confirms Maori fishing rights. | Maori TV begins broadcasting, committed to NZ content, and Maori language and culture. |

condemnation of the French act brought middle NZ in behind the antinuclear policy, which became associated with national independence. Other New Zealanders were uneasy about the new economic approach, but failed to come up with a convincing alternative. Revelling in new freedom, NZ investors engaged in a frenzy of speculation, then suffered heavy losses in the economic crash of 1987.

The economy remained fairly stagnant until the late 1990s, when recovery began. In politics, a National (conservative) government replaced Labour in 1990, and introduced proportional representation in 1996. Labour, led by Helen Clark, returned to office in 1999, and was re-elected in 2002 and 2005. The Clark years saw improvements in the labour market (NZ had its lowest unemployment rate ever in 2007), and a massive real estate boom across the country. In 2008, however, Labour was ousted by the Nationals under new prime minister John Key, whose image as a likeable Kiwi bloke still serves him well.

The early 21st century is an interesting time for NZ. Like food and wine, film and literature are flowering as never before and multiculturalism is creating wonders in music and the arts. There are continuities, too – the pub, the rugby, the bush, the beach and the bach – that remain part of the reason people like to come here.

| 2005 | 2008 | 2011 |
|---|---|---|
| Helen Clark is returned in NZ's third successive Labour government. The Maori Party takes four seats. | John Key's National Party ousts Clark's Labour after nine years in government. | New Zealand hosts the Rugby World Cup – will the All Blacks deliver on home turf? |

# MAORI CULTURE John Huria

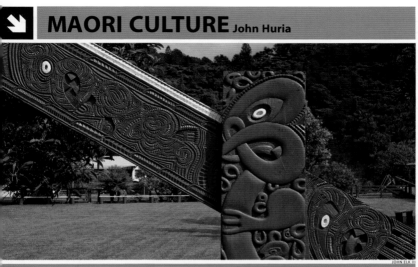

JOHN ELK III

Maori wood carving, Koriniti Pa, Whanganui

f you're looking for a Maori experience in New Zealand you'll find it – a performance, a conversation, an art gallery, on a tour...Maori are a diverse people. Some are engaged with traditional cultural networks and pursuits; others are occupied with adapting tradition and placing it into a dialogue with our rapidly globalising culture.

Maori are New Zealand's *tangata whenua* (people of the land); their relationship to their country has developed over hundreds of years. The Maori concept of *whanaungatanga* (family relationships) is important to the culture. Families spread out from the *whanau* (extended family) to the *hapu* (subtribe) and *iwi* (tribe) and even, in a sense, beyond the human world and into the natural and spiritual worlds.

## MAORI THEN

Three millennia ago people began moving eastwards into the Pacific, sailing against the prevailing winds and currents (hard to go out, easier to return safely) in large, double-hulled ocean-going craft. Some stopped at Tonga and Samoa; others settled the central East Polynesian tropical islands.

The first arrival in Aotearoa (NZ's Maori name) was the great navigator Kupe, whose wife Kuramarotini gave Aotearoa its name: '*He ao, he ao tea, he ao tea roa!*' (A cloud, a white cloud, a long white cloud!).

The early settlers moved around a lot, but when they settled, Maori established *mana whenua* (regional authority), whether by military campaigns or by peaceful intermarriage and diplomacy.

Maori lived in *kainga* (small villages) with associated gardens. From time to time people would leave their home base and go to harvest seasonal foods. When peaceful life was interrupted by conflict, Maori would withdraw to a *pa* (fortified village).

Then Europeans arrived… See p343 for more.

## MAORI TODAY

Today's culture is marked by new developments in arts, business, sport and politics. Many historical grievances still stand, but some *iwi* (Ngai Tahu and Tainui, for example) have settled historical grievances and are major forces in the NZ economy. Maori have also addressed the decline in Maori language use by establishing *kohanga reo, kura kaupapa Maori* and *wananga* (Maori-medium schools). Maori radio stations abound; **Maori Television** (www.maoritelevision.com) and the Maori-language station **Te Reo** (www.tereo.tv) occupy TV screens. In late May or early June, Matariki (Maori New Year) is a time for learning, planning and preparing as well as singing, dancing and celebrating.

## RELIGION

Christian churches and denominations are important in the Maori world: there are televangelists, mainstream churches for regular and occasional worship, and two major Maori churches (Ringatu and Ratana).

But in the (non–Judaeo Christian) beginning there were the *atua Maori,* the Maori gods, and for many Maori the gods remain a vital and relevant force. They are spoken of on the *marae* and in wider Maori contexts. The traditional Maori creation story is well known and widely celebrated.

## VISITING MARAE

As you travel around NZ, you will see many *marae* complexes; they should only be visited by arrangement with the owners. *Marae* complexes include a *wharenui* (meeting house), which often embodies an ancestor. Its ridge is the backbone, the rafters are ribs, and it shelters the descendants.

*Hui* (gatherings) are held at *marae*. Issues are discussed, classes conducted, milestones celebrated and the dead farewelled. *Te reo Maori* (the Maori language) is prominent, sometimes exclusively so.

### ⟶ THE HONGI

The Maori *hongi* greeting involves pressing the forehead and nose together firmly, shaking hands, and perhaps offering a greeting such as 'Kia ora' or 'Tena koe'. Some prefer one press (for two or three seconds, or longer); others prefer two shorter (press, release, press).

If you visit a *marae* as part of an organised group, you'll be welcomed in a *powhiri* – a process involving a ceremonial *wero* (challenge), a *karanga* (ceremonial call) between women, *whaikorero* (speech making) and a *waiata*. The visitors' speaker then places *koha* (a gift, usually an envelope of cash) on the *marae*. The hosts then invite the visitors to *hariru* (shake hands) and *hongi*. Visitors and hosts are now united and share food and drink.

# THE ARTS

Some of the largest collections of Maori arts (or *taonga,* meaning treasures) are at Wellington's Te Papa Museum (p146), the Auckland Museum (p63) and Canterbury Museum (p251) in Christchurch.

## TRADITIONAL MAORI ARTS

### CARVING

Traditional Maori carving, with its intricate detailing and curved lines, can transport the viewer. It's quite amazing to consider that it was done with stone tools, themselves painstakingly made, until the advent of iron (nails suddenly became very popular). The apex of carving today is the *whare whakairo* (carved meeting house), with traditional motifs used to interpret stories and embody ancestors.

### WEAVING

Weaving was an essential art that provided clothing, nets and cordage, footwear, mats and *kete* (bags). Some woven items were major works – *korowai* (cloaks) could take years to finish. Woven predominantly with flax and bird feathers, they

PAUL KENNEDY

Carving, Auckland Museum (p63)

are worn now on ceremonial occasions. Flax was (and still is) the preferred medium for weaving, but contemporary weavers use everything in their work: raffia, copper wire, rubber – even polar fleece and garden hoses!

### HAKA

As any All Blacks rugby fan will tell you, experiencing the awe-inspiring, uplifting *haka* – chanted words, vigorous body movements and *pukana* (when performers distort their faces, eyes bulging with the whites showing, perhaps with tongue extended) – can get the adrenaline flowing. The *haka* isn't just a war dance – it's also used to welcome visitors, honour achievement, express identity or to present strong opinions.

### TA MOKO

*Ta moko* is the Maori art of tattoo, traditionally worn by men on their faces, thighs and buttocks, and by women on their chins and lips. Historically, *moko* were tapped into the skin using pigment and a bone chisel, but the modern tattooist's gun is more common now. Many Maori wear *moko* with quiet pride and humility; see www.tamoko.org.nz for more info.

## CONTEMPORARY MAORI ARTS

A distinctive theme in much contemporary Maori art is the tension between traditional Maori ideas and modern artistic mediums and trends. For general information on Maori arts today, see www.maoriart.org.nz.

### WRITING

Key Maori authors to scan the shelves for include Patricia Grace (*Potiki, Cousins, Dogside Story, Tu*), Witi Ihimaera (*Pounamu, Pounamu; The Matriarch; Bulibasha; The Whale Rider*), Keri Hulme (*The Bone People, Stonefish*), Alan Duff (*Once Were Warriors*) and James George (*Hummingbird, Ocean Roads*). Poetry buffs should seek out anything by the late, lamented Hone Tuwhare (*Deep River Talk: Collected Poems*).

### THEATRE

Theatre is a strong area of the Maori arts today. Instead of dimming the lights and immediately beginning the performance, many Maori theatre groups begin with a stylised *powhiri* (see p352), with space for audience members to respond to the play, and end with a *karakia* (blessing or prayer) or farewell.

Taki Rua (www.takirua.co.nz) is a prominent theatre group and veteran independent producer of Maori work worth looking out for.

### FILM

Barry Barclay's *Ngati* (1987) was NZ's first nondocumentary, feature-length movie by a Maori director. Mereta Mita was the first Maori woman to direct a fiction feature – *Mauri* (1988). Other films with significant Maori input include the harrowing *Once Were Warriors* and the uplifting *Whale Rider*. Oscar-shortlisted Taika Waititi wrote and directed *Eagle vs Shark* and *Boy*.

The New Zealand Film Archive (www.filmarchive.org.nz) in Auckland and Wellington is a great place to experience Maori film, with most showings either free or inexpensive.

### DANCE

Contemporary Maori dance often takes its inspiration from *kapa haka* and traditional Maori imagery. The exploration of pre-European life also provides inspiration.

NZ's leading specifically Maori dance company is the Atamira Dance Collective (www.atamiradance.co.nz), which produces critically acclaimed, beautiful and challenging work.

◥ **THE BEST**

HOLGER LEUE

Maori performers, Waitangi (p105)

**PLACES TO EXPERIENCE HAKA**

- Whakarewarewa Thermal Village (p129)
- Waitangi Treaty Grounds (p106)
- Mitai Maori Village (p131)
- Te Puia (p129)
- Auckland Museum (p63)

# ⮔ SUSTAINABLE TRAVEL

TIM BARKER

Southern Alps, between Queenstown and Milford Sound

The Maori proverb '*Whatungarongaro te tangata toitu te whenua*' translates as: 'People pass on, but the land remains'. New Zealand has earned a reputation for its pristine environment, but this status is threatened by the 2.5 million international travellers passing through every year. You can help reduce your impact on the land by making a few simple, informed choices about how you travel.

## OUT & ABOUT

Consider carbon-offsetting your flights to/from NZ. Support NZ businesses by eating at local restaurants and buying from farmers markets that sell locally sourced produce. Instead of hiring a care, you might consider car-pooling from town to town. You can also stay at hotels and hostels that actively engage in recycling and waste reduction.

## RESPONSIBLE TRAMPING

If you can, time your NZ hike to avoid peak season: less people equals less stress on the environment (and fewer snorers in the huts). Treat NZ's forests and native wildlife with respect. The land is sensitive; if a track passes through a muddy patch, just plough straight on through — skirting around the outside increases the size of the bog.

### RUBBISH

Carry out *all* your rubbish (including unglamorous items such as condoms, tampons and toilet paper). Burying rubbish disturbs soil and vegetation, encourages erosion

## ⇘ GREENDEX

The GreenDex (p397) at the back of this book has listings of ecofriendly tours and places to explore, stay and eat, selected by Lonely Planet authors because they demonstrate active sustainable-tourism policies.

and animals will probably dig it up anyway. Pick up other people's rubbish, too (there's nothing worse than finding a muesli-bar wrapper on a mountaintop).

### HYGIENE

Don't use detergents, shampoo or toothpaste in or near watercourses – go at least 50m away. Wash scuzzy breakfast bowls with a scourer, sand or snow instead of detergent. If you need to scrub your bod, use biodegradable soap and a bucket. Spread waste water around widely to help the soil filter it. Where there isn't a toilet, dig a hole and bury your by-product (at least 15cm deep, 100m from any watercourse). Cover it up with soil and a rock. In snow, dig down until you're into the dirt.

### FIRES

Don't depend on open fires for cooking. Instead, use lightweight kerosene, alcohol or Shellite (white gas) stoves; avoid disposable butane gas canisters. If fires are allowed, use only dead, fallen wood in existing fireplaces (collecting firewood around campsites strips the forest bare). Keep fires small, don't surround them with rocks, and leave extra wood for the next happy camper. Douse fires with water and check the ashes before leaving.

### FOOD

Keep food-storage bags out of reach of scavengers by tying them to rafters or trees. If something comes a-sniffing, don't kill it – chances are it'll be a protected native critter. Feeding wildlife can lead to unbalanced populations and diseases – keep your dried apricots to yourself!

## FREEDOM CAMPING

Your first option for camping out should be a commercial campsite or DOC campsite (see www.doc.govt.nz). If you must 'freedom camp', choose a place with appropriate facilities (if your van doesn't have a toilet, camp somewhere that does). Never just assume it's OK to camp somewhere — always ask first (try the local i-SITE, DOC office or commercial holiday park). And please, treat the area with respect. See www.camping.org.nz for more tips on freedom camping.

## INTERNET RESOURCES

Online, www.lnt.org is a great resource for low-impact tramping tips. Look for ecofriendly NZ businesses listed by Qualmark Green (www.qualmark.co.nz) or Organic Explorer (www.organicexplorer.co.nz).

# ↘ DIRECTORY & TRANSPORT

# DIRECTORY
## ACCOMMODATION

Across New Zealand, you can bed down at night in guest houses that creak with history; in facility-laden hotels; comfortably uniform motel units; beautifully situated campsites; and hostels that range in character from clean-living and relaxed to tirelessly party-prone.

If you're travelling during peak tourist seasons, book your bed well in advance. Accommodation is most in demand (and at its priciest) during the summer holidays from Christmas to late January, at Easter, and during winter in snowy resort towns like Queenstown. At other times, weekday rates may be cheaper than weekend rates (except in business-style hotels in larger cities, where the reverse applies), and you'll certainly discover that low-season rates abound.

### B&BS & GUEST HOUSES

Guest houses are usually spartan, cheap, 'private' (unlicensed) hotels, mostly low-key places patronised by people who eschew the impersonal atmosphere of many motels. Some guest houses are reasonably fancy and offer self-contained rooms.

### ⤦ BOOK YOUR STAY ONLINE

For more accommodation reviews and recommendations by Lonely Planet authors, check out the online booking service at www.lonely planet.com. You'll find the true, insider lowdown on the best places to stay. Reviews are thorough and independent. Best of all, you can book online.

Although breakfast is included at genuine B&Bs, it may or may not feature at guest houses. Your morning meal may be 'continental' (cereal, toast and tea or coffee), 'hearty continental' (add yoghurt, fruit, home-baked bread or muffins) or a stomach-loading cooked meal including eggs, bacon and sausages. Some B&B hosts, especially in isolated locations or within the smaller towns where restaurants are limited, may cook dinner for guests and advertise dinner, bed and breakfast (DB&B) packages.

Tariffs are typically in the $120 to $180 bracket (per double), though some places charge upwards of $300 per double. New Zealand's *Bed and Breakfast Directory* (www.bed-and-breakfast.co.nz) and *Bed & Breakfast Book* (www.bnb.co.nz) are available online, and at bookshops and visitor information centres.

### CAMPING & CAMPERVAN PARKS

Campers and campervan drivers alike converge upon NZ's hugely popular 'holiday parks', slumbering peacefully in powered and unpowered sites, cheap bunk rooms (dorm rooms), cabins and self-contained units (often called motels or tourist flats).

The nightly cost of holiday-park camping is usually between $15 and $18 per adult, with children charged half-price; powered sites are a couple of dollars more. Cabin/unit accommodation normally ranges from $60 to $120 per double. Unless noted otherwise, the prices we've listed for campsites, campervan sites, huts and cabins are for two people.

If you'll gladly swap facilities for wilder, less-developed locations such as national parks, head for one of the 250-plus, vehicle-accessible camping grounds managed by the **Department of Conservation** (DOC;

## WWOOFING

If you don't mind getting your hands dirty, an economical way of travelling around NZ involves doing some voluntary work as a member of Willing Workers on Organic Farms (WWOOF; ☎ 03-544 9890; www.wwoof.co.nz). Down on the farm, in exchange for a hard day's work, owners provide food, accommodation and some hands-on organic farming experience. Contact farm owners a week or two beforehand to arrange your stay, as you would for a hotel or hostel – don't turn up unannounced!

There are plenty of places where 'freedom camping' is permitted in NZ, but you should never just *assume* it's OK to camp somewhere. Always ask a local first. Check at the local i-SITE or DOC office, or even with local commercial camping grounds. See www.camping.org.nz for more tips on freedom camping.

## FARMSTAYS

Farmstays open the door on the agricultural side of NZ life, with visitors encouraged to get some dirt beneath their fingernails at orchards, and dairy, sheep and cattle farms. Costs can vary widely, with B&B generally ranging from $80 to $120.

Farm Helpers in NZ (FHINZ; www.fhinz. co.nz) produces a booklet ($25) that lists around 190 farms throughout NZ providing lodging in exchange for four- to six-hours work per day. Rural Holidays NZ ( ☎ 03-355 6218; www.ruralholidays.co.nz) lists farmstays and homestays throughout the country on its website.

## HOSTELS

NZ is packed to the rafters with backpacker hostels, ranging from small, homestay-style affairs with a handful of beds to refurbished hotels with scuffed facades and the towering modern structures you'll find in the big cities. Hostel bed prices listed throughout this book are the non-membership rates.

If you're a Kiwi travelling in your own country, be warned that some hostels (typically inner-city places) only admit overseas travellers. If you encounter such discrimination, either try another hostel or insist that you're a genuine traveller and not a bedless neighbour.

Backpacker establishments typically charge $20 to $30 for a dorm bed, $40 to $50 for a single and $50 to $80 for a twin or double room (usually with shared bathroom facilities). Some also have space for a few tents.

## HOTELS & MOTELS

The least expensive form of NZ hotel accommodation is the humble pub. In the cheapest pubs, singles/doubles might cost as little as $30/50 (with a shared bathroom down the hall), though $50/70 is more common.

At the other end of the hotel scale are five-star international chains, resort complexes and architecturally splendorous boutique hotels, all of which charge a hefty premium for their mod cons, snappy service and/or historic opulence.

NZ's towns have a glut of nondescript, low-rise motels and 'motor lodges', charging between $80 and $160 for double rooms. These tend to be squat structures congregating just outside CBDs, or skulking by highways on the edge of towns.

## RENTAL ACCOMMODATION

The basic Kiwi holiday home is called a 'bach' (short for 'bachelor' as they were often used by single men as hunting and fishing hideouts); in Otago and Southland they're known as 'cribs'. These are simple self-contained cottages that can be rented in rural and coastal areas, often in isolated locations. Prices are typically $80 to $130 per night, which isn't bad for a whole house or self-contained bungalow.

Good websites to help you find a bach or holiday house include www.holiday homes.co.nz and the AA's www.booka bach.co.nz; for swanky self-contained apartments try www.newzealand-apartments.co.nz.

## CLIMATE CHARTS

See p44 for further information on choosing the best time of year for your visit to New Zealand.

## CUSTOMS REGULATIONS

For the low-down on what you can and can't bring into NZ, see the **New Zealand Customs Service** (www.customs.govt.nz) website.

When entering NZ you can bring most articles in free of duty provided customs is satisfied they're for personal use and that you'll be taking them with you when you leave. There's a per person duty-free allowance of 1125mL of spirits or liqueur, 4.5L of wine or beer, 200 cigarettes (or 50 cigars or 250g of tobacco) and dutiable goods up to the value of $700.

Customs officers are obviously fussy about drugs, so declare all medicines. Biosecurity is another customs buzzword – authorities are serious about keeping out any diseases that may harm NZ's agricultural industry. Tramping gear such as boots and tents will be checked and may need to be cleaned before being allowed

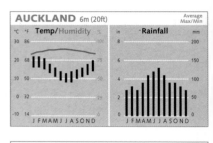

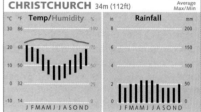

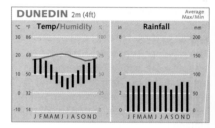

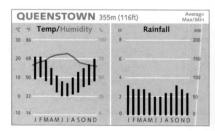

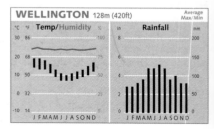

in; ditto golf clubs and bicycles. You must declare any plant or animal products (including anything made of wood), and food of any kind. You'll also come under greater scrutiny if you've arrived via Africa, Southeast Asia or South America. Weapons and firearms are either prohibited or require a permit and safety testing.

## DANGERS & ANNOYANCES

Although it's no more dangerous than other developed countries, violent crime does happen in NZ, so it's worth taking sensible precautions on the streets at night or if staying in remote areas.

Theft, primarily from cars, is a *major* problem around NZ, and travellers are viewed as easy marks. Avoid leaving valuables in vehicles, no matter where it's parked; the worst places to tempt fate are tourist parking areas and the car parks at trailheads.

Don't underestimate the dangers posed by NZ's unpredictable, ever-changing climate, especially in high-altitude areas; see p324 for information.

NZ has thankfully been spared from the proliferation of venomous creatures found in neighbouring Australia (spiders, snakes, jellyfish etc). Sharks hang out in NZ waters, but are well fed by the abundant marine life and rarely nibble on humans. Much greater hazards in the ocean, however, are the rips and undertows that plague some beaches and can quickly drag swimmers out to sea.

The islands' roads are often made hazardous by speeding locals, wide-cornering campervans and traffic-ignorant sheep. Set yourself a reasonable itinerary instead of careening around the country at top speed and keep your eyes on the road no matter how photogenic the scenery may be. If you're cycling, take care – motorists can't always overtake easily on skinny roads.

In the annoyances category, NZ's sandflies are a royal pain. Lather yourself with insect repellent in coastal areas. (See the boxed text, below.)

## DISCOUNT CARDS

The **International Student Travel Confederation** (ISTC; www.istc.org) is an international collective of specialist student travel organisations and the body behind the internationally recognised

---

### SANDFLIES  SIR IAN MCKELLEN

As an unpaid but enthusiastic proselytiser on behalf of all things Kiwi, including the New Zealand tourist industry, I hesitate to mention the well-kept secret of sandflies. I first met them en masse at the glorious Milford Sound, where visitors (after the most beautiful drive in the world) are met, at least during the summer, by crowds of the little buggers. There are patent unctions that cope, and tobacco repels them too, but I would hope that travellers find them an insignificant pest compared with the glory of their habitat.

Oddly, when actually filming scenes for *Lord of the Rings,* I don't recall being bothered by sandflies at all. Honestly. Had there been, we would have set the orcs on them.

Sir Ian McKellen is a UK-based actor who spent several years in NZ filming and has become something of an unofficial ambassador for NZ tourism.

## PRACTICALITIES

- For weights and measures, NZ uses the metric system.
- DVDs and videos viewed in NZ are based on the PAL system – the same system used in Australia, the UK and most of Europe.
- Use a three-pin adaptor (the same as in Australia; different to British three-pin adaptors) to plug yourself into the electricity supply (230V AC, 50Hz).
- For news, leaf through Auckland's *New Zealand Herald,* Wellington's *Dominion Post* or Christchurch's *The Press* newspapers, or check out www.stuff.co.nz.
- Tune in to Radio National for current affairs and Concert FM for classical and jazz (see www.radionz.co.nz for frequencies). Kiwi FM (www.kiwifm.co.nz) plays 100% NZ music; Radio Hauraki (www.hauraki.co.nz) cranks out the classic rock (too much Split Enz is barely enough…).
- Watch one of the national government-owned TV stations (TV One, TV2, TVNZ 6, TVNZ 7, Maori TV and the 100% Maori language Te Reo) or the subscriber-only Sky TV (www.skytv.co.nz).

International Student Identity Card (ISIC). The card is issued to full-time students aged 12 years and over and provides red-hot discounts on accommodation, transport and admission to attractions. The ISTC also produces the International Youth Travel Card (IYTC), available to folks between 12 and 26 who are not full-time students, and gives equivalent benefits to the ISIC. Cards (NZ$25 each) are available online at www.isiccard.co.nz or from student travel companies like STA Travel (www.statravel.co.nz).

Another option is the New Zealand Card (www.newzealandcard.com), a $35 discount pass that'll score you between 5% and 50% off a range of accommodation, tours, sights and activities.

## EMBASSIES & CONSULATES

Most principal diplomatic representations to NZ are in Wellington, with a few in Auckland. Embassies, consulates and high commissions include:

**Australia** (Map p158; ☎ 04-473 6411; www. australia.org.nz; 72-76 Hobson St, Thorndon, Wellington)

**Canada** (Map p158; ☎ 04-473 9577; www. newzealand.gc.ca; L11, 125 The Terrace, Wellington)

**Fiji** (Map p158; ☎ 04-473 5401; www.fiji.org.nz; 31 Pipitea St, Thorndon, Wellington)

**France** (Map p158; ☎ 04-384 2555; www.ambafrance-nz.org; 34-42 Manners St, Wellington)

**Germany** (Map p158; ☎ 04-473 6063; www. wellington.diplo.de; 90-92 Hobson St, Thorndon, Wellington)

**Ireland** (Map p62; ☎ 09-977 2252; www.ireland.co.nz; L7, Citigroup Bldg, 23 Customs St E, Auckland)

**Israel** (Map p158; ☎ 04-471 0079; L13, Greenock House, 102 Lambton Quay, Wellington)

**Japan** (Map p158; ☎ 04-473 1540; www. nz.emb-japan.go.jp; L18 & L19, The Majestic Centre, 100 Willis St, Wellington)

**Netherlands** (Map p158; ☎ 04-471 6390; www.netherlandsembassy.co.nz; L10, Investment House, cnr Featherston & Ballance Sts, Wellington)

**UK** (Map p158; ☎ 04-924 2888; www.britain.org.nz; 44 Hill St, Thorndon, Wellington)

**USA** (Map p158; ☎ 04-462 6000; http://wellington.usembassy.gov; 29 Fitzherbert Tce, Thorndon, Wellington)

# FESTIVALS & EVENTS

For general festival and event info, check out the **Tourism New Zealand** (www.newzealand.com/travel) website – click on Sights, Activities & Events, then Events Calendar. See also www.nzlive.com, www.eventfinder.co.nz and the Events Calendar on p46 for further listings.

# GAY & LESBIAN TRAVELLERS

The G&L tourism industry in NZ isn't as high-profile as in neighbouring Australia, but homosexual communities are prominent in the main cities of Auckland and Wellington, with myriad support organisations across both islands. NZ has relatively progressive laws protecting the rights of gays and lesbians; the legal minimum age for sex between consenting persons is 16. Generally speaking Kiwis are fairly relaxed and accepting about homosexuality, but that's not to say that homophobia doesn't exist.

There are loads of websites dedicated to gay and lesbian travellers. **Gay Tourism New Zealand** (**www.gaytourismnewzealand. com**) is a good starting point, with links to various sites. Other worthwhile queer websites include www.gaynz.com, www.gaynz.net.nz and www.lesbian.net.nz. For accommodation listings see www.gaystay.co.nz. Queenstown visitors should check out www.gayqueenstown.com.

Check out nationwide magazines like *express* (www.gayexpress.co.nz) every second Wednesday and *Out!* (www.out.co.nz) published every two months for the latest happenings, reviews and listings on the NZ gay scene.

# HEALTH Dr David Millar

New Zealand is one of the healthiest countries in the world in which to travel. The risk of diseases such as malaria and typhoid are unheard of and, thanks to NZ's quarantine standards, even some animal diseases such as rabies have yet to be recorded. The absence of poisonous snakes and other dangerous animals makes this a very safe region to get off the beaten track and out into the beautiful countryside.

## BEFORE YOU GO

Bring medications in their original, clearly labelled containers. A signed and dated letter from your physician describing your medical conditions and medications, including generic names, is also a good idea. If carrying syringes or needles, be sure to have a physician's letter documenting their medical necessity.

### INSURANCE

If your current health insurance doesn't cover you for medical expenses incurred overseas, you should think about getting extra insurance – check out www.lonelyplanet.com for more information. Find out in advance if your insurance plan will make payments directly to providers or reimburse you at a later date for overseas health expenditures. (In many countries doctors expect payment in cash.)

### RECOMMENDED VACCINATIONS

NZ has no vaccination requirements for any traveller. The World Health Organization recommends that all travellers should be covered for diphtheria, tetanus, measles, mumps, rubella, chickenpox and polio, as well as hepatitis B, regardless of their destination. Planning to travel abroad is an ideal time to ensure that all routine vaccination cover is complete. The consequences of these diseases can be severe and while NZ has high levels of childhood vaccination coverage, outbreaks of these diseases do occur.

DIRECTORY

HEALTH

## INTERNET RESOURCES

Tthere's a wealth of travel health advice available on the internet. For further information on health, **Lonely Planet** (www.lonelyplanet.com) is a good place to start. The **World Health Organization** (www.who.int/ith/) publishes an excellent book called *International Travel and Health,* which is revised annually and is available online at no cost.

Another good website of general interest is **MD Travel Health** (www.mdtravelhealth.com), which provides complete travel health recommendations for every country and is updated daily.

# IN NEW ZEALAND
## AVAILABILITY & COST OF HEALTH CARE

Health insurance is essential for all travellers. While health care in NZ is of a high standard and not overly expensive by international standards, considerable costs can be built up and repatriation can be extremely expensive. See p363 for insurance information.

NZ does not have a government-funded system of public hospitals. All travellers are, however, covered for medical care resulting from accidents that occur while in NZ (eg motor vehicle accidents, adventure activity accidents) by the Accident Compensation Corporation (ACC). Costs incurred by treatment of a medical illness that occurs while in NZ will only be covered by travel insurance. For more details see www.moh.govt.nz and www.acc.co.nz.

NZ has excellent specialised public health facilities for women and children in the major centres. No specific health concerns exist for women but greater care for children is recommended to avoid environmental hazards such as heat, sunburn, cold and marine hazards.

The 24-hour, free-call **Healthline** (☎ 0800 611 116) offers health advice throughout NZ.

## ENVIRONMENTAL HAZARDS
### HYPOTHERMIA

This is a significant risk, especially during the winter months or year-round in the mountains of the North Island and all of the South Island. Mountain ranges and/or strong winds produce a high chill factor which can result in hypothermia, even in moderately cool temperatures. Early signs include the inability to perform fine movements (such as doing up buttons), shivering and a bad case of the 'umbles' (fumbles, mumbles, grumbles, stumbles). The key elements of treatment are changing the environment to one where heat loss is minimised, changing out of any wet clothing, adding dry clothes with wind- and water-proof layers, adding insulation and providing fuel (water and carbohydrate) to allow shivering to build the internal temperature. In severe hypothermia, shivering actually stops; this is a medical emergency requiring rapid evacuation in addition to the above measures.

### SPIDER BITES

NZ has two poisonous spiders, the native katipo (not very poisonous and uncommon to the point of being endangered) and the introduced (thanks, Australia) white-tailed spider (also uncommon). White-tailed spider bites have been known to cause ulcers that are very difficult to heal. Clean the wound thoroughly and seek medical assistance if an ulcer develops.

### SURF BEACHES & DROWNING

NZ has exceptional surf beaches, particularly on the western, southern and eastern coasts. The power of the surf can fluctu-

seabed at many beaches. Check with local surf life-saving organisations before entering the surf and be aware of your own limitations and expertise.

## ULTRAVIOLET LIGHT EXPOSURE

NZ has one of the highest rates of skin cancer in the world, so you should monitor UV exposure closely. UV exposure is greatest between 10am and 4pm – avoid skin exposure during these times. Always use SPF30+ sunscreen, making sure you apply it 30 minutes before exposure and that you reapply regularly to minimise sun damage.

## WATER

Tap water is universally safe in NZ. Increasing numbers of streams, rivers and lakes, however, are being contaminated by bugs that cause diarrhoea, making water purification when tramping essential.

The simplest way of purifying water is to boil it thoroughly. You should also consider purchasing a water filter. It is very important when buying a filter to read the specifications so that you know exactly what it removes from the water and what it doesn't. Simple filtering will not remove all dangerous organisms, so if you cannot boil water it should be treated chemically. Chlorine tablets will kill many pathogens, but not parasites such as giardia or amoebic cysts. Iodine is more effective in purifying water. Follow the directions carefully and remember that too much iodine can be harmful.

# HOLIDAYS
## PUBLIC HOLIDAYS

NZ's main public holidays:
**New Year** 1 & 2 January
**Waitangi Day** 6 February
**Easter** Good Friday & Easter Monday; March/April
**Anzac Day** 25 April
**Queen's Birthday** 1st Monday in June
**Labour Day** 4th Monday in October
**Christmas Day** 25 December
**Boxing Day** 26 December

In addition, each NZ province has its own anniversary-day holiday. The dates of these provincial holidays vary – when these holidays fall between Friday and Sunday, they're usually observed the following Monday; if they fall between Tuesday and Thursday, they're held on the preceding Monday – the great Kiwi tradition of the 'long weekend' continues.

Provincial anniversary holidays:
**Southland** 17 January
**Wellington** 22 January
**Auckland** 29 January
**Northland** 29 January
**Nelson** 1 February
**Otago** 23 March
**Taranaki** 31 March
**South Canterbury** 25 September
**Hawke's Bay** 1 November
**Marlborough** 1 November
**Chatham Islands** 30 November
**Westland** 1 December
**Canterbury** 16 December

## SCHOOL HOLIDAYS

The Christmas holiday season, from mid-December to late January, is part of the summer school vacation. It's the time you'll most likely find transport and accommodation booked out, and long, grumpy queues at tourist attractions. There are three shorter school-holiday periods during the year: from mid- to late April, early to mid-July, and mid-September to early October.

For exact dates see the **Ministry of Education** (www.minedu.govt.nz) website.

# INSURANCE

A watertight travel insurance policy covering theft, loss and medical problems is essential. Some policies specifically exclude designated 'dangerous activities' such as scuba diving, parasailing, bungy jumping, white-water rafting, motorcycling, skiing, and even bushwalking. If you plan on doing any of these things (a distinct possibility in NZ), make sure the policy you choose covers you fully.

You may prefer a policy that pays doctors or hospitals directly rather than you having to pay on the spot and claim later. If you have to claim later make sure you keep all documentation. Check that the policy covers ambulances and emergency medical evacuations by air.

It's worth mentioning that under NZ law, you cannot sue for personal injury (other than exemplary damages). Instead, the country's **Accident Compensation Corporation** (ACC; www.acc.co.nz) administers an accident compensation scheme that provides accident insurance for NZ residents and visitors to the country, regardless of fault.

Worldwide cover for travellers from over 44 countries is available online at www.lonelyplanet.com/bookings /insurance.do.

# INTERNET ACCESS

Getting online in NZ is easy in all but the most remote locales.

Internet cafes in the bigger urban centres or tourist areas are usually brimming with high-speed terminals. Facilities are a lot more haphazard in small, out-of-the-way towns, where a so-called internet cafe could turn out to be a single terminal in the corner of a video store.

Most hostels make an effort to hook you up, with internet access sometimes free for guests. Many public libraries have free internet access too, but there can be a limited number of terminals – head for an internet cafe first.

Internet access at cafes ranges anywhere from $4 to $6 per hour – the lowest rates can be found in cities where competition and traveller numbers generate dirt-cheap prices.

Increasingly, you'll be able to find wi-fi access around the country, from hotel rooms to pub beer gardens to hostel dining rooms. Usually you have to be a guest or customer to access the internet at these locations – you'll be issued with a code, a wink and a secret handshake to enable you to get online. Sometimes it's free; sometimes there's a charge.

# LEGAL MATTERS

Marijuana (aka 'New Zealand Green', 'electric puha' or 'dac') is widely indulged in but illegal, and anyone caught carrying this or other illicit drugs will have the book thrown at them. Even if the amount of drugs is small and the fine minimal, a conviction will still be recorded against you, which may affect your visa status.

Always carry your licence when driving. Drink-driving is a serious offence and remains a significant problem in NZ despite widespread campaigns and severe penalties. The legal blood alcohol limit is 0.08% for drivers over 20, and 0.03% for those under 20.

If you are arrested, it's your right to consult a lawyer before any formal questioning begins.

# MAPS

Top-notch maps are widely available throughout NZ – from detailed street maps and atlases to topographic masterpieces.

The **Automobile Association** (AA; www. aa.co.nz) produces excellent city, town, regional, island and highway maps, available from their local offices. Other reliable countrywide atlases, available from visitor information centres and bookshops, are published by Hema, KiwiMaps and Wises.

Online, log onto **AA SmartMap** (www.aamaps.co.nz) or the **Yellow Maps** (maps.yellowpages.co.nz) to pinpoint exact addresses in NZ cities and towns.

# MONEY

## ATMS & EFTPOS

Branches of the country's major banks, including the Bank of New Zealand, ANZ, Westpac and ASB, have 24-hour ATMs that accept cards from other banks and provide access to overseas accounts. You won't find ATMs everywhere, but they're widespread across both islands.

Many NZ businesses use electronic funds transfer at point of sale (Eftpos), a convenient service that allows you to use your bank card (credit or debit) to pay directly for services or purchases, and often withdraw cash as well. Eftpos is available practically everywhere, even in places where it's a long way between banks. Just like an ATM, you need to know your personal identification number (PIN) to use it.

## CREDIT & DEBIT CARDS

Perhaps the safest place to keep your NZ travelling money is inside a plastic card! The most flexible option is to carry both a credit and a debit card.

Credit cards (Visa, MasterCard etc) are widely accepted for everything from a hostel bed to a bungy jump. Credit cards are pretty much essential if you want to hire a car. They can also be used for over-the-counter cash advances at banks and from ATMs, depending on the card, but be aware that such transactions incur charges. Charge cards such as Diners Club and Amex are not as widely accepted.

Apart from losing them, the obvious danger with credit cards is maxing out your limit and going home to a steaming pile of debt. A safer option is a debit card with which you can draw money directly from your home bank account using ATMs, banks or Eftpos machines. Any card connected to the international banking network (Cirrus, Maestro, Visa Plus and Eurocard) should work, provided you know your PIN. Fees for using your card at a foreign bank or ATM vary depending on your home bank; ask before you leave. Companies such as Travelex offer debit cards (Travelex calls them Cash Passport cards) with set withdrawal fees and a balance you can top-up from your personal bank account while on the road – nice one!

## CURRENCY

NZ's currency is the NZ dollar, comprising 100 cents. There are 10c, 20c, 50c, $1 and $2 coins, and $5, $10, $20, $50 and $100 notes. Prices are often still marked in single cents and then rounded to the nearest 10c when you hand over your money.

## MONEY CHANGERS

Changing foreign currency or travellers cheques is usually no problem at banks throughout NZ or at licensed money changers such as Travelex (formerly Thomas Cook) in the major cities. Money changers can be found in all major tourist areas, cities and airports, and conveniently tend to stay open beyond normal business hours during the week (often until 9pm).

## TAXES & REFUNDS

The Goods and Services Tax (GST) is a flat 15% tax applied to all domestic goods and services. Prices in this book include GST, but look out for any small print announcing that the price is GST-exclusive. There's no GST refund available when you leave NZ.

## TIPPING
Tipping is completely optional in NZ, and staff do not depend on tips for income – the total at the bottom of a restaurant bill is all you need to pay (note that sometimes there's an additional service charge). That said, it's totally acceptable to reward good service and the tip you leave depends entirely on your satisfaction – between 5% and 10% of the bill is the norm.

## TRAVELLERS CHEQUES
The ubiquity of debit- and credit-card access in NZ can make travellers cheques seem rather old-hat. Nevertheless, Amex, Travelex and other international brands of travellers cheques are easily exchanged. You need to present your passport for identification when cashing them. Fees per transaction for changing foreign-currency travellers cheques vary from bank to bank, while Amex or Travelex perform the task commission-free if you use their cheques.

# SHOPPING
NZ isn't one of those countries where it's necessary to buy a T-shirt to help you remember your visit; the spectacular landscapes are mementoes in themselves. But there are numerous locally crafted items you can purchase for their own unique qualities.

## CLOTHING
The main cities of Auckland, Wellington and Christchurch boast fashion-conscious boutiques ablaze with the sartorial flair of young and well-established NZ designers. Check out www.fashionz.co.nz for up-to-date information on the hottest designers and labels and where to find them. Keep an eye out for labels such as Zambesi, Kate Sylvester, Karen Walker, Trelise Cooper, NOM D and Little Brother.

In Auckland, head to places like Newmarket, Ponsonby Rd and High St; Wellington offers retro mix-and-match boutiques on Cuba St and high fashion along Lambton Quay. In Christchurch, pick up new duds on Colombo, High or Cashel Sts, then parade yourself along self-important Oxford Tce.

From the backs of NZ sheep come sheepskin products such as footwear (including the much-loved ugg boot) and beautiful woollen jumpers (jerseys or sweaters) made from hand-spun, hand-dyed wool. Other knitted knick-knacks include hats, gloves and scarves. Look for garments made from a lovely soft yarn that's a combination of merino wool and possum fur.

## MAORI ARTS
For some brilliant examples of Maori *whakairo rakau* (woodcarving), check out the efforts of artisans at Te Whakarewarewa cultural area (p129) in Rotorua, then browse the town's Maori craft shops; in some cases you may be able to buy directly from the artist. Avoid buying poor examples of the craft that line the souvenir shops in Auckland.

Maori artisans have always made bone carvings in the shape of humans and animals, but nowadays they cater to the tourist industry. Bone fish-hook pendants, carved in traditional Maori and modernised styles, worn on a leather string around the neck, are most common.

To confirm the authenticity of any Maori-made piece, see if it's accompanied by the trademark **toi iho** (www.toiiho.com), a symbol created by a Maori arts board to identify the output of individual artists or groups of artists of Maori descent. Do note that not all Maori artists are registered with this scheme.

## PAUA

Abalone shell, called paua in NZ, is carved into some beautiful ornaments and jewellery and is often used as an inlay in Maori carvings. Lovers of kitsch and general tackiness will find that it's also incorporated into generic souvenirs, often in delightfully unattractive ways. Shells are used as ashtrays in places where paua is plentiful. Be aware that it's illegal to take natural paua shells out of the country – only processed ornaments can be taken with you.

## POUNAMU

Maoris consider *pounamu* (greenstone, or jade or nephrite) to be a culturally invaluable raw material. It's found predominantly on the west coast of the South Island – Maoris called the island Te Wahi Pounamu (The Place of Greenstone) or Te Wai Pounamu (The Water of Greenstone).

You're unlikely to come across any *mere* (war clubs) in *pounamu* studios or souvenir shops, but you will find lots of stony green incarnations of Maori motifs. One of the most popular is the *hei tiki,* which literally means 'hanging human form' – in Maori legend, Tiki was the first man created and *hei* is 'to hang'. Other popular motifs are the *taniwha* (monster) and the *marakihau* (sea monster).

Traditionally, *pounamu* is bought as a gift for another person, not for yourself. Ask a few questions to ensure you're buying from a local operator who crafts local stone, not an offshore company selling imported (usually Chinese or European) jade.

# TELEPHONE

**Telecom New Zealand** (www.telecom.co.nz) is the country's key domestic player and also has a stake in the local mobile (cell) market. Another mobile network option is **Vodafone** (www.vodafone.co.nz).

## LOCAL & INTERNATIONAL CALLS

### INFORMATION & TOLL-FREE CALLS

Numbers starting with ☎ 0900 are usually recorded information services, charging upwards of $1 per minute (more from mobiles); these numbers cannot be dialled from payphones.

Toll-free numbers in NZ have the prefix ☎ 0800 or ☎ 0508 and can be called free of charge from anywhere in the country, though they may not be accessible from certain areas or from mobile phones. Telephone numbers beginning with ☎ 0508, ☎ 0800 or ☎ 0900 cannot be dialled from outside NZ.

### INTERNATIONAL CALLS

Payphones allow international calls but the cost and international dialling code for calls will vary depending on which provider you're using.

The toll-free Country Direct service connects callers in NZ with overseas operators to make reverse-charge (collect) or credit-card calls. Country Direct numbers and other details are listed in the front of telephone directories or are available from the NZ international operator. The access number varies, depending on the number of phone companies in the country you call, but is usually ☎ 000-9 (followed by the country code).

To make international calls from NZ you need to dial the international access code (☎ 00), the country code, and the area code (without the initial 0). So for a London number you'd dial ☎ 00-44-20, then the number. Certain operators will have you dial a special code to access their service.

If dialling NZ from overseas, the country code is ☎ 64, followed by the appropriate area code minus the initial zero.

### LOCAL CALLS

Local calls from private phones are free! Local calls from payphones cost 50c, though coin-operated payphones are scarce – you'll need a phonecard. Both involve unlimited talk time. Calls to mobile phones attract higher rates and are timed.

### LONG-DISTANCE CALLS & AREA CODES

NZ uses regional area codes for long-distance calls, which can be made from any payphone.

If you're making a local call (ie to someone else in the same town), you don't need to dial the area code. But if you're dialling within a region (even if it's to a nearby town) you do have to dial the area code, regardless of the fact that the place you're calling has the same code as the place you're dialling from.

### MOBILE PHONES

Local mobile phone numbers are preceded by the prefix ☎ 021, ☎ 025 or ☎ 027. Mobile phone coverage is good in cities and towns and most parts of the North Island, but can be patchy away from urban centres on the South Island.

If you want to bring your own phone and use a prepaid service with a local SIM card, **Vodafone** (www.vodafone.co.nz) is a practical option. Any Vodafone shop (found in most major towns) will set you up with a SIM card and phone number (about $35, including $10 worth of calls); top-ups can be purchased at newsagen-

cies, post offices and shops practically anywhere.

If you don't bring your own phone from home, you can rent one from **Vodafone Rental** (www.vodarent.co.nz) priced from $6/25 per day/week, with pick-up and drop-off outlets at NZ's major airports. You can also rent a SIM card for $2.50 per day (minimum charge $10) or $40 per month. You can arrange this in advance via the website. We've also had some positive feedback on **Phone Hire New Zealand** (www.phonehirenz.com), who hire out mobile phones, SIM cards, modems and GPS systems.

### PHONECARDS

NZ has a wide range of phonecards available, which can be bought at hostels, newsagencies and post offices for a fixed dollar value (usually $5, $10, $20 and $50). These can be used with any public or private phone by dialling a toll-free access number and then the PIN on the card. It's worth shopping around – call rates vary from company to company.

## TIME

NZ is 12 hours ahead of GMT/UTC and two hours ahead of Australian Eastern Standard Time.

In summer, NZ observes daylight-saving time, where clocks are wound forward by one hour on the last Sunday in September; clocks are wound back on the first Sunday of the following April.

So (excluding the duration of daylight saving), when it's noon in NZ it's 10am in Sydney, 8am in Singapore, midnight in London and 5pm the previous day in San Francisco.

## TOURIST INFORMATION

Almost every Kiwi city or town – whether it has any worthwhile attractions or not –

seems to have a visitor information centre. The bigger centres stand united within the outstanding **i-SITE** (www.newzealand.com/travel/i-sites) network, which is affiliated with Tourism New Zealand (the official national tourism body), and have trained staff, abundant information on local activities and attractions, and free brochures and maps. Staff also act as travel agents, booking activities, transport and accommodation.

Bear in mind that many information centres only promote accommodation and tour operators who are paying members of the local tourist association, while others are ironically hamstrung by the demands of local operators that they be represented equally. In other words, sometimes information centre staff aren't supposed to recommend one activity or accommodation provider over another, a curious situation that exists in highly competitive environments.

There's also a network of **Department Of Conservation** (DOC; www.doc.govt.nz) visitor centres to help you plan your recreation activities and make bookings. DOC visitor centres are found in national parks, major regional centres and in each of the major cities.

**Tourism New Zealand** ( ☎ 04-917 5400; www.newzealand.com) has representatives in various countries around the world. A good place for pretrip research is the official website (emblazoned with the hugely successful 100% Pure New Zealand branding), which has information in several languages (including German and Japanese). Overseas offices:

**Australia** ( ☎ 02-8299 4800; L12, 61 York St, Sydney)

**UK & Europe** ( ☎ 020-7930 1662; New Zealand House, 80 Haymarket, London, UK)

**USA & Canada** ( ☎ 310-395 7480; 501 Santa Monica Blvd, Santa Monica, USA)

# TRAVELLERS WITH DISABILITIES

Kiwi accommodation generally caters fairly well for travellers with disabilities, with a significant number of hostels, hotels, motels and B&Bs equipped with wheelchair-accessible rooms. Many tourist attractions similarly provide wheelchair access, with wheelchairs often available at key attractions with advance notice.

Tour operators with accessible vehicles operate from most major centres. Key cities are also serviced by kneeling buses (buses that hydraulically stoop down to kerb level to allow easy access) and taxi companies offer wheelchair-accessible vans. Large car-hire firms (Avis, Hertz etc) provide cars with hand controls at no extra charge; advance notice is required. Mobility parking permits are available from branches of **CCS Disability Action** ( ☎ 0800 227 200, 04-384 5677; www.ccsdisabilityaction.org.nz) in the main centres.

For good general information, see NZ's **disability information website** (www.weka.net.nz). Outdoor enthusiasts should check out www.accessiblewalks.co.nz and www.disabledsnowsports.org.nz.

# VISAS

Visa application forms are available from NZ diplomatic missions overseas, travel agents or through **Immigration New Zealand** ( ☎ 0508 558 855, 09-914 4100; www.immigration.govt.nz). Immigration New Zealand has over a dozen offices overseas; consult the website.

## VISITOR'S VISA

Citizens of Australia don't need a visa to visit NZ and can stay indefinitely (provided they have no criminal convictions). UK citizens don't need a visa either and can stay in the country for up to six months.

Citizens of another 56 countries that have visa-waiver agreements with NZ don't need a visa for stays of up to three months, provided they have an onward ticket, sufficient funds to support their stay (NZ$1000 per month, or NZ$400 per month if accommodation has been prepaid) and a passport valid for three months beyond the date of their planned departure from NZ. Nations in this group include Canada, France, Germany, Ireland, Japan, the Netherlands and the USA.

Citizens of other countries must obtain a visa before entering NZ. Visas come with three months' standard validity and cost NZ$100 if processed in Australia or certain South Pacific countries (eg Samoa, Fiji), or NZ$130 if processed elsewhere in the world.

### WORK VISA

It's illegal for foreign nationals to work in NZ on a visitor's visa, except for Australians who can legally gain work without a visa or permit. If you're visiting NZ to find work, or you already have an employment offer, you'll need to apply for a work visa, which translates into a work permit once you arrive and is valid for up to three years. You can apply for a work permit after you're in NZ, but its validity will be backdated to when you entered the country. The fee for a work visa ranges from NZ$180 to NZ$280 depending on where it's processed and the type of application.

## WOMEN TRAVELLERS

NZ is generally a very safe place for women travellers, although the usual sensible precautions apply. It's best to avoid walking alone late at night in any of the major cities and towns, and never always keep enough money aside for a taxi back to your accommodation. The same applies in rural towns where there may be a lot of unlit, semideserted streets between you and your bed. Lone women should also be wary of staying in basic pub accommodation unless it looks safe and well managed.

Sexual harassment is not a widely reported problem in NZ, but of course it does happen.

See www.womentravel.co.nz for more information.

# TRANSPORT

New Zealand's peaceably isolated location in a distant patch of the South Pacific is a major drawcard, but it also means that unless you travel from Australia, you have to contend with a long-haul flight to get there. As NZ is serviced by good airline and bus networks, travelling around the country is a much less taxing endeavour.

Flights, tours and rail tickets can be booked online at www.lonelyplanet.com/bookings.

## GETTING THERE & AWAY

### ENTERING THE COUNTRY

Disembarkation in NZ is generally a straightforward affair, with only the usual customs declarations to endure (see Customs Regulations, p360) and the uncool scramble to get to the luggage carousel first. Recent global instability has resulted in increased security in NZ airports, in both domestic and international terminals, and you may find customs procedures time-consuming. One procedure has the Orwellian title Advance Passenger Screening, a system whereby documents that used to be checked after you touched down in NZ (passport, visa etc) are now

make sure all your documentation is in order so your check-in is stress-free.

## PASSPORT

There are no restrictions when it comes to foreign citizens entering NZ. If you have a current passport and visa (or don't require one; see p371), you should be fine.

# AIR

There's a number of competing airlines servicing NZ and a wide variety of fares to choose from if you're flying in from Asia, Europe or North America, though ultimately you'll still pay a lot for a flight unless you jet in from Australia. NZ's inordinate popularity and abundance of year-round activities mean that at almost any time of year airports can be swarming with inbound tourists – if you want to fly at a particularly popular time of year (eg Christmas), book well in advance.

The high season for flights into NZ is during summer (December to February), with slightly less of a premium on fares over the shoulder months (October/November and March/April). The low season generally tallies with the winter months (June to August), though this is still a busy time for airlines ferrying ski bunnies and powder hounds.

## AIRPORTS

Seven NZ airports handle international flights, with Auckland receiving most traffic:

**Auckland** (AKL; ☎ 0800 247 767, 09-275 0789; www.aucklandairport.co.nz)
**Christchurch** (CHC; ☎ 03-358 5029; www.christchurchairport.co.nz)
**Dunedin** (DUD; ☎ 03-486 2879; www.dnairport.co.nz)
**Hamilton** (HLZ; ☎ 07-848 9027; www.hamiltonairport.co.nz)

**Palmerston North** (PMR; ☎ 06-351 4415; www.pnairport.co.nz)
**Queenstown** (ZQN; ☎ 03-450 9031; www.queenstownairport.co.nz)
**Wellington** (WLG; ☎ 04-385 5100; www.wellingtonairport.co.nz)

## TICKETS

Automated online ticket sales work well if you're doing a simple one-way or return trip on specified dates, but are no substitute for a travel agent with the low-down on special deals, strategies for avoiding layovers and other useful advice.

For online ticket bookings, start with the following websites:

**Air Brokers** (www.airbrokers.com) This US company specialises in cheaper tickets. To fly LA-Tahiti-Auckland-Sydney-Bangkok-Hong Kong-LA costs around US$2200 (excluding taxes).
**Cheap Flights** (www.cheapflights.com) Informative site with specials, destination information and flight searches from the USA.
**Cheapest Flights** (www.cheapestflights.co.uk) Cheap worldwide flights from the UK; get in early for the bargains.
**Expedia** (www.expedia.com) Microsoft's travel site; good for USA-related flights.

## DEPARTURE TAX

An international departure tax of NZ$25 applies when leaving NZ at all airports except Auckland, payable by anyone aged 12 and over (NZ$10 for children aged two to 11, free for those under two years of age). The tax is not included in the price of airline tickets, but must be paid separately at the airport before you board your flight. Pay via credit card or cash.

**Flight Centre International** (www.flight
centre.com) Respected operator handling
direct flights, with sites for NZ, Australia,
the UK, the USA, Canada and South
Africa.

**Flights.com** (www.flights.com) International site for flights; cheap fares and
an easy-to-search database.

**Roundtheworldflights.com** (www.round
theworldflights.com) This excellent site allows you to build your own trip from
the UK with up to six stops. A six-stop
trip including Asia, Australia, NZ and the
USA costs from UK£550 in the NZ winter.

**STA Travel** (www.statravel.com) Prominent
in international student travel (but you
don't have to be a student). Linked to
worldwide STA sites.

**Travel Online** (www.travelonline.co.nz) Good
place to check worldwide flights from NZ.

**Travel.com.au** (www.travel.com.au) Good
Australian site; look up fares and flights
to/from the country.

**Travelocity** (www.travelocity.com) US site
that allows you to search fares (in US
dollars) from/to practically anywhere.

# GETTING AROUND
## AIR

Those who have limited time to get between NZ's attractions can make the most
of a widespread network of intra- and
inter-island flights.

### AIRLINES IN NEW ZEALAND

The country's major domestic carrier,
Air New Zealand, has an aerial network
covering most of the country. Australia-
based Jetstar also flies between main
urban areas.

Regional operators include the
following:

**Air Fiordland** ( ☎ 0800 107 505, 03-249 6720;
www.airfiordland.com) Services around Milford Sound, Te Anau and Queenstown.

**Air New Zealand** ( ☎ 0800 737 000, 09-357
3000; www.airnewzealand.co.nz) Offers flights
between 26 domestic destinations.

**Air West Coast** ( ☎ 0800 247 937, 03-738
0524; www.airwestcoast.co.nz) Flies between
Greymouth and Christchurch and runs
charter flights.

**Air2there.com** ( ☎ 0800 777 000, 04-904
5130; www.air2there.com) Connects destinations across Cook Strait, including Blenheim, Napier, Nelson and
Wellington.

**Jetstar** ( ☎ 0800 800 995; www.jetstar.com)
Joins the dots between key tourism
centres: Auckland, Wellington, Christchurch and Queenstown.

**Soundsair** ( ☎ 0800 505 005, 03-520 3080
www.soundsair.co.nz) Hops across Cook
Strait between Wellington and Picton
up to 16 times per day. Also links Wellington with Blenheim and Nelson.

## BICYCLE

Touring cyclists proliferate in NZ, particularly over summer – the roads and trails
run thick with fluoro-clad creatures with
aerodynamic heads. The country is popular with cyclists because it's clean, green
and relatively uncrowded, and has lots of
cheap accommodation (including camping) and easily accessible freshwater. The
roads are generally in good nick, and the
climate generally not too hot or too cold
(except on the South Island's rain-soaked
West Coast). The many hills make for hard
going at times, but there are expansive
flats and lows to accompany the highs. As
in any country, road traffic is the biggest
danger, and you'll hear numerous cyclists'
tales about inconsiderate or unsafe behaviour from drivers. Trucks overtaking
too close to the cyclist are a particular
threat. Take care! Bikes and cycling gear
(to rent or buy) are readily available in the
main centres, as are bicycle repair shops.

Rates offered by most outfits for renting road or mountain bikes are anywhere from $10 to $20 per hour and $30 to $50 per day.

## BOAT

NZ may be an island nation but there's virtually no long-distance water transport around the country. Obvious exceptions include the boat services between Auckland and various islands in the Hauraki Gulf (see p86), the inter-island ferries that chug across Cook Strait between Wellington (p166) and Picton (p217).

## BUS

Bus travel in NZ is relatively easy and well organised, with services transporting you to the far reaches of both islands (including the start/end of various walking tracks), but it can be expensive, tedious and time-consuming. The bus 'terminals' in smaller places usually comprise a parking spot outside a prominent local business.

The dominant bus company is **InterCity** ( ☎ Auckland 09-583 5780, Wellington 04-385 0520, Christchurch 03-365 1113, Dunedin 03-471 7143; www.intercity.co.nz), which also has an extra-comfort travel and sightseeing arm called **Newmans Coach Lines** ( ☎ 09-623 1504; www.newmanscoach. co.nz). InterCity can drive you to just about anywhere on the North and South Islands, from Invercargill and Milford Sound in the south to Paihia and Kaitaia in the north.

Smaller regional operators running key routes or covering a lot of ground on the North Island include:

**Alpine Scenic Tours** ( ☎ 07-378 7412; www.alpinescenictours.co.nz) Has services around Taupo and into Tongariro National Park, plus the ski fields around Mt Ruapehu and Mt Tongariro.

**Bay Xpress** ( ☎ 0800 422 997, 06-873 4984; www.bayxpress.co.nz) Connects Wellington with Hastings and Napier via Palmerston North.

**Dalroy Express** ( ☎ 0508 465 622, 06-759-0197; www.dalroytours.co.nz) Operates a daily service between Auckland and Hawera via New Plymouth and Hamilton. Also runs from Auckland to Pahia, and from Hamilton to Rotorua and Taupo.

**Go Kiwi Shuttles** ( ☎ 07-866 0336; www.go-kiwi.co.nz) Links places like Auckland, Rotorua and Hamilton with various towns across the Coromandel Peninsula.

**Magic Travellers Network** ( ☎ 09-358 5600; www.magicbus.co.nz) Has a useful collection of passes available, covering both islands or each individually.

**Naked Bus** ( ☎ 0900 625 33; www.nakedbus. com) Low-cost routes across the North (and South) Island, from Auckland to Wellington and most places in between.

**Waitomo Wanderer** ( ☎ 0508 926 337, 03-477 9083; www.waitomotours.co.nz) Does a loop from Rotorua to Waitomo.

**White Star City to City** ( ☎ 06-759 0197; www.whitestarbus.co.nz) Shuttles between Wellington, Palmerston North, Whanganui and New Plymouth.

South Island shuttle-bus companies:

**Abel Tasman Coachlines** ( ☎ 03-548 0285; www.abeltasmantravel.co.nz) Traverses the tarmac between Nelson, Motueka, Golden Bay, and Kahurangi and Abel Tasman National Parks.

**Atomic Shuttles** ( ☎ 03-349 0697; www. atomictravel.co.nz) Has services throughout the South Island, including to Christchurch, Dunedin, Invercargill, Picton, Nelson, Greymouth/Hokitika, Te Anau and Queenstown/Wanaka.

**Cook Connection** ( ☎ 0800 266 526; www. cookconnect.co.nz) Triangulates between Mt Cook, Twizel and Lake Tekapo.

**East West Coaches** (☎ 0800 142 622, 03-789 6251) Offers a service between Christchurch and Westport, running via the Hanmer Springs turn-off, Maruia Springs and Reefton.

**Hanmer Connection** (☎ 0800 242 663; www.atsnz.com) Provides services between Hanmer Springs and Christchurch, and three services weekly between Hanmer and Kaikoura.

**Knightrider** (☎ 03-342 8055; www.knight rider.co.nz) Runs a nocturnal service from Christchurch to Invercargill via Dunedin. David Hasselhoff nowhere to be seen…

**Naked Bus** (☎ 0900 625 33; www.nakedbus. com) Low-cost routes across the South (and North) Island, from Nelson to Invercargill and most places in between.

**Scenic Shuttle** (☎ 0800 304 333, 03-477 9083; www.scenicshuttle.co.nz) Drives between Te Anau and Invercargill via Manapouri.

**Southern Link Travel** (☎ 0508 458 835; www.southernlinkkbus.co.nz) Roams across most of the South Island, taking in Christchurch, Nelson, Picton, Greymouth, Queenstown and Dunedin, among others.

**Topline Tours** (☎ 03-249 8059; www.top linetours.co.nz) Connects Te Anau and Queenstown.

**Tracknet** (☎ 0800 483 262, 03-249 7777; www.tracknet.net) Daily track transport (Milford, Routeburn, Hollyford, Kepler etc) between Queenstown, Te Anau, Milford Sound, Invercargill, Fiordland and the West Coast.

**West Coast Shuttle** (☎ 03-768 0028; www. westcoastshuttle.co.nz) Daily bus from Greymouth to Christchurch and back.

## INTERCITY BUS PASSES
**InterCity** (☎ Auckland 09-583 5780, Wellington 03-471 7143; www.intercity.co.nz) offers bus passes, covering either the whole country, or the North and South Islands separately. If you're covering a lot of ground, passes can be cheaper than paying as you go, but they lock you into using InterCity buses (rather than, say, the convenient shuttle buses that cover much of the country).

## NATIONWIDE PASSES
InterCity's pan-NZ **Travelpass** (☎ 0800 339 966; www.travelpass.co.nz) combines bus travel with a Cook Strait ferry crossing. There are three hop-on/hop-off passes available, each valid for a year. Adult and child prices are the same:

**Kia Ora New Zealand** ($579; 7-day minimum travel) A one-way trip between Auckland and Christchurch via Rotorua, Wellington, Dunedin, Queenstown and Milford Sound. Available in both directions.

**Kiwi Explorer** ($623; 9-day minimum travel) A one-way trip between Auckland and Christchurch via Rotorua, Napier, Wellington, the West Coast, Milford Sound and Queenstown. Available in both directions.

**Aotearoa Adventurer** ($1283; 14-day minimum travel) A monster loop from Auckland to Milford Sound and back, via Northland, Rotorua, Wellington, Christchurch, Queenstown, the West Coast and Napier.

The appropriately named **Flexi-Pass** (☎ 0800 222 146; www.flexipass.co.nz) is valid for one year and allows you to travel pretty much anywhere (and in any direction) on the InterCity network; you can get on and off wherever you like and can change bookings up to two hours before departure without penalty. The pass is purchased in five-hour blocks of travel up to a maximum of 60 hours ($605) — the average cost of each block becomes cheaper the more hours you buy. You can top up the pass if you need more time.

## NORTH ISLAND PASSES

There are seven InterCity North Island passes:

**Thermal Explorer** ($39; 1-day minimum travel) Rotorua to Taupo return.

**Bay Escape** ($106; 1-day minimum travel) Auckland to Paihia and back, via Whangarei.

**Eastern Wanderer** ($119; 3-day minimum travel) Rotorua to Napier circuit via Whakatane, Gisborne and Taupo.

**Maui's Catch** ($169; 3-day minimum travel) Auckland to Wellington via Waitomo, Rotorua, Taupo, Napier and Palmerston North. Available in both directions.

**Volcanic Explorer** ($184; 2-day minimum travel) Auckland to Rotorua loop via Tauranga, Taupo and Waitomo.

**Northland Explorer** ($205; 3-day minimum travel) Auckland to Paihia return via Whangarei, with a daytrip to Cape Reinga.

**North Island Discovery** ($243; 4-day minimum travel) Auckland to Wellington return via Waitomo, Rotorua, Taupo, Napier, Palmerston North and Hamilton. Available in both directions.

## SOUTH ISLAND PASSES

There are 10 InterCity South Island passes:

**Kaikoura Discovery** ($40; 1-day minimum travel) Christchurch to Kaikoura and back.

**West Coast Passport ex-Greymouth** ($135; 2-day minimum travel) Greymouth to Queenstown via Franz Josef Glacier, Fox Glacier and Wanaka. Available in both directions.

**West Coast Passport ex-Nelson** ($155; 2-day minimum travel) Nelson to Queenstown via Greymouth, Franz Josef Glacier, Fox Glacier and Wanaka. Available in both directions.

**West Coast Passport ex-Picton** ($180; 3-day minimum travel) Picton to Queenstown via Nelson, Greymouth, Franz Josef Glacier, Fox Glacier and Wanaka. Available in both directions.

**Southern Trail** ($188; 3-day minimum travel) Greymouth to Christchurch via Franz Josef Glacier, Fox Glacier, Wanaka, Queenstown and Tekapo. Available in both directions.

**Greenstone Encounter** ($189; 2-day minimum travel) Christchurch to Milford Sound via Tekapo, Queenstown and Te Anau. Available in both directions.

**Goldminers Trail** ($221; 2-day minimum travel) Christchurch to Milford Sound via Dunedin, Queenstown and Te Anau. Available in both directions.

**Te Hamo's Adventure** ($259; 2-day minimum travel) Christchurch to Milford Sound via Aoraki/Mt Cook, Queenstown and Te Anau. Available in both directions.

**Maui's Canoe** ($442; 5-day minimum travel) South Island circuit starting/ending in Christchurch via Queenstown, Milford Sound, Fox Glacier, Franz Josef Glacier, Nelson and Kaikoura. Available in both directions.

**Alpine Discovery** ($539; 5-day minimum travel) South Island circuit starting/ending in Christchurch via Aoraki/Mt Cook, Queenstown, Te Anau, Milford Sound, Fox Glacier, Franz Josef Glacier, Greymouth, Nelson and Kaikoura. Available in both directions.

## SEAT CLASSES

There are no allocated economy or luxury classes on NZ buses; smoking is a no-no.

## RESERVATIONS

Over summer, school holidays and public holidays, book well ahead on more popular routes. At other times you should have few problems accessing your preferred service, but if your long-term travel plans rely on catching a particular bus, book at least a day or two ahead just to be safe.

InterCity fares vary widely depending on availability and how the tickets are booked (online or via an agent). The best prices are generally available online, booked a few weeks in advance.

## CAR & MOTORCYCLE

The best way to explore NZ in depth is to have your own transport, which allows you to create your own leisurely, flexible itinerary. Good-value car- and campervan-hire rates are not hard to track down; alternatively, consider buying your own set of wheels.

### AUTOMOBILE ASSOCIATION

NZ's **Automobile Association** (AA; ☎ 24hr **road service 0800 500 222; www.aa.co.nz**) provides emergency breakdown services, excellent touring maps and detailed guides to accommodation (from holiday parks to motels and B&Bs).

Members of foreign automobile associations should bring their membership cards – many of these bodies have reciprocal agreements with NZ's AA.

### DRIVING LICENCE

International visitors to NZ can use their home country's driving licence – if your licence isn't in English, it's a good idea to carry a certified translation with you. Alternatively, use an International Driving Permit (IDP), which will usually be issued on the spot (valid for 12 months) by your home country's automobile association.

### FUEL

Fuel is available from service stations with the well-known international brand names. Prices vary from place to place, but basically petrol (gasoline) isn't pumped cheaply in NZ, with per-litre costs at the time of research averaging around $1.65. More remote destinations may charge a small fortune to fill your tank and you're better off getting fuel before you reach them – places in this category include Milford Sound (fill up at Te Anau) and Mt Cook (buy fuel at Twizel or Lake Tekapo).

## HIRE
### CAMPERVAN

Check your rear-view mirror on any far-flung NZ road and you'll likely see a shiny white campervan (aka mobile home, motor home, RV) packed with liberated travellers, mountain bikes and portable barbecues cruising along behind you.

Campervanning around NZ is big business. It's flexible and affordable, and you can leave the trampled tourist trails behind and crank up the AC/DC as loud as hell! Most towns of any size have a camping ground or campervan park with powered sites for around $35 per night. There are also places where 'freedom camping' is permitted, but you should never just *assume* it's OK to camp somewhere. Always ask a local first. Check at the local i-SITE or DOC office, or even with local commercial camping grounds. If you are freedom camping, please treat the area with respect – if your van doesn't have toilet facilities, find a public loo. See www.camping.org.nz for more tips on freedom camping.

You can hire campervans from assorted companies, prices varying with time of year, how big you want your home-on-wheels to be, and length of rental. Major operators:

**Britz** ( ☎ **0800 831 900, 09-255 3910; www.britz.co.nz**)

**Kea Campers** ( ☎ 0800 520 052, 09-441 7833; www.keacampers.com)

**Maui** ( ☎ 0800 651 080, 09-255 3910; www.maui. co.nz)

A small van for two people typically has a mini-kitchen and fold-out dining table, the latter transforming into a double bed when dinner is done 'n' dusted. Larger 'superior' two-berth vans include shower and toilet. Four- to six-berth campervans are the size of trucks (and similarly sluggish) and, besides the extra space, usually contain a toilet and shower.

Over summer, rates offered by the main rental firms for two-/four-/six-berth vans start at around $160/290/320 per day, dropping to as low as $50/80/95 in winter for month-long rentals; industry infighting often sees even lower rates.

## CAR

Competition between car-rental companies in NZ is torrid — rates tend to be variable and lots of special deals come and go (we've heard of discounted rates as low as $15 per day, so shop around). Car rental is most competitive in Auckland, Christchurch, Wellington and Picton. The main thing to remember when assessing your options is distance — if you want to travel far, you need unlimited kilometres. Some (but not all) companies require drivers to be at least 21 years old — ask around.

Sizable multinational companies, with offices or agents in most major cities, towns and larger airports:

**Avis** ( ☎ 0800 655 111, 09-526-2847; www.avis. co.nz)

**Budget** ( ☎ 0800 283 438, 09-529 7784; www. budget.co.nz)

## BACKPACKER VAN RENTALS

There are several budget players in the campervan industry, offering slick deals and funky, well-kitted-out vehicles to attract young, independent travellers (the kind who would shun the larger, more traditional box-on-wheels). All companies offer living, sleeping and cooking equipment, 24-hour roadside assistance, and maps and travel tips. Rates are competitive (from $35 per day May to September; from $70 per day December to February). Check out the following:

- **Backpacker Sleeper Vans** ( ☎ 0800 325 939, 03-359 4731; www.sleepervans.co.nz) Low-cost family-run business.
- **Escape Rentals** ( ☎ 0800 216 171; www.escaperentals.co.nz) 'The freedom to sleep around' — loud, original artwork on van exteriors, pitched squarely at young travellers after something different. DVDs, TVs and outdoor barbecues available for rent.
- **Jucy** ( ☎ 0800 399 736, 09-374 4360; www.jucy.co.nz) The flashpacker's vehicle of choice.
- **Spaceships** ( ☎ 0800 772 237, 09-526 2130; www.spaceshipsrentals.co.nz) The customised 'Swiss Army Knife of campervans', with extras including DVD and CD players, roof racks and solar showers.
- **Wicked Campers** ( ☎ 0800 246 870; www.wicked-campers.co.nz) Spray-painted vans bedecked with everything/everyone from Mr Spock to Sly Stone.

**Europcar** (☎ 0800 800 115, 03-357 0920; www.europcar.co.nz)

**Hertz** (☎ 0800 654 321, 03-520 3044; www.hertz.co.nz)

**Thrifty** (☎ 0800 737 070, 03-359 2720; www.thrifty.co.nz)

Local rental firms and firms with limited locations can be found in the *Yellow Pages* – see the regional chapters in this guide. These are almost always cheaper than the big boys – sometimes half the price – but the cheap rates may come with serious restrictions, vehicles are often older, and with less formality sometimes comes less protective legal structure for renters.

Affordable, independent operators with national networks:

**Ace Rental Cars** (☎ 0800 502 277, 09-303 3112; www.acerentalcars.co.nz)

**Apex Rentals** (☎ 0800 939 597, 03-379 6897; www.apexrentals.co.nz)

**Ezy Rentals** (☎ 0800 399 736, 09-374 4360; www.ezy.co.nz)

**Go Rentals** (☎ 0800 467 368, 09-525 7321; www.gorentals.co.nz)

**Omega Rental Cars** (☎ 0800 525 210, 09-377 5573; www.omegarentalcars.com)

**Pegasus Rental Cars** (☎ 0800 803 580, 03-548 2852; www.rentalcars.co.nz)

Most car-hire firms suggest (or insist) that you don't take their vehicles between islands on the Cook Strait ferries. Instead, you leave your car at either Wellington or Picton terminal and pick up another car once you've crossed the strait. This saves you paying to transport a vehicle on the ferries, and is a pain-free exercise.

The major companies offer a choice of either unlimited kilometres, or 100km (or so) per day free plus so many cents per subsequent kilometre. Daily rates in main cities typically start at around $40 per day for a compact, late-model, Japanese car, and around $75 for medium-sized cars (including GST, unlimited kilometres and insurance). Local firms start at around $30 per day for the smallest option. It's cheaper if you rent for a week or more and there are often low-season and weekend discounts. Credit cards are the usual payment method.

## MOTORCYCLE

Born to be wild? NZ has great terrain for motorcycle touring, despite the fickle weather in some regions.

Most of the country's motorcycle-hire shops are in Auckland and Christchurch, where you can hire anything from a little 50cc moped (aka nifty-fifty) for zipping around town, to a throbbing 750cc touring motor-cycle and beyond. Recommended operators:

**New Zealand Motorcycle Rentals & Tours** (☎ 09-634 9118; www.nzbike.com) Yamahas, BMWs, Hondas and Harleys from $120 to $395 per day. Rates vary with size of bike, length of rental and season. Guided tours also available.

**Te Waipounamu Motorcycle Tours** (☎ 03-372 3537 www.motorcycle-hire.co.nz) Yamahas, Ducatis, Kawasakis, BMWs, Hondas and Suzukis from $115 to $300 per day. Guided tours also available.

## INSURANCE

When it comes to renting a vehicle, know exactly what your liability is in the event of an accident. Rather than risk paying out a large amount of cash if you do have an accident (minor collisions are common in NZ), you can take out your own comprehensive insurance policy, or (the usual option) pay an additional daily amount to the rental company for an 'insurance excess reduction' policy. This brings the amount of excess you must pay in the event of an accident down from around $1500 or $2000 to around $150 or $200. Smaller operators offering cheap rates often have a compulsory insurance excess, taken as a credit-card bond, of around $900.

Most insurance agreements won't cover the cost of damage to glass (including the windscreen) or tyres, and insurance coverage is often invalidated on beaches and certain rough (4WD) unsealed roads – always read the fine print.

For information on the country's no-fault Accident Compensation Corporation scheme, see p366.

### ROAD RULES

Kiwis drive on the left-hand side of the road and all cars are right-hand drive. A 'give way to the right' rule applies and is interpreted to a rather strange extreme here – if you're turning left and an oncoming vehicle is turning right into the same street, you have to give way to it.

Speed limits on the open road are generally 100km/h; in built-up areas the limit is usually 50km/h. An 'LSZ' (Limited Speed Zone) sign on the open road means that the speed limit is reduced from 100km/h to 50km/h in certain conditions – this applies when conditions are unsafe due to bad weather, limited visibility, pedestrians, cyclists or animals on the road, excessive traffic, or lousy road conditions. Speed cameras and radars are used extensively.

At single-lane bridges (of which there are a surprisingly large number), a smaller red arrow pointing in your direction of travel means that *you* give way, so slow down as you approach and pull a little to the side if you see a car approaching the other end of the bridge.

## LOCAL TRANSPORT

### BUS, TRAIN & TRAM

Most of NZ's urban buses have been privatised. Larger cities have fairly extensive bus services but, with a few honourable exceptions, they are mainly daytime, weekday operations; on weekends, particularly on Sunday, bus services can be hard to find or may cease altogether. Negotiating the inner-city area in Auckland is made easier by the Link and City Circuit buses, and in Christchurch by the Shuttle Bus service and the historic tramway. Most main cities have a late-night bus service roaming central entertainment districts on boozy, end-of-week nights.

The only city with a decent train service is Wellington, which has five suburban routes.

### TAXI

The main cities have plenty of taxis and even small towns may have a local service. Taxis cruise the busy areas in Auckland, Wellington and Christchurch, but elsewhere you usually have to either phone for one or find a taxi rank.

### TRAIN

With the exception of Wellington's suburban trains, NZ train travel is about the journey, not about getting anywhere in a hurry. **Tranz Scenic** ( ☎ 0800 872 467, 04-495 0775; www.tranzscenic.co.nz) operates several visually stunning routes: the *Overlander* between Auckland and Wellington; the *TranzCoastal* between Christchurch and Picton; and the *TranzAlpine,* which rattles over the Southern Alps between Christchurch and Greymouth. All routes run in both directions daily. It also operates the weekday *Capital Connection* commuter service between Palmerston North and Wellington.

Reservations can be made through Tranz Scenic directly, or at most train stations (notably *not* at Palmerston North or Hamilton), travel agents and visitor information centres, where you can also pick up booklets detailing timetables. Ask about discount fares – reductions apply for children (50% off standard fares), seniors and students (30% off), and holders of backpackers cards (20% off). Discounts don't apply on the *Overlander* or *Capital Connection* services.

## TRAIN PASSES

Given NZ's limited rail network, buying a train pass isn't particularly good value.

Tranz Scenic's **Scenic Rail Pass** (www. tranzscenic.co.nz) allows unlimited travel on all of its rail services (with the exception of the *Capital Connection*), with the option of including passage on the Interislander ferry between Wellington and Picton. A pass (with ferry trip) lasting two weeks costs $517/394 per adult/child.

# ↘ GLOSSARY

This glossary is a list of abbreviations, 'Kiwi English', Maori, and slang terms and phrases you may hear in New Zealand.

**AA** – NZ's Automobile Association; provides road information and roadside assistance

**All Blacks** – NZ's revered national rugby union team

**Aoraki** – Maori name for Mt Cook, meaning 'Cloud Piercer'

**Aotearoa** – Maori name for NZ, most often translated as 'Land of the Long White Cloud'

**B&B** – 'bed and breakfast' accommodation

**bach** – holiday home, usually a wooden cottage (pronounced 'batch')

**black-water rafting** – rafting or tubing underground in a cave

**BYO** – 'bring your own' (usually applies to alcohol at a restaurant or cafe)

**chillie bin** – cooler; esky; large insulated box for keeping food and drinks cold

**dairy** – small corner store that sells milk, bread, newspapers, ice cream and pretty much everything else

**DB&B** – 'dinner, bed and breakfast' accommodation

**DOC** – Department of Conservation (or *Te Papa Atawhai*); government department that administers national parks and thus all tracks and huts

**farmstay** – accommodation on a *Kiwi* farm where you're encouraged to join in the typical day-to-day activities

**Great Walks** – a set of nine popular tramping tracks within NZ

**greenstone** – jade; *pounamu*

**haka** – any dance, but usually refers to the traditional challenge; war dance

**handle** – beer glass with a handle

**hangi** – oven made by digging a hole and steaming food in baskets over embers in the hole; a feast of Maori food

**hokey pokey** – delicious variety of vanilla ice cream with butterscotch chips

**homestay** – accommodation in a family house where you're treated as one of the family

**hongi** – Maori greeting; the pressing of foreheads and noses, and sharing of life breath

**Interislander** – large ferries crossing Cook Strait between Wellington and Picton

**i-SITE** – information centre

**iwi** – large tribal grouping with common lineage back to the original migration from Hawaiki; people; tribe

**K Rd** – Karangahape Rd in Auckland

**kai** – food; almost any word with *kai* in it has a connection with food

**kapa haka** – traditional Maori group singing and dancing

**kauri** – native pine

**Kiwi** – A New Zealander; an adjective to mean anything relating to NZ

**kiwi** – the flightless, nocturnal brown bird with a long beak that is the national symbol

**kiwi fruit** – small, succulent fruit with fuzzy brown skin and juicy green flesh; a Chinese gooseberry; never called a *kiwi*
**kumara** – Polynesian sweet potato; a Maori staple food

**Maori** – indigenous people of NZ
**Maoritanga** – Maori culture
**marae** – literally refers to the sacred ground in front of the Maori meeting house, more commonly used to refer to the entire complex of buildings
**motorway** – freeway or expressway

**nga** – the (plural); see also *te*
**ngai/ngati** – literally, 'the people of' or 'the descendants of'; tribe (on the South Island it's pronounced 'kai')

**pa** – fortified Maori village, usually on a hill top
**Pacific Rim** – term used to describe modern NZ cuisine; cuisine with an innovative use of local produce, especially seafood, with imported styles
**Pakeha** – Maori for a white or European person
**paua** – abalone; tough shellfish pounded, minced, then made into patties (fritters), and available in almost every NZ fish-and-chip shop; the beautiful, iridescent *paua* shell is often used in decoration and jewellery
**pavlova** – meringue cake, usually topped with cream and *kiwi fruit;* the quintessential *Kiwi* dessert

**PI** – Pacific Islander
**pipi** – common edible bivalve
**poi** – ball of woven flax
**poi dance** – women's formation dance that involves singing and manipulating a *poi*
**pounamu** – Maori name for *greenstone*
**powhiri** – traditional Maori welcome onto a *marae*

**tane** – man
**tangata whenua** – people of the land; local people
**te** – the (singular); see also *nga*
**Te Papa** – literally 'our place'; the national museum in Wellington
**Te Papa Atawhai** – Maori name for *DOC*
**tiki** – short for *hei tiki;* carved, stylised human figure worn around the neck representing the first human and supposed to bring good luck
**tramp** – bushwalk; trek; hike
**tuatara** – prehistoric reptile dating back to the age of dinosaurs

**wahine** – woman
**waiata** – song
**waka** – canoe
**whanau** – family
**whare** – house
**whitebait** – tiny translucent fish that is scooped up in nets and eaten whole (head, eyes and all!) or made into patties

# ⬎ BEHIND THE SCENES

## THE AUTHORS
### CHARLES RAWLINGS-WAY

**Coordinating Author, This Is New Zealand, New Zealand's Top 25 Experiences, Itineraries, Planning Your Trip, Waikato & the King Country, Taranaki, Rotorua & the Bay of Plenty, Directory & Transport**

English by birth, Australian by chance, All Blacks fan by choice: Charles considers himself a worldly lad, but his early understanding of Aotearoa was less than comprehensive. He realised there was more to NZ when a wandering uncle returned with a faux-jade *tiki* in 1981. He wore it with pride until he saw the NZ cricket team's beige uniforms in 1982... Mt Taranaki's summit, Raglan's breaks and Whanganui's charm have helped him forgive. He's once again smitten with the country's landscapes, locals, and determination to sculpt its own political and indigenous destiny. Roll on Rugby World Cup 2011!

*Author thanks*
Thanks to the many generous, knowledgeable and quietly self-assured Kiwis I met on the road, especially the staff at NZ's i-SITEs who flew through my questions with the greatest of ease. Thanks to Errol Hunt and Suzannah Shwer for signing me up, and the in-house LP staff who schmoozed this book through production. Humongous gratitude to my tireless, witty and professional co-authors – Sarah, Peter, Brett and Scott – who infused this book with local lowdown. Thanks also to Eloise Jones for the buttered date loaf and tea. Most of all, thank you Meg, Ione and Remy, my three (very patient) road-trippin' sweethearts.

### BRETT ATKINSON
Christchurch, Canterbury, Dunedin, Otago, Fiordland & Southland

Although he's lived in Auckland for four decades, Brett never misses a chance to explore the rugged mountains, lakes, and coastline of NZ's South Island. On his second extended research trip to the 'Mainland', he kayaked Doubtful Sound, shared the

## LONELY PLANET AUTHORS

Why is our travel information the best in the world? It's simple: our authors are passionate, dedicated travellers. They don't take freebies in exchange for positive coverage so you can be sure the advice you're given is impartial. They travel widely to all the popular spots, and off the beaten track. They don't research using just the internet or phone. They discover new places not included in any other guidebook. They personally visit thousands of hotels, restaurants, palaces, trails, galleries, temples and more. They speak with dozens of locals every day to make sure you get the kind of insider knowledge only a local could tell you. They take pride in getting all the details right, and in telling it how it is. Think you can do it? Find out how at **lonelyplanet.com**.

BEHIND THE SCENES

audacious scenery of Banks Peninsula and the Catlins with his family, and unearthed more than a few places to drink NZ's excellent microbrewed beers. Brett has contributed to guidebooks covering four of the planet's continents, and covered more than 40 countries as a freelance travel writer. See www.brett-atkinson.net for his latest work.

## SARAH BENNETT
The East Coast, Wellington Region, Marlborough & Nelson

Raised among the cherry trees of Marlborough, Sarah migrated to Wellington at 16 and has lived there ever since, except for various travels and a stint in London working in Lonely Planet's UK office. An arguably flawed guidebook writer due to eternal optimism and irrepressible nationalism ('New Zealand...what's not to like?'), she has done her best to find fault wherever she can, especially in regard to ill-chosen garnish and inadequate beer selection. Sarah's other books are *The Best of Wellington, Let's Go Camping* and *The New Zealand Tramper's Handbook,* all of which she co-authored with her husband, Lee Slater.

## PETER DRAGICEVICH
Auckland Region, Northland, the Bay of Islands, Coromandel Region, Taupo & the Central Plateau

After nearly a decade working for off-shore publishing companies, Peter's life has come full circle, returning to West Auckland where he was raised. As managing editor of Auckland-based *Express* newspaper he spent much of the '90s writing about the local arts, club and bar scene. This is his second time researching his homeland NZ, and after co-authoring 17 books for Lonely Planet, it remains his favourite gig.

## SCOTT KENNEDY
The West Coast, Queenstown & Wanaka

Scott grew up in the mountains of Western Canada and has always been drawn to wild places. When he first set foot in NZ a decade ago he knew he'd found the place he was looking for. For the last eight years he's called Queenstown home and jumped at the chance to pass on the inside story to Lonely Planet readers. A passionate fan of the outdoors, Scott is an avid skier, mountain biker, rock climber, tramper, runner and surfer. When Scott isn't travelling the world penning guidebooks for Lonely Planet he works as a freelance writer, photographer and filmmaker – with a focus on adventure of course. Scott's website is www.adventureskope.com.

## CONTRIBUTING AUTHORS

**Professor James Belich** wrote the History feature (p342). James is one of NZ's pre-eminent historians and the award-winning author of *The New Zealand Wars, Making Peoples* and *Paradise Reforged.* He has also worked in TV – *New Zealand Wars* was screened in NZ in 1998.

**John Huria** (Ngai Tahu, Muaupoko) wrote the Maori Culture section (p351). John has an editorial, research and writing background with a focus on Maori culture. He was senior editor for Maori publishing company Huia (NZ) and now runs an editorial and publishing services company, Ahi Text Solutions Ltd (www.ahitextsolutions.co.nz).

**Lauraine Jacobs** wrote the Food & Drink section (p340). Lauraine is an award-winning food writer, and food editor of *Cuisine* magazine.

**Dr David Millar** wrote the Health section (p363). David is a travel-medicine specialist, diving doctor and lecturer in wilderness medicine.

**Gareth Shute** wrote the Music section (p332). Gareth is the author of four books, including *Hip Hop Music in Aotearoa* and *NZ Rock 1987–2007*. He is also a musician and has toured the UK, Europe and Australia as a member of The Ruby Suns. He now plays in The Conjurors, The Investigations and The Cosbys.

**Vaughan Yarwood** wrote the Environment section (p335). Vaughan is an Auckland-based writer whose most recent book is *The History Makers: Adventures in New Zealand Biography*. He has written widely for NZ and international publications and is the former associate editor of *New Zealand Geographic,* for which he continues to write.

Thanks to: Sir Ian McKellen (Sandflies boxed text, p361); Nandor Tanczos, whose contribution to *New Zealand* 15 informs the Environmental Issues section in the Environment feature (p335) in this book; Grace Hoet, for her contribution to the Maori Culture feature (p351); and all the New Zealand regional tourism organisations, for their help with pre-research briefings.

## THIS BOOK
This 1st edition of *Discover New Zealand* was coordinated by Charles Rawlings-Way, and researched and written by Charles, Brett Atkinson, Sarah Bennett, Peter Dragicevich and Scott Kennedy. This guidebook was commissioned in Lonely Planet's Melbourne office, and produced by the following:

**Commissioning Editors** Errol Hunt, Suzannah Shwer
**Coordinating Editors** Susan Paterson, Dianne Schallmeiner
**Coordinating Cartographers** Hunor Csutoros, Alex Leung
**Coordinating Layout Designer** Jim Hsu
**Managing Editors** Imogen Bannister, Liz Heynes
**Managing Cartographers** David Connolly, Corey Hutchison
**Managing Layout Designer** Indra Kilfoyle
**Assisting Editors** Chris Girdler, Angela Tinson, Gina Tsarouhas, Jeanette Wall
**Cover Research** Naomi Parker, lonelyplanetimages.com
**Internal Image Research** Rebecca Skinner, lonelyplanetimages.com

**Thanks to** Jane Hart, Lisa Knights, John Mazzocchi, Averil Robertson, Jane Thompson, Juan Winata, Celia Wood.

**Internal photographs** p4 Mt Taranaki, David Wall; p10 The Remarkables mountain range, Otago, David Wall; p12 Surfers, Bay of Plenty, Tourism Bay of Plenty; p31 Vineyard, Marlborough, Micah Wright; p39 Te Matua Ngahere (Father of the Forest)

BEHIND THE SCENES

THIS BOOK

kauri tree, Waipoua Kauri Forest, Northland, Anders Blomqvist; p50 Auckland Harbour, Paul Kennedy; p89 Glowworm tour, Tourism Bay of Plenty; p143 Artwork at Te Papa, Wellington, Richard I'Anson; p199 Kayaking, Marlborough, Destination Marlborough; p235 Church of the Good Shepherd, Lake Tekapo, David Wall; p275 Mitre Peak, Milford Sound, David Wall; p322 Tunnel Beach, Dunedin, David Wall; p357 Queen Charlotte Sound ferry, John Elk III.

All images are copyright of the photographer unless otherwise indicated. Many of the images in this guide are available for licensing from Lonely Planet Images: www.lonelyplanetimages.com.

# ↘ INDEX

INDEX

B-C

000 Map pages
000 Photograph pages

INDEX

G-I

INDEX

M-O

INDEX

O-S

**INDEX**

**S-T**

000 Map pages
000 Photograph pages

INDEX

W-Z

# GREENDEX
## GOING GREEN

As Kermit the Frog asserts, it's not easy being green, but in tourism these days everyone wants to be 'eco'. But how can you know which businesses are legitimately ecofriendly and which are just jumping on the sustainable bandwagon?

The following listings have been selected by Lonely Planet authors because they demonstrate active sustainable-tourism policies. Some are involved in conservation or environmental education; many are owned and operated by local and indigenous operators, thus preserving local identity and culture. Some are also accredited by **Qualmark Green** (www.qualmark.co.nz) or listed by **Organic Explorer** (www.organicexplorer.co.nz).

All national parks and reserves and DOC–controlled areas preserve native bush and fauna, and are by their very nature 'green'.

If you think we've omitted someone or you disagree with our choices, email us at talk2us@lonelyplanet.com.au. For more information about sustainable tourism and Lonely Planet, see www.lonelyplanet.com/responsibletravel.

# MAP LEGEND

## ROUTES

| | |
|---|---|
| **Tollway** | One-Way Street |
| **Freeway** | Mall/Steps |
| **Primary** | Tunnel |
| Secondary | Pedestrian Overpass |
| Tertiary | Walking Tour |
| Lane | Walking Tour Detour |
| Under Construction | Walking Path |
| Unsealed Road | Track |

## TRANSPORT

| | |
|---|---|
| Ferry | Rail/Underground |
| Metro | Tram |
| Monorail | Cable Car, Funicular |

## HYDROGRAPHY

| | |
|---|---|
| River, Creek | Canal |
| Intermittent River | Water |
| Swamp/Mangrove | Dry Lake/Salt Lake |
| Reef | Glacier |

## BOUNDARIES

| | |
|---|---|
| International | Regional, Suburb |
| State, Provincial | Marine Park |
| Disputed | Cliff/Ancient Wall |

## AREA FEATURES

| | |
|---|---|
| Area of Interest | Forest |
| Beach, Desert | Mall/Market |
| Building/Urban Area | Park |
| Cemetery, Christian | Restricted Area |
| Cemetery, Other | Sports |

## POPULATION

| | |
|---|---|
| **CAPITAL (NATIONAL)** | **CAPITAL (STATE)** |
| **LARGE CITY** | **Medium City** |
| Small City | Town, Village |

## SYMBOLS

### Sights/Activities

| | |
|---|---|
| Buddhist | |
| Canoeing, Kayaking | |
| Castle, Fortress | |
| Christian | |
| Confucian | |
| Diving | |
| Hindu | |
| Islamic | |
| Jain | |
| Jewish | |
| Monument | |
| Museum, Gallery | |
| Point of Interest | |
| Pool | |
| Ruin | |
| Sento (Public Hot Baths) | |
| Shinto | |
| Sikh | |
| Skiing | |
| Surfing, Surf Beach | |
| Taoist | |
| Trail Head | |
| Winery, Vineyard | |
| Zoo, Bird Sanctuary | |

### Information

| | |
|---|---|
| Bank, ATM | |
| Embassy/Consulate | |
| Hospital, Medical | |
| Information | |
| Internet Facilities | |
| Police Station | |
| Post Office, GPO | |
| Telephone | |
| Toilets | |
| Wheelchair Access | |

### Eating

| | |
|---|---|
| Eating | |

### Drinking

| | |
|---|---|
| Cafe | |
| Drinking | |

### Entertainment

| | |
|---|---|
| Entertainment | |

### Shopping

| | |
|---|---|
| Shopping | |

### Sleeping

| | |
|---|---|
| Camping | |
| Sleeping | |

### Transport

| | |
|---|---|
| Airport, Airfield | |
| Border Crossing | |
| Bus Station | |
| Bicycle Path/Cycling | |
| FFCC (Barcelona) | |
| Metro (Barcelona) | |
| Parking Area | |
| Petrol Station | |
| S-Bahn | |
| Taxi Rank | |
| Tube Station | |
| U-Bahn | |

### Geographic

| | |
|---|---|
| Beach | |
| Lighthouse | |
| Lookout | |
| Mountain, Volcano | |
| National Park | |
| Pass, Canyon | |
| Picnic Area | |
| River Flow | |
| Shelter, Hut | |
| Waterfall | |

# LONELY PLANET OFFICES

**Australia**
Head Office
Locked Bag 1, Footscray, Victoria 3011
☎ 03 8379 8000, fax 03 8379 8111
talk2us@lonelyplanet.com.au

**USA**
150 Linden St, Oakland, CA 94607
☎ 510 250 6400, toll free 800 275 8555,
fax 510 893 8572
info@lonelyplanet.com

**UK**
2nd fl, 186 City Rd,
London EC1V 2NT
☎ 020 7106 2100, fax 020 7106 2101
go@lonelyplanet.co.uk

**Published by Lonely Planet Publications Pty Ltd**
ABN 36 005 607 983

© Lonely Planet 2010
© photographers as indicated 2010

Printed by Toppan Security Printing Pte. Ltd.
Printed in Singapore

Lonely Planet and the Lonely Planet logo are trademarks of Lonely Planet and are registered in the US Patent and Trademark Office and in other countries.

Lonely Planet does not allow its name or logo to be appropriated by commercial establishments, such as retailers, restaurants or hotels. Please let us know of any misuses: lonelyplanet.com/ip.

**Mixed Sources**
Product group from well-managed forests and other controlled sources
www.fsc.org  Cert no. SGS-COC-005002
© 1996 Forest Stewardship Council